Photoshop® Elements 5 Workflow

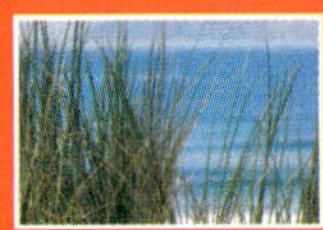

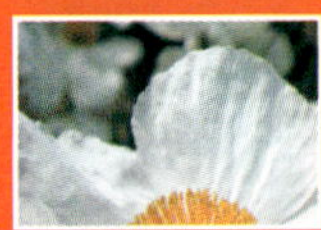

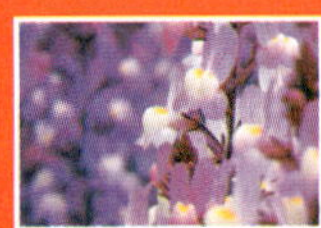

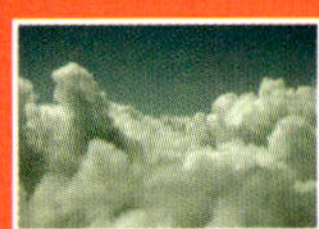

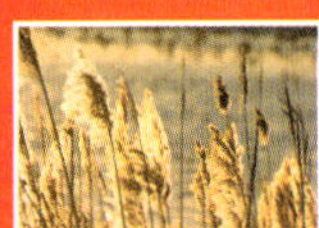

Photoshop® Elements 5 Workflow

The Digital Photographer's Guide

Tim Grey

Peter K. Burian

BICENTENNIAL 1807 WILEY 2007 BICENTENNIAL

WILEY PUBLISHING, INC.

Acquisitions Editor: Pete Gaughan
Development Editor: Kim Wimpsett
Technical Editor: Mara Zebest
Production Editor: Sarah Groff-Palermo
Copy Editor: Sharon Wilkey
Production Manager: Tim Tate
Vice President and Executive Group Publisher: Richard Swadley
Vice President and Executive Publisher: Joseph B. Wikert
Vice President and Publisher: Neil Edde
Book Designer: Franz Baumhackl
Compositor: Maureen Forys, Happenstance Type-O-Rama
Proofreader: Nancy Riddiough
Indexer: Ted Laux
Anniversary Logo Design: Richard Pacifico
Cover Designer: Ryan Sneed
Cover Image: Tim Grey

The following photos are by Peter Burian: Chapter 2 opener (clowns); 2.3, page 21, 2.4, 2.11, 2.12, 2.13, 2.14, 2.15, 2.16, 2.17, 2.18, 2.19, 2.20. 2.21, 6.2, 6.4, 6.15, 7.2, 7.4, 7.6, 7.7, 7.10, 7.11, 7.12, 7.14, page 22, 7.16, 8.10, 8.11, 8.12, Chapter 11 opener (flag), 11.1–11.16, page 248; 12.1113.5, 13.8, 13.9, 13.10, and 13.11.

All photos not otherwise attributed are by Tim Grey.

Published simultaneously in Canada

ISBN: 978-0-4701-0086-8

For general information on our other products and services or to obtain technical support, please contact our Customer Care Department within the U.S. at (800) 762-2974, outside the U.S. at (317) 572-3993 or fax (317) 572-4002.

Wiley also publishes its books in a variety of electronic formats. Some content that appears in print may not be available in electronic books.

Library of Congress Cataloging-in-Publication Data is available from the publisher.

10 9 8 7 6 5 4 3 2 1

Dear Reader,

Thank you for choosing *Photoshop Elements 5 Workflow.* This book is part of a family of premium-quality Sybex graphics books, all written by outstanding authors who combine practical experience with a gift for teaching.

Sybex was founded in 1976. More than 30 years later, we're still committed to producing consistently exceptional books. With each of our graphics titles we're working hard to set a new standard for the industry. From the writers and artists we work with to the paper we print on, our goal is to bring you the best graphics books available.

I hope you see all that reflected in these pages. I'd be very interested to hear your comments and get your feedback on how we're doing. Feel free to let me know what you think about this or any other Sybex book by sending me an email at nedde@wiley.com, or if you think you've found an error in this book, please visit http://wiley.custhelp.com. Customer feedback is critical to our efforts at Sybex.

Best regards,

NEIL EDDE
Vice President and Publisher
Sybex, an Imprint of Wiley

To Miranda, with love. I'm proud of you.
—Tim Grey

For Bev, Julie, and Kate, who wondered if this book would ever be finished so I could get back to working only 50 hours per week. I love you, sweeties!
—Peter K. Burian

Acknowledgments

First, I thank my wife, Bev, and daughters, Kate and Julie, who often wondered what I was doing every evening while working on this book. But the extra effort paid off, and now that it's finished, I resolve to spend a lot more time with them.

For her technical advice over the years, I'm grateful to Ellen Anon, a friend who is a superlative nature photographer, coauthor of several books for Sybex and Wiley, and an incredibly patient imaging software instructor. Ellen was the first person to take me beyond what I had learned about Photoshop and Photoshop Elements by reading and experimenting. Several years ago, she gently forced me to try "complicated" techniques and tolerated my occasional abuse of her Mac laptop computer. Ellen Anon also provided some guidance, as well as beautiful images, for my part of a chapter of this Workflow book, and for that too I am grateful.

Although my family is convinced that I'm a workaholic, it's always great to to be motivated during any major project such as this book. My development editor, Kim Wimpsett, was always there with a reminder about deadlines and a few helpful suggestions. Of course, the technical editor, Mara Zebest, was also a great asset, forcing me to take a step beyond the first draft, with insistence on maximum technical depth and the greatest value for the reader. And finally, I would be remiss if I failed to acknowledge my coauthor, Tim, who has forgotten more about imaging software than most of us will ever learn. This book would definitely have been impossible without the valuable content and direction he provided. By the way, Tim, thank you for being a friend.

—Peter K. Burian

About the Authors

Tim Grey A lifetime of working with computers and a love of photography combine as the perfect passion for Tim Grey. He got started with computers at a very early age, writing animation programs in BASIC for his Commodore 128 at about 10 years old. Not too long after that, he got his first experience with a PC and started writing database software. When Microsoft Windows 3.0 launched, he became enamored of the graphical user interface and quickly shifted his programming efforts to take advantage of the benefits offered by this interface.

In high school Tim signed up for a photography class and quickly fell in love. While dabbling in college, he started tinkering with Adobe Photoshop, helping others learn how to use the software. Since then his passion for all things related to photography and digital imaging has grown exponentially.

Tim loves learning as much as he possibly can about digital imaging, and he loves sharing that information even more. He does so through his writing and speaking appearances. His articles have been published in *Outdoor Photographer*, *PC Photo*, and *Digital Photo Pro* magazines, among others. He is the author of *Photoshop CS2 Workflow* (Sybex, 2005) and of *Color Confidence: The Digital Photographer's Guide to Color Management, Second Edition* (Sybex, 2006); he's also a coauthor of *Photo Finish: The Digital Photographer's Guide to Printing, Showing, and Selling Images* (Sybex, 2004) and of *Real World Digital Photography, Second Edition* (Peachpit Press, 2003). He also presents seminars and workshops at a variety of industry trade shows and other venues.

Tim publishes a regular "Digital Darkroom Questions" email list, where he answers questions related to digital imaging for photographers. To add your email address to the list, visit www.timgrey.com.

When he isn't working to meet deadlines on his latest book, Tim enjoys venturing out with his digital SLR to find new subjects. When traveling on business around the country and the world, he capitalizes on any "downtime" to go out walking with camera in hand capturing whatever catches his eye, which typically includes urban subjects on such trips.

He also enjoys photographing nature's beauty during outings near his home in Bellevue, Washington. And one of these days, when caught up on book projects, he plans to pick up his guitar again to really learn how to play and get current on his pilot's license so he can once again take to the skies in the pilot's seat.

Peter K. Burian An outdoor, travel, and lifestyles photographer who supplies three stock agencies with images, Peter K. Burian is also a regular contributor to photographic magazines in Canada, the United States, and Australia. He contributes monthly articles on photographic and imaging techniques, as well as many equipment test reports, to publications including *Photo Life*, *Shutterbug*, *Here's How!*, and *Australian Photography*. In addition, he teaches two online courses for BetterPhoto.com, one about mastering the EOS Digital Rebel cameras (EOS 300D, 350D, and 400D) and the other about all aspects of digital photography and imaging.

This is a second career for Peter, who had a "past life" as an insurance claims adjuster, supervisor, and then manager for a national property and casualty company in Canada. During the last five years of that tenure, he was already writing frequently for two magazines and for more than two years was editor of a quarterly publication, *Shutterbug's Outdoor & Nature Photography*. Hence, it was not difficult for him to begin stock photography and writing on a full-time basis, having developed the contacts and markets to make these pursuits into a full-time occupation.

Peter was initially attracted to photography by the high-tech gadgets such as the first commercially successful 35mm autofocus SLR camera, the Minolta Maxxum 7000. As the initial fascination with the technology wore off, he became more interested in photography for its own sake, to capture colorful scenes in exotic locations such as Brazil and Costa Rica and people involved in fast-paced activities such as cycle racing and whitewater kayaking. Although primarily self-taught in both 35mm and digital photography, he acknowledges the value of night-school courses that he took at Sheridan College in Oakville, Ontario, in the early 1990s.

About five years ago, he switched from 35mm photography to digital almost totally, both in testing equipment for the magazine *Reviews* and in his own choice of equipment. Although Peter admits he still has five years of work on color slide film that he needs to scan, his digital photographs are up-to-date in terms of image optimization and cataloging.

Previous to his work on this book written with Tim Grey, who has been a friend for several years, Peter has co-written a dozen other books. He wrote the *National Geographic Photography Field Guide: Secrets to Making Great Pictures, Second Edition* (National Geographic, 2003) with Bob Caputo, and 11 other books about specific 35mm and digital SLR camera systems (for Lark Books, with various coauthors). His single-author book, *Mastering Digital Photography and Imaging* (Sybex, 2004), received favorable reviews from a wide range of print publications and digital camera websites.

Although he claims to be chained to a computer most of his life, Peter manages to travel quite often and to generate new work frequently, both in distant locations and closer to his home in the Toronto area. Recent stock photography trips include Bavaria in Germany, Paris, New York City, and the American Southwest. As this book was nearing completion, he was checking for discounts on tickets for a major trip, a Mediterranean cruise, with his wife of 33 years, Bev, who is a schoolteacher. Frankly, Bev and daughters Julie and Kate have never quite understood why Peter gave up his first career or why he enjoys spending hours optimizing even their digital snapshots. They insist that he's a workaholic, ignoring his suggestion that "digital imaging is not just work; it's also my hobby." In his spare time, Peter enjoys traveling with Bev, entertaining friends on their spacious back deck, or cruising the twisty country roads in a high-powered sports coupe searching out scenes that will eventually make for great subjects, or backgrounds, for his digital photographs.

Contents

Introduction *xiv*

Part I **Getting Started** 1

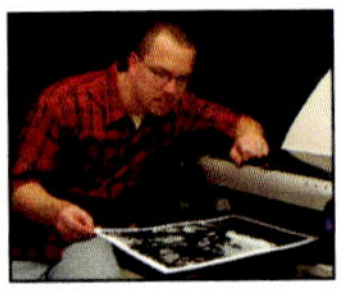

Chapter 1 **Workflow Foundations** **3**

Understanding the Importance of Workflow 4
Quality 4
Efficiency 5
Consistency 7

Establishing a Workflow 7
Determine Priorities 7
Focus on Results 9
Maintain Flexibility 10

Revising Your Workflow 13
Nothing Is Permanent 13
Requirements Will Evolve 13

Creating a Workflow That Works 15

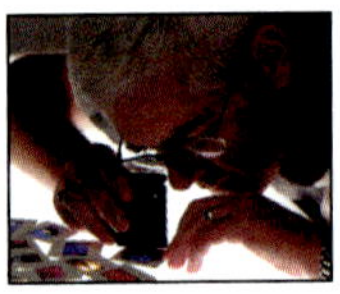

Chapter 2 **Download and Sort** **17**

Safe Downloading 18
Creating a Master Folder 18
Using Adobe Photo Downloader 19
Using Third-Party Software 23
Using Windows XP Wizard 23
Manual Copying 25
Confirming a Successful Transfer 26
Archiving 28
Reformatting Memory Cards 28

Sorting Images in Organizer 29
Light Table Analogy 29
Sorting Strategy 30
Applying Tags 34
Other Organizer Features 35

Reviewing Images for Evaluation 37
Zoom Tool 38
Hand Tool 38
Navigator Palette 41
Keyboard Shortcuts 42

Printing Contact Sheets 44

Ready to Work 45

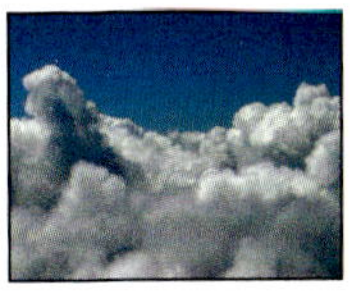

Chapter 3 **RAW Conversion** **47**

Understanding the Benefits of RAW 48
Getting Accurate White Balance 48
Correcting Exposure Errors 50
Capturing High-Bit Data 51

Converting with Adobe Camera Raw 51
Adobe Camera Raw Settings 53
Navigation Tools 53
White Balance 54
Tonal Adjustments 58
Noise Reduction 61
Ready to Convert 63

Archiving RAW Captures 64

Part II **Basic Adjustments** 67

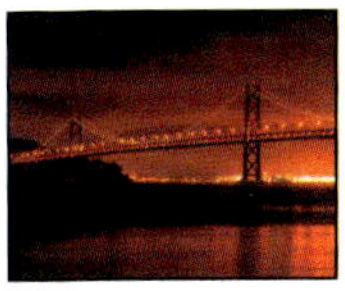

Chapter 4 **Rotate and Crop** **69**

Basic Rotation 70

Basic Cropping 72
Cropping from a Selection 73
Using the Crop Tool 76

Custom Rotation 82
Rotating with the Crop Tool 83
Using the Custom Rotate Tool 86
Using the Straighten Tool 88

Right-Side Up 89

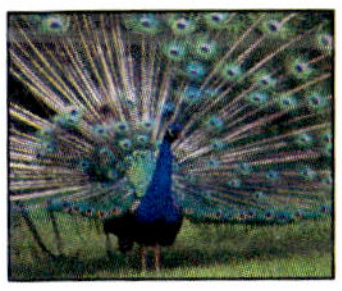

Chapter 5 **Tone and Color** **91**

Increasing Saturation for Evaluation 92

Prioritizing Adjustments 93

Making Tonal Adjustments 95
Brightness/Contrast 95
Levels 102

Making Color Adjustments 112
Color Balance 112
Basic Saturation 118

Using Quick Fix Adjustment Tools 119

Basically Done 121

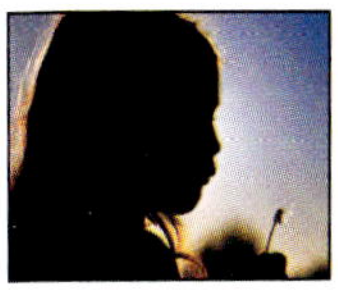

Chapter 6 **Image Cleanup** **123**

Cleanup Workflow 124

Clone Stamp 125
Getting Started 125
Cloning Pixels 130
Fixing Cloning Mistakes 134

Healing Brush 136
Getting Started 136

Healing Pixels 137
Minimizing Healing 138

Spot Healing Brush 140

A Clean Image. 141

Part III **Advanced Adjustments** 67

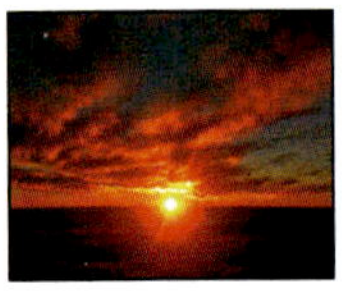

Chapter 7 **Advanced Tonal Adjustments** **145**

Shadows/Highlights. 146

Adjust Color Curves 153

Selective Adjustments 155
Setting Up 157
Painting with Light 160
Dodge and Burn Tools 162
Correcting Mistakes 164

Fine-Tuned Tonality 165

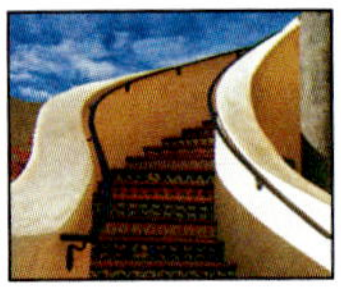

Chapter 8 **Advanced Color Adjustments** **167**

Hue/Saturation 168
Using Preset Color Ranges 168
Customizing Ranges 169
Defining Inverse Ranges 173

Color Casts 176
Solid Color 178
Average Color Removal 180

Targeted Color Painting 183

Targeted Saturation Painting 187

Ready to Get Selective. 189

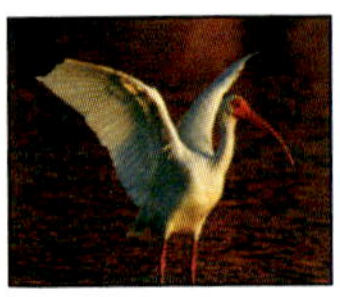

Chapter 9 **Making Selections** **191**

Understanding the Selection Tools. 192
Marquee 193
Lasso 198
Polygonal Lasso 200
Magnetic Lasso 203
Selection Brush 205
Magic Selection Brush 207
Magic Wand 207

Using the Threshold Technique 213

Modifying Selections 215

Saving and Loading Selections. 216

Putting Selections to Use 217

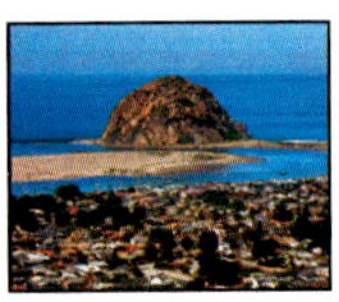

Chapter 10 **Targeted Adjustments** **219**

Introducing Masking. 220

Masking from a Selection 221

Masking by Painting 224
Alternative Methods of Placing Pixels 226
Applying a Gradient to a Mask 226

Hitting Your Target 229

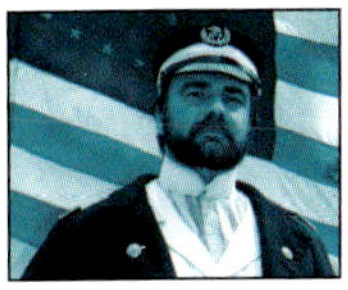

Chapter 11 **Creative Adjustments** **231**

Getting Creative 232

Colorize 232

Grayscale Conversion 235
Using Convert To Black And White 236
Grayscale Hue Shift 239

High Pass Sharpening 241

Filters 243
Filter Gallery 243

Just the Beginning 245

Part IV **Finishing the Workflow** 247

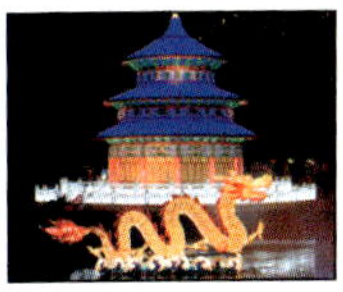

Chapter 12 **Saving Files** **249**

Master Image Concept 250

Filenames, Locations, and Formats 252
Photoshop PSD Format 254
TIFF Format 255
Choosing between PSD and TIFF 257

Safely Saved 257

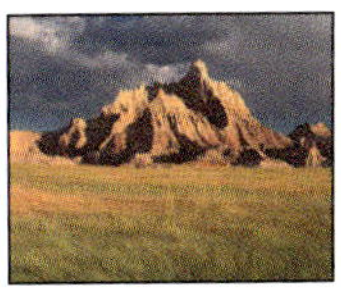

Chapter 13 **Output Processing** **259**

Following an Output Workflow 260

Preserving the Master Image 261

Processing a Working Copy 262
Duplicate Image 263
Flatten Image 263
Image Size 265

Sharpening Your Images 267
Unsharp Mask 268
Adjust Sharpness 270
Image Output 272

Saving a Copy 273

Workflow Complete! 273

Appendix **Sample Workflow Checklist** **275**

Index *278*

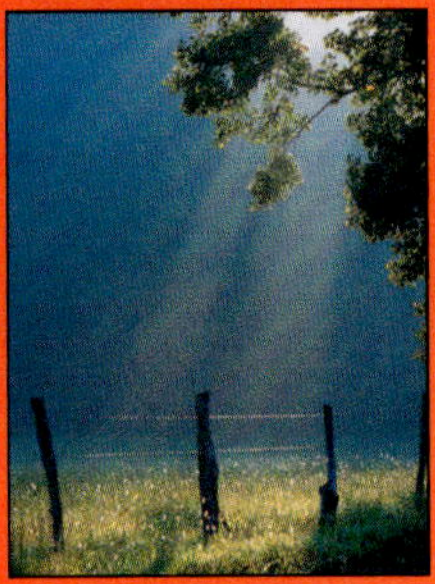

“We want this book not only to promote logical workflow and

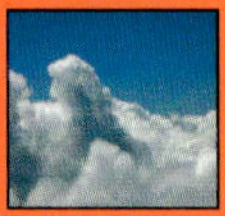

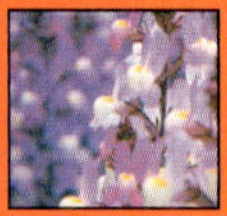

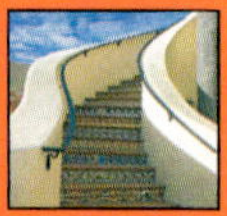

the most suitable methods for image optimization but also to encourage readers to open new doors to creativity.”

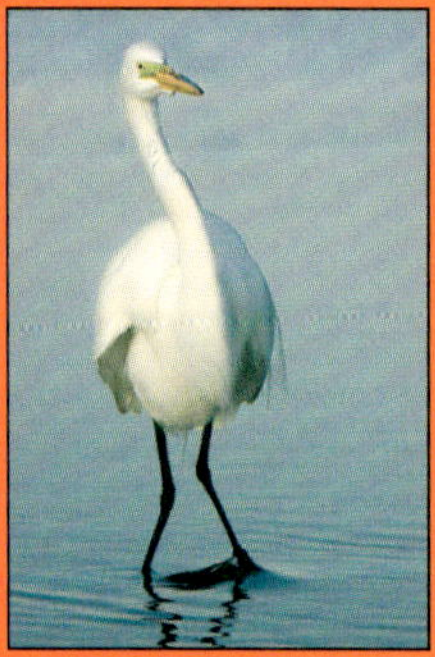

Introduction

The debate about whether digital photography will replace film has been put to rest, and the winner is clear. But although digital photography exceeds all expectations year after year, many photographers—especially hobbyists—think they aren't making the most of the opportunities. In particular, they find it challenging to make the most of their digital photographs after they were captured.

Adobe Photoshop has long been a clear leader for the optimization of digital images, but it is considered by many to be too difficult to easily learn. It is an incredibly powerful tool, but because it requires an investment of time (and money) to use proficiently, it is a tool generally reserved for professional or advanced amateur users.

Adobe Photoshop Elements provides a solution for those who want a tool that is easy to use while still providing the features they need to optimize their photographic images. Early versions were generally considered to represent Photoshop with many features removed. However, with recent updates—culminating in the current version 5 covered in this book—it has become much easier to use. It has become a tool that not only represents an excellent solution for those who don't have the time to become experts in Photoshop but also meets the needs of relatively advanced users who are looking for a more cost-effective way to meet their digital imaging needs.

In this book, we present a structure you can follow—and modify as your own needs and preferences dictate—when optimizing your images in Photoshop Elements 5. Although it may be presented as a formula in some respects, based on methods that have proven successful for us, it's definitely not an absolute structure. Consider it as a basic workflow that will guide you in developing your own version. Try our approach, and you'll discover what works perfectly for your own images and temperament and what needs to be fine-tuned to meet your own specific needs.

Besides encouraging you to develop a logical flow in making adjustments to images, we will emphasize the techniques that will allow you to do so in a nondestructive manner. Whenever possible, we'll present adjustments that will preserve the original information in your images while still affording you maximum flexibility in optimizing the images, enabling you to make the most of your creative vision.

We hope it becomes obvious as you read this book that we are both passionate about digital photography and image optimization in Elements. We want this book not only to promote logical workflow and the most suitable methods for image optimization but also to encourage readers to open new doors to creativity. If our passion for the art and craft of photography and image editing is infectious, we'll have done our jobs effectively.

Who Should Use This Book

Photoshop Elements 5 Workflow really covers the full spectrum of adjustments you'll want to apply to photographic images in Photoshop Elements. As a result, it is appropriate for photographers of all skill levels who would like some guidance in creating the best workflow for image optimization. Beginning users will build a strong foundation and then be able to move on to more-advanced topics, while expert users will gain a greater understanding of the issues affecting workflow as well as some new techniques they can use on their images.

This book was written based on Adobe Photoshop Elements 5, but it's also applicable for users of prior versions of Elements (though some new features will obviously not be available). We've included keyboard shortcuts for both Windows and Mac versions of Elements, though at press time the Mac version of Elements 5 had not yet been released.

If you're a digital photographer who doesn't feel totally confident that you're getting the most benefit from your image optimization in Elements, this is the book for you.

What's Inside

Part I, "Getting Started," consists of the following chapters:

Chapter 1: Workflow Foundations will help you understand the principles of a good foundation and will get you thinking about your priorities in an image-optimization workflow.

Chapter 2: Download and Sort provides guidance on the process of getting digital captures onto your computer and then sorting and organizing them.

Chapter 3: RAW Conversion shows you how to process your RAW captures to retain maximum detail.

Part II, "Basic Adjustments," consists of the following chapters:

Chapter 4: Rotate and Crop provides the basics of cropping your images as well as rotating them to set the proper orientation or to fix crooked horizons.

Chapter 5: Tone and Color guides you through the basic adjustments that affect tone and color in your images.

Chapter 6: Image Cleanup helps you master the art of fixing dust spots and flaws in your images to help them look their best.

Part III, "Advanced Adjustments," consists of the following chapters:

Chapter 7: Advanced Tonal Adjustments takes things a bit further with tonal adjustments, showing you some of the advanced options available.

Chapter 8: Advanced Color Adjustments offers a look at some of the advanced options available for fine-tuning color in your images.

Chapter 9: Making Selections includes many methods for creating selections, from the basic tools to the more advanced methods.

Chapter 10: Targeted Adjustments lets you put your selections, as well as other techniques, to use so you can apply adjustments to specific areas of your images.

Chapter 11: Creative Adjustments gives you an opportunity to exercise a little creative license with your images by using techniques that go beyond the basic photo optimization.

Part IV, "Finishing the Workflow," consists of the following chapters:

Chapter 12: Saving Files covers the basics of saving your files to ensure that all the work you've put into the image is retained.

Chapter 13: Output Processing finishes up the workflow by discussing how to prepare your images for final output.

Finally, the appendix, "Sample Workflow Checklist," gives you a quick-reference guide to our recommended workflow, telling you where you'll find each process step covered in the book.

The Book and the Authors, Online

Sybex strives to keep you supplied with the latest tools and information you need for your work. Please check its website at www.sybex.com, where we'll post additional content and updates that supplement this book if the need arises. Enter **elements workflow** in the Search box (or type the book's ISBN, **978-0-470-10086-8**), and click Go to access the book's update page.

To provide feedback about this book or offer input on the types of books you'd like to see from Tim Grey in the future, you can contact him via email at tim@timgrey.com. You can find more information about his writing and appearances at www.timgrey.com. Should you want to know more about Peter Burian's work or his online digital courses, visit www.peterkburian.com; you can also take advantage of the Contact option at that site in order to write to him.

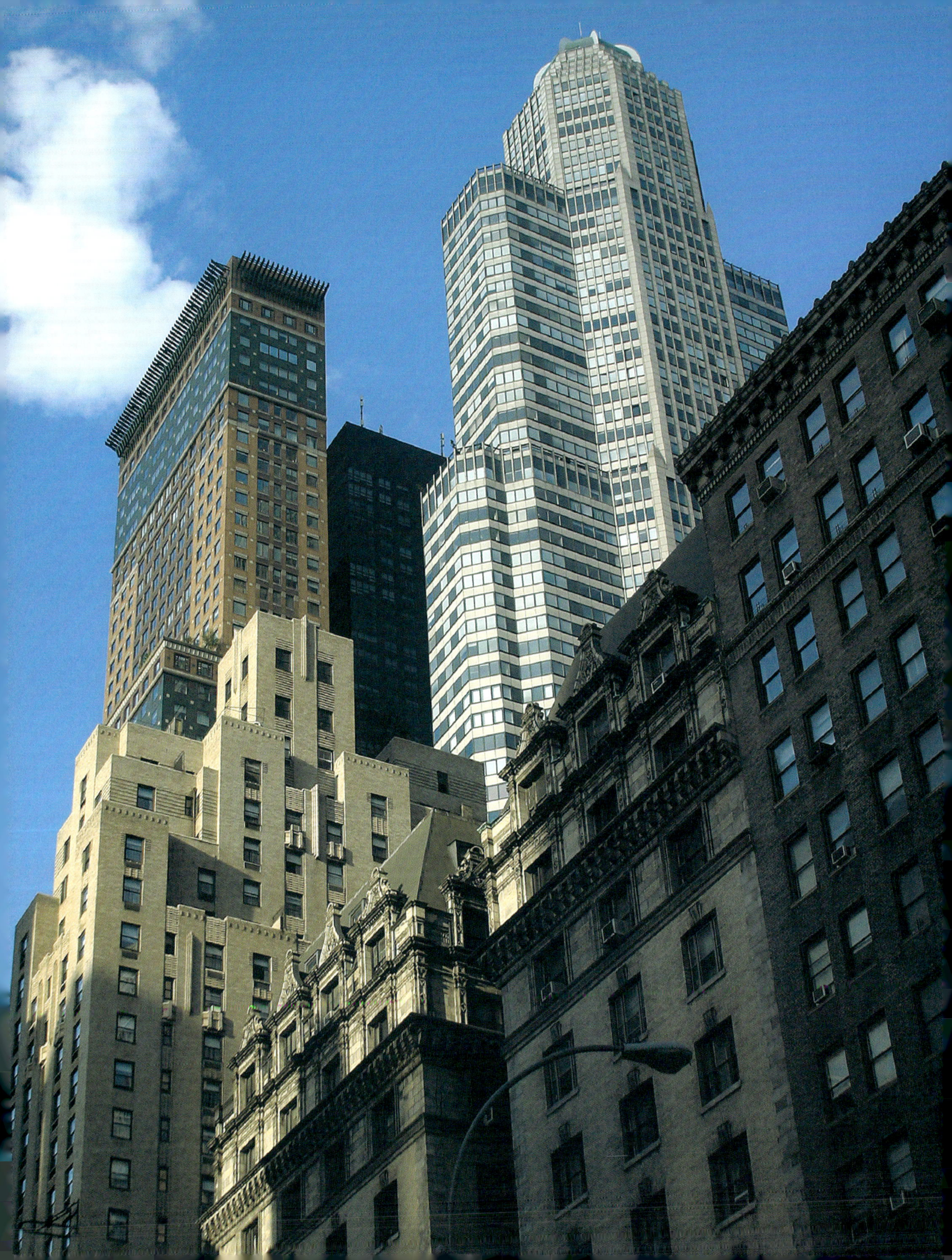

I

Getting Started

Digital photography has opened up a whole new level of control for photographers. Never before has it been so easy to exercise so much control over your photographic images. And yet, when many photographers start using digital tools, they don't know where to begin. In this part, we'll examine the first steps in establishing and implementing a digital workflow to help you start down the right path to optimizing your photographic images.

Chapter 1 **Workflow Foundations**

Chapter 2 **Download and Sort**

Chapter 3 **RAW Conversion**

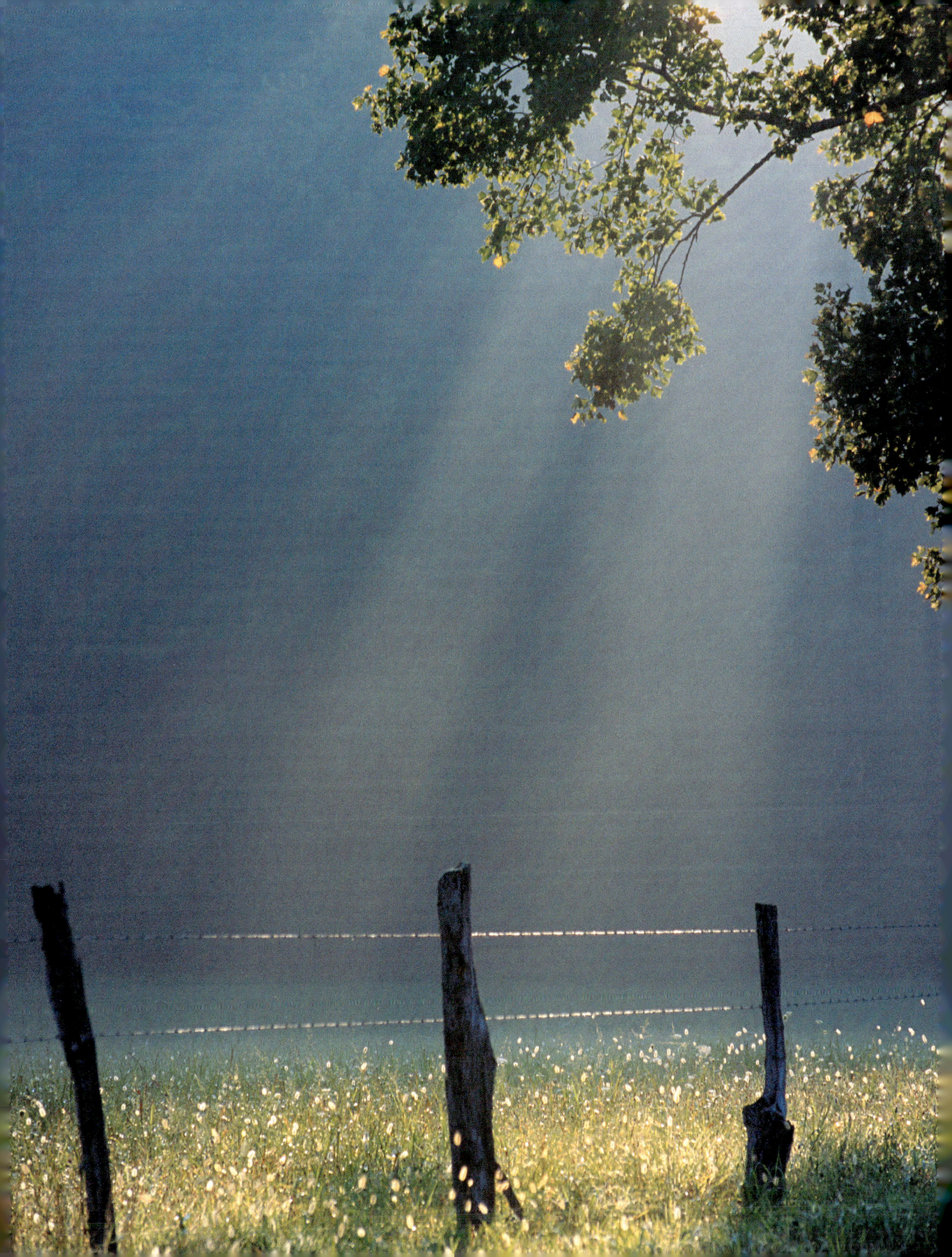

Workflow Foundations

If you've ever worked in a wet darkroom (and a great many readers of this book probably started with digital and never set foot in a wet darkroom), you know that there is a normal order, or flow, *to the work that must be performed to create an image. The paper is exposed from the negative, then slid into the developer where the image magically appears, then into a stop bath to cease the development process, and finally into a fixer to ensure a permanent image before the image gets washed and dried. When you're working with pixels in the digital darkroom, the process has more options and variables, making an unlimited number of possible paths for optimizing your images. Establishing a workflow provides an efficient method of working on your images to help ensure the highest quality possible.*

1

Chapter Contents

Understanding the Importance of Workflow
Establishing a Workflow
Revising Your Workflow
Creating a Workflow That Works

Understanding the Importance of Workflow

The term *workflow* has become a buzzword in the world of digital imaging, and with good reason. Many photographers feel overwhelmed when they set out to optimize some of their favorite digital captures. Besides not being sure where to begin, they don't know how the process should unfold.

Having a plan for your digital imaging workflow is important not only for making the process more efficient for you but also for ensuring the best quality in the image. Understanding the benefits of a consistent and optimized workflow will help you appreciate the importance of establishing one.

Quality

For most photographers, the quality of the final image is of paramount importance. The potential quality of the final image is directly determined by the quality of the original capture. So the first step in producing the best images in the digital darkroom is to make the best captures before you even sit down in front of the computer.

One of the first steps toward achieving that goal is to ensure that you have selected the largest/finest JPEG combination if using JPEG capture. Naturally, you might also consider using RAW captures for reasons to be discussed in a moment; a RAW file certainly provides the best possible quality. Although it may be tempting to opt for a lower JPEG size or quality level—because more of the smaller files will fit on a memory card—the trade-off for size is lower quality. If you decide to shoot with a small JPEG size or low-JPEG-quality level, you may regret it later if you capture a once-in-a-lifetime photo. The level of detail may not be adequate even for an excellent 5″×7″ print. Memory cards have become relatively inexpensive, so buy several 1- or 2-gigabyte (GB) cards in order to have an ample supply of storage space and set the largest/finest JPEG quality available, or switch to RAW capture for peace of mind.

Also, be sure to take advantage of in-camera overrides (particularly when using JPEG or TIFF capture) to make images that are reasonably accurate in terms of exposure (brightness) and white balance, and pleasing in terms of color saturation and contrast. That's much less important when shooting in RAW capture, as you'll see, because you can modify most image parameters with Photoshop Elements 5, using the special software that's designed for adjusting RAW files. Still, it's worth developing serious photography habits and making the technically best possible images in-camera.

When reading the recommendation for using the RAW capture mode, you might have wondered, "What is RAW?" Not all digital cameras with built-in lenses provide a RAW capture mode, but all digital single-lens reflex (SLR) cameras do. Think of a RAW capture as the equivalent of a digital negative. When you choose a JPEG or TIFF capture mode, the camera processes the image and makes choices for you, and the result is the final JPEG or TIFF. But RAW capture results in a file that contains all the raw data and information off the camera sensors—with little or no in-camera processing. When you open a RAW file in Elements, the program launches a dialog box that enables you to make choices about how you want the image to look (how to process it). You will find that process to be extremely fun and rewarding as you see the kinds of results you can achieve with a RAW file. And because RAW is a digital negative, you can come back to this file over and over again and process it differently each time. Maybe you will want one version that's grayscale, for instance, and another version that's full color.

Think of it this way—if you take a traditional negative to different store locations for processing, your photos developed by one store might come back looking slightly different than those from another store (depending on the processing choices and machine settings of each store)—but your negative is still intact and hasn't changed or been altered. The same is true of RAW. You can open it as many times as you want, process it differently each time, and then save the processed file as TIFF, JPEG, or any file format of your choosing. Elements preserves the original RAW file without changing the original data it contains. RAW is covered more thoroughly in chapter 3.

After you bring the images into your digital darkroom, a proper workflow helps ensure optimal image quality for professional results. When you have a plan for your workflow, it means you're thinking about the order in which you're performing adjustments and the methods you use to make those adjustments. These are both key factors that affect the quality of the final image, and having a plan focused on optimal quality will give you much better results than adjusting your images in a haphazard fashion.

For example, one of the factors often used to determine overall image quality is the amount of detail visible in the image (Figure 1.1). To ensure minimal detail loss, you can certainly exercise caution when making your adjustments, but a proper workflow will also help in this goal.

Note: Quality can be a subjective factor in many images, especially when using unique photographic methods or special effects. Although the definition of optimal quality can vary by photographer or even by photographic image, your workflow should focus on maintaining the quality and aesthetics of your original image as you captured it, while producing an improvement in the final result.

As you are fine-tuning the workflow you use to optimize your images, consider the effect of the particular methods you're using, as well as the order in which you perform particular tasks, to see whether you can improve the image quality in any way. Throughout this book we'll share methods for achieving exactly those high-quality results with your digital workflow.

Efficiency

Although image quality tends to be a chief concern for most photographers (as it should be), efficiency is also important. As much as most photographers love working with their images—seeing them transformed from good captures to remarkable images—generally they don't want to sit in front of the computer all day. They'd much rather be out taking new pictures.

By developing a general workflow, you can work much more efficiently. You won't have to stop and think about what the next step is. Although certain images will certainly require extra attention, and at times you will need to try various techniques before achieving the desired results, an established workflow you are comfortable with will make the work of perfecting your images go relatively quickly.

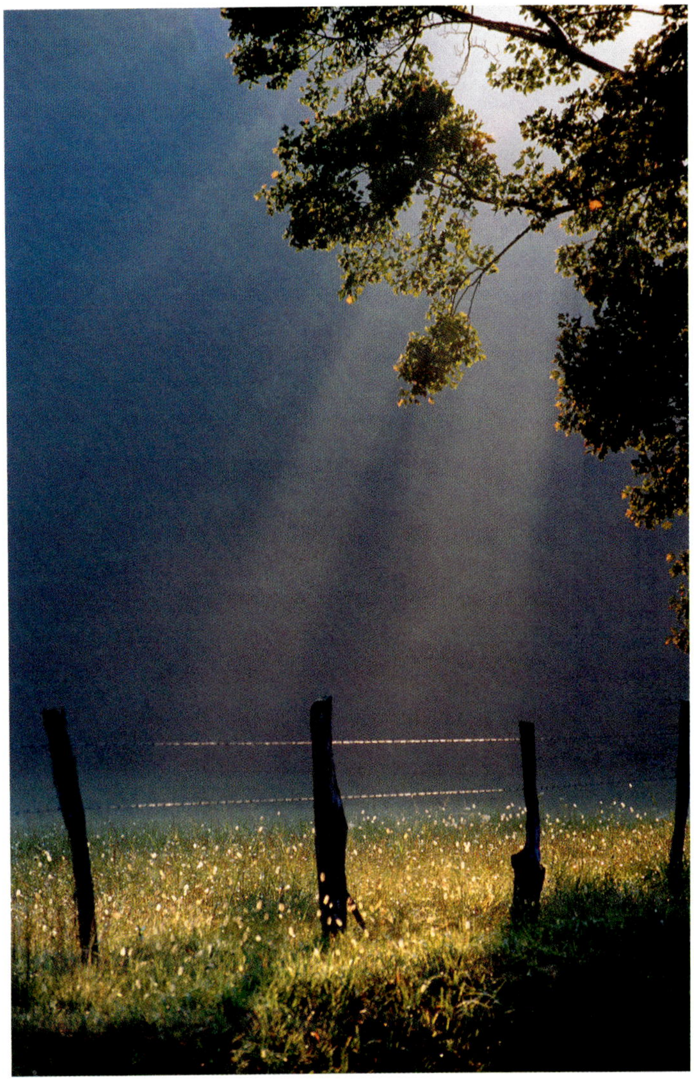

Figure 1.1
Maintaining maximum detail in an image is one of the factors commonly considered to represent good quality, and is a key concern when the image includes relatively dark shadows. A proper workflow will help you maintain detail and quality in your images. (Photo by Gabby Salazar)

When Tim teaches workshops on digital imaging (see www.timgrey.com for a schedule of upcoming appearances), it may take an hour to fully discuss the details of one particular adjustment, whereas making the adjustment as part of your normal workflow may require mere seconds or a few minutes at most. However, the time spent understanding how the adjustment works is well worth it. When you're familiar with the tools available in Elements, you're able to use them much more efficiently. Similarly, throughout this book we'll be presenting methods for working with the various tools to optimize your images. It may take some time for you to fully grasp all the details, but by taking the time to truly understand how the tools work, you'll be much more efficient without compromising the quality of your images.

Consistency

Another benefit of a consistent workflow is—no surprise here—consistency. This relates to the two previous topics: by maintaining a consistent workflow, you'll ensure consistent quality in your images and ensure a familiarity that will improve your efficiency. When you find a workflow that works, that workflow (with obvious variations as needed for specific images) will work well for all of your images.

Note: Keep in mind that an established workflow doesn't define absolute rules of what adjustments you must make to all of your images, but rather provides a road map that guides you through the best way to approach your images for optimization.

In effect, if it makes sense to establish a workflow for optimizing your images (and we certainly think it makes a lot of sense), it makes sense to be consistent in your use of that workflow. In other words, make a plan and stick to it in order to achieve the maximum benefits.

Establishing a Workflow

Because you're reading this book, we're assuming you already appreciate the value of establishing a workflow for optimizing your digital images. We also assume you aren't completely comfortable with the process you're currently using or you are new to Elements 5. As you work your way through this book, that will change.

As you start toward creating a workflow that works for you, we strongly recommend making duplicate copies of a couple of favorite images that could use some work and going through the process of experimenting with the adjustments that will form the foundation of your workflow. Because they're just copies of your images, you don't have to worry about whether you produce a good final result, and you can focus on practicing the steps involved and figuring out what works best for you.

Note: Although this chapter is about establishing a workflow for your images, you won't find details of a specific workflow here. That's because this entire book is about the workflow process, and by going through the book in its entirety, you'll learn what steps you need to include in your own workflow and in what order you'll likely apply them.

Determine Priorities

Your priorities in optimizing your images probably reflect the topics covered in the beginning of this chapter. In particular, you probably want to ensure maximum quality in your images while maintaining efficiency with your workflow. However, you may also have other priorities for your images, which you'll want to consider when fine-tuning your workflow.

The first step in establishing a digital workflow is to think about what is important to you and how you prefer to work. Some of this relates to overall strategies. For example, we strongly recommend becoming familiar with the Layers palette and using adjustment layers or separate image layers for all adjustments. We'll emphasize this approach throughout this book by using a layer-based method for every adjustment presented. Another aspect to consider is the general flow of your adjustments. Do you prefer to clean up dust and other blemishes before you get started or move right into tonal adjustments first? This book will present recommendations on what order you should use to make your adjustments and under which circumstances you should change that order.

Of course, your priorities will depend in large part on the type of work you're doing and the deadline under which you're operating. For example, photojournalists usually have speed as their utmost concern. For them, a workflow that focuses on methods to speed up the process of preparing images is optimal. For a nature photographer producing large prints, quality is the greatest concern, even if that means taking considerably longer to process an image. For a given photographer, the optimal workflow may even vary based on the particular project. The key is to define a workflow that meets your typical production needs but to remain flexible so you can revise your workflow based on changing needs.

One suggestion that may help you determine the basic structure of your workflow is to focus on solving the problem that requires the most significant adjustment first and work your way down from there (Figure 1.2). The specific problem you'd define as the greatest for a given image will obviously be different from one image to the next. Some images will have significant tonal problems because of an error in exposure, for example. Others will need major color correcting because of lighting issues or a problem with your white balance setting in the digital camera. For scans of older film, the biggest problem may be considerable dust or scratches on the original. In each case there is a logical order to correcting the image based on prioritizing which problems are of greatest concern.

Although the most serious problem for each image will vary, as you work on more and more images you'll find that most tend to have a similar order of priorities for problems that need to be fixed. For example, with digital captures we usually find that the color is pretty accurate, so any tonal adjustments tend to be the most significant adjustment we'll make. For that reason, we usually find that it makes sense to start with broad tonal adjustments, then move on to broad color adjustments, and then move on to fine-tuning adjustments.

All this talk about "problems" may lead you to believe that this book is all about working on your very worst images—or that we suspect you are a terrible photographer! That's not the case. In fact, the problems in an image may be minor. Often, you may open an image and think it really doesn't need any significant changes. That is the ideal starting point, because such an image allows you to explore how you can make a great photo breathtaking, rather than trying to salvage a bad photo. Even when the image starts off looking great, a proper workflow will help ensure that you can produce the best results possible from that image.

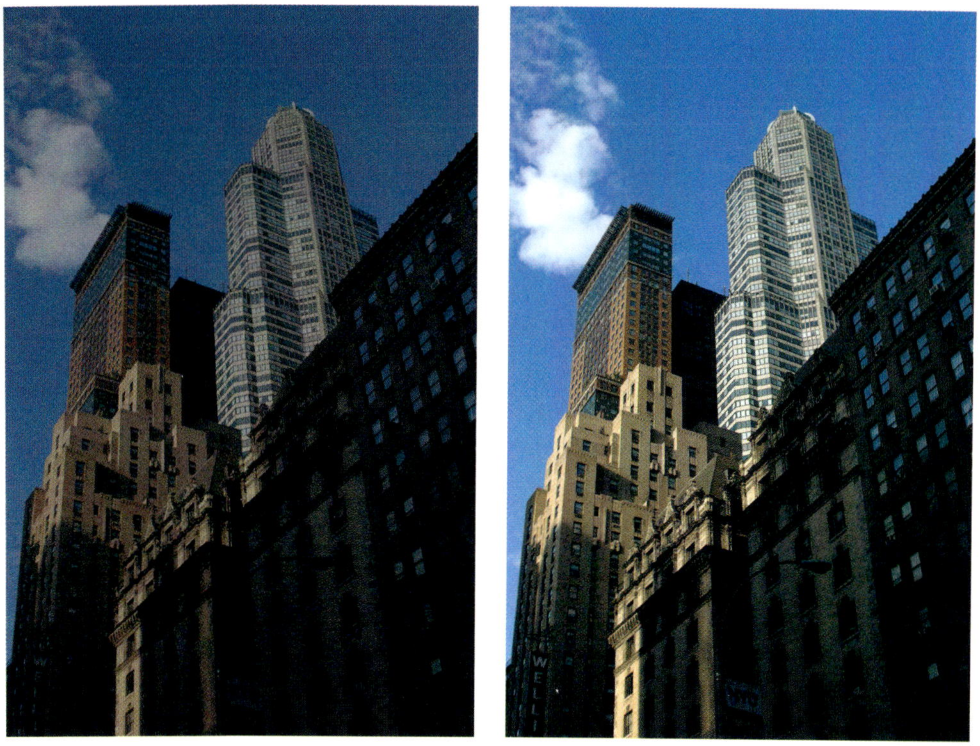

Figure 1.2 For many digital images, the tonal adjustments tend to be the most significant required. Therefore, a typical workflow may include basic tonal adjustments as the first step.

Focus on Results

Although workflow is all about a process, the real purpose of that process is to create the final result (Figure 1.3). Photographers typically capture images because they want to produce beautiful prints or other output to share with as many viewers as possible. We want that final output to be impressive, both because of the content of the image and because of the quality of the final display. As such, it is important that you are thinking about the final result when you're optimizing your images, as well as when you're figuring out your workflow in the first place.

We want to produce the best images possible, and a proper workflow will ensure that you are able to maintain that quality throughout the process. However, you should also consider your intent for the final appearance of your images. How you want your images to look at the end of the process can determine the steps you take to adjust the images during that process. For example, if you are preparing an image for a brochure and need it to be a real attention-grabber, you might boost the saturation and kick up the contrast. You may need to tone down the same image used for a restaurant menu to achieve a more subtle appearance. A general workflow that is layer based will provide the flexibility to adjust the image either way, but the actual process may be different for each.

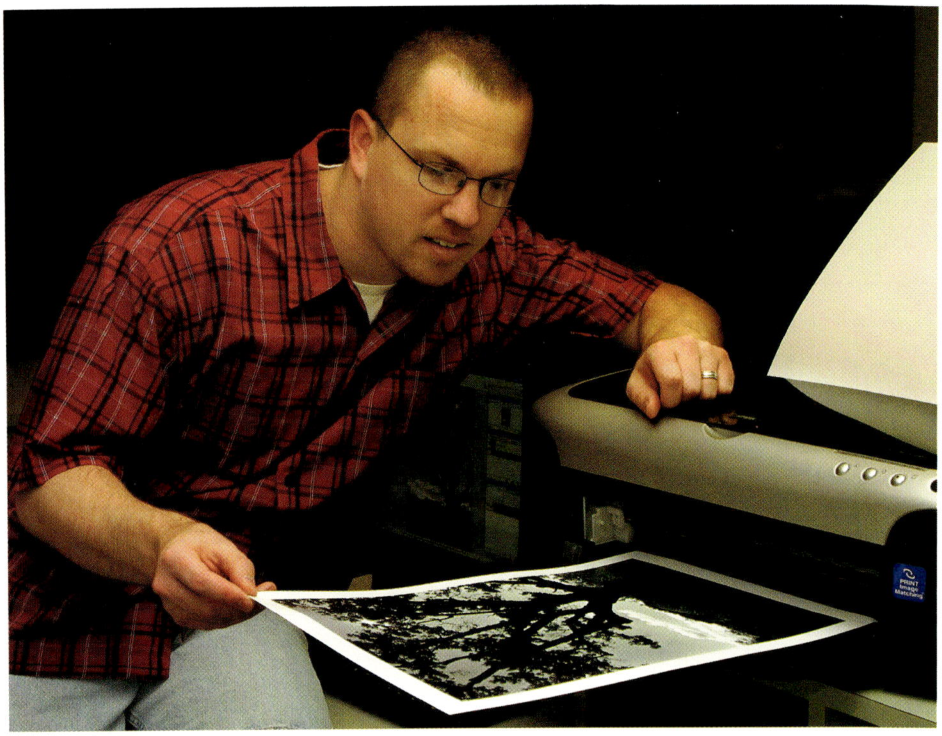

Figure 1.3 For most photographers, the ultimate result of their digital workflow is a high-quality print they are proud to display for all to see.

As you think about the results you are trying to achieve, and the typical order of priorities in producing the best results, you'll get a sense of how you might organize the process of optimizing your images. Give some thought to the order in which you should be making your adjustments and the factors that are particularly important to you when it comes to your images. As you think about these topics, you'll start to get a sense of what a workflow means as well as determine a workflow that will be a good fit for you and your images.

Note: We are not suggesting that you need to write your own manual on how to apply a workflow to your images (especially because this book can guide you through the workflow process). Still, it might make sense to write the basic steps you think are important as you develop your own workflow. Also, be sure to see the appendix at the back of this book for a workflow guide you can use as you develop your own workflow.

Maintain Flexibility

Another important consideration for your workflow is flexibility. You want to be sure your workflow is making your image-optimization process more efficient and that it allows you to change your mind about what you want the image to look like.

A Flexible Attitude

One aspect of maintaining flexibility in your workflow is a state of mind. It is important that you don't get caught in the trap of always applying the same effects to every image. Each image is unique and deserves to be optimized based on what you judge to be the best result for that particular image. Some photographers apply the same adjustments with the same settings in the same order to every single image. This robotic approach to image editing would not demand too much of your time, but it also wouldn't ensure optimal image quality. Some images may be improved by those particular adjustments, while others may be harmed.

Even if you find that certain settings for some adjustments seem to work best for every image, keep in mind that the workflow you establish is a basic guideline for the general order in which you'll perform your adjustments. Don't think of your workflow as a rigid set of rules that dictate what steps should be taken and in what order.

Even after you've established a workflow that helps you achieve exceptional results with your images, don't be afraid to change the process around for a particular image. Some images will have unique problems that you need to address early in the workflow to maintain high quality. In other situations you'll simply want to depart from your typical workflow to produce a creative variation (Figure 1.4). Whatever the situation, you'll have to depart from your typical workflow to achieve certain goals. Treat your workflow as a guide for producing the best results with your typical images, but maintain the flexibility to change your process when you think it will benefit the final result.

Layer-Based Workflow

Another aspect of maintaining flexibility is ensuring that you'll be able to change your mind and revise the adjustments you've made to an image without reducing the image quality or causing an excessive loss of detail. Using layers to optimize your images will ensure that you always maintain this flexibility.

We strongly advocate using layers for all adjustments to your images (Figure 1.5). Layers are available when you select Edit And Enhance Photos (also called Full Edit) in Elements 5 but *not* available when you select Quickly Fix Photos (also called Quick Fix). Throughout this book you'll find techniques for applying many adjustments, all performed with adjustment layers whenever possible. When an adjustment layer doesn't provide the tools needed to achieve a particular change, we'll employ separate image layers with particular properties to use. As a last resort, when the particular technique doesn't lend itself to using an adjustment layer or empty image layer for the adjustment, create a duplicate of the background image layer for the purposes of applying the change.

By following this recommendation, you'll ensure that you maintain the original image data contained in the background layer. The result is that you can always return to the image and remove particular adjustments or fine-tune them if you've changed your mind about the adjustment itself. You may have experienced a situation where you've optimized an image and then opened it at a later date only to wonder what you were thinking when you made the original adjustments. By working with layers, you can ensure that such situations don't represent a need to compromise the overall quality of the image, but rather represent opportunities to make the image even better than it was the first time you worked on it.

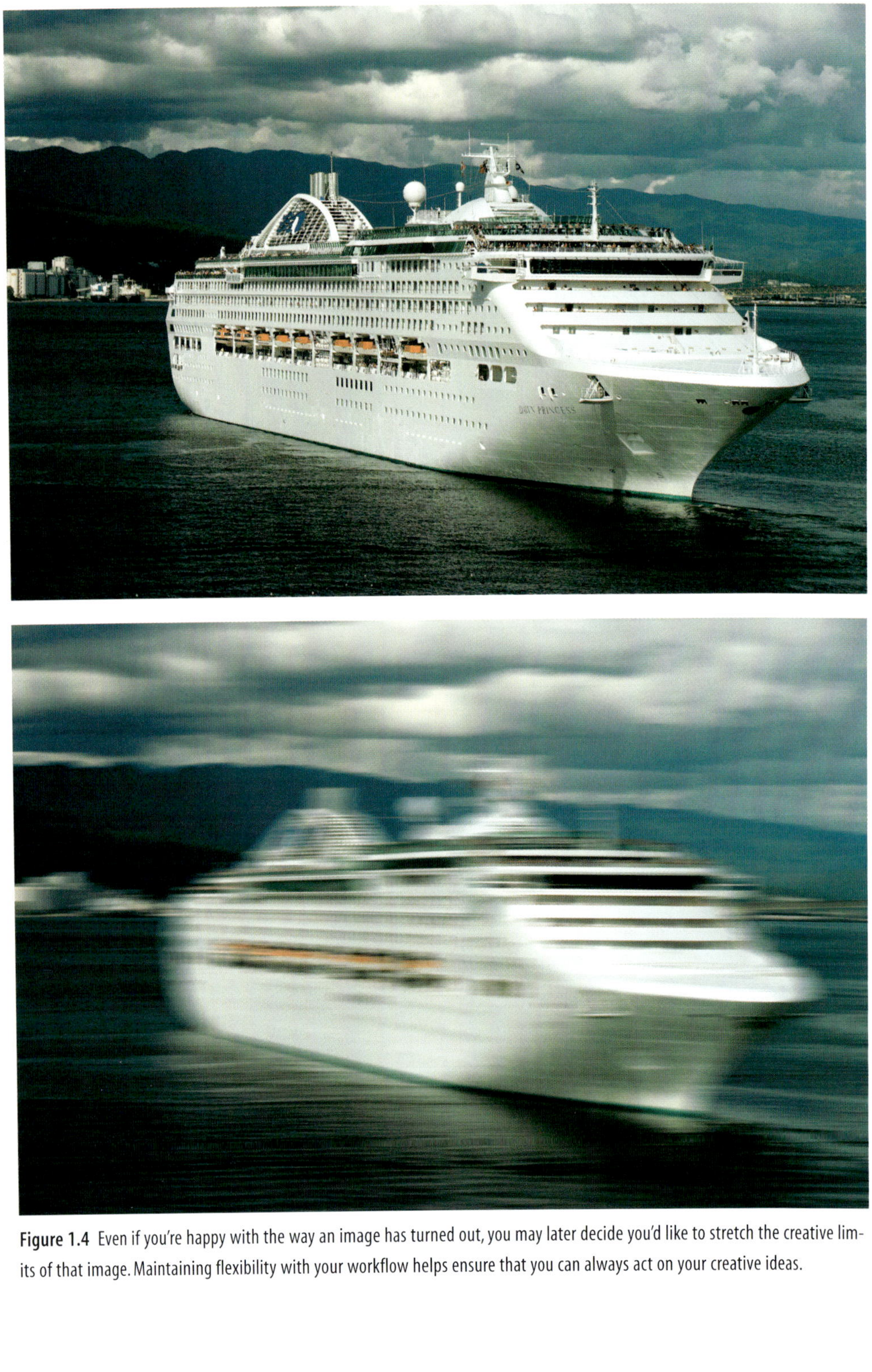

Figure 1.4 Even if you're happy with the way an image has turned out, you may later decide you'd like to stretch the creative limits of that image. Maintaining flexibility with your workflow helps ensure that you can always act on your creative ideas.

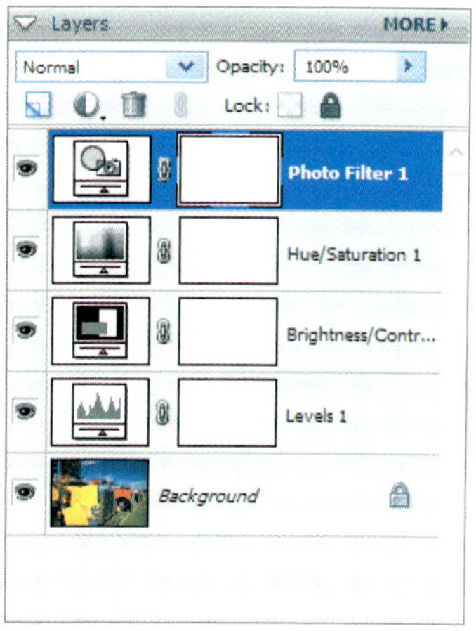

Figure 1.5
By using layers in your workflow, you'll maintain the flexibility to revise the adjustments you've made at any time without risking a loss of detail or quality in the image.

Revising Your Workflow

We recommend thinking of a digital imaging workflow as a living entity. That's not because we have some weird fascination with workflow, but because we realize that your typical workflow will change over time. You need to be comfortable revising your workflow to take advantage of new techniques you learn.

Nothing Is Permanent

A variety of factors may lead you to revise the way you work on your images. For starters, as you learn new image-editing techniques, you may want to incorporate them into your workflow. As you read more books, take workshops, or just talk to others who are also involved in digital photography, you'll discover new methods that provide a more efficient way to achieve similar results or a way to produce completely new variations of your images.

A general workflow provides the flexibility to incorporate new methods into the process of optimizing your images, because it is simply a guideline for general adjustments. However, in many cases you may develop a very specific workflow that will call for performing specific actions (with variable settings) in a specific order. To ensure that you are always able to achieve the best results, be willing to revise your workflow to incorporate new skills as you learn them.

Another factor that can change your workflow is changes in software. With each new version of Elements, or with the release (or discovery) of new plug-ins and filters, you'll find ways to add efficiency and creativity to your normal workflow.

The key is to be willing to revise your workflow when appropriate. If you learn a way to make your workflow more efficient or to provide even better results, by all means change your workflow to include such techniques.

Requirements Will Evolve

As you continue working with your images, you'll likely find that your own requirements will evolve. In our estimation, these changing requirements fall into two general categories.

The first category represents actual changes to the results you need to produce. For example, if you've been producing only ink-jet prints but now need to be able to prepare your images for offset press output, you may need to revise your workflow to be sure you're producing the best results for that type of output. If you create a website to share your images, you may also need to alter your workflow to include steps for preparing smaller versions of the images as well as thumbnail representations. Whatever the reasons, you'll likely find that the requirements placed on your images change over time, and you'll want to be sure your workflow is always ready to meet those demands.

The second category has to do with the likelihood that standards will get higher with time. If you've been working with digital imaging for any length of time, you can probably relate to this from your own experience. When the first photo ink-jet printers became available, most of us were thrilled with the quality they could provide. But if you compare that early output to what today's photo ink-jet printers are able to achieve, you'd consider those older models totally inadequate (Figure 1.6). What used to be considered excellent quality is now rated as garbage. As we see what is now possible, what used to be possible is no longer good enough.

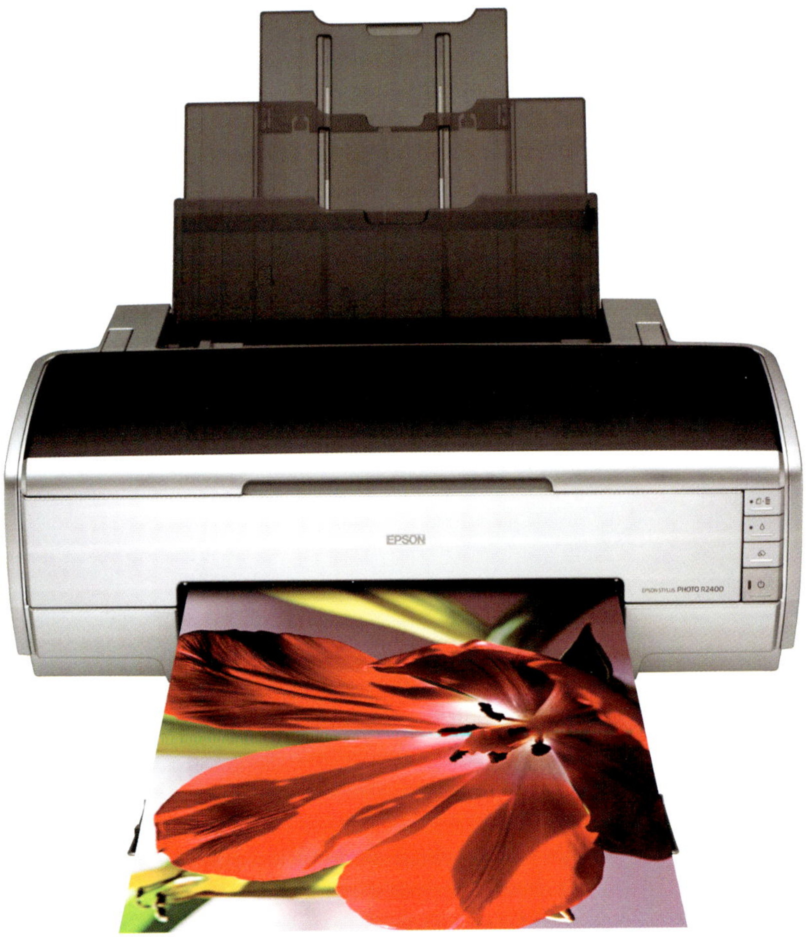

Figure 1.6 Today's photo ink-jet printers produce considerably better quality than those of just a few years ago. Similarly, your capabilities will improve with time, and you may want to revise your workflow over time so you always meet or exceed your own standards.

Similarly, you'll likely find that your own standards increase over time. As you become more skilled in the optimization of your images, you may open older images and wonder how you ever let yourself print them because you know you can do so much better today. As such, your developing skills in image optimization will call for revisions to your overall workflow.

Creating a Workflow That Works

The workflow you use to optimize your images will continue to evolve over time. The most important step is to actually implement a workflow so it can evolve. Evaluate your images, consider the adjustments that are necessary to achieve the results you desire, and think about a logical way to apply those adjustments that will provide an efficient way to produce consistently high-quality results.

By taking the time to develop such a workflow, you'll ensure that the process is working for you, rather than creating a situation where you are working hard but not producing the consistent quality you desire. With a proper workflow—as you'll find throughout the rest of this book—you'll be able to unleash the great potential of the pixels in your images.

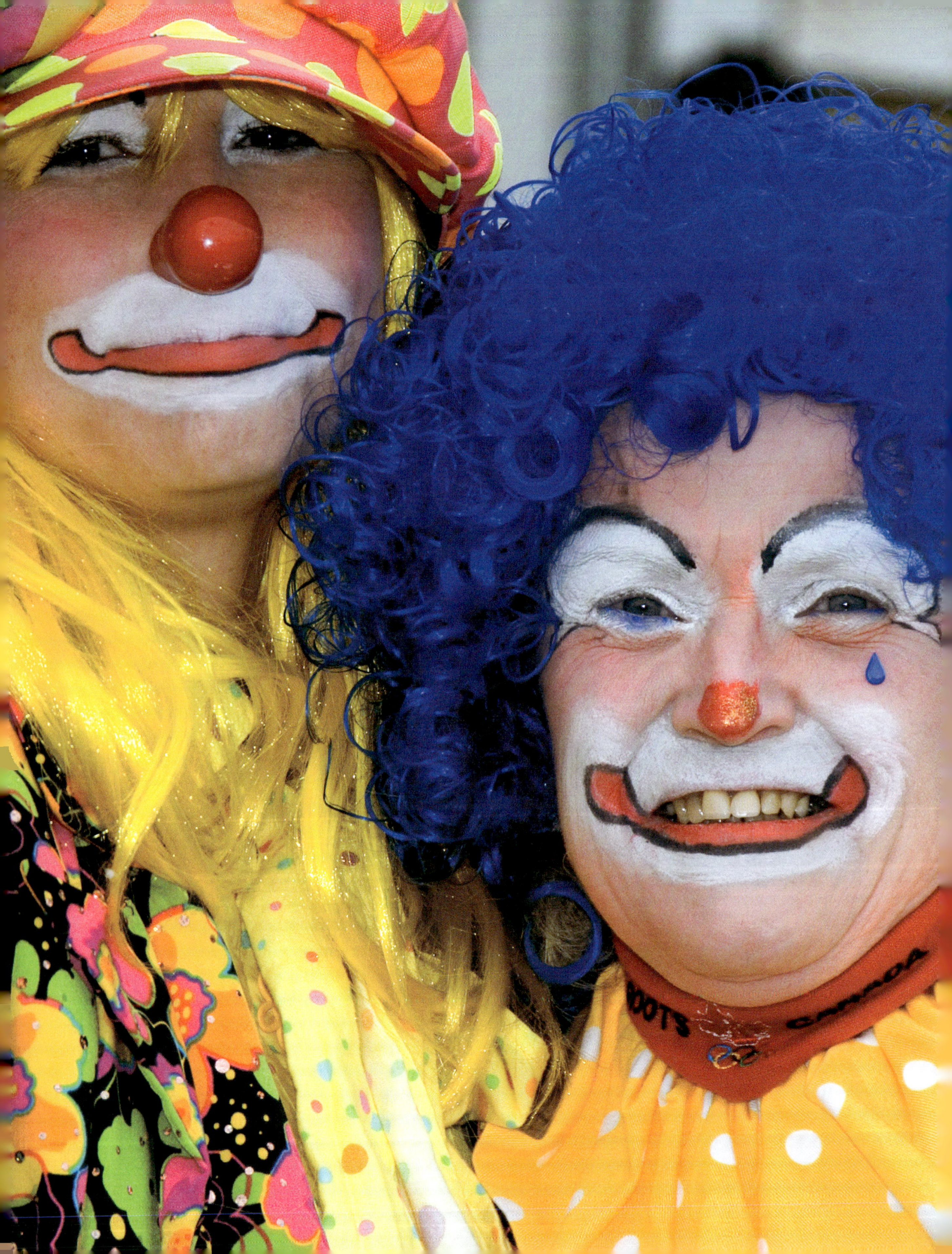
ROOTS
CANADA

Download and Sort

2

The real workflow for your digital photos starts before the images even reach your computer—before you press the shutter release button to capture an image. Of course, the actual workflow of optimizing starts with the process of downloading and sorting your images. Proper techniques ensure that you'll safeguard your images and keep your growing collection of them organized.

Chapter Contents

Safe Downloading
Sorting Images in Organizer
Reviewing Images for Evaluation
Printing Contact Sheets

Safe Downloading

After returning from a trip or other photo shoot, we're all anxious to review the images that we have made. Granted, we have glimpsed them already on the camera's LCD display, but that isn't the same as taking a closer and more detailed look on a computer monitor (Figure 2.1). Besides examining the images closely and starting the sorting process, we want to make sure that the images are safely downloaded to a computer.

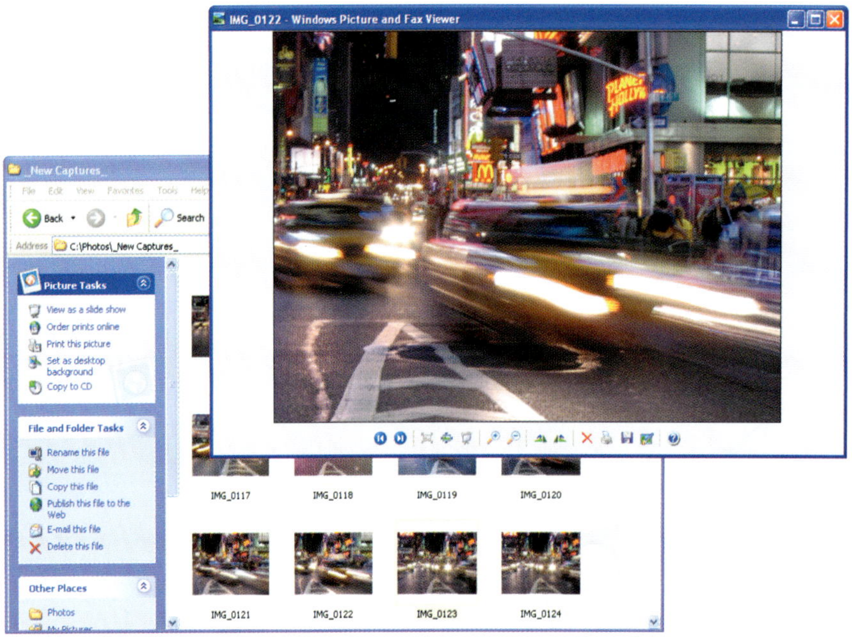

Figure 2.1 After you've downloaded your photos from memory cards onto your computer, you can perform a more detailed review of those images.

The basic goal is to transfer all of the images and collect them in one place on your computer. This makes it easier to sort through the images, determine which you want to delete and which you want to keep, and start to get an idea of which images you'd like to work with further. After you have safely downloaded your files, you can get organized and process your images with the workflow covered throughout this book.

Creating a Master Folder

Before you start downloading images, think about an organizational system for those files. You may have already started creating a folder structure to organize your images by subject matter, geographic location, or capture date. This is a great way to maintain a basic organizational system so you don't get overwhelmed with trying to find a particular image when you need it. Having such as system in place, in advance, will help streamline the overall process and make sure you are able to stay organized as you continue to take more pictures.

Regardless of how you'll be organizing images after sorting them, we recommend creating a master folder, perhaps called New Captures, to serve as the preliminary destination for downloaded images (Figure 2.2). This keeps the new images separate from your normal organizational folder structure and provides a familiar location for your downloaded photos. You can use the New Captures folder (and subfolders as needed) for initially storing all new photos when you don't have time to sort through them right away. You can then continue taking more pictures or working on other tasks, returning to this download destination folder when you're ready to sort through the images. We recommend naming the New Captures folder in such a way that it will always be listed first when sorted alphabetically, such as by placing an underscore as the first character in the folder name.

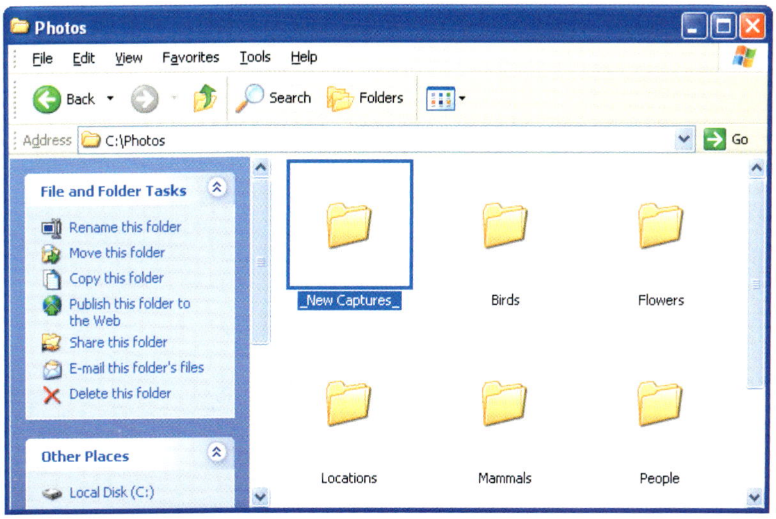

Figure 2.2 Creating a folder for storing new photos will help you stay organized. Name your download folder alphabetically, such as _New Captures_, and it will always be the first item in your list of folders.

Note: If you've filled several high-capacity memory cards and therefore have a particularly large number of digital photos to sort through, you may not want to download all of them to a single New Captures folder. Doing so will require considerable processing power to build thumbnail previews and can slow down the sorting process. Instead, you may want to create subfolders in your New Captures folder, each named by date, so that any one folder will contain a manageable number of images.

Using Adobe Photo Downloader

After you've established the New Captures folder as the first destination for your downloaded images, you're ready to start copying images from memory cards onto your computer. You can use various methods, including Adobe Photo Downloader, which was available as an option when you installed Photoshop Elements 5 from the CD. This software recognizes JPEG and TIFF captures as well as RAW files from cameras that are supported by Adobe Camera Raw. (Previous versions of Photo Downloader did not provide RAW support, but the current version does, when used with Elements 5.)

After you connect your camera or a memory card reader to your computer, Photo Downloader should launch when it automatically detects the device containing image files. Click the Advanced Dialog button, and a larger dialog box opens (Figure 2.3), showing thumbnails of images on the memory card. You can clear the checkbox under any images that should not be downloaded because of serious exposure or other problems. A Browse button is available, allowing you to specify where your images should be copied—in your New Captures folder, for example. You can also create subfolders by shot date, by today's date, or with a custom name. The latter allows you to create a subfolder named for the location and date where you took the photos, the event you photographed, the name of the subject, and so on, to help you stay organized.

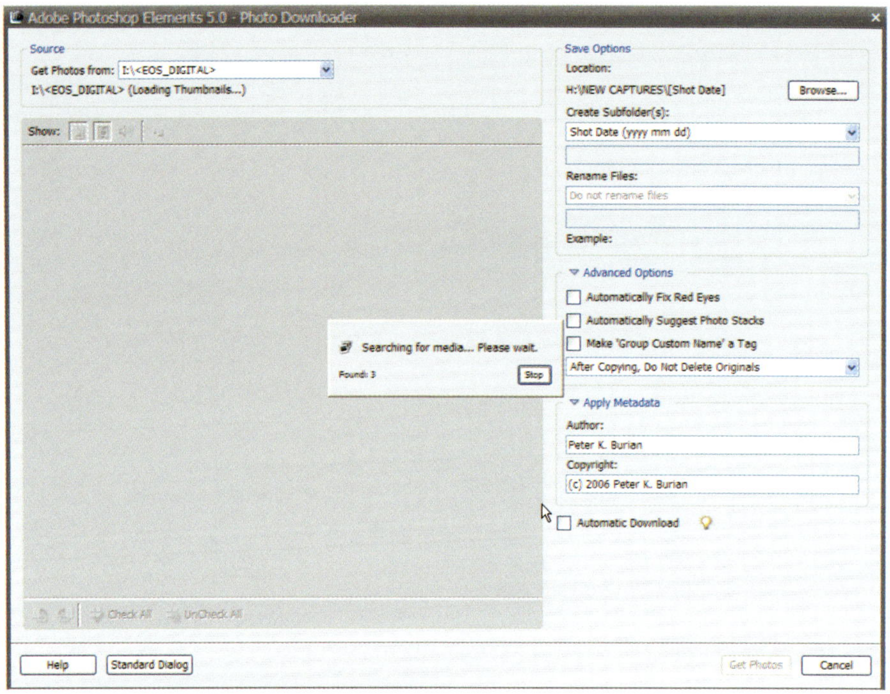

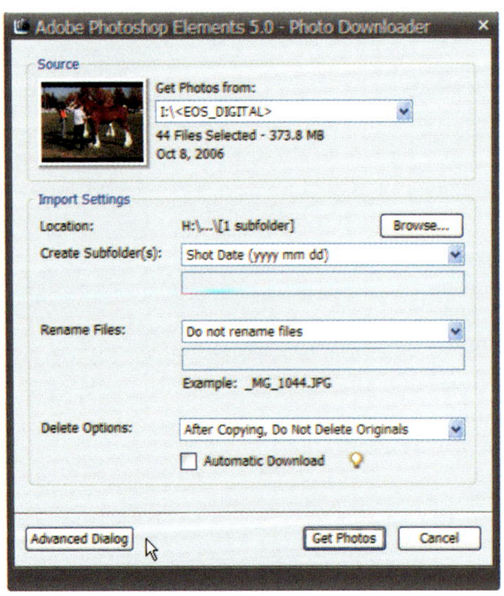

Figure 2.3 You can set Adobe Photo Downloader to automatically launch when it detects that a device including a memory card has been connected to your computer. This software provides a user-friendly method for downloading your images, with a Standard and Advanced Dialog box providing useful options.

> **Note:** Adobe Photo Downloader was not included in the Macintosh version of Photoshop Elements 4. At the time of this writing, Elements 5 was not yet available for the Mac.

If Photo Downloader did not automatically launch when you connected your camera or card reader, simply click the Organize button in Elements to launch the Organize interface. From there, choose Edit > Preferences > Camera Or Card Reader. In the Preference dialog box under the Download Options section, make sure the Auto Launch Adobe Photo Downloader On Device Connect checkbox is selected. Click OK. If you still need to manually load Photo Downloader, choose File > Get Photos. Then choose the source of your images such as your camera, mobile phone, and so on.

Photo Downloader can also rename the files for you as they are being downloaded. Simply select the Rename Files To checkbox, and choose one of the options, including Custom (which allows you to set your own filenames). The files will be renamed accordingly, and a sequence number will be appended.

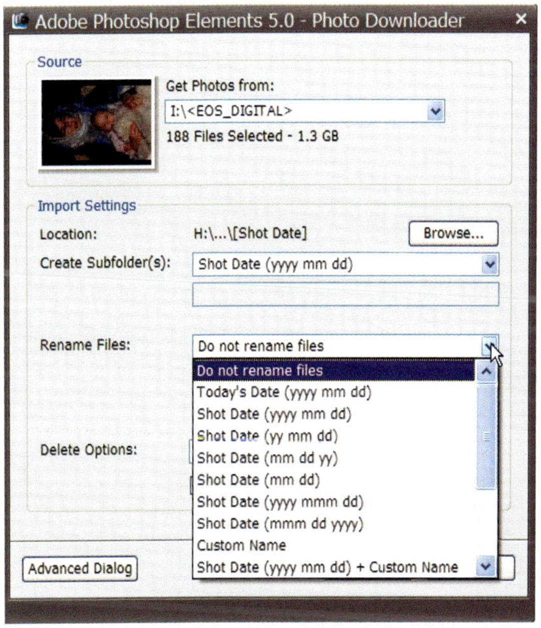

Other available features include Automatically Fix Red Eyes, Automatically Suggest Photo Stacks, and Make Group Custom Name A Tag. The automatic red-eye correction option slows the downloading process because the software looks for red-eye in all your images; consequently, we recommend against that option.

Photo Stacks organizes images that Photo Downloader determines are visually similar into stacks that appear in the browser, which can help keep your photos more organized. Use this option if you prefer to group similar photos together. The similar images will appear as one thumbnail in Organizer rather than displayed as separate thumbnails. Use this option with caution if you prefer to see separate thumbnails of all the images. If images are stacked, you can always right-click the thumbnail and choose Stack > Unstack Photos to view them as separate thumbnails again.

The third option, Make Group Custom Name A Tag, is a personal preference based on whether you want to use the Group Custom Name as a tag. Use this option only if you have chosen to assign custom groups. A tag is another means available to organize your photos further. You can choose keywords to organize photos by attaching a tag label such as Family, Friends, Places, and so on.

There is a Tag palette in Organizer that allows you to sort and find images based on these tag names. You have controls within the palette to create new tag names or fine-tune the default tag name options already available. If you do not select Make Group Custom Name A Tag, you can always tag your images manually by dragging the tag name from the palette onto the thumbnail images within Organizer. You can then use the Tag palette to find or sort images based on the Tag name categories.

You can also specify that Photo Downloader should automatically delete all images on the memory card after the download, but we don't recommend that. Instead, it's best to select the After Copying, Do Not Delete Originals option as a safety measure. After you are certain that all images have been transferred, you can reformat the card in your camera as per the instructions in your camera owner's manual.

Finally, under the Apply Metadata heading, you can type your name as the photographer and add copyright information, such as © 2007 T. J. Wilson. This may not provide a significant value in terms of protecting your image, but at least it will notify anyone who receives a copy that you are the copyright owner.

After establishing all settings, click the Get Photos button, and Photo Downloader begins transferring the images. After that has been completed, Elements automatically launches Organizer, if you have checked the Open Organizer When Finished item under Advanced Options in the Photo Downloader dialog box. All of the images that you downloaded will then be displayed (Figure 2.4).

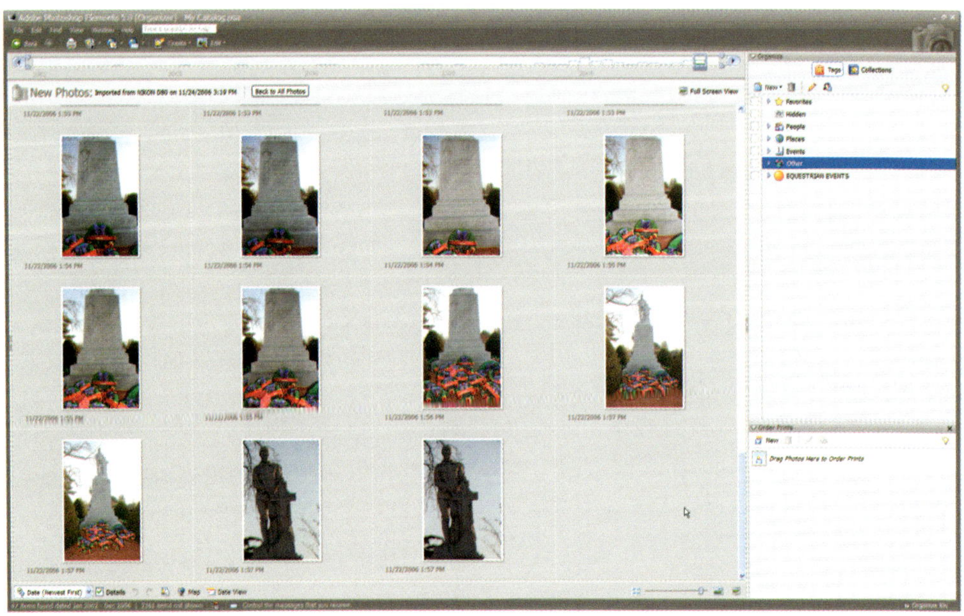

Figure 2.4 After Photo Downloader successfully downloads your images, Photoshop Elements automatically launch Organizer , showing the images that were downloaded.

Using Third-Party Software

Although Photo Downloader is convenient, you can use other methods for transferring files from your memory card to the computer. These include aftermarket software that is similar in concept to Photo Downloader and manual transfer discussed in a subsequent section. There are many third-party programs, including Tim's favorite, the particularly versatile Downloader Pro from Breeze Systems (www.breezesys.com). This one will particularly appeal to photographers who want numerous file-renaming options as part of their organizational workflow. You can also use the wizard included with Windows XP or navigate in Windows Explorer or in My Computer to select files from a memory card and transfer them to the hard drive.

> **Note:** In addition to the Adobe Photo Downloader and third-party programs such as ACDSee Photo Manager from ACD Systems, most digital cameras include basic or advanced software that includes a feature for downloading images from a memory card reader or directly from your camera. The features within the downloader vary widely depending on the software that your camera maker provides. Some include all of the solutions discussed in this section while others are very basic and provide few workflow or efficiency benefits.

Using Windows XP Wizard

For Windows XP users, the included Scanner And Camera Wizard provides a convenient method for downloading image files from a digital camera or a memory card reader. If downloading from a camera, you may first need to install the "driver" software that is on the CD packaged with the camera.

Accessing the Scanner And Camera Wizard is as easy as inserting a media card into the card reader. Windows will recognize that a card has been inserted and will ask you what action you'd like to perform (Figure 2.5). Select the "Copy pictures to a folder on my computer using Microsoft Scanner And Camera Wizard" option and click OK to start the process. If Windows doesn't prompt you for an action, you can go to My Computer and right-click the drive letter for your card reader. Select AutoPlay from the menu that pops up, and the prompt will be displayed.

The first page of the wizard simply confirms the drive you are copying from and provides some basic information about the process. Click Next to proceed. The next page (Figure 2.6) shows you thumbnails of images on the card. By default all of the images are selected for download, but you can clear the checkbox for any you don't want to copy. This is a great way to filter out the images you know you definitely don't want based on the thumbnail preview, such as an obviously bad exposure that can't be salvaged or a shot taken with the lens cap on. Click Next to continue.

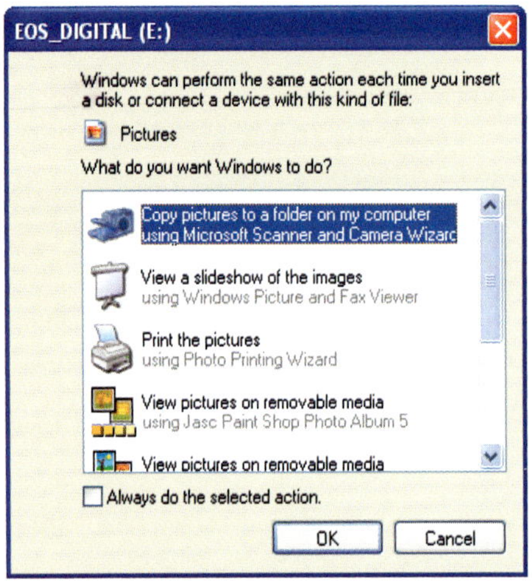

Figure 2.5 When you insert a card into a card reader, Windows XP prompts you for the action you'd like to perform.

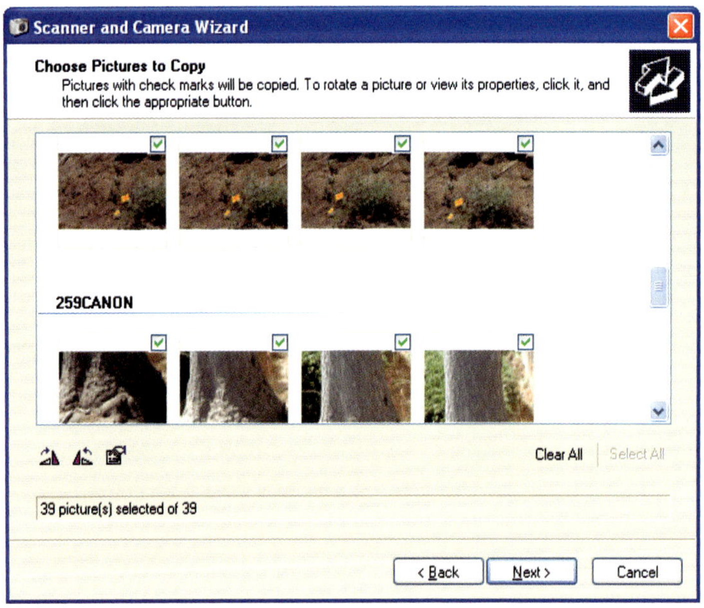

Figure 2.6 The Scanner And Camera Wizard allows you to select the specific files you'd like to download.

The next page provides options for the filename structure and location for the images you will be downloading (Figure 2.7). The first option asks for a name for the group of photos. Whatever you type into this field will have a number added to it to create filenames for *all* images as they are downloaded. To specify a destination folder for the images, click the Browse button and select the desired location in the Browse For Folder dialog box. This page also includes an option to delete the image files from your media card when downloading is complete. However, we don't recommend this option because it's wise to confirm that all files have been transferred safely before deleting; also, there is some benefit to reformatting the memory card often, making that a suitable way to delete all files.

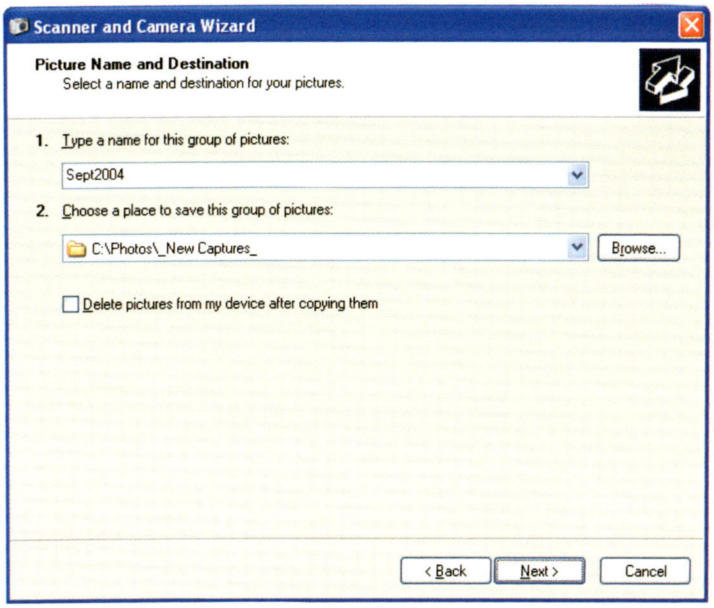

Figure 2.7 The Picture Name And Destination page of the Scanner And Camera Wizard allows you to specify the filename structure and location for images to be downloaded.

Note: Reformatting your card in the camera re-initializes the card to help avoid the potential for accumulated file corruption (which could ultimately cause you to lose files). During this process, all files are erased, so this is the recommended method for deleting all images when you're ready to do so.

After you click Next on the Picture Name And Destination page of the wizard, the process of copying your images begins. A progress page is displayed, showing you the status of the current image as well as the complete process. When the copying is completed, you'll be asked whether you'd like to perform another task. To finish, select the Nothing option and click Next. A final summary page is displayed, which you can close by clicking the Finish button. After you do so, Windows automatically displays a folder view of the destination folder you used for the Scanner And Camera Wizard so you can immediately review the downloaded images.

Note: The Windows Scanner And Camera Wizard renames all files it downloads from your camera, so be sure this isn't a problem for your particular workflow before using this download utility.

Manual Copying

Another option for transferring images from a memory card to a computer is to simply copy them manually through your operating system. Start by inserting the card into your card reader. In Windows a folder view may appear automatically, or you can double-click the card reader's drive letter in My Computer or in Windows Explorer.

Most digital cameras use the standard DCIM folder as the main folder on the media card, so at first this is the only thing you'll see. If you open DCIM, you'll see one or more subfolders that contain images, often named to indicate the camera manufacturer and a sequence number, such as 156CANON and 157CANON. You may also see a folder (with a name such as CANONMSC) containing miscellaneous files that are used only by the camera and do not need to be downloaded.

With the folders containing images visible, you now need to open the destination folder on your computer, such as the New Captures folder. When both are visible, select all image folders on the media card and drag and drop them to the destination folder (Figure 2.8). They will then be copied to that location.

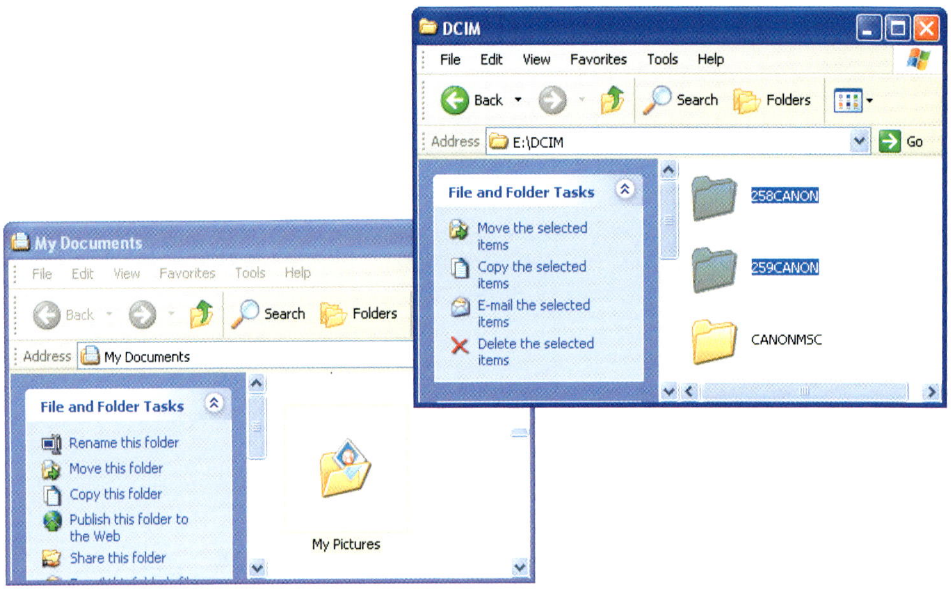

Figure 2.8 To copy files manually from your media card, open a folder view of the card itself and the destination folder, and then drag and drop from the source to the destination the folders that contain images.

The advantage of copying the files manually from your cards is being able to see for yourself that all images have been selected for copying. Some photographers prefer the sense of control this provides. However, others employ different methods. We suggest experimenting to determine which you find to be most logical and convenient.

Confirming a Successful Transfer

Although any of the methods for downloading files from a memory card are highly reliable, your images are important enough to warrant taking a moment to confirm a full, successful download. Open the destination folder where you have copied new captures and confirm that the folder contains all the images you are expecting. Selecting a thumbnail preview mode for JPEG or TIFF images within your operating system provides a quick way to confirm that the images you were expecting have been downloaded safely (Figure 2.9).

If you are working with RAW captures, you should use Organizer in Elements, or other software that supports your camera's RAW captures, to confirm that all have been downloaded.

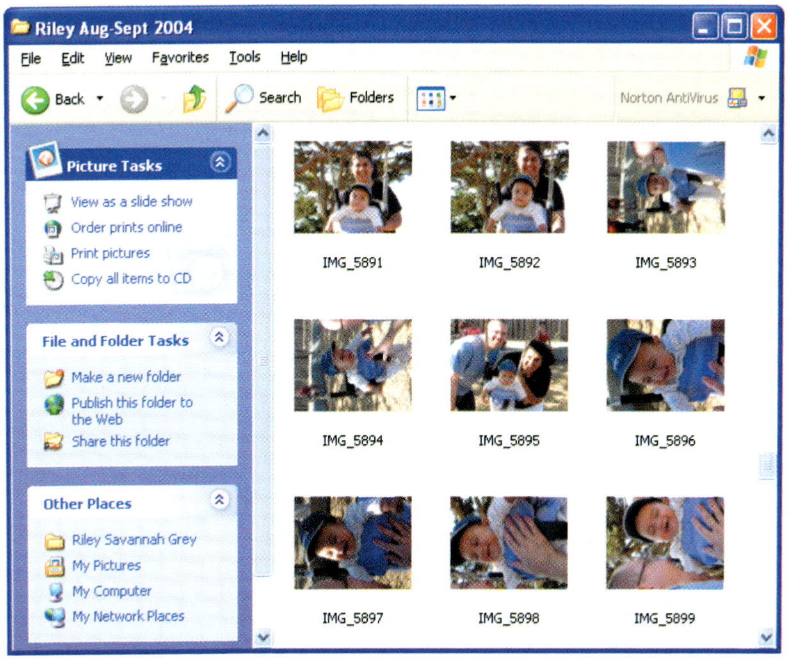

Figure 2.9 Simply browsing the list of files or a thumbnail view of the folder where you copied your images (including RAW captures if the software supports your camera's format) is a great way to confirm that they were all copied successfully.

You may not be able to confirm that every image on your memory card has been downloaded just by looking at the images themselves. However, you can usually confirm success by looking at the number of images that were downloaded and viewing the first and last few. Doing so will likely jog your memory about what had been captured, and you'll be better able to confirm their successful download. You can also select the files that were downloaded to confirm the count and hard-disk space consumed, and then compare that to the properties of the folder(s) on your card to ensure that all the image data has been transferred.

Note: If you used a camera's RAW+JPEG capture, there may be two distinct files for each photo that you made—one in the RAW format and the other as a JPEG. However, that does not apply for every digital camera. Some models embed the JPEG image into the RAW file; in that case, only one file, the RAW capture, will appear per image. When you later decide to open your image files in Elements or other software that supports your camera's RAW format, both the RAW and JPEG photo will be available.

Archiving

Besides getting the new captures into your computer, it's wise to implement a backup system that produces an archival copy right from the beginning of your workflow. It's best to create an archival (permanent) copy of all images immediately upon download, but you may prefer to wait until you have reviewed the photos closely and deleted any that are not satisfactory. In either case, create a duplicate copy on CD, DVD, external hard disk, or other media early in the workflow process.

The workflow that we'll discuss in this book will eventually produce a master image file in which the original capture data is maintained unaltered. Still, it is a great idea to create a duplicate copy of the original captures as a last-resort backup. You may never need to access them—but if you do, you'll be glad you kept them.

We usually recommend retaining the original filenames for the backup copies of your images. However, this can lead to a problem if you need to find a particular backup copy of an image later; a filename such as `_MG2201.CR2` or `MG2201.tif` will mean nothing to you a few months from now. That's another reason why you might want to rename image files *prior* to the download, an option available with the Adobe software and some aftermarket programs.

We recommend either that you keep the original capture name as *part* of the filename—adding additional text as appropriate for each set of new images—or that you rename the files immediately upon downloading and then create a backup copy with the new names. This step will ensure that the archived backup files have the same filename reference as your master files, making it easier to find a specific image when you need it.

Because the backup copy is intended only for insurance, you may never need to access it. Therefore, find a method that is convenient for quickly copying the files and storing the resulting media. Although high-grade or archival CD-R or DVD-R media can be convenient for recording a group of files from a particular photo shoot, the discs can accumulate quickly and require a fair amount of storage space. (The rewriteable RW discs are not as archival as the R discs.) We recommend obtaining a high-capacity external hard drive for this purpose, using it exclusively for backing up your images after downloading them to your computer.

Reformatting Memory Cards

After you have copied all images from your card and confirmed that all are in the destination folder, you're ready to clear the card so it will be ready for your next photo shoot. Just be sure to safely eject the card or camera from your operating system to avoid potential data problems. We strongly recommend reformatting the cards in the camera rather than deleting or formatting within your operating system. The latter is the more serious mistake because reformatting in the computer could make the card unusable by the camera, although reformatting it in the camera should solve that problem. This can occur because of differences in the file system used by your operating system and by the camera. With most digital cameras, the Format option can be accessed from the menu that appears on the LCD monitor after you press the Menu or similar button.

Formatting the card in-camera erases the images as part of the process, and is generally faster than any of the other methods for deleting all images from the card. It also re-initializes the card with a new "table of contents." Doing so helps prevent accumulated corruption of the card's file system, helping to ensure you won't experience any read or write problems in the future.

Note: Because the memory card serves as an effective backup of the images you downloaded from it, you may want to wait to reformat the card until just before you need to use it again. This precaution will allow you to recover images if they are inadvertently deleted from your computer. That potential risk exists and it also reinforces the benefit of creating an archival copy of all images immediately after downloading them.

Sorting Images in Organizer

Getting your digital images onto your computer is certainly a start. But as you've probably noticed, those files seem to accumulate quickly, and keeping them organized can be a bit of a chore, especially if you have a backlog of images stored in many folders. After downloading your latest batch of photos to a New Captures or similar folder, you'll probably want to get started right away working with them. The first step, of course, is to figure out what you have and which images you'd like to start optimizing first.

Note: The Organizer available with Elements 5 can be selected from the main screen by clicking the Organize button at the top if you are already in Full Edit or Quick Fix. Although more professionally oriented software is available, the Adobe solution is easy to use and allows for sorting, organizing, tagging, and later finding specific images as we will explain shortly. For example, you will have no difficulty finding images by the date (month and year) taken. However, you will also be able to assign "tags" to your photos to categorize them in sections such as People, Family, Friends, Places, and Events. After tagging, it will be easy to find images in any category, simply by selecting that category in Organizer.

Light Table Analogy

Most (though certainly not all) photographers who are now capturing images with a digital camera started off with film photography. For those who used slide film, the concept of a light table sorting method is quite clear, and so this has been used countless times as an analogy for sorting digital images.

With 35mm slides, for example, the basic process of sorting involved laying out the slides on a light table, starting with an overall review to delete obviously bad images, and then getting a closer look with a loupe (magnifier accessory) to further evaluate those that remained (Figure 2.10). In the process, slides could be grouped based on criteria such as favorites, subject matter, the person or family in the photos, or other factors. This allowed the photographer to get organized while working to slim down the number of images. A similar process works quite well when sorting digital images.

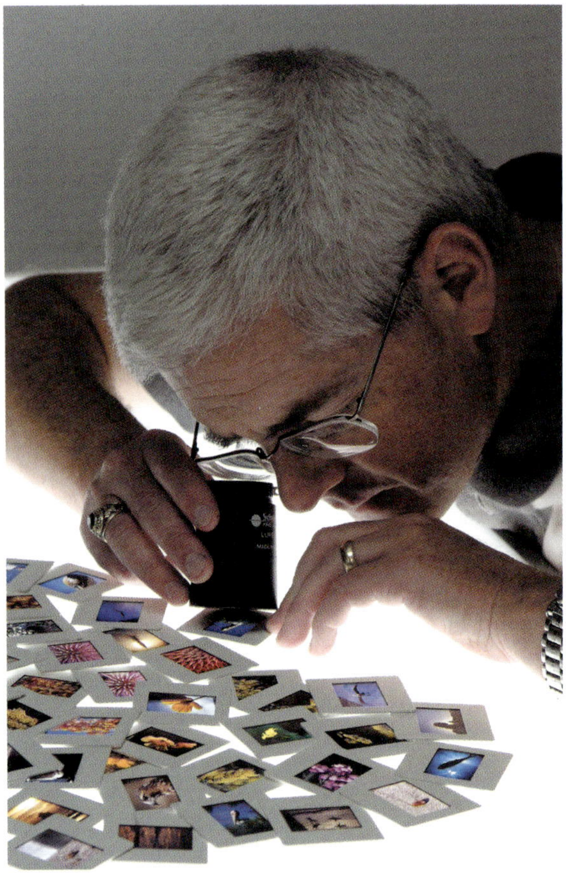

Figure 2.10 A light table provides an appropriate analogy for the process of sorting digital images.

Sorting Strategy

Before you start sorting, you'll want to consider a basic strategy for doing so. This will help you work more efficiently, and will help prevent you from feeling overwhelmed when you have a large number of images to process. While viewing a series of images in Organizer, taken during the past month for example, consider taking the following steps as you begin sorting through your images. Remember that double-clicking any image will toggle between a very large thumbnail view and the sort view. Both views provide a Rotate Right and Rotate Left tool under the image. The steps are as follows:

1. **Rotate verticals:** Images captured vertically will appear sideways, making them a little more difficult to evaluate. Rotating them to their proper orientation allows you to review the images as they should appear, without tilting your head or imagining how they will look when rotated.
2. **Discard unsatisfactory images:** Part of sorting through images is getting rid of those you know you'll never use. It can sometimes be difficult to delete photos that didn't turn out well, but if you want to get better organized you'll have to

take a serious look at the images and decide which you really don't need. We recommend a two-step process for discarding photos: remove the obviously poor images in a first pass, and later inspect the "less than ideal" images with greater scrutiny as discussed later in this chapter.

3. **Select the keepers:** After you have narrowed the images down to those you definitely want to keep, start deciding which images you'll want to work with for a particular project or simply to print or share with others. You can do this by moving your favorite images into a particular folder, or simply tagging them in Organizer in much the same way that film photographers have marked slide mounts and slide protector pages by using a grease pencil.
4. **Organize images:** You'll want to start organizing the images you're keeping so you'll be better able to locate just the right image whenever you need it. Depending on the software you're using, that can mean moving images into categorized folders or renaming the files. More-involved strategies can utilize specialized image-management software to provide a higher level of organization, or updating metadata (adding data that will be embedded in the image file) to reflect details that you want to be able to search on later.

Lightbox View

For the first pass of sorting, when you want to get an overall look at the images and start deleting the obviously unacceptable photos, we recommend using a *lightbox view* of the images in the current folder. That calls for making maximum use of the available space, by removing the Tools palette so the image thumbnails can fill a greater area. To achieve that, simply slide the vertical bar that divides the palettes pane from the thumbnails pane to the right so you can see nothing but thumbnails (Figure 2.11).

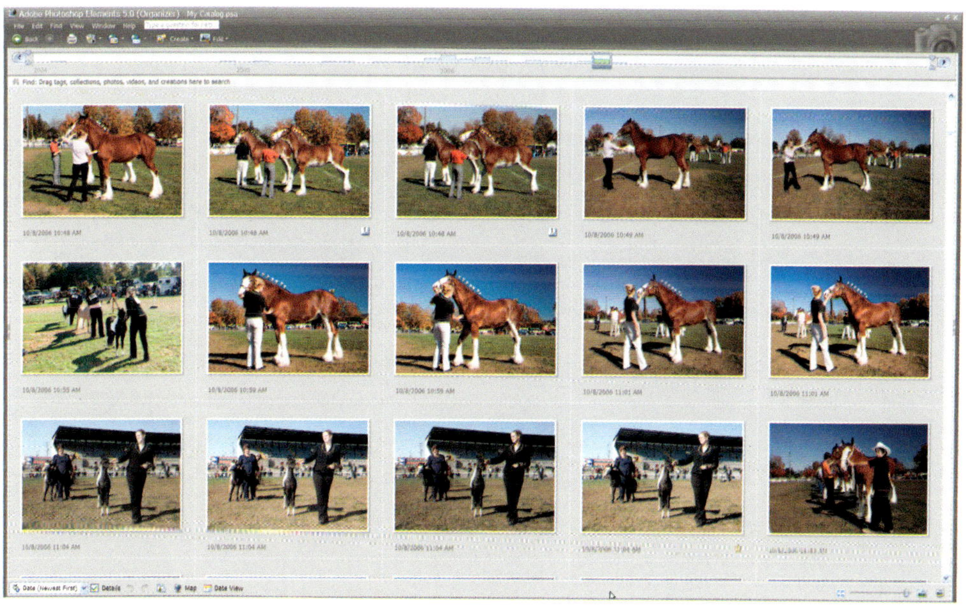

Figure 2.11 The lightbox view allows you to get an overview of the images in the current folder, and to start deleting those you can tell you don't want to keep simply by looking at the thumbnails.

With this display, you have an overview of the images and a better sense of exactly what you had captured. For larger or smaller thumbnails, use the Adjust Size Of Thumbnail slider, in the bottom-right corner of the screen. This is a suitable opportunity to start thinking about which subjects or particular types of images within the current collection seem to have the most potential. You will also want to rotate your verticals so they appear with the proper orientation. To rotate images, simply select them and click the appropriate rotation control near the lower-left corner of the Organizer window.

While scanning moderately large thumbnails, you'll notice that some stand out because of obviously poor exposure or other problems that make them candidates for immediate deletion. To remove those images, identify them and press the Delete key on your keyboard; you can also right-click the image and choose the Delete From Catalog option from the pop-up menu that appears. A dialog box appears, to alert you that the image will be deleted from the catalog. An additional option is available to select if you wish to have the image deleted from the hard drive at the same time.

If you aren't sure whether an image should be deleted just by looking at the thumbnail, you can double-click it for a larger display in Single Photo View mode (Figure 2.12), although that may still not allow you to make a final decision.

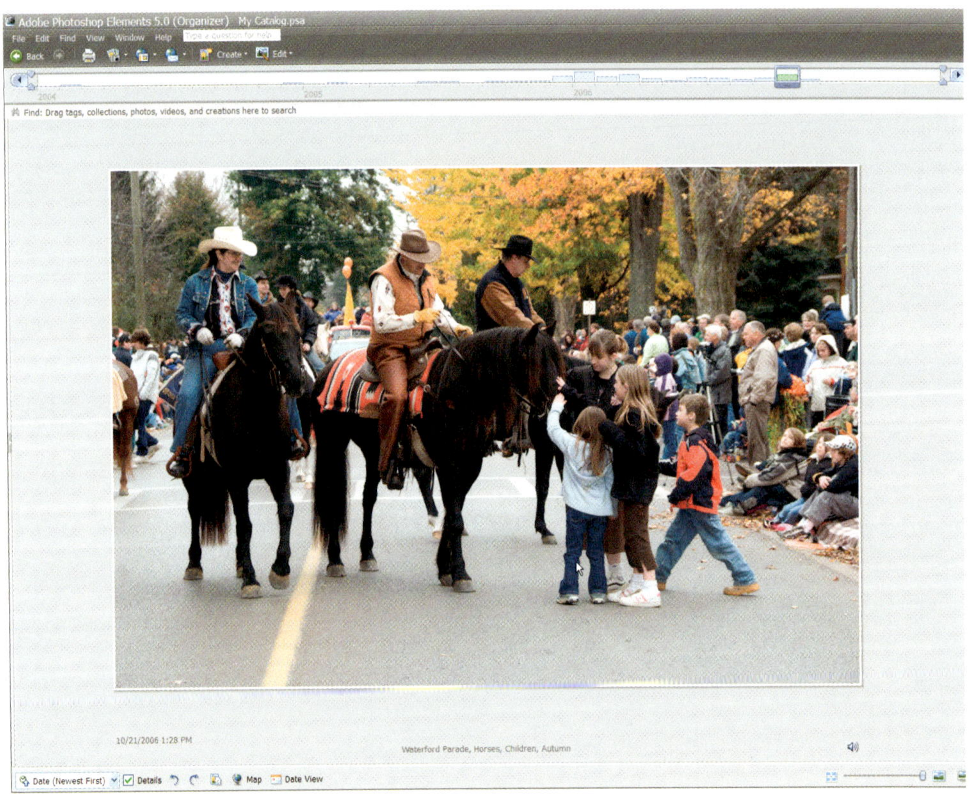

Figure 2.12 The Single Photo View mode can be useful for getting a closer look at a larger image, but that's not necessary yet in this early stage of the process. Save this option for later when cleaning up or sharpening the image.

You can get an even larger display of an image. While viewing a photo, click the Full Screen View button, near the bottom-right corner of the screen, or press the F11 key. The image then fills your monitor and a dialog box appears with various slideshow options, the primary use of the Full Screen View. To return to the organizer screen from Full Screen, press the Esc key on your keyboard.

However, all of that single image viewing can be time-consuming, and this first stage review is not the ideal time for close scrutiny. For now, we recommend simply viewing the thumbnails. When in doubt, don't delete any image just yet; you'll have an opportunity to do a more detailed review later. This first stage is a rough edit designed to clean out the collection of images you don't want to waste time scrutinizing.

Preview View

After you've taken an overall look at the images and deleted and rotated as needed, you're ready to start taking a closer look to decide which should be deleted and which should be tagged or otherwise identified. For this next step, we suggest an approach that we call the *preview view* of the images.

To get as large a preview image as possible, drag the vertical divider bar over to leave enough space for viewing a single column of thumbnails (Figure 2.13). This provides a great method for reviewing your images with more scrutiny than on your first pass, while still maintaining an easy way to navigate through the collection.

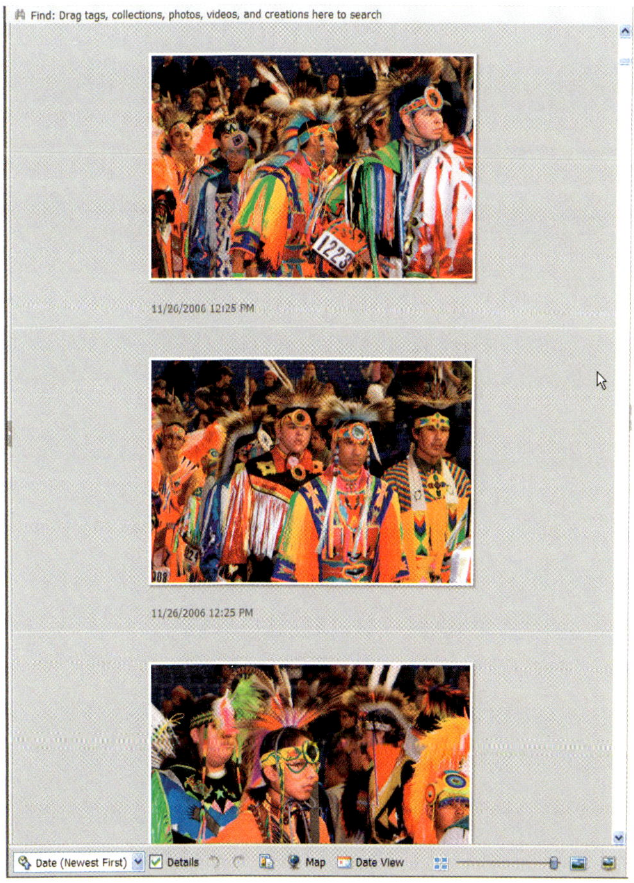

Figure 2.13 Adjusting the panes within Organizer so you are able to see a few large thumbnails at one time is an excellent way to review photos with greater scrutiny than your first review pass.

Instead of using your mouse to click the images that you want to view in more detail, we recommend taking a close look at all of the images in your collection. Click the first image on the list (scroll to the top of the list if necessary) and then use the up and down arrow keys on your keyboard to navigate through the images. As you move up and down, the preview updates based on the currently active image. This gives you a much better idea of the overall composition, exposure accuracy, and image quality, so you can make more-educated decisions as to which images should be deleted and kept. You can also start to get a better idea of which images deserve more attention as you sort through them.

Applying Tags

As you sort through the images, deleting those not worth keeping, you'll start getting an idea of which are the best, which you want to include in a particular project, or which deserve to be printed as soon as possible. Trying to remember your favorites can be a challenge if you're working with a large number of photos at once. Click the Tags tab and you'll find that the tagging feature in Organizer enables you to designate images in various categories: Favorites (with a one-to-five-star rating), People, Places, and Events. These premade tags are fine, but you can also click the New button to create your own New Tabs, New Categories, or New Sub Categories to be added to existing tabs. You might create tags such as Equestrian Events, San Francisco, or Joe and Mary's Wedding, for example. You can also right-click the existing Tag items for more options to change, delete, or add to the existing default tag labels.

To assign a tag, you simply select one and drag and drop it on any thumbnail image. An icon of the tag then permanently appears under that thumbnail of the image. You can drag and drop the same tag to many images, such as all of your photos of a specific wedding. You can also assign multiple tags to any image: Equestrian Events and Horse Jumping and Mary Competing, for example. To do so, hold down the Ctrl/⌘ key on your keyboard and click the tag items that are appropriate. Release the Ctrl/⌘ key and you can drag all of those tags to any image.

You may also want to quickly tag a series of photos. Identify several photos by holding the Ctrl/⌘ key while clicking the image thumbnails you want to select. Release the key when all have been identified. Now, drag and drop the pertinent tag icon—or several tag icons as a group, if multiple tags have been selected—to one of the selected photos. Release the mouse, and the tag(s) will be attached to all the selected images (Figure 2.14).

The tagging process is quicker than it might seem from our description. The most time-consuming aspect is creating new Tabs, Categories, or Sub Categories, but after a few weeks of using the custom feature, you'll have created most of the tags you will ever need.

This extra effort will pay off later, when you decide that you want to view all images in a Category or Sub Category, such as People, Events, or Horse Jumping, simply by double-clicking the category name in the list of Tags. A binoculars icon will then appear, and the display will exhibit only images with the pertinent tag. This is a great way to review photos that you considered "keepers" in a particular series and then

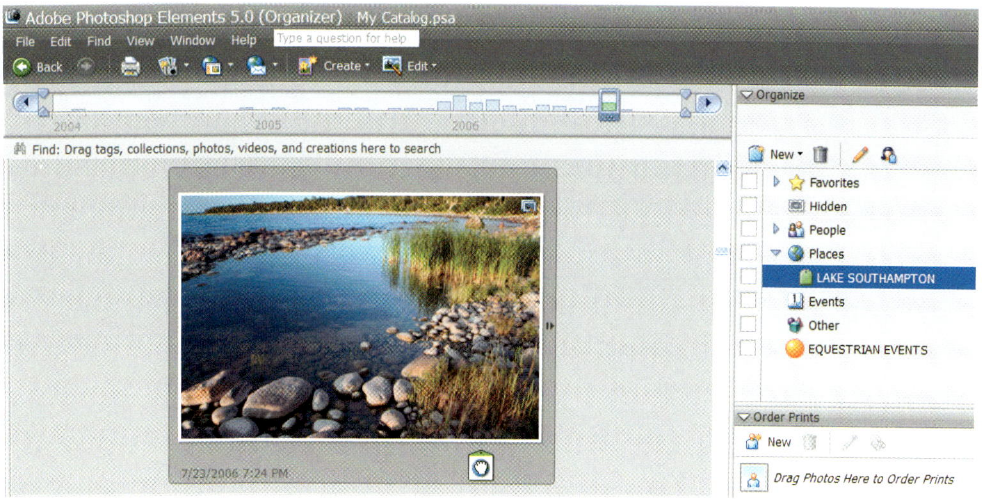

Figure 2.14 After you tag an image, one or more icons will appear below the thumbnail display to confirm the tag or tags that you have assigned.

scrutinize them to determine which are redundant and which should be removed. Whenever you wish to remove a tag from an image, right-click the photo, and select Remove From Category from the drop-down menu that appears. To view all of your images in Organizer again, click Back To All Photos near the top of the screen.

Note: When sorting through a large collection of images, you often may end up tagging similar images that weren't near each other in the list of images because of the order in which they were captured. This is one of the great things about tagging images: you can identify favorites but then further evaluate that group to determine which images will make the final cut in a Category.

If tagging images seems remarkably simple, that's because it is. But this simplicity is part of what makes the feature so elegant. You can quickly shift back and forth between similar images, for example, until you decide which is best. Then you can tag one with a Sub Category tag, such as Equestrian Feb 2007. 07 Best, so you'll know it was your favorite, and you don't need to scrutinize that pair again. You can also use Organizer to sort images and mark the ones you'd like to utilize for a particular project.

Other Organizer Features

Organizer offers a variety of additional features, although they are not all essential to the workflow concepts to be discussed in this book. Date View allows you to quickly review images made during a specific month/year. Click Date View at the bottom of the screen to bring up a calendar; specify a certain day and you can view images made on that date. For more-targeted searching, you could try options such as Face Tagging (Find > Find Faces For Tagging) that automatically locates all images that include a human face. Another option, Find By Visual Similarity, tries to locate photos with attributes that are similar to those in an image that you identify in terms of subject type, color similarity, or orientation. None of these search features is foolproof, but both can be useful when you quickly need to locate certain types of images.

Mentioned earlier, metadata (also called EXIF) is data that is recorded by the camera during shooting and embedded into the image file. You can view that information for any image by clicking the icon resembling the letter *i* in the Properties palette. If the Properties palette is not in view, click the Show or Hide Properties button located next to the rotate buttons at the bottom of the screen. Brief data will appear, but you can also select the Complete option if you want to view a vast amount of data. More importantly, you can add data to be embedded in image files by clicking the first icon under the Properties label, called General. Type in a Caption as well as Notes if desired. (You can also add a caption to any image while viewing it in Single Photo View mode; select the Caption option below the image.)

Adding such data will provide another method for quickly locating specific images. After adding information for many photos, you can choose Find > Find By Caption Or Note and specify what terms should be searched: a name, a place, or some noun or adjective that you recall using in captions or notes for pertinent photos. Organizer will find the relevant images and display them on a separate screen for your review.

The Find command (Figure 2.15) is also useful when you want Organizer to locate files by using other attributes: File Name or History (when it was emailed or printed), for example. It's worth exploring the various Find options because some of them are likely to be useful at some time in the future, when you want to locate one specific image or certain types of images for a project.

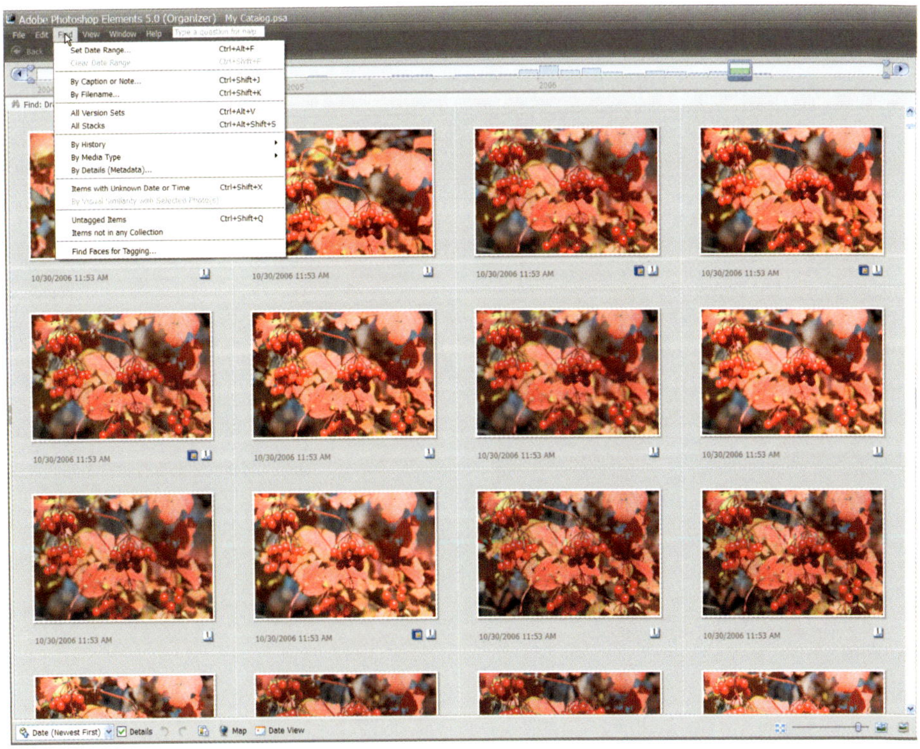

Figure 2.15 The many options under Find enable you to locate specific images based on parameters such as date, filename, details, media type (audio or video, for example), faces, and visual similarities.

And finally, Organizer offers a feature called Collections (next to the Tags icon). After tagging many of your photos, you might want to take advantage of this option by creating a collection of your very finest images. Select Collections, click New, and a dialog box appears (Figure 2.16). Enter a name for your collection, plus some notes if you wish. After creating a Collection, you can drag any desired image, or many images identified by Ctrl/⌘+clicking, to the icon for a Collection; those photos will then be copied to the collection and numbered sequentially. Any time you want to use those photos or simply show them to a friend, for example, they're available immediately by clicking the pertinent Collection icon.

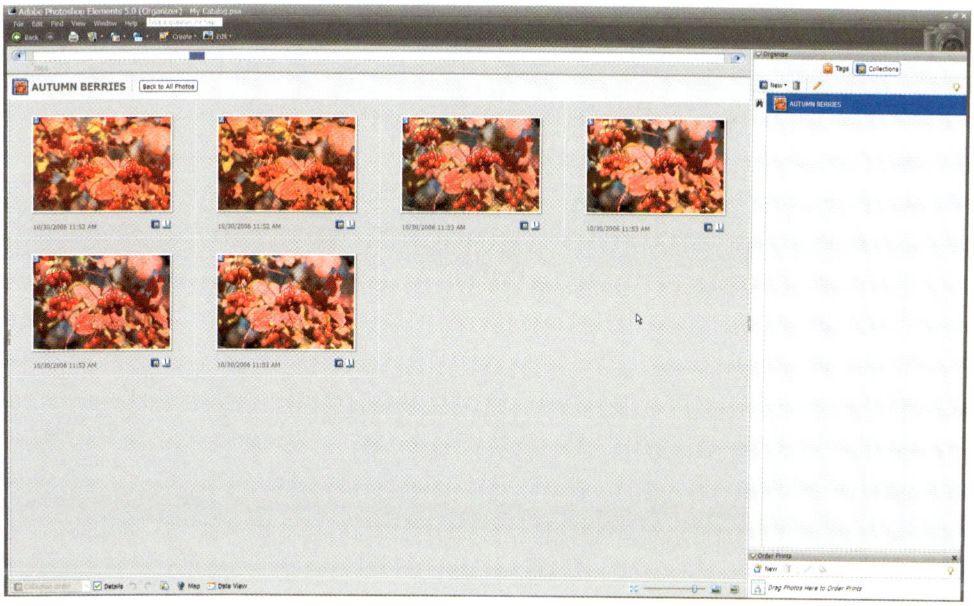

Figure 2.16 The ability to create Collections can be useful for a specific project, such as making an album of the very best photos from a special event or trip.

Reviewing Images for Evaluation

Although Organizer is useful for sorting and organizing your images, it doesn't offer a full-zoom review option so it's not ideal for making a critical analysis of issues such as overall sharpness or focus on the primary subject. Hence, it's not intended for decision making as to whether an image is worth the effort of putting through your full optimization workflow. To perform the best evaluation, you'll want to open the image in Elements and use the many tools for navigation and for a full evaluation.

Elements allows you to zoom in and out to various magnification levels and move your view around to look at individual areas within the image. There are many options, and which works best depends on how you prefer to work and the particular situation. We recommend getting familiar with all the available options so you can navigate quickly and easily for the most efficient evaluation possible. These skills will also help you throughout the image-optimization workflow.

When you open a file, Elements determines the zoom percentage so the entire image can be displayed. This is a perfect feature to allow you to perform an overall evaluation before much closer scrutiny. Are you satisfied with the composition? Do the tonal range and exposure seem appropriate? Is the color accurate or visually pleasing? Do you like the image overall, or do you wonder why you ever made it? Are the problems you notice something you can fix easily with the tools available in Elements? After you've evaluated the overall image, it is time to take a closer look at various areas to make a more critical evaluation. The navigation tools allow you to perform just that sort of review.

Zoom Tool

The most basic of navigation tools, the Zoom tool does include some hidden features that can be very helpful. To select the Zoom tool, click the magnifying glass icon on the Tools palette or press Z on your keyboard.

In the most basic use, you can click the Zoom tool anywhere in your image to zoom in, or magnify, by one preset percentage level. When you do so, not only will the image be enlarged on the screen, but the point you clicked will become the center of the new display. If you need to zoom out, to make the displayed image smaller instead of larger, select the minus option on the Options bar above the image area. Alternatively you can use a shortcut: simply hold down the Alt/Option key while you click. When zooming out, the same basic behavior occurs in reverse. The image will zoom out by one level, and the area you clicked will become the center of the new display.

The Zoom tool provides a suitable way to perform basic zooming on your image but it also offers a capability that makes it incredibly powerful. If you click and drag with the Zoom tool, you'll create a *marquee* (dashed box) on your image that specifies a certain area. When you release the mouse, the area you dragged the box around will be zoomed to fill the document window (Figure 2.17). This is an excellent way to zoom in on a particular area of your image to give it a closer look.

Another handy hidden feature of the Zoom tool is the ability to quickly go to a 100% view of your image, which is an excellent way to evaluate sharpness and look for small problems such as dust spots. To quickly return the zoom percentage to 100%, simply double-click the Zoom tool's icon on the Tools palette. You can also right-click and select any of the options that appear in a drop-down: Fit On Screen, Actual Pixels (100% view), Print Size (not useful until the image has been sized for making a print), and either Zoom In or Zoom Out.

Hand Tool

The Hand tool provides a way to navigate around your image when the magnification is relatively high and the image spills over the document window. You can think of this tool as behaving the way your own hand would if you were evaluating a mural-size print on a huge table. Instead of moving your head around to look at different areas of the image, you could simply move the print with your hand. This behavior is mimicked with the Hand tool. You can activate the Hand tool by clicking its icon in the Tools palette or by pressing H on your keyboard.

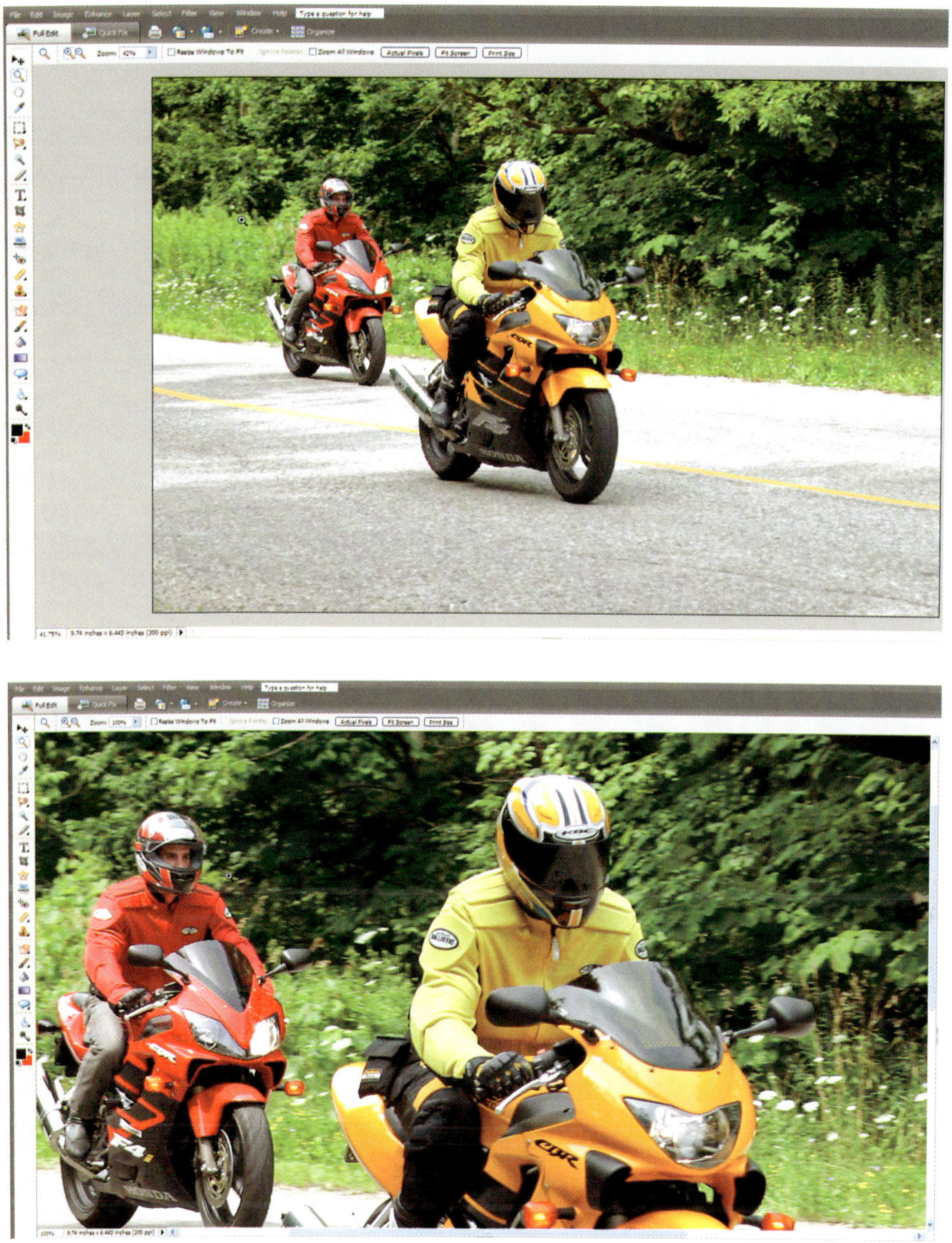

Figure 2.17 Dragging with the Zoom tool defines the area you want to take a closer look at. (Note the zoom percentage in the title bars.)

With the Hand tool active, you can move around within your image by clicking and dragging on the image. The image will move in the direction you drag, with the display being updated in real time so you can watch the image slide around as you move the mouse. Release the mouse when the most important image area is in the center of the screen.

Note: The Hand tool can't move your image around if the image is zoomed out to the extent that you can see the entire image at once. This setting is also called Fit On Screen magnification level.

Another handy trick is to use the Hand tool to quickly display your image at a magnification that allows it to fit within the space available without being obstructed by the palettes (if they are docked to the side of the screen) or to fill the screen display area (if they are not), resizing the image window if necessary. To do so, double-click the Hand tool in the Tools palette. This returns image magnification to the Fit On Screen level and is useful for a quick evaluation of the image's overall composition, tonality, and color.

Evaluating Sharpness

Determining whether an image is critically sharp is a major aspect of the image review process that leads up to the actual optimization workflow. Many photographers have a difficult time evaluating sharpness of a digital image displayed on a monitor, especially those who have spent many years evaluating the sharpness of images on film by utilizing a high-powered loupe.

The first step to evaluating sharpness for a given image is to view it at 100% magnification (or Actual Pixels). To do this, you can use the methods mentioned earlier or the keyboard shortcut Ctrl+Alt+0 / ⌘+Option+0. At this magnification, a single image pixel is represented by a single monitor pixel. As a result, you are seeing all of the actual pixels within the image for the area that can be displayed on the monitor. If you don't have the display set to 100% magnification, the monitor either is using more than a single pixel to represent each pixel in the image (if the zoom percentage is higher than 100%) or is not showing all pixels for a given area within the image (if the zoom percentage is lower than 100%).

When viewing the image at 100% magnification, check whether the edges within the subject matter of the image have good contrast. This is the key attribute of an image with crisp focus. The actual level of sharpness depends on your camera; some apply more sharpening than others during JPEG processing. Many cameras—as well as RAW file converter programs—allow you to set a desired sharpening level by using a menu item, from very low to very high. Also, as the final step in your workflow, you will often want to apply sharpening by using the tools available in Elements. We'll discuss these issues and techniques later in this book, but for now, it's important to be aware of this aspect of "sharpness" when evaluating images.

You'll primarily be checking the images to confirm correct focus and to confirm that they are not blurred by camera shake or subject motion. Learning to see what a sharp image looks like on a monitor display takes some practice, and the only way to accumulate that practice is to evaluate a large number of images. Besides simply reviewing photos on your monitor, it can be helpful to first make prints of some of your images, and then compare the printed image (where you'll have an easier time evaluating sharpness) to the image on the monitor at 100% magnification. Do so before you apply any sharpening in Elements. Comparing the electronic display to the print will give you a better idea of how the monitor display translates into actual image sharpness.

Navigator Palette

The Navigator palette consolidates the features of the Zoom and Hand tools into a single package, and provides an efficient method for navigating around your image to evaluate various portions of it. If the Navigator palette isn't visible, choose Window > Navigator from the menu to make it active.

The Navigator palette provides a thumbnail preview of the currently active image (Figure 2.18). A red box indicates which portion of the image is being displayed within the document window, so you always have a sense of what portion of the image you are viewing. The top-left corner of the palette includes a zoom, or magnification, percentage indicator for reference.

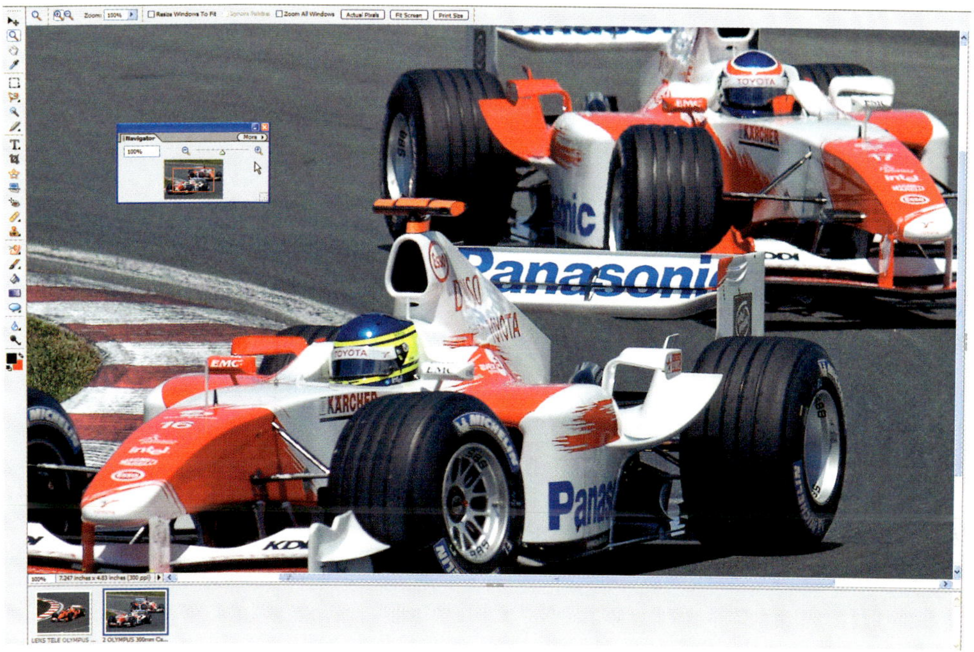

Figure 2.18 The Navigator palette incorporates the basic features of the Zoom and Hand tools into one convenient window, providing an efficient way to navigate around your image.

If you want to zoom while using the Navigator palette, simply move the slider control above the image thumbnail in the palette. This allows you to increase or decrease magnification by tiny increments as small as one percentage level. You can exercise greater control over the zooming process by adjusting the slider toward the left (to zoom out) or the right (to zoom in).

Within the thumbnail display for your image, the red box not only indicates which area of the image is being viewed, but also provides a way to change the view to a different area of the image. If you drag the boxed area around within the thumbnail display, the document display will change in real time to reflect the area defined by the box. This is similar to the use of the Hand tool for navigating around your image, but most users find it more convenient.

Note: The red box in the thumbnail in the Navigator palette cannot be moved if the entire image is currently visible. This setting is also called Fit On Screen magnification level.

Besides dragging the red box within the Navigator palette, you can also point your mouse to a particular area of the thumbnail and click to center the red box on that spot. This is a great method to use when you want to spot-check various portions of the image. For example, if you're trying to evaluate critical sharpness, you may want to check various areas of the subject and even areas at various distances from the camera to see the effect of depth of field. By simply clicking on various points in the thumbnail of the Navigator palette, one at a time, you can check multiple areas of the image quickly and easily.

One last trick in the Navigator palette allows you to reproduce the effect of drawing a marquee on your image with the Zoom tool, so you can quickly fill the screen with a particular portion of your image. To do so, hold the Ctrl/⌘ key and click and drag within the thumbnail display of the Navigator palette to draw a red box over the area you want to view. When you release the mouse, the image will automatically be zoomed and repositioned so the area you selected with the red box will fill the available space in the document window (Figure 2.19).

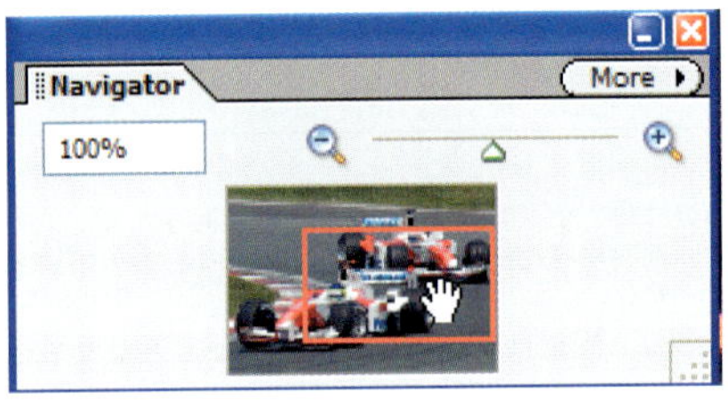

Figure 2.19 The marquee feature available in Navigator allows for convenient review of various image areas by dragging the red box to elements that you want to scrutinize.

The Navigator packs a lot of power into a small palette window, and represents an excellent way to navigate around your image as you evaluate it before embarking on your optimization workflow. Getting comfortable with the Navigator will make this process go much more smoothly and give you the sense of being able to view any portion of your image as needed almost instantly.

Keyboard Shortcuts

Some computer users love using keyboard shortcuts to speed up their workflow. Elements provides a variety of such options for navigating around your images during the evaluation process (as well as during your actual optimization workflow). If you tend to keep one hand on the keyboard as you work, this may be your preferred way to navigate.

Even if you prefer to use the mouse as much as possible, remembering a few of these keyboard shortcuts can help improve your workflow by adding to your arsenal of tricks for working with your images. Table 2.1 lists the most common navigational shortcuts.

Table 2.1 Keyboard Shortcuts for Image Navigation

Windows Shortcut	Macintosh Shortcut	Action
H	H	Activates the Hand tool
Z	Z	Activates the Zoom tool
Ctrl++	⌘++	Zooms in
Ctrl+–	⌘+–	Zooms out
Ctrl+0	⌘+0	Zooms document window to fit on screen
Ctrl+Alt+0	⌘+Option+0	Zooms to 100% magnification (Actual Pixels)
Spacebar	Spacebar	Temporarily activates the Hand tool regardless of currently active tool (with the exception of the Text tool)
Ctrl+spacebar	⌘+spacebar	Temporarily activates the Zoom tool regardless of currently active tool
Ctrl+Alt+spacebar	⌘+Option+spacebar	Temporarily activates the Zoom tool in Zoom Out mode regardless of the currently active tool

To zoom in and out on your image, you can hold the Ctrl/⌘ key and press the plus key (+) to zoom in or the hyphen key (-) to zoom out. This produces the same effect as zooming one level at a time with the Zoom tool, but without changing the center of the view because you aren't clicking on an area of the image when using this keyboard shortcut.

To quickly view the image at 100% magnification (Actual Pixels) for evaluating critical sharpness or other detailed aspects of the image, hold the Ctrl+Alt / ⌘+Option keys and press the zero (0) key. To get an overall view of the image to evaluate overall composition, tone, and color issues, hold the Ctrl/⌘ key and press the zero (0) key.

If you want to take advantage of the special capabilities of the Zoom tool, especially the ability to draw a marquee around a particular area of the image and have that portion automatically zoomed to fill the document window, press Ctrl/⌘+spacebar to temporarily access the Zoom tool, no matter what tool is currently active. Similarly, you can hold the spacebar at any time to access the Hand tool regardless of which tool is currently active (with the exception of the Text tool). When the Text tool is active, pressing the spacebar will type a space—go figure.

As you've seen in this section, there are many options for navigating around your images during the evaluation and optimization processes. Instead of trying to decide which particular methods work best for your needs, make an effort to become familiar with all of them. Doing so will ensure that you have the maximum number of techniques available for any given situation. What you'll likely find is that although you have your favorite methods for navigating around your images, in certain situations other methods are more convenient. By being comfortable with all of the available methods, you'll have maximum flexibility and control when working on your images.

Printing Contact Sheets

After you've sorted through your photos and determined those that should be optimized, you might want to print a contact sheet of certain images. These sheets of multiple images can be useful both for your own reference and for sharing with others. To start the process, open the desired images in Elements and choose File > Print Multiple Photos. That causes Organizer to launch, and a Print Photos dialog box appears, though not immediately. Your identified photos will be shown as thumbnails along the left side of the box and one will appear in the center of a "sheet" of paper (Figure 2.20).

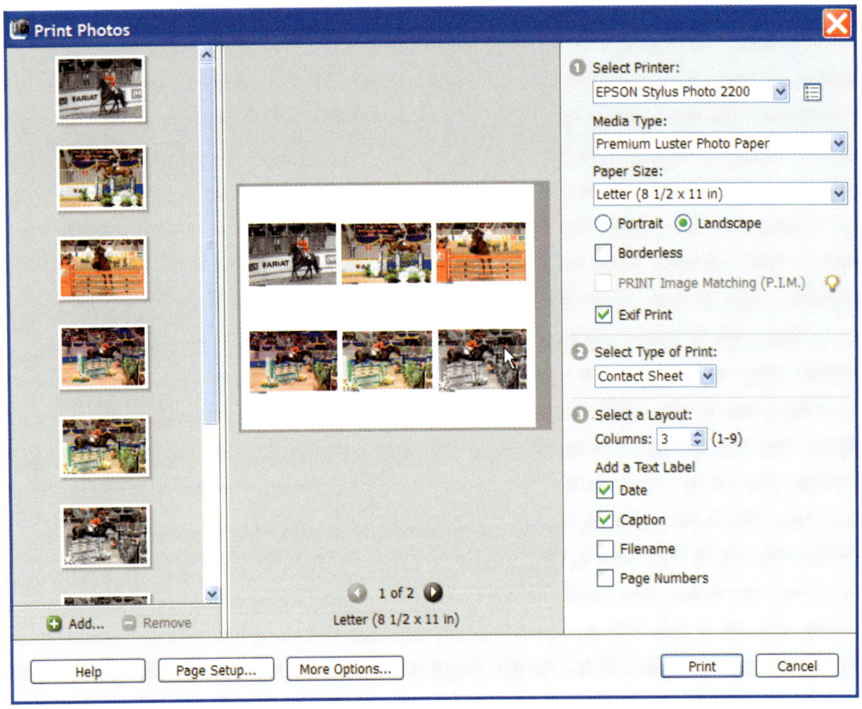

Figure 2.20 The automated Contact Sheet feature in Elements allows you to quickly and easily build contact sheets of images that you want to print in order to share with others. Your screen may vary slightly depending on the type of printer installed for your system.

In the Select Type Of Print drop-down box, specify the Contact Sheet option to see a preview of the contact sheet, showing all of your open images in a default layout. Click the Page Setup button at the bottom to access the Printer Properties dialog box and fine-tune additional settings such as the Media Type (for example, Photo Glossy) and the Paper Size you plan to use for printing (for example, 8.5″×11″ paper). Specify the printer to be used and a Portrait or Landscape orientation. You can select Borderless if that is supported by the printer and paper combination that you selected. Keep in mind that many features available are dependent on the type of printer and printer driver installed on the computer system.

Under Select A Layout, enter a number for Columns. The smaller the number entered, the fewer the images that will be included in one contact sheet. The layout of your preview contact sheet will change each time you change the number of images to be included. Experiment with various layouts until you find one that is satisfactory.

Click the More Options button to add other specifications, including Adobe RGB color space, an ideal choice for ink-jet printing (Figure 2.21).

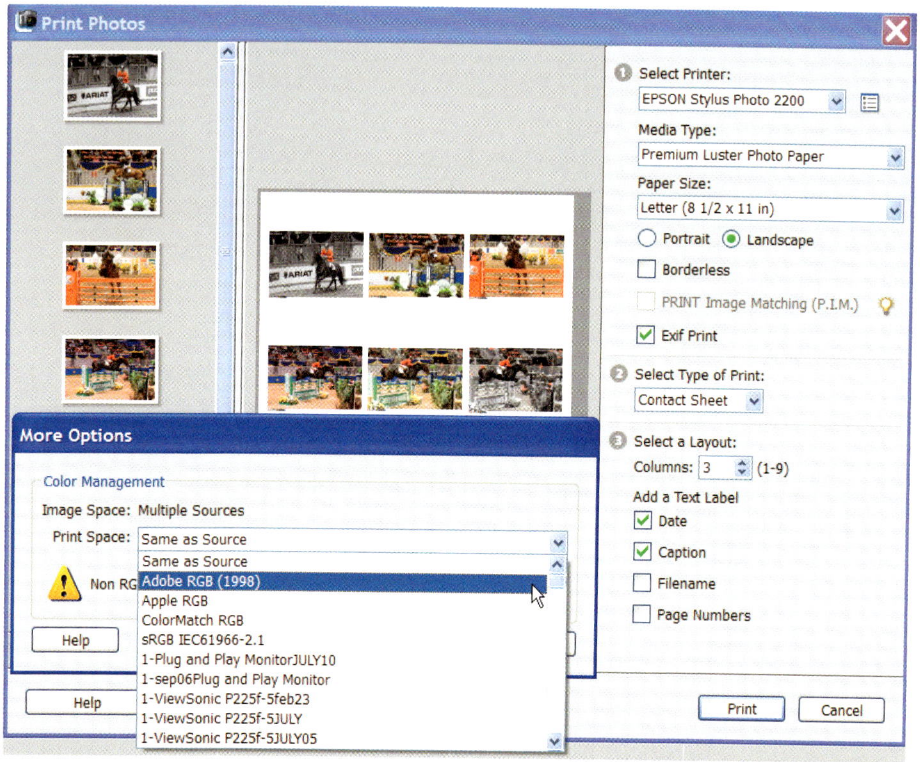

Figure 2.21 The additional options available with the Contact Sheet feature in Elements allow you to select the sRGB or Adobe RGB color space. Naturally, your computer system may not provide the various monitor profiles shown in this illustration but the Color Space options will be available.

You can also specify whether you want text printed on the contact sheet such as filenames, dates, page numbers, or the captions you had added, as discussed earlier under Metadata. (Page numbering can also be specified, if the number of images and the layout require more than one contact sheet to be printed.) The filename is certainly useful because it will later let you determine exactly which image file on your computer represents a particular photo on the contact sheet. Should you decide that you do not want to include one or more images after all, simply click them, and then click Remove under the thumbnails. Those image files will then be closed and will no longer appear. If you decide that you want a few more images for contact sheet printing, click Add and specify the images in the Add Photos dialog box. When the settings are adjusted to your satisfaction, click the Print button near the bottom-right corner of the dialog box.

Ready to Work

With your images downloaded, sorted, and evaluated, you're ready to move on to optimizing your images. At this point you should be feeling confident about the images you are getting ready to work with, because you have narrowed the field to those that most deserve to be optimized in order to produce excellent output for sharing.

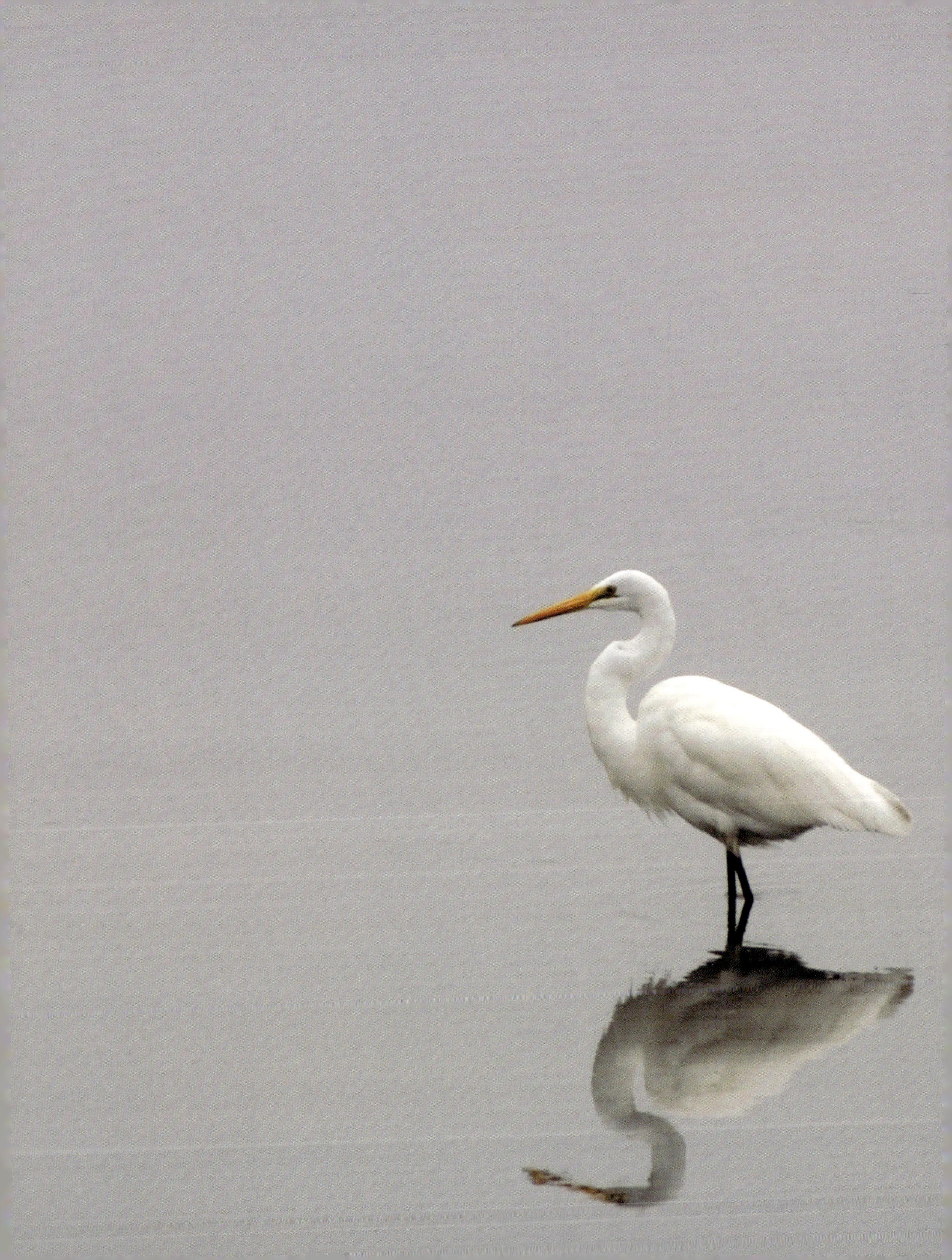

RAW Conversion

When you select a digital camera's RAW capture mode, the camera captures raw data directly from the sensor and applies little or no processing. In fact, the processing is done later, in imaging software such as Adobe Camera Raw (available in Photoshop Elements 5). This software enables you to adjust the raw data file and convert it to a familiar format such as TIFF. RAW capture offers many benefits to the digital photographer and provides the best opportunity for maximum image quality and detail with a proper RAW conversion. Of course, the advantages of RAW capture come at a price: the step of RAW conversion added to the workflow. Still, when you need to maintain optimal quality in your images, a slight reduction in overall workflow efficiency is well worth the benefits you can achieve with RAW capture.

3

Chapter Contents

Understanding the Benefits of RAW
Converting with Adobe Camera Raw
Archiving RAW Captures

Understanding the Benefits of RAW

Photographers take a lot of steps to ensure the absolute best quality in their images. Using a tripod, employing mirror lockup, selecting lenses with image stabilization or similar technology, and using the lowest ISO (International Organization for Standards) setting possible on a digital camera are all examples of such steps. Capturing in the RAW mode offered by many digital cameras is yet another way to help ensure the best image quality.

The quality benefits of RAW capture derive from several factors, including white balance, exposure, and high-bit data. Each of these represents a potential benefit to the photographer as well as the quality of the final image.

Note: Remember that although RAW capture offers potential benefits, it still isn't a replacement for using the best photographic techniques. You still should start with the best photograph possible even when capturing in RAW.

Getting Accurate White Balance

Digital cameras introduced the need for photographers to deal with color temperature and white balance in an electronic manner. Film photographers have to choose film appropriately balanced for the lighting conditions or use colored filters for a pleasing color balance under certain lighting conditions. With a digital camera, however, you can control color temperature electronically. Using the various white balance features, you can set the camera to compensate for the color of the light, which is measured as a color temperature in degrees Kelvin (Figure 3.1). In a general sense, you can think of this as a way to make a white sheet of paper look neutral no matter what type of lighting is illuminating it.

The color of light can vary significantly from yellow/red (household lamps) to green (certain fluorescent lamps) to blue (on a dark, overcast day), and so on. Most digital cameras do an acceptable to exceptional job of automatically determining the appropriate compensation for the lighting conditions when you use the Auto White Balance (AWB) feature. The system is most reliable outdoors or when flash is the primary light source; under artificial lighting, however, AWB rarely produces an ideal color balance. That's why cameras include white balance presets such as Shade, Tungsten, Fluorescent, and so on; each option was designed to produce a more accurate white balance—minimizing a color cast or tint—than AWB under a specific type of lighting condition.

When you use the camera's RAW capture mode, however, you can trust the AWB setting completely. Even if the camera does a poor job of adjusting for a certain color of light, you will be able to correct the image in the RAW converter software with absolutely no penalty in image quality. In fact, this process will produce the same effect as if you had used the camera's appropriate white balance preset for the type of lighting at the time you were making an image. The RAW converter software also offers other white balance adjustment features for additional control over this aspect of the image.

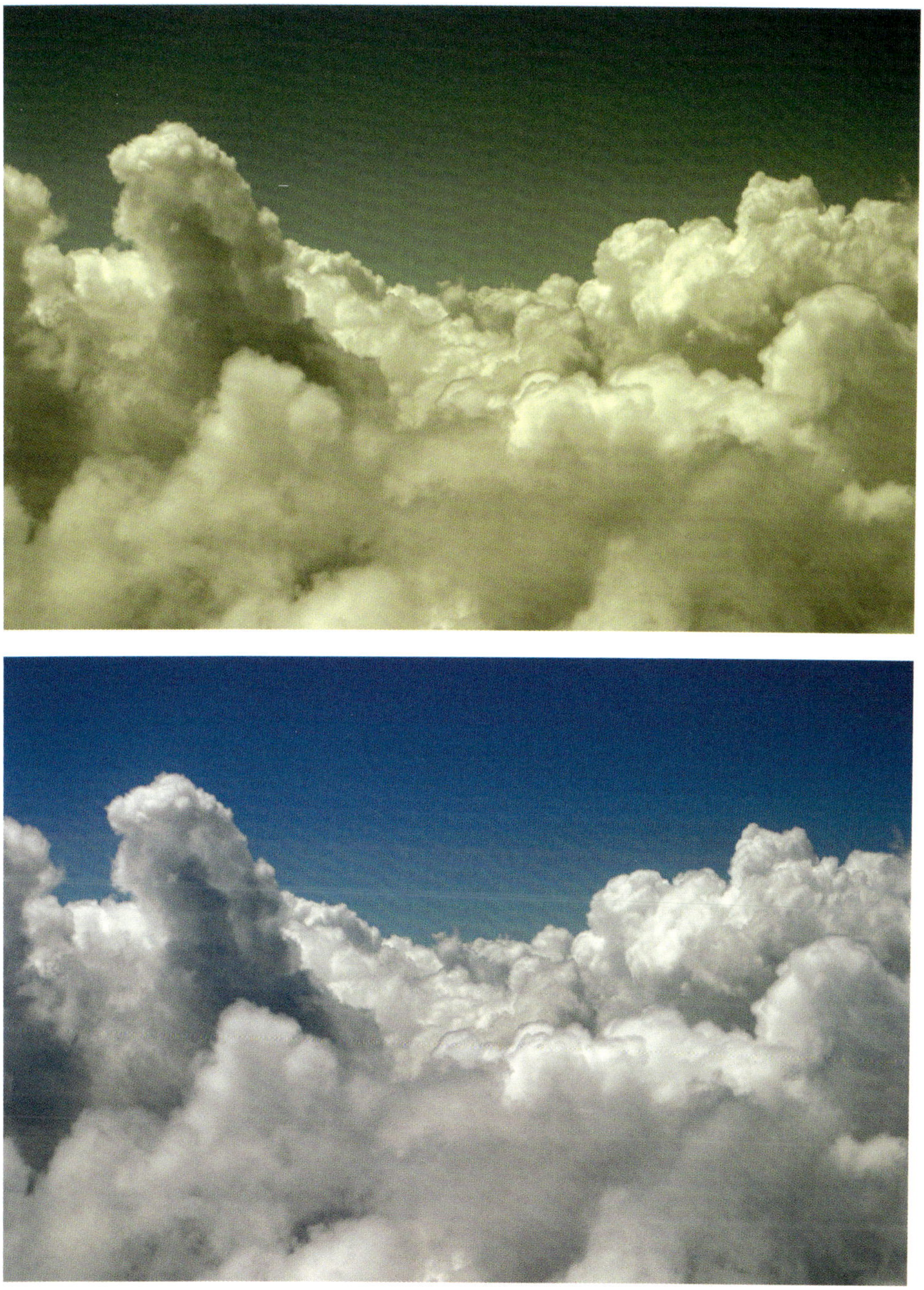

Figure 3.1 Digital cameras need to compensate for the color temperature of the lighting so that the effect of the color of that light is neutralized in the final image.

Note: Although you can certainly keep your camera set to Auto White Balance when capturing in RAW with the confidence that you can fix any errors in the RAW converter software, this can slow down your workflow. If you plan to take a large number of images under a certain lighting condition, you may want to use your camera's Custom White Balance feature to minimize the effort that will be necessary later, during the RAW conversion process.

Correcting Exposure Errors

Because RAW captures are recording the amount of light that reaches the imaging sensor during exposure and aren't being converted immediately to a standard image file format, they offer more exposure latitude than a JPEG capture. The best digital single-lens reflex (SLR) cameras offer about six stops of exposure latitude. RAW capture adds about three stops of potential latitude. However, it is important to realize that the final image file will still be able to contain only about six stops of latitude. RAW simply offers the ability to extract more detail from the image and make adjustments to recover from exposure errors.

In general, it is possible to compensate for an exposure error of about one stop overexposed or two stops underexposed by using RAW capture (Figure 3.2) and RAW adjustment in software such as Adobe Camera Raw, available in Elements 5. That doesn't mean you'll always avoid blown highlights (loss of detail in bright areas) if you overexposed by one stop. It also doesn't mean quality will be maintained at the same level as though the exposure were correct to begin with. For example, if the exposure is dark and needs to be brightened considerably in the RAW converter software, you'll still have a higher risk of noise and posterization in the darker shadow areas of the image.

Note: Just because RAW capture provides greater exposure latitude doesn't mean it offers a panacea for exposure problems. Quality can suffer if you make extreme corrections to RAW captures in the RAW converter software, so always make an effort to achieve the most accurate exposure possible.

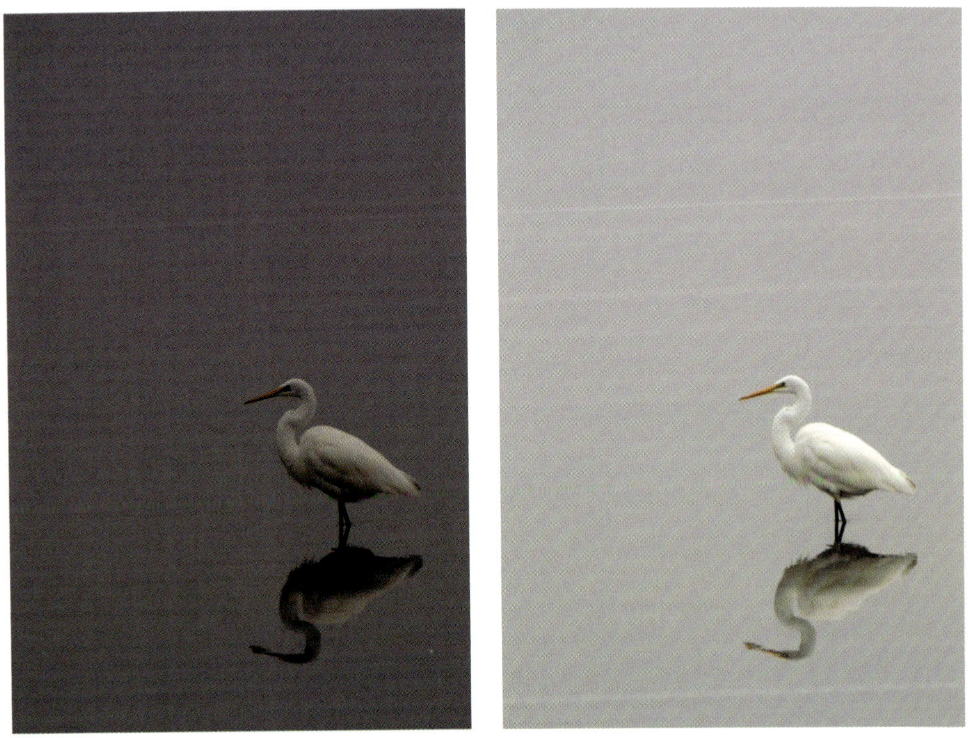

Figure 3.2 RAW capture makes it possible to recover from exposure errors at capture, provided they aren't too extreme.

Think of this capability as a way to recover from some exposure mistakes, within reason, as well as a way to fine-tune the exposure after the fact. It won't necessarily save the day with captures that have bad exposures, but it can help make mediocre exposures look exceptional.

Capturing High-Bit Data

The final major advantage of RAW capture is that high-bit data (typically 10- or 12-bit data stored in a 16-bit file) is preserved in the capture and can be preserved in the conversion process. This means that more discrete tonal and color values are being recorded and retained in the final image. This is a twofold benefit.

For one thing, the higher bit-depth used for the in-camera analog-to-digital conversion results in more information, so that smooth gradations of tone and color can be maintained. In short, more detail is retained within the image because there are more available values for each pixel. Second, by converting the RAW capture to a high-bit image file (such as a TIFF), you will maintain the benefit of being able to make significant adjustments to the image without risking posterization (Figure 3.3).

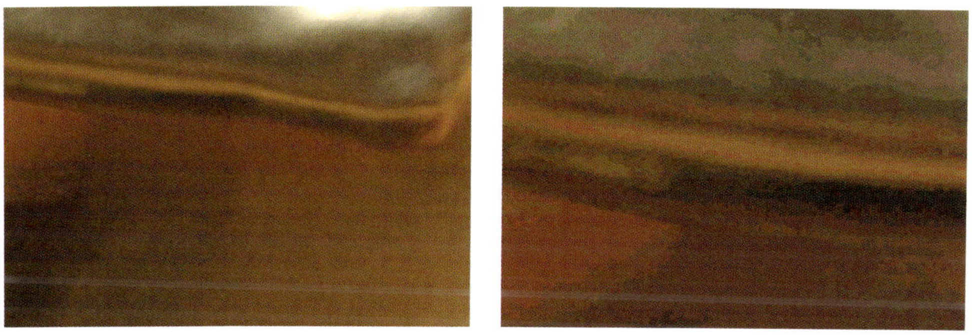

Figure 3.3 The high-bit data of a digital capture helps ensure that you don't encounter posterization with your images, even with extreme adjustments. The image on the left shows smooth gradations, while the image on the right shows posterization.

For images captured with proper exposure, the high-bit advantage is a minor one. However, whenever you need to make significant adjustments to achieve your vision for an image, starting with high-bit data will help you maintain maximum quality throughout the process to the final print.

Note: Because Elements does not support adjustment layers for high-bit files, you'll be limited in what you can do if you decide to take advantage of high-bit with RAW capture. Because we feel that working in layers is so critical, we prefer to work in 8-bit in Elements.

Converting with Adobe Camera Raw

When your digital camera records in RAW format, it isn't actually creating an image file. Rather, it is creating a data file in a proprietary format such as Canon's CR2, Sony's ARW, Pentax's PEF, or Nikon's NEF. The data file contains the information collected by each individual photodiode on the imaging sensor during exposure. This is the reason

RAW captures will need to be converted to an actual image file format, using Adobe Camera Raw (ACR) or another RAW converter software program.

Before the raw data is converted to a conventional image file format, you will have an opportunity to optimize the image. By making careful adjustments in the RAW converter software, you will be able to produce the best quality possible. If you are using a newly released digital camera, it is possible that Adobe Camera Raw doesn't yet support that model; in other words, it does not recognize the proprietary raw data format used by that camera. However, Adobe provides regular updates to Adobe Camera Raw to provide support for new cameras, so check its website (www.adobe.com/digitalimag) for the latest plug-in that you can download and install in Elements 5.

Utilizing Adobe Camera Raw within Elements 5 provides convenience and workflow efficiency. Organizer (the included file browser) allows you to preview your RAW captures by double-clicking any RAW file. You can then open a RAW file with any of these three methods:

- Choose Edit > Go To Full Edit.
- Use the Ctrl+I shortcut.
- Right-click the image and select Go To Full Edit from the drop-down menu.

The image then opens in the Adobe Camera Raw dialog box. The Adobe Camera Raw interface is designed efficiently to allow you to work quickly when establishing the optimal settings for RAW conversion (Figure 3.4).

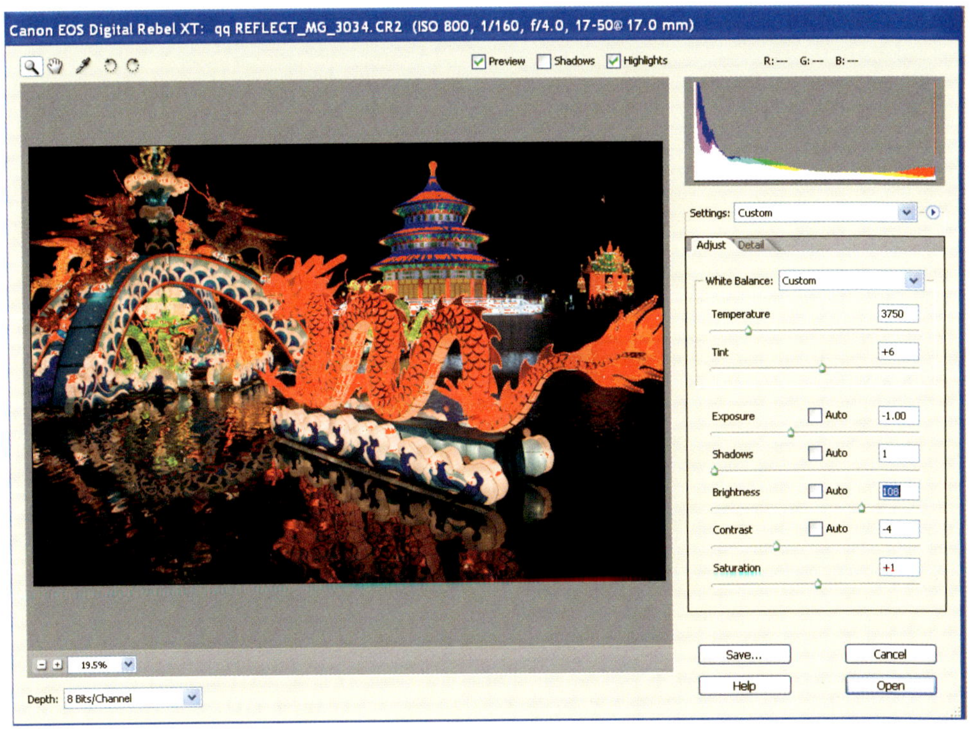

Figure 3.4 The Adobe Camera Raw dialog box provides an efficient interface for establishing the optimal settings for RAW conversion.

To get started with Camera Raw, simply open a RAW capture either from the Organizer as mentioned, or from the Elements 5 Editor by choosing File > Open. The RAW capture then appears in the Adobe Camera Raw dialog box.

Adobe Camera Raw Settings

When opening a RAW file in ACR for the first time, we recommend you remove the sharpening that is always applied by default. To do so, select the Detail tab; then set Sharpness to zero. Finally, click the side menu button and choose Save New Camera Raw Defaults. Now, whenever you open a new RAW file, the sharpening level will automatically be set to zero; you can change that at any time for a specific image if you want.

We strongly recommend using zero sharpening in RAW conversion for three reasons. First, using a single slider to adjust sharpening doesn't provide nearly the degree of control that you will want to exercise over the sharpening process. Second, the default setting is simply too aggressive and often creates halo artifacts at high-contrast edges within the image. Finally, we both prefer not to apply any sharpening until the image is being prepared for final output, as will be discussed in greater detail in Chapter 13, "Output Processing."

In addition to the sharpening setting, we recommend selecting all three checkboxes at the top of the Adobe Camera Raw dialog box so you can see the effects of your adjustments and see whether you are clipping any data. 

The Preview checkbox enables you to see the effect of any adjustments as you make them; turning it off and on provides a convenient method for viewing a "before" and an "after" view of the image. The Shadows and Highlights checkboxes allow you to see a color overlay in your image that identifies areas where you've clipped (lost) detail based on the exposure or adjustments. By having these checkboxes turned on, you get some guidance as to the adjustments you might want to make in order to prevent the loss of important highlight or shadow detail to the extent possible.

Navigation Tools

You're now ready to start the "real" process of working with your image. But first, you may want to evaluate various areas of your image, similar to the process of navigating discussed in Chapter 2, "Download and Sort."

Camera Raw provides the Zoom and Hand tools in the top-left corner of the dialog box (Figure 3.5). These tools function the same as the tools by the same name found within Elements 5. All of the same tricks and keyboard shortcuts are available, so be sure to review these topics in Chapter 2 if you're not familiar with them. You can then zoom in to get a closer look at any portion of the image you'd like as you're making decisions about the best settings to use in ACR.

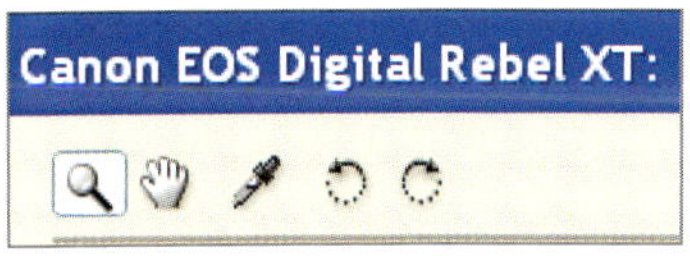

Figure 3.5
The Zoom and Hand tools on the toolbar in the Camera Raw dialog box behave the same as those on the Tools palette in Photoshop.

White Balance

One of the most convenient aspects of the Adobe Camera Raw dialog box is that it presents the controls in a logical order that matches the order we recommend for making adjustments (Figure 3.6).

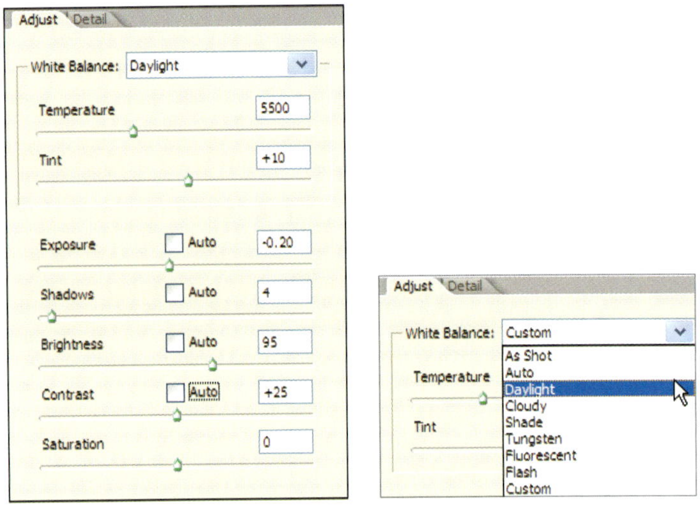

Figure 3.6 The controls under the Adjust tab (left) are arranged in the recommended order of adjustments before converting RAW captures. The drop-down at the top of the White Balance section (right) allows you to select presets that match those available in your digital camera.

Note: You can make dependable color adjustments—including White Balance adjustment—only if you are working with a calibrated and profiled monitor display. For complete details on color management workflow, including calibration and profiling, see *Color Confidence, Second Edition* by Tim Grey (Sybex, 2006).

The first among these, found under the Adjust tab along the right side of the dialog box, is the White Balance section. As its name indicates, this section provides controls that allow you to adjust the compensation applied to the image based on the color of the light that illuminated the subject when you took the photo. This can be used to compensate for a shortcoming of the camera's Automatic or Preset White Balance feature, or to fine-tune the image to warm it up or otherwise change, in effect, the color of the light used to illuminate the scene.

Note: Although the White Balance presets are the first option under the Adjust tab, we actually recommend skipping this option (leaving it at the As Shot setting) and moving directly to the Temperature and Tint sliders discussed later in this section.

Using White Balance Presets

The first White Balance section is a drop-down list that contains preset options. The default is As Shot, meaning the white balance settings will be left at the setting used in the camera when the picture was taken. For example, if the camera was set to Auto White Balance, the sliders will reflect the values based on the camera's reading of the light.

In addition to the As Shot setting, additional presets will be listed that match those available within the camera, such as Daylight, Cloudy, Shade, Tungsten, Fluorescent, and others. You'll also notice that Auto is listed as an available preset. It is important to keep in mind that the Auto setting available from the White Balance drop-down does not correspond to the Auto White Balance setting found on your camera. Instead, this setting will tell Adobe Camera Raw to evaluate the image and make its own decision, using its own algorithms, about the best settings. It often does a very good job in correcting a color cast, but it is important to remember that the correction is based on an evaluation of the color values found within the image, not a measurement of the color temperature by the camera.

The final item in the White Balance drop-down is a Custom option. You don't really need to select this directly, because it will be set automatically whenever you adjust the Temperature or Tint slider.

Although the presets available from the White Balance drop-down provide a quick way to effectively tell Adobe Camera Raw what the lighting conditions were at the time of capture, chances are selecting one of these options won't produce a perfect result. In other words, the image may still have a color cast or it may not exhibit the color balance that is most visually pleasing. Because you'll need to adjust the Temperature and Tint sliders for most images anyway, we recommend leaving the drop-down set to As Shot, the default setting.

Adjusting White Balance

Another option for quickly establishing white balance settings is to use the White Balance Tool at the top-left of the Camera Raw dialog box (the eyedropper icon in Figure 3.5); use it to click an area of the image that should be neutral. When you do so, the Temperature and Tint sliders will automatically be adjusted so that the pixel you clicked will be perfectly neutral. Ideally, that should cause all other colors to be accurate as well. When using the White Balance tool in selecting a neutral point, the goal is to click an area that should be slightly off-white (not pure white).

Note: Unlike other implementations of the eyedropper icon, the White Balance Tool in Adobe Camera Raw is not affected by the Sample Size setting for the eyedropper that you might have set in Elements 5.

Although this can be a great way to establish optimal settings when you have an area within the image that should definitely be neutral (off-white or light gray), the process is rarely quite so simple. Instead, it tends to turn into a process of clicking repeatedly on the preview image as you try to find a spot that should indeed be perfectly neutral. This is much less efficient than it would seem at first glance. If you find that after a few clicks with the White Balance tool you haven't found a good white balance for the image, move on to a manual adjustment instead and select As Shot from the drop-down menu to return to the original settings. Then, get ready to work with the Temperature and Tint sliders.

Adjusting Temperature and Tint

Although the White Balance drop-down and White Balance tool (eyedropper icon) provide the potential to correct a color cast quickly and easily, these simplified options contradict the very benefit of RAW capture: the ability to exercise greater control over your images. We strongly recommend skipping the White Balance drop-down and White Balance tool, and instead starting with the Temperature and Tint sliders. In the vast majority of RAW conversions you'll probably want to fine-tune these sliders anyway, so it makes sense to start with them and achieve the best results possible in your image.

The Temperature slider allows you to adjust the color temperature of the lighting, within a blue/yellow balance using degrees Kelvin as a guide. In theory, that means you simply want to adjust the slider to the color temperature of the lighting under which the image was captured. Of course, chances are you have no idea (or just a general idea) of what that color temperature was. Also, you don't necessarily want to simply compensate for the lighting that was used. Instead, you should take advantage of the capability to fine-tune the blue/yellow balance to provide the best image in terms of aesthetics with no penalty in terms of image quality. This enables you to interpret the image as you desire, rather than simply neutralizing a color cast.

As you get started with the Temperature slider, we recommend moving it between extremes to get a sense of how the adjustment will affect the overall image and to get a preview of what variations might be possible (Figure 3.7). Moving to the left will cool down the image, compensating for "warm" lighting (light with a lower Kelvin temperature). Moving the slider to the right will warm up the image, compensating for "cool" lighting (light with a higher Kelvin temperature). Obviously, the extremes aren't likely to be an appropriate choice, but the perspective of those extremes helps you determine whether you will need a warmer or cooler effect.

After sliding through the extremes, start to settle down on the area of the Temperature scale that seems to represent the most pleasing color balance for the image. After you have moved the slider to the point that seems to provide the best color, release the mouse and use the up and down arrow keys on your keyboard to fine-tune the adjustment. This makes it easier to make subtle adjustments (in extremely small increments of 50 K) as you make a decision about the best "look" for the image in terms of color balance.

After establishing the Temperature value, you can move to the Tint slider. This tool adjusts the color balance between green and magenta for a final fine-tuning. As with the Temperature slider, try sliding through the extremes to get a sense of how the image is being affected, even though you won't use those extremes for the final setting. Adjust the slider to taste based on the preview image, and then use the up/down arrow keys for fine-tuning as you did with the Temperature slider.

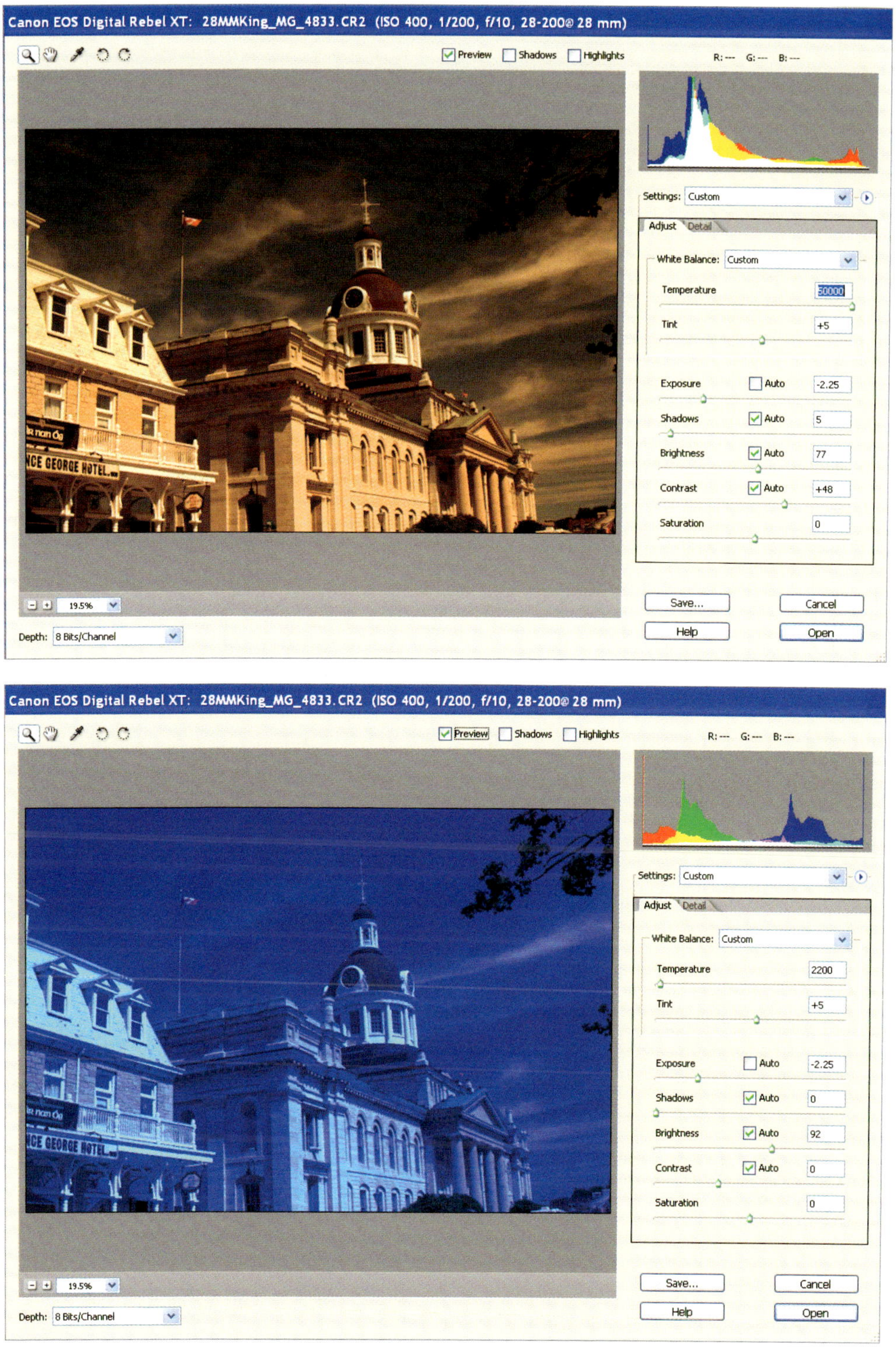

Figure 3.7 Moving the Temperature slider through the extremes to compensate for cool lighting (high Kelvin temperature, top) and warm lighting (low Kelvin temperature, bottom) allows you to get a better sense of how the adjustment will affect the overall image as you settle on a final value.

With both the Temperature and Tint sliders established, the overall color balance of the image should look pretty accurate. Of course, accuracy is in the eye of the beholder. In fact, you will sometimes adjust the sliders to introduce a desired color cast, such as a warm glow, instead of focusing exclusively on compensating for the color of light that illuminated the scene.

Tonal Adjustments

With the White Balance settings established, you're ready to move on to the overall tonal adjustments for the image. When doing so, it is important to keep in mind that the basic goal of tonal adjustments in the RAW converters should be to optimize dynamic range for maximum detail in highlight and shadow areas. In other words, you shouldn't be concerned at this point with producing an image that is ready to print, because that will be dealt with during the rest of your workflow in Elements 5. Instead, you should be looking to maximize the amount of detail within the image so you will have as much flexibility as possible when optimizing the image.

When making tonal adjustments in Adobe Camera Raw, the three key controls are Exposure, Shadows, and Brightness. Together these allow you to optimize tonal range while maintaining detail, as well as adjusting the overall appearance of the image.

Note: The Exposure, Shadows, and Brightness sliders discussed here include an Auto checkbox that when clicked will cause Adobe Camera Raw to adjust the setting to a value it deems appropriate. Although this can be helpful for getting started, we recommend simply adjusting the controls manually as described throughout the rest of this section.

Adjusting Exposure

The Exposure slider allows you to adjust, in effect, the brightness of the image, using as its scale an Exposure Value. In other words, a +1 value is equivalent to a +1 exposure compensation level that you might have used in the camera. Likewise, setting the slider to –1 would produce a similar effect to darkening the exposure by one stop, by setting a –1 compensation level, in the camera. This would lead most photographers to believe that the Exposure control should be used as a basic brightness adjustment (and would probably make them wonder why there is also a Brightness slider in the same dialog box).

The behavior of the Exposure slider makes it ideal for establishing the white point within your image. By adjusting this slider, you can effectively determine which pixel value within the image should be set to white. This is virtually identical to the behavior of the white point slider in Levels, as you'll see in Chapter 5, "Tone and Color."

As a general rule, we recommend setting the Exposure slider to maximize the white point for the image without clipping any important detail. In other words, use Exposure to brighten the image just to the threshold before you start to lose detail in the highlights. You can watch the histogram display as you adjust the Exposure slider, but it can be a challenge to determine when you've actually started to lose detail. Fortunately, by having the Highlights checkbox at the top of the Camera Raw dialog box selected, you'll have a visual indication when you lose detail in the image. With the checkbox selected, raising the Exposure setting to a value where clipping occurs will cause a red overlay to be shown in those areas. Adjust the Exposure slider to the point just before this overlay starts to appear.

Although setting the Exposure to make the brightest pixels nearly white works with many images, that doesn't mean it should be adjusted this way for all images. You need to evaluate the image itself to make sure the adjustment is a good one, providing a pleasing visual effect.

Note: If the clipping preview display shows that you have lost detail without an Exposure adjustment, you may be able to recover that detail by reducing the Exposure setting. For specular highlights (such as reflections from glass or metal) this may not be a significant concern. Such areas do not contain important detail, and usually they are so bright that it would be impossible to recover the detail in any event.

Adjusting Shadow Detail

After setting the white point with the Exposure slider, the black point can be established with the Shadows slider. This effectively sets the black point for the image, very similar to the behavior of the black point slider in the Levels adjustment you'll see in Chapter 5. When you know how to use the Exposure slider, the Shadows slider is suddenly easy to master as well, because it works in virtually the same manner.

As with Exposure, make sure the Shadows checkbox at the top of the ACR dialog box is selected. You can then use the clipping display (which shows up as a blue overlay) while making your Shadows adjustment to see when you lose shadow detail in your image.

Although it is often beneficial to sacrifice some shadow detail to optimize contrast in an image, we don't recommend giving up this detail during the RAW conversion. Instead we recommend saving that sort of adjustment for your full workflow in Elements 5. Therefore, the basic process is to adjust the Shadows slider to the right until blue pixels start to appear. Then move the slider back to the left until the blue overlay disappears. This will ensure that you have maximized tonal range for the image without clipping detail in the shadows (Figure 3.8).

Note: Even if you don't intend to produce an image with maximum tonal range, we recommend using the preceding procedures outlined for Exposure and Shadows with most images, because this will maximize the amount of information in the image. You can always reduce the tonal range with adjustments in Elements 5 later, but you can't recover information after the fact unless you reprocess the original RAW capture with different settings.

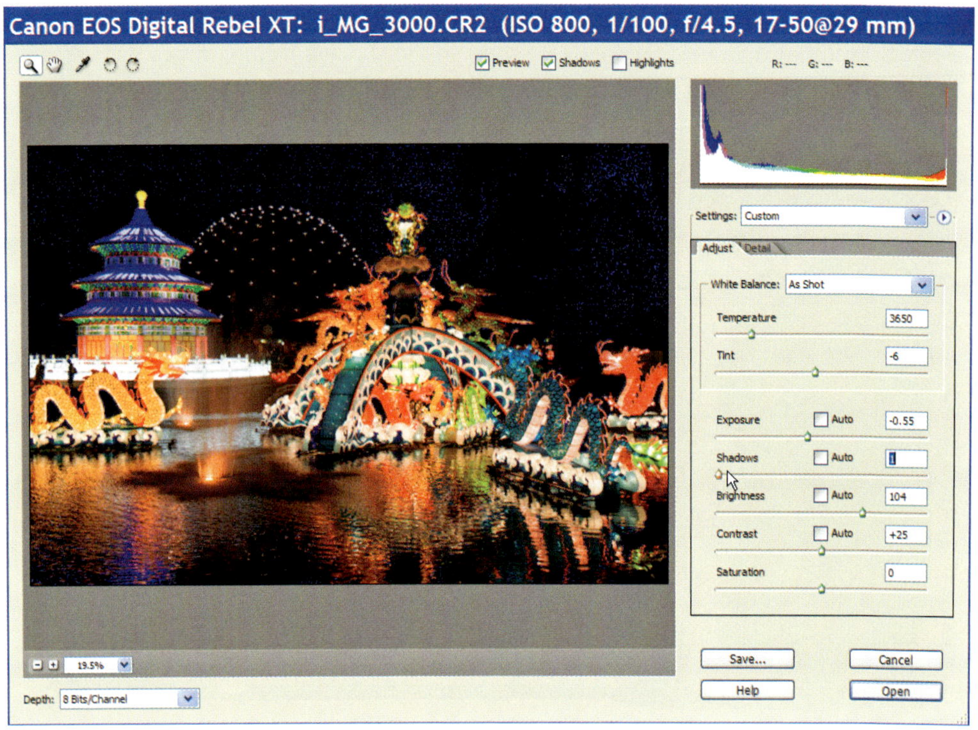

Figure 3.8 The clipping preview for Shadows allows you to accurately establish a setting that optimizes the black point without sacrificing shadow detail.

Adjusting Brightness

The preceding methods discussed for the Exposure and Shadows sliders will expand the tonal range within your image but may not produce optimal overall brightness. The Brightness slider allows you to correct that problem. You may already be familiar with the Levels adjustment (which will be covered in great detail in Chapter 5), and the Brightness slider is like the middle-tone slider in Levels. It allows you to adjust the overall brightness of an image without affecting the established black and white points. As such, you don't have to worry about your Brightness adjustment causing any problems with the settings you've already defined for Exposure and Shadows.

The Brightness control doesn't support the clipping preview, because making this adjustment won't cause any detail to be clipped. Therefore, you should simply adjust the slider based on a visual review of the preview, making a decision about the best overall brightness for the image. You'll have an opportunity to fine-tune the results during the rest of your workflow in Elements 5.

Fine-Tuning Contrast

Many photographers like to boost the contrast of their images, and in fact many images benefit from an increase in contrast. However, in the case of a RAW conversion we don't recommend boosting the contrast to the point that the image seems ready to print, simply because it means you are sacrificing too much information in the image at this early stage. Also, you've already established a basic contrast adjustment for the image by adjusting the Exposure and Shadows sliders as outlined earlier. Therefore, we recommend that you do not adjust the Contrast slider at all. Doing so will only undo the careful work you did to expand tonal range with the Exposure and Shadows adjustments.

Adjusting Saturation

Digital cameras vary in the level of color saturation (richness) that they produce at default settings. Most serious photographers prefer moderate (as opposed to high) saturation because they know they have much greater control over the final results during the workflow process in Elements 5. Excessively high saturation is not problematic with RAW captures because you can adjust this parameter in Adobe Camera Raw, although that does add an extra step to the workflow. If your camera produces excessively high saturation, it makes sense to simply set it for a lower Color Saturation level, an option that is available with virtually all of today's cameras.

The Saturation slider at the bottom of the Adjust tab in the Adobe Camera Raw dialog box provides a method for moderating saturation for a more "natural" look. You can also use it for increasing saturation to intensify the colors and for a 100% decrease in saturation to remove color, bringing the image closer to grayscale. However, we do not recommend either of those two techniques.

There is no benefit to boosting saturation during the RAW conversion process. Note too that this tool is not very versatile because it allows only for an *overall* saturation adjustment without the ability to adjust individual colors as in the Hue/Saturation utility in Elements 5. Furthermore, because a significant increase in saturation could cause loss of detail in one or more of the color channels, it is best to use an adjustment layer in Elements 5 after RAW conversion for saturation adjustment. And if one of your plans is to work with monochrome images, you will find a better utility in Elements 5 for converting color images to black-and-white and then varying the monochrome effects, as discussed in Chapter 11, "Creative Adjustments."

Noise Reduction

In some situations, especially with longer exposures or when you use a relatively high ISO setting, you'll find that your digital captures contain a certain amount of noise. This is most often exhibited as a random variation in pixel color values (producing a mottled color effect), but it can also show up as variations in tonal values (somewhat similar to grain in high ISO film). The variations are on the pixel level, so you'll need to zoom in relatively close to see them. You'll most likely be able to see a noise pattern in the shadow areas of your images when it does occur.

Although there are a variety of methods to minimize or eliminate noise in your images after RAW conversion, the Adobe Camera Raw dialog box also includes options to help minimize noise. Under the Detail tab you'll find sliders for Luminance Smoothing and Color Noise Reduction for this purpose.

The Luminance Smoothing slider allows you to compensate for noise exhibited as tonal variations at the pixel level. This isn't common, but it does occur. When using the Luminance Smoothing slider, zoom in to a 100% scale (double-click the Zoom tool to quickly change to a 100% view) and view an area of the image that exhibits luminance noise. Then slowly increase the Luminance Smoothing slider to clear up the noise.

When adjusting Luminance Smoothing, keep a close eye on various areas of the image. Besides reducing luminance noise, this adjustment also can produce a softening effect in the image and lead to posterization.

For the more common color noise, the appropriately named Color Noise Reduction slider will help (Figure 3.9). The default value is 25, which does minimize a small amount of noise. In general, the Color Noise Reduction slider doesn't have a significant effect on sharpness, but it can soften the image slightly when used with a high setting. Use the lowest setting that produces an acceptable reduction in noise within the image. As with Luminance Smoothing, zoom in at a 100% view while looking at dark shadow areas and other places you can see noise while adjusting the Color Noise Reduction slider.

Figure 3.9 The Color Noise Reduction slider in Camera Raw allows you to compensate for color noise within your images, which is often found in shadow areas of an image especially when a high ISO setting was used in capture.

Batch Processing Images

Adobe Camera Raw does not provide a batch processing function in any version of Elements as it does in Photoshop CS2. However, there is one method for applying exactly the same adjustments to any number of images, as each is individually opened in Adobe Camera Raw. This can be useful if you took many pictures under the same circumstances, and all will require the same white balance and tonal corrections.

Start by opening one of the RAW files in Adobe Camera Raw; complete all adjustments and click Open to complete the processing and conversion. Now, open another of the RAW files from the series. Under the Settings side menu, select the Previous Conversion option. When you do so, ACR will automatically apply all of the same adjustments as you had made to the previous RAW file. Continue the same process for all of the RAW images that require exactly the same adjustments. Although this technique does not offer the same speed and convenience as batch processing, it does help to alleviate the tedious and slow process of repeatedly making similar adjustments.

Deciding on Bit Depth

After you've established all the settings to produce the optimal RAW conversion, the only remaining option is for either 8-bits per color channel or 16-bits per color channel from the Depth pop-up menu in ACR. One of the major benefits of RAW capture is that you are able to retain 16-bit data, so you might consider selecting the 16-bit option. That certainly makes sense in Photoshop CS2 because that program supports layers and all core features for images with 16-bit color depth. However, Elements 5 provides no layers support whatsoever for a 16-bit image. It does allow you to use most core features for tonal and color adjustments, as well as many filters, but requires you to work directly on the pixels.

Consequently, we do not recommend the 16-bit option for Elements 5 owners. Do your best to achieve a wide dynamic range and accurate tonal values in Adobe Camera Raw, and convert the file to an image with 8-bit color depth. This will allow you to work with layers as discussed in several subsequent chapters.

Ready to Convert

As you can see, the adjustments you'll need to make within the Adobe Camera Raw dialog box are best approached with a logical progression. In general, approach the process by solving the biggest problem with your image first and working your way down. Because the controls are arranged in a way that makes sense for most images, you'll generally just work your way from the top of the Adjust tab to the bottom when adjusting your RAW images.

As you become more comfortable with the adjustments within ACR, you'll find that the process can be quick. Using the techniques described here, you can move from slider to slider on the Adjust tab quickly without compromising quality. And be sure to take advantage of the Previous Conversion option when working on a series of RAW images that all require the same adjustments.

When all settings have been established for a given image, you can simply click the Open button to start the image processing; that will take a few seconds, and the image will be ready for you to view and Save As a TIFF or other file format. You can then employ the additional optimizing steps in Elements 5, as discussed throughout the rest of this book.

Do note that you have two other options, denoted by the buttons marked Save and Cancel. The latter simply closes Adobe Camera Raw without performing any adjustment tasks. The Save button allows you to save the adjusted file as a Digital Negative (DNG) format (another RAW file format) for archival purposes. This is an option some photographers take advantage of because they are concerned about the proprietary nature of RAW file formats. Because DNG is a documented file format, there is a greater sense of security that the file format will be supported long-term.

Adobe Camera Raw is extremely flexible in allowing you to undo adjustments you have made. If you are ever dissatisfied with the look of an image in ACR after making adjustments and would like to start again, hold down the Alt/Option key to change the Cancel button into a Reset button. Unlike Cancel, which closes the ACR dialog box and the image entirely, the Reset option simply acts as a "revert" control, undoing all the adjustments you have made to the RAW file.

Conversion Alternatives

This book is all about workflow within Elements 5, and Adobe Camera Raw certainly provides an efficient way to process your RAW captures from within Elements. However, there are other alternatives for converting your RAW captures. For one thing, your digital camera will include software for converting RAW captures. In general, the software from camera manufacturers provides excellent quality, but its image processing tends to be relatively slow and the program may not be very versatile or user-friendly.

Another excellent option is the Capture One PRO software from Phase One (www.phaseone.com). The company also offers Capture One LE, without some of the most advanced features, at a lower price; this program would also meet most imaging enthusiasts' needs.

The Phase One software is relatively expensive and less convenient than Adobe Camera Raw, primarily because it requires you to utilize different software for the RAW conversion than for the image optimization. This isn't a major issue, but one that can hinder the efficiency of your overall workflow. Still, the Phase One converter programs are exceptionally versatile and also provide an efficient workflow in their own right. The Pro or LE program is worth considering if you're looking for an alternative to Adobe Camera Raw. It produces images of exceptional quality, in some cases providing better shadow detail and overall image sharpness than Adobe Camera Raw is able to achieve.

Regardless of the solution you choose to utilize for RAW adjustment and conversion, the key is to develop a workflow that helps you produce the best results efficiently so you have the best starting point for the rest of your optimization workflow in Elements 5.

The same also applies to nearly all dialog boxes in Elements. After you complete some adjustment, such as color saturation, you can hold down the Alt/Option key to change the function of the Cancel key to a Reset key. Click Reset, and all adjustments you have made in that utility, Hue/Saturation in this example, are undone, but the utility remains open so you can start again. (If you use the Cancel key instead, your adjustments are not only canceled but the utility also closes.) This shortcut is quicker than using the Edit > Undo command.

Archiving RAW Captures

After you have processed your RAW captures to produce images that are ready to put through your full workflow in Elements 5, you may feel that you no longer need the original RAW capture files. The file you'll save after optimizing your image will become your new master, used as the basis of all prints and other output. However, we strongly recommend that you keep all of your original RAW captures. Just as you wouldn't throw away your original slides or negatives just because you have scanned them into the computer, the original RAW captures are still worth saving.

There is a good chance you won't need your original RAW captures later if you did a good job converting and optimizing them, saving them as a new file. However, saving those original captures provides another level of backup, allowing you to reconvert later, with different adjustments. That can be useful if you change your mind about how the image should be interpreted or if better tools become available in the future for RAW file optimization.

When archiving your RAW captures, we recommend keeping the original filenames intact. In fact, you may want to use the original filename as part of the filename for the new master image that you created after adjusting the RAW file; this will make it easy to refer to the original RAW capture file in the future, if needed.

Because you will not need to access the RAW capture files on a regular basis, there's no need to have them taking up space on your hard disk. Instead, you can archive them to CD, DVD, or an external hard disk, and store them in a safe place. Be sure to label the media adequately so that if you do ever need the RAW captures, you'll be able to locate them easily.

Note: Archiving RAW files in the camera manufacturer's RAW file format is certainly straightforward. However, many photographers prefer to save the files in the "universal" DNG raw data format instead, because DNG is more likely to be supported in the long run. Adobe Camera Raw—and an increasing number of other brands of imaging programs—can open DNG format RAW files. Also, Adobe also provides a free DNG converter, available for download from www.adobe.com/digitalimag. That software allows you to drag a multiple number of RAW files for batch conversion processing; in other words, you can convert all the RAW files in a particular folder to the DNG (raw data) format in one easy maneuver.

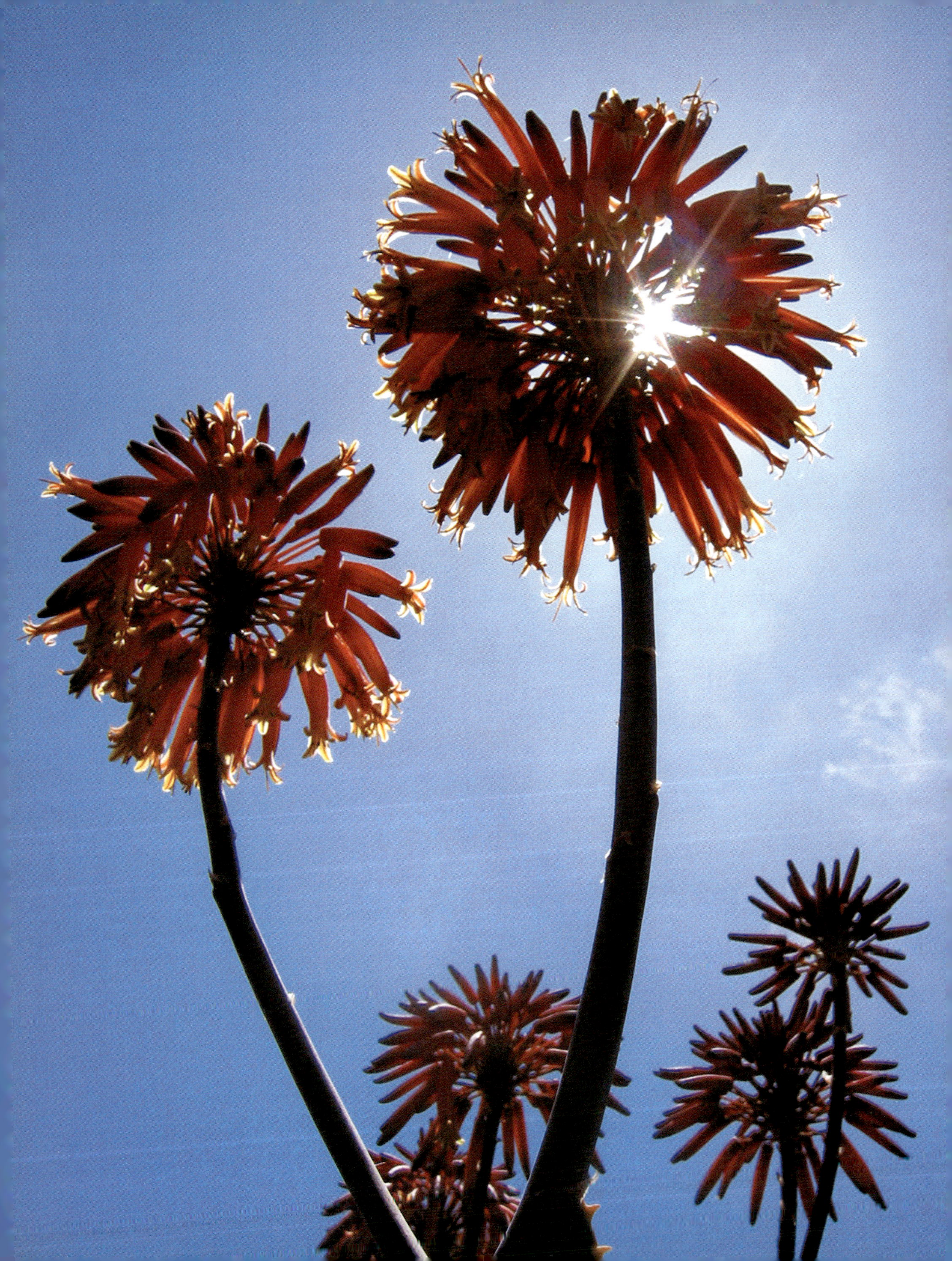

II

Basic Adjustments

In Part I, we covered some of the issues you'll need to deal with before you start the process of optimizing your images in Photoshop Elements 5. In Part II, we'll cover the basic workflow that is the foundation of the optimization process. This will provide you with strong knowledge of the fundamentals so you'll be ready to move on to more-advanced adjustments later in the book.

Chapter 4 **Rotate and Crop**

Chapter 5 **Tone and Color**

Chapter 6 **Image Cleanup**

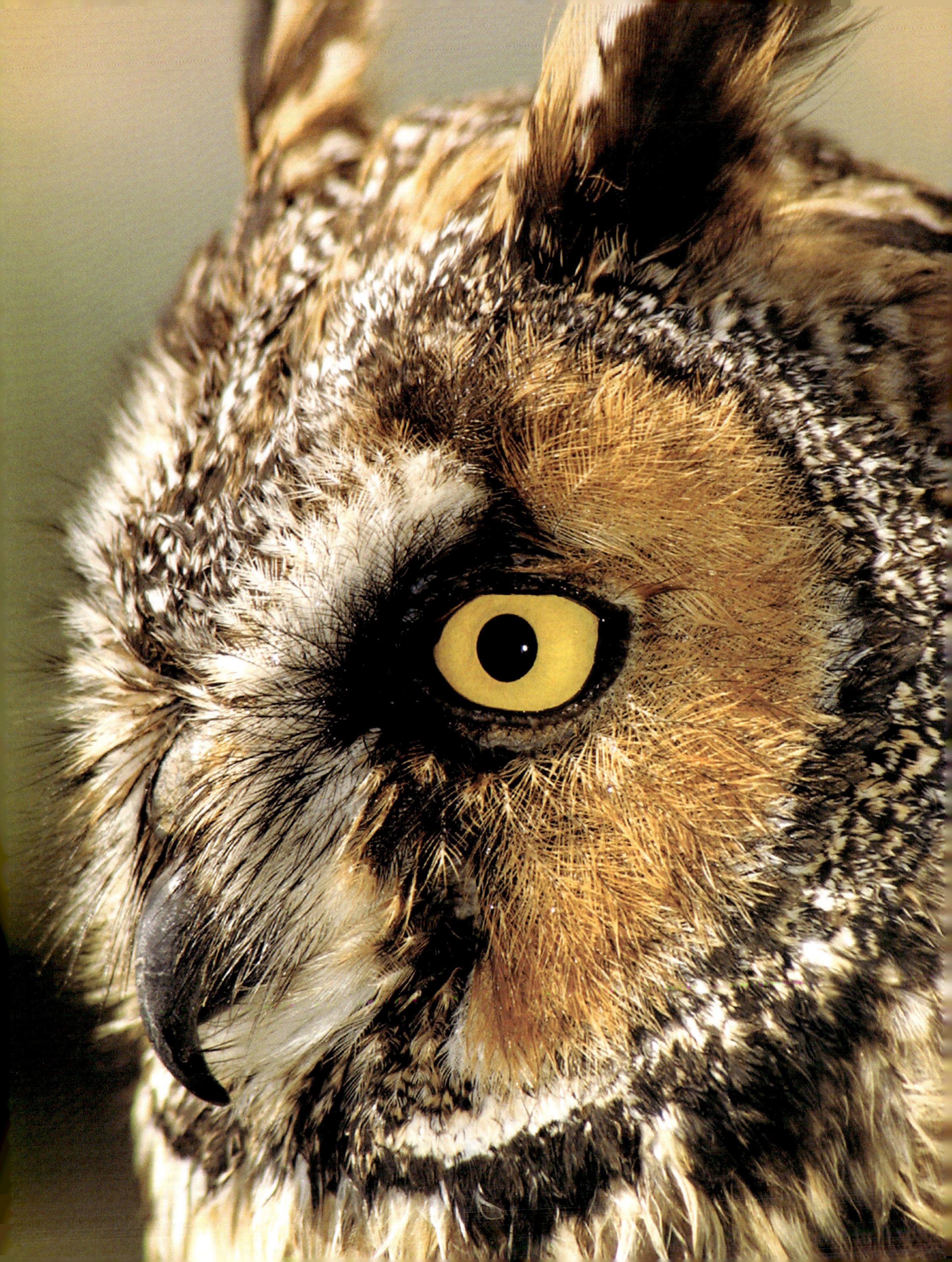

4 Rotate and Crop

Rotation and cropping are methods for correcting the presentation of an image. Rotation *ensures that the image will be viewed in the proper orientation and that it isn't perceived as being crooked.* Cropping *cuts unwanted peripheral elements that may clutter the image or draw attention away from the intended subject. It makes sense to perform these tasks early in your image-optimization workflow so you'll be making later adjustments based on an accurate view of the image.*

Chapter Contents

Basic Rotation
Basic Cropping
Custom Rotation

Basic Rotation

The most basic form of rotation is done in 90-degree increments to correct the orientation of the image. For example, if you forgot to properly rotate the image in your film scanner, or if you are working with a digital camera that doesn't include an automatic rotation capability, you'll need to correct the image yourself.

We recommend performing this basic rotation early in your workflow simply because it can be challenging to assess tonal and color adjustments in an image when it isn't properly oriented. As soon as you start working on an image, it's worth getting it properly rotated so you can better evaluate it and thereby make better decisions about the adjustments you might want to make.

Note: Many digital cameras now include a sensor that can detect when you are capturing an image in portrait vs. landscape mode; such cameras add a tag to the image's metadata indicating that the image needs to be rotated. Elements 5 will look for this metadata tag and automatically rotate the image appropriately when it is opened.

The first step in performing a basic rotation is to determine which direction the image needs to be rotated, and by how much. This is a relatively simple matter of looking at the image and deciding how you'd have to rotate it to turn it "right-side up" (Figure 4.1).

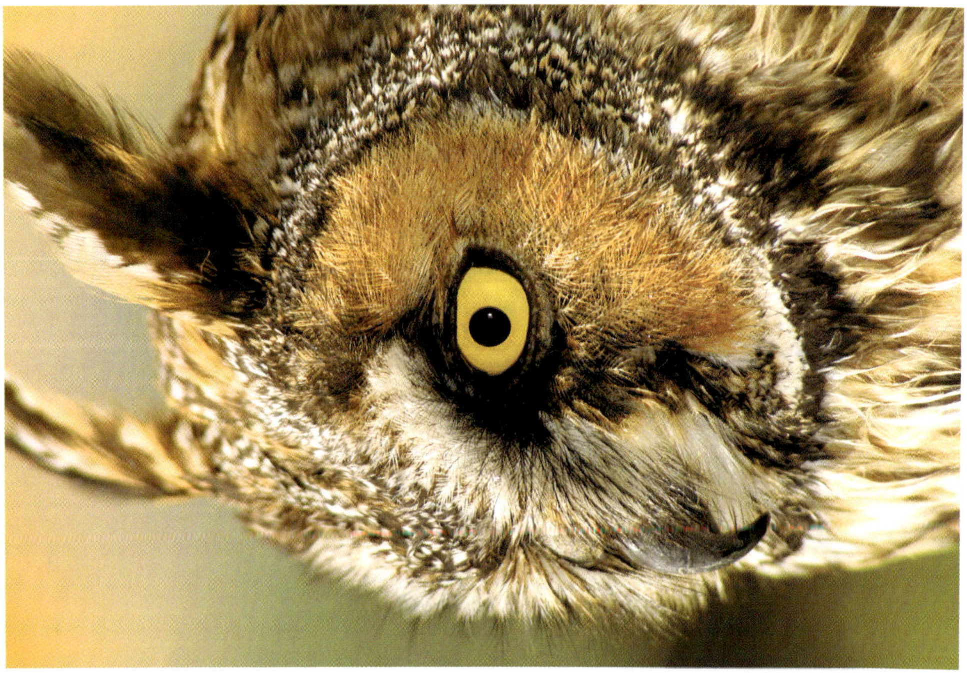

Figure 4.1 When you look at an image that needs to have a basic rotation applied, it is relatively clear in which direction and by how much it needs to be rotated.

Note: Keep in mind that "flipping" an image is not the same as rotating. When you rotate the image, the orientation is changed but the relationships between objects within the image are not. Flipping creates a mirror image in the direction of the flip, changing the relationships between objects in the image. Flipping should not be substituted for rotation, and should be done only when you wish to produce a mirror image.

After you've determined how an image needs to be rotated, doing so is as easy as selecting the appropriate option from the menu. In Elements 5, the options for basic rotation are found in the Image > Rotate menu. You'll find options to rotate the image 180 degrees (180° on the menu), 90 degrees right, and 90 degrees left.

When you select an option from the menu, the image will be rotated based on that option. At this point the image should be right-side up, in the proper general orientation (Figure 4.2).

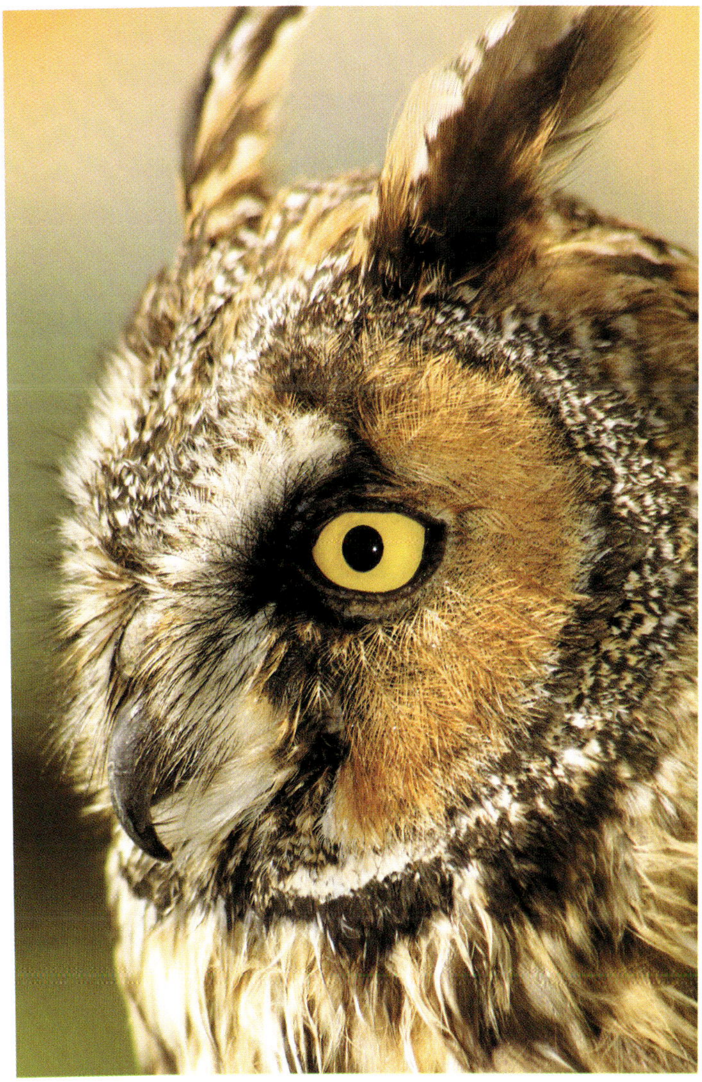

Figure 4.2 When you have applied the proper basic rotation to your image, it should appear in the proper orientation.

Basic Cropping

With the image properly oriented, you can make a more effective evaluation of its composition. In doing so, you may decide that certain areas of the image should be cropped (removed) to strengthen the composition. You may want to eliminate a distracting element, tighten up the overall framing, or change the aspect ratio (relationship between height and width) for aesthetic reasons. For images scanned from film, this is also the point at which you should use cropping to remove the entire slide frame so that only the actual image area is preserved.

You might want consider an approach that Tim uses; he divides cropping into two basic categories. The first is *corrective* cropping, which corrects problems with the image. For example, cropping out the edge of a slide frame of a scanned image would fall into this category. The second category is *artistic* cropping. This changes the artistic effect or compositional appearance of the image.

Corrective cropping is something that usually can't be avoided. Artistic cropping, on the other hand, is purely subjective. You'll probably want to separate the two; complete the essential cropping first and then apply artistic cropping as a separate process. In that second step, you'll focus more on how various amounts or types of cropping will change the interpretation of the image.

Note: If you are performing artistic cropping on an image, be certain you want to eliminate the area being cropped before committing the crop. If you aren't sure, save the artistic cropping for later in your workflow, after you've been able to spend more time with the image. You may find that the areas you wanted to crop earlier suddenly add to the image after applying adjustments throughout your workflow.

For example, you might start with a corrective cropping to eliminate areas of the image that would be a problem if they were included in the final print (Figure 4.3). If someone were standing right at the edge of the frame in a beautiful landscape shot, or if a bad reflection caused an undesirable glare in one corner of the image, you'd certainly want to exclude that distracting element from the scene.

After cropping to correct problems such as these, you can then move on to artistic cropping. Perhaps you'd like to go so far as to change a horizontal image into a vertical by cropping most of the sides. Or maybe you just need to fine-tune the aspect ratio to emphasize certain elements, such as cropping a little off the top of a landscape scene to emphasize the sweeping horizon. You could also simply focus more attention on the main subject matter by cropping out distracting elements from the peripheral areas of the image.

Cropping is often seen as a minor part of your overall workflow. However, the way you crop an image can have a dramatic effect on its final interpretation. By applying a crop, you are able to move beyond the limitations imposed by the aspect ratio of your film or digital imaging sensor. Making a change to the aspect ratio of your image—presenting something different than the viewer is accustomed to—can add visual impact to your images. Even when you don't think you need to crop an image, you might spend some time working with the Crop tool to see whether there are new ways to present the image that you haven't thought about but that would produce a more aesthetically appealing final result.

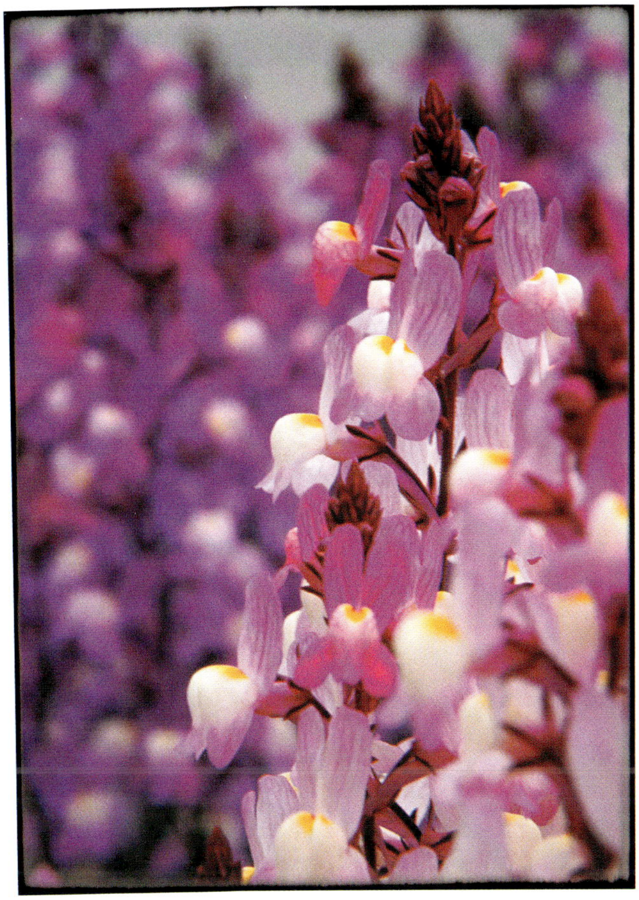

Figure 4.3 When you are working with a film scan, it is important to crop the slide edge from the entire perimeter of the image.

Cropping from a Selection

One of the most straightforward methods of cropping an image is to use a selection as the basis of the crop. Of course, because it is such a simple process, it doesn't offer significant functionality. However, in a variety of situations, starting from a selection is an easy way to crop your image. Creating selections will be covered in extensive detail in Chapter 9, "Making Selections." In the meantime, we'll show you a basic way to create a selection for cropping. After you learn to utilize other selection methods, you can use those for cropping as well.

When using a selection to crop an image, you are defining the outer boundaries of the crop. No matter what the shape of the selection, the final crop will always be to a rectangle. In effect, the cropped image will have outer dimensions defined by the point at which the selection extends farthest in each direction, horizontally and vertically.

The first step is to create a selection that defines the area of the image you want to keep. Start by choosing the Rectangular Marquee tool from the Tools palette or by pressing M (in Full Edit, but not available in Quick Fix). Click and drag on your image to define a rectangular shape, starting in one corner and finishing in the opposite corner (Figure 4.4). The resulting shape should define the area you want to keep, so that only those elements of the image you want to eliminate fall outside the rectangle.

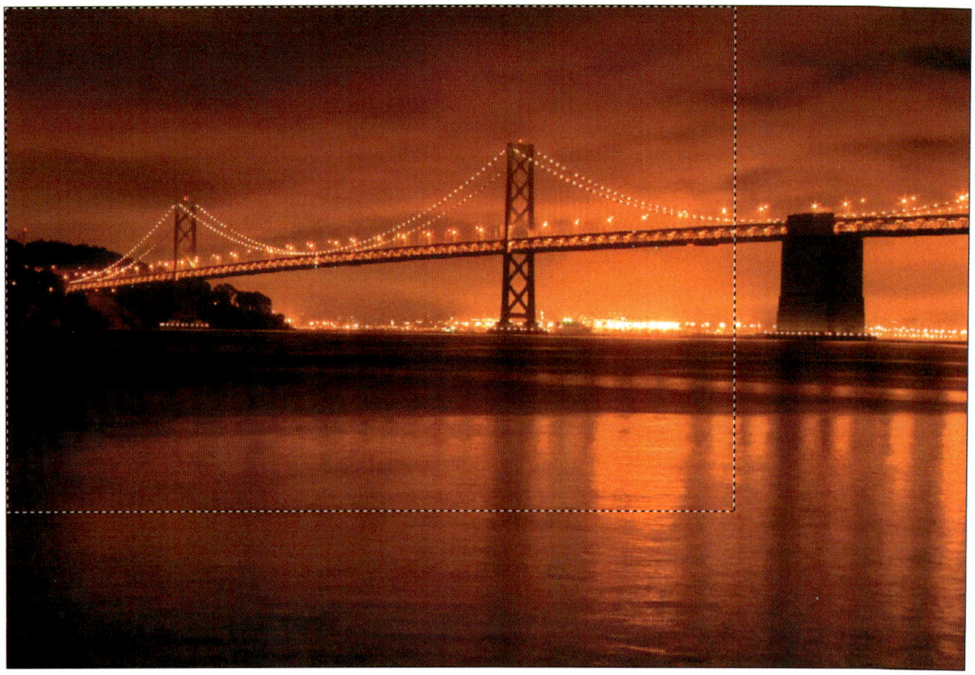

Figure 4.4 You can use the Rectangular Marquee tool to create a selection that defines the area you'd like to crop in an image.

After defining a selection within the image, you can crop based on that selection by choosing Image > Crop from the menu. This causes the image to be cropped so the selection defines the new edge of the image. In other words, this eliminates everything outside that selection edge (Figure 4.5). After cropping, or if you simply decide not to proceed, you can deselect the Rectangular Marquee tool with any of these four methods:

- Right-click the image area and choose Deselect.
- Press Ctrl/F+D.
- Choose Select > Deselect.
- Choose Edit > Undo Rectangular Marquee.

Of course, the selection doesn't need to be rectangular just because the cropped image will be. As you'll see in Chapter 9, you can make selections from a wide variety of shapes, and you can use any of them to create a selection for cropping your image. Just keep in mind that whatever the shape of the selection, the final crop will always be a rectangle that coincides with the outermost points of the selection (Figure 4.6).

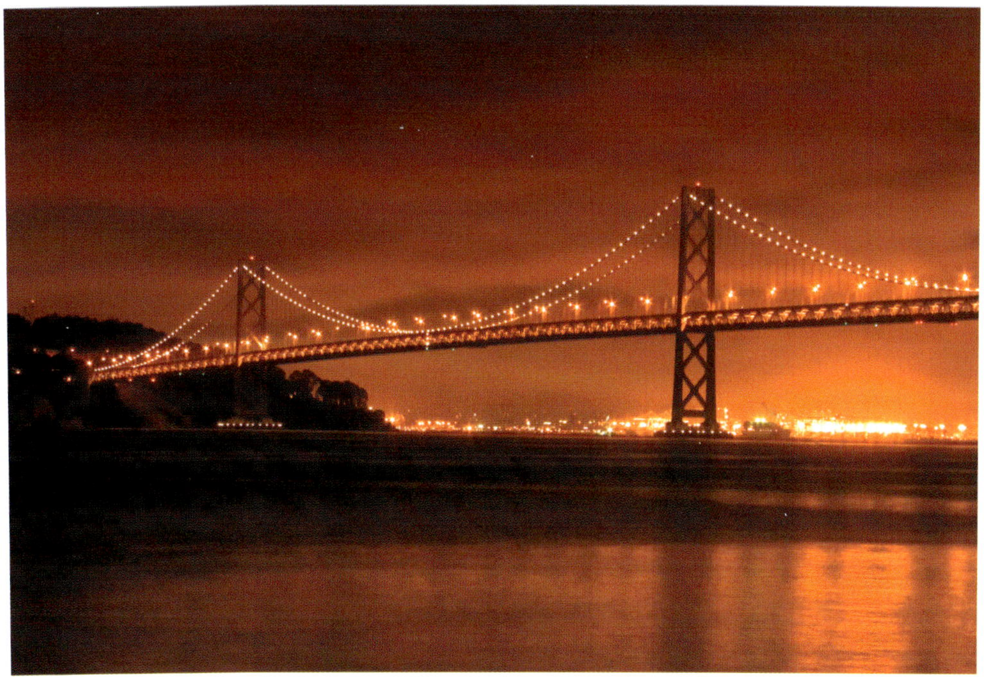

Figure 4.5 After you've defined a selection, you can choose Image > Crop from the menu, and the image will be cropped to the outer edge of your selection.

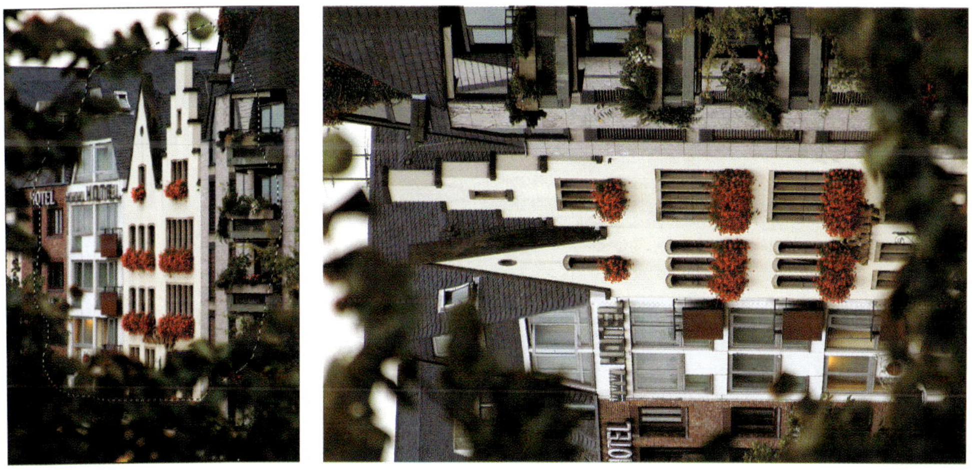

Figure 4.6 You don't need to create a rectangular selection as the basis of a crop, even though the final crop will be rectangular. We've sketched a selection using the Lasso tool that simply defines areas we want to keep in the image, without following a rectangular shape (left). After applying the nonrectangular selection as a crop, the result is a rectangular image that is cropped to the edges of the selection (right).

It may seem pointless to crop an image by using a selection with a nonrectangular shape when the final crop will be rectangular. However, in certain situations you may find it easier to think about cropping an image by determining the specific areas you want keep, tracing those areas to produce the selection, and then cropping to match that shape. In other situations you may create a nonrectangular selection for another purpose and then realize that the selection provides a perfect basis for a crop. The key to remember is that you have a high degree of flexibility when using selections for cropping, so don't think you always need to use a rectangular selection.

Using the Crop Tool

In many cases cropping from a selection is a preferred method because of its flexibility of allowing you to crop from a selection of any shape (though the resulting crop will still be rectangular). However, the Crop tool is generally the most appropriate choice for most cropping tasks because it is specifically designed for that purpose.

To get started with the Crop tool, select it from the Tools palette or press C on your keyboard. This changes the Options bar (above the image area on your screen) to include the settings that are specific to this tool (Figure 4.7). You'll start with a basic crop, so if necessary, delete any data in the Width, Height, and Resolution fields to make sure no sizing options are set. From the Aspect Ratio drop-down menu, select No Restriction. You'll see how to put the various settings to use a little later.

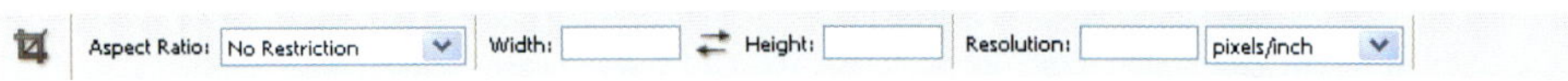

Figure 4.7 When you select the Crop tool, the Options bar will be updated to reflect the options for this tool.

Similar to the use of the Rectangular Marquee tool described in the previous section, you can click and drag across your image with the Crop tool to define the crop area. This action produces a rectangular box, or *marquee*, that defines the area to be kept. Anything outside the crop box will be removed from the image after you apply the crop.

With the crop box defined, you can adjust the shape of the crop to fine-tune the result you're trying to achieve. At each corner, and at the halfway point of each border line of the crop box, you'll see a small square handle. You can drag these handles to change the outer dimensions of the crop box. You can also grab any edge of the crop box to drag and resize. If you click and drag one of the handles at the midway point of a border, you'll change the position of that border line only, not affecting the other lines. Dragging a corner handle will change the position of that corner, and thus affect the two lines that intersect at that corner. If you hold the Shift key while adjusting one of the corner handles, you can change the position of that corner without changing the aspect ratio of the crop.

When you are cropping an image, the display darkens the area around the crop, so you can get a better idea of how the image will appear after you apply the crop. The default settings cause the black shield to be displayed at 75% opacity. This considerably darkens the area to be discarded, making it easy to visualize the result. However, you can change the color of the shield, as well as the opacity (darkness of the color) in the Edit > Preferences > Display & Cursors dialog box to blue, for example (Figure 4.8).

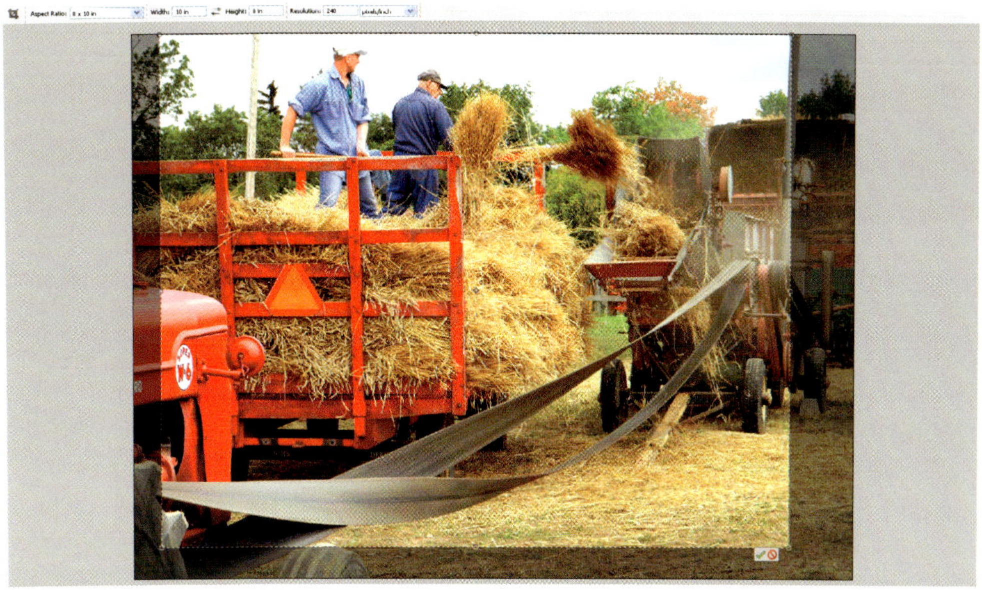

Figure 4.8 The shaded area, or *shield*, for the Crop tool makes it easier to see what the effect of the crop will be on the resulting image. You can switch to another color, such as blue in this case, by using the Display & Cursors dialog box, one of the options under Preferences.

When working on a black-and-white photo, you may find that a very dark-toned shield blends into the image; in that case, you may prefer a shield of a lighter color. You can also adjust the Opacity of the shield: the degree to which you are able to see through the area that is going to be cropped. If you set the Opacity to 100% when using a black shield, for example, you won't see the image through the crop shield at all; instead, it will appear to be matted with the selected color as a border. We recommend using a lighter-toned shield, or reducing the Opacity setting, so you can better see the area of the image you are cropping while deciding exactly what areas should be eliminated.

If you prefer not to see the shield, you can temporarily deselect it by pressing the forward slash (/) key on your keyboard. This key serves as a toggle to turn the shield off and on. Although the shield is helpful for visualizing the effect of a crop, it can interfere at times. For example, you may sometimes find that it makes it difficult to see exactly where the edge of a crop falls on the image. In those cases, you might want to turn it off temporarily to evaluate the image, and then turn it back on to view the overall crop.

It is important to check the area you are cropping to make sure you're eliminating extraneous elements, such as the edge of the slide frame in a scan. Use the crop handles (denoted by small rectangles) to move the crop selection area as desired but make sure that the crop box doesn't extend outside the image area. Any extension would cause additional pixels to be added around the edge of the image with the background color defined in the Tools palette. We recommend zooming in close to check the corners of your crop and possibly checking the full perimeter if necessary to ensure you are producing the best crop possible.

Because you are in the middle of a crop process when you check the edges of your crop area, you can't switch to other tools used for navigation. However, keyboard shortcuts provide efficient ways to check the image. If you hold the Ctrl/F key and the spacebar, the Zoom tool is activated no matter what tool you're currently using.

You can then click and drag a box around a corner of the image while still holding those keys. This will cause the image to be zoomed in so that area fills the available display area. To return to a view showing the full image, hold Ctrl/F and press 0 (the zero key). Repeat this process for each corner of the image to check for appropriate cropping, adjusting the position of the crop box corner as needed. If you want to check the full perimeter of the crop box, you can hold the spacebar after you've zoomed in to activate the Hand tool, which can then be used to drag the image around while you examine the edge of the crop.

After you have defined the crop that will be most effective for an image, you're ready to apply that crop by clicking the Commit button ✓ under the image. Alternatively, you can press Enter/Return on the keyboard, or you can double-click inside the crop box. Any of these steps causes the image to be cropped based on the current crop box, with the pixels outside the crop box discarded.

If you decide you don't want to apply the crop, you can click the Cancel button ⊘ under the image or press the Esc key on your keyboard. The crop will not be applied, and the crop box will go away. You can then start over with a new crop, or simply move on to using other tools if you decide you don't want to crop the image at all.

Crop Size

The Crop tool also provides a variety of options that allow you to specify the aspect ratio of the final crop, as well as the size of the image after cropping. If you decide to use them, you must establish these settings before you create the crop box. So be sure to apply these settings first, or if you are already in the middle of a crop and realize you need to select a specific size, cancel the crop and set these options before starting the crop process again.

The controls for establishing a specific aspect ratio or image size are quite simple. You can select one of the few standard print size options available from the Aspect Ratio drop-down menu, and the size will automatically appear in the Width and Height fields. This feature provides only a few specific size options, so it is very restrictive. There is another option, Use Photo Ratio, but that is even less useful because it sets an arbitrary size *and* resolution value that will rarely meet your intentions. For greater control, select No Restriction in the drop-down menu and enter any desired value for Width and Height, such as **8.5 in** (for inches) and **11 in** for an 8.5″×11″ print. You can also enter dimensions in centimeters or millimeters by using the abbreviation cm or mm, respectively.

You can enter a value in the Resolution field. However, you don't always need to include the Resolution option, and in some cases you may want to exclude it. When you set a size without establishing a Resolution, the image will be cropped to the aspect ratio defined by the Width and Height settings. The number of pixels within the cropped area will not be changed: no interpolation will be applied. In other words, Elements will not increase or decrease the image file size.

On the other hand, if you do include a value for Resolution in addition to Width and Height, the image will be cropped and resized in one step, so that the cropped image has exactly the dimensions and resolution you specified. This means interpolation will be applied if necessary to change the image file size to the exact dimensions and resolution you have specified.

Whenever you enter values for Width and Height, or use an Aspect Ratio option, the crop will be constrained. In other words, the crop box you create will be limited to the specific aspect ratio defined by those size values.

For example, let's say you have entered dimensions for an 8″×10″ print (or a 10″×8″ print for a vertical image) before creating your crop box (Figure 4.9). By leaving the Resolution value blank, only the aspect ratio is being constrained, and the pixels you choose to keep, based on the final crop, will not be altered. When you click and drag on the image to establish the crop, the shape of the crop box will be determined by the aspect ratio represented by the Width and Height settings you've established. The size isn't limited, and you can make the crop box as big or small as your image will allow. However, no matter what direction you drag the box, the aspect ratio of the crop box will be fixed, to the correct aspect ratio for an 8″×10″ print in this example.

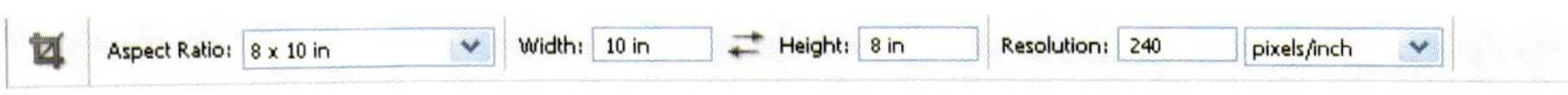

Figure 4.9 The Width, Height, and Resolution settings on the Options bar for the Crop tool provide a way for you to set a final image size for a crop.

Between the Width and Height settings, you'll see a double-arrow icon that, when clicked, will swap those two values. This is handy if, for example, you are creating a collage and want all of the images to be the exact same size, but some are horizontal and some are vertical.

If you want the image file after cropping to be a specific size, not just set for specific dimensions, you'll need to include a value for Resolution, in pixels per inch or per centimeter. With all three values established, the exact size and resolution of the image after cropping is known, and you can crop and resize in one step. This is a great way to crop an image to fit a specific output size, such as when you need to print an image to fit a particular frame and know that you want to print at a specific resolution such as 240 pixels per inch.

When cropping to a specific image size, be sure to set the Resolution value to whatever you will be using for the print, because the image will be interpolated based on the values you enter. This will be covered in greater detail in Chapter 13, "Output Processing," but when in doubt you should use a Resolution setting between 240 pixels/inch and 300 pixels/inch, suitable values for ink-jet printers.

Note: It is a good practice to always clear the Width, Height, and Resolution field's values after cropping an image to a specific size; also select No Restriction in the Aspect Ratio drop-down. This will ensure that you will be starting with default behavior the next time you decide to use the Crop tool.

Perspective

Elements 5 includes a utility called Correct Camera Distortion under the Filter menu item. When you select that utility, the image appears in a dialog box. You can then use the available tools to correct perspective problems or to introduce a change in perspective to add a creative twist. This option is most often used to correct perspective errors, such as those caused by tilting a lens upward to record an entire tall subject in a photo as is often seen when you use a wide-angle lens to capture an image of a building (Figure 4.10).

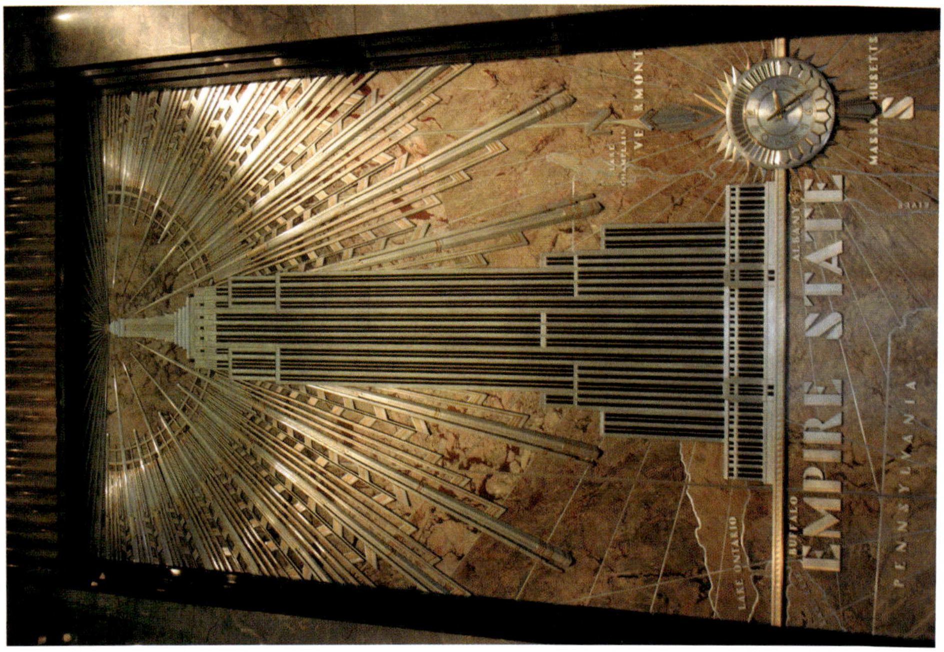

Figure 4.10 When capturing images by pointing a lens upward, especially with a wide-angle lens, you'll often see perspective errors that can be distracting from the image.

We recommend that you duplicate the image layer before using the Correct Camera Distortion filter. Select Layer > Duplicate Layer and rename it, perhaps to Distortion Correction, so you will remember exactly why you created this additional layer. When you use Correct Camera Distortion, experiment with the Vertical Perspective and Horizontal Perspective tools; make adjustments in small increments until the image looks just right. To make it easier to judge the adjustments that you should make, click the Show Grid checkbox at the bottom of the Correct Camera Distortion dialog box to enable the Grid display. This displays a grid pattern over your image, which you can use to better judge the amount of perspective change that will produce the desired results (Figure 4.11).

Note: Although we are discussing perspective correction after the Cropping section, we recommend using the Correct Camera Distortion filter before you do any cropping. That's because you will need to crop the image after using this utility, and it simply makes sense to crop only once in order to achieve exactly the desired cropping effect.

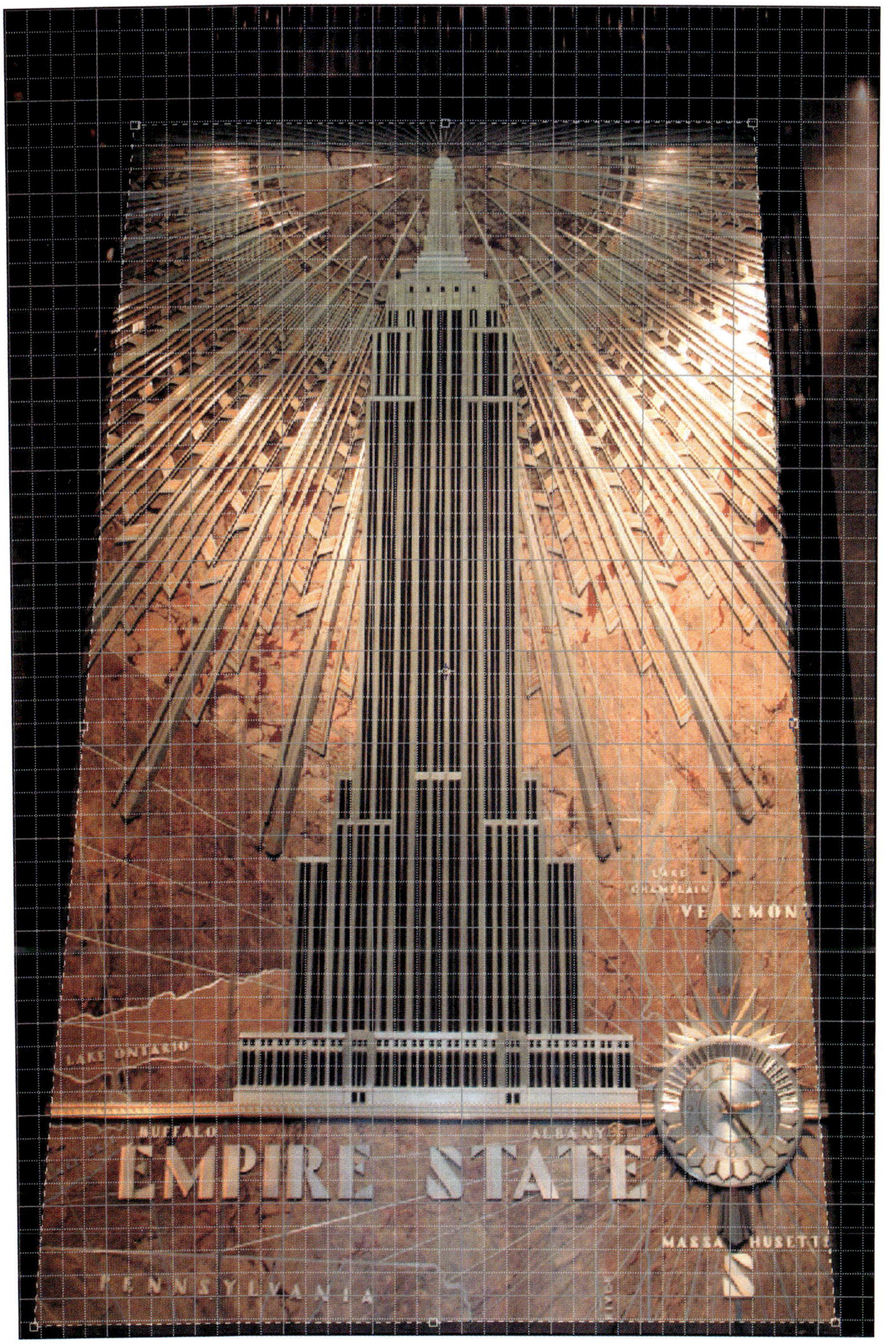

Figure 4.11 Using the Correct Camera Distortion utility in Elements 5 allows you to correct perspective before cropping with the Crop tool. Turning on the grid display (at the bottom of the dialog box) can help you better judge the perspective correction amounts that will produce the desired effect.

When you're finished working in this utility, click OK. The image, with the new perspective, appears in the standard Edit screen. You will need to crop it to include only the desired image area. Unrestricted cropping works best for this process (Figure 4.12). Afterward, you may decide to do additional cropping, to create a specific print size, by using the Width and Height options.

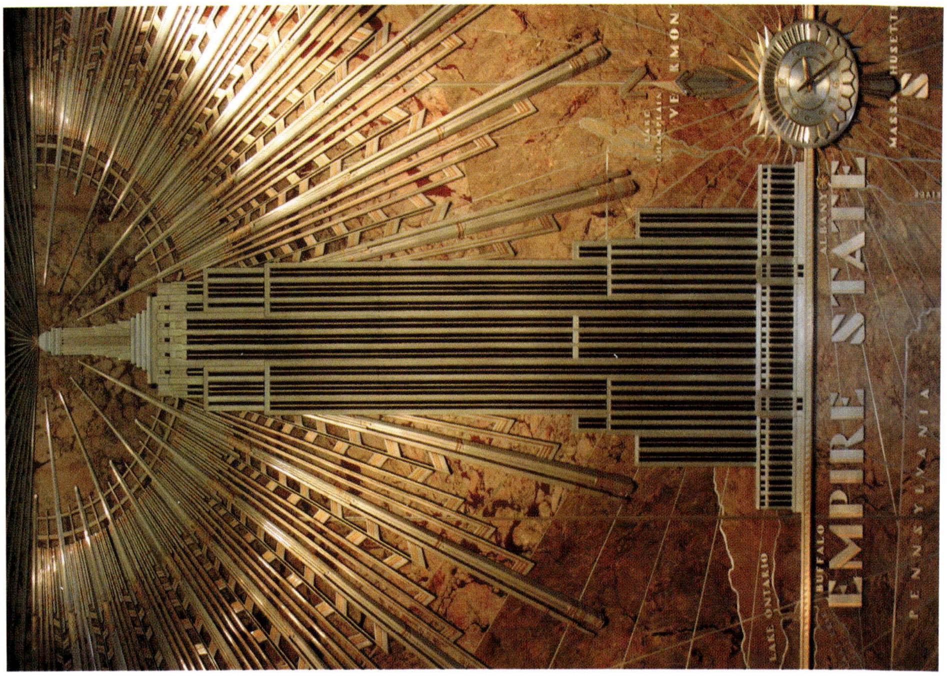

Figure 4.12 After you have established the proper perspective by using the Correct Camera Distortion filter, the image will be skewed by Elements to correct for the distortion. This will require cropping.

Note: It can take a great deal of practice to get the best results with the Correct Camera Distortion filter. If you're not happy with the results you achieve, undo the filter by choosing Edit > Undo Correct Camera Distortion from the menu and try again.

Custom Rotation

At the beginning of this chapter we mentioned rotating your image in 90-degree increments to correct its overall orientation. However, sometimes you'll want to rotate the image by an entirely different number of degrees. That can be useful for correcting a crooked horizon or an object that should be perfectly horizontal or vertical but appears slightly crooked, or off-kilter (Figure 4.13). One method for achieving this effect is to rotate the cropping border while using the Crop tool, but Elements 5 offers two other tools that are more convenient, and far more precise, for achieving exactly the desired effect: the Custom Rotate tool and the Straighten tool.

After you rotate an image by other than 90-degree increments, cropping will be necessary. This is because the resulting image is always a rectangle, and if you have rotated the image by a few degrees, you'll end up with part of the image hanging outside that rectangle. You may also find areas within the image rectangle that don't have any actual pixel values (in which case these areas will be replaced with the current background color set in the Tools palette).

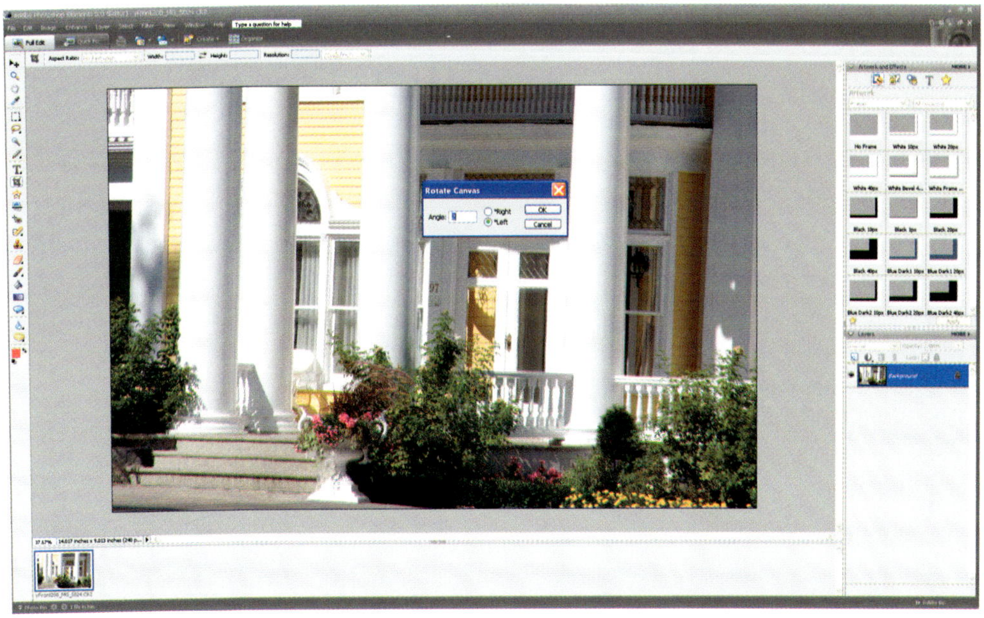

Figure 4.13 When an object within the image that should be horizontal or vertical isn't straight, you can use custom rotation to correct the problem.

Rotating with the Crop Tool

Because you'll have to crop the image anyway after you apply an arbitrary amount of rotation, it makes sense to use the Crop tool for both the rotation and the cropping. Fortunately, this tool provides exactly that capability.

If you're going to apply an arbitrary rotation to an image, we recommend that you not perform any cropping in advance; this ensures that you will have as many pixels to work with as possible when you're applying the arbitrary rotation. Using the Crop tool to apply a basic arbitrary rotation is rather easy, and the process starts just as it would for a normal crop.

Start by selecting the Crop tool and clicking and dragging on the image to define a basic crop box. To apply a rotation, move the mouse pointer outside the crop box. The mouse pointer becomes a double-headed curved arrow. When you click and drag, you'll see that the crop box rotates. This allows you to define the exact angle that the eventual image should be.

Note: The small target icon that appears in the middle of the crop box defines the center of rotation. In most cases you'll want the center of the crop box to coincide with the center of rotation. However, if you'd like the box to rotate around a different point, you can click and drag this target to a different position.

The best method is to first find something in the image that should be perfectly horizontal or vertical. This may be a horizon line, the edge of a building, or some other object. In some situations it may be difficult to see exactly where that line is, such as a landscape on a hazy day. However, you'll need to select something within the image to use as your reference line.

With that reference line selected, the next step is to drag one of the edges of the crop box toward that line (Figure 4.14). For vertical objects you'd move the left or right edge of the box inward, and for horizontal objects you'd bring the top or bottom edge in. Simply point your mouse to the edge itself or the square handle on the edge, and click and drag inward. Put the edge relatively close to the reference line, but not right on top of it. If it is right on top of the reference line, it is difficult to evaluate how close they are to being parallel. All you really need is for the two lines to be close enough to decide when they are parallel to each other.

With the edge dragged inward near your reference line, move the mouse pointer outside the crop box and click and drag to rotate (as in the second image of Figure 4.14). Rotate the crop box until the edge of the box and your reference line in the image are perfectly parallel. At this point your angle of rotation is established (Figure 4.15). However, because you brought one of the edges of the crop box inward, you now need to adjust the edges. Also, the rotation may have caused one or more corners of the crop box to move outside the image. Therefore, you need to adjust all four corners so that you are including as much of the image as possible (or as much as is desired) within the crop area, and that all four of the corners are inside the available image area.

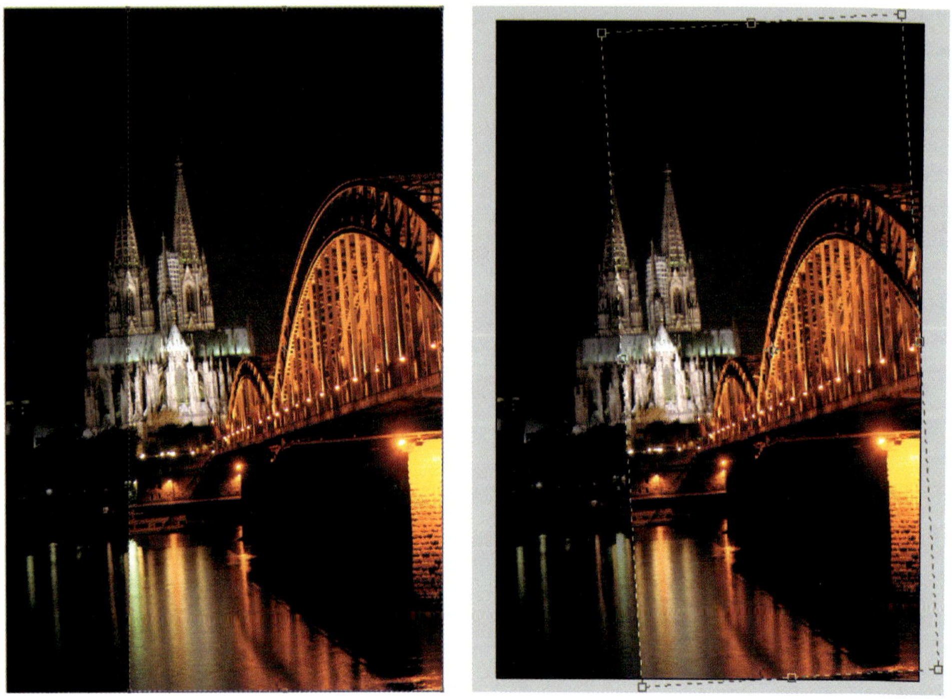

Figure 4.14 The first step in applying arbitrary rotation with the Crop tool is to bring one of the crop box edges in toward your reference line within the image (left). Then rotate the crop box so its edge is parallel with the reference line within the image that should be horizontal or vertical, such as the horizon line or the steeple of the cathedral in this case (right).

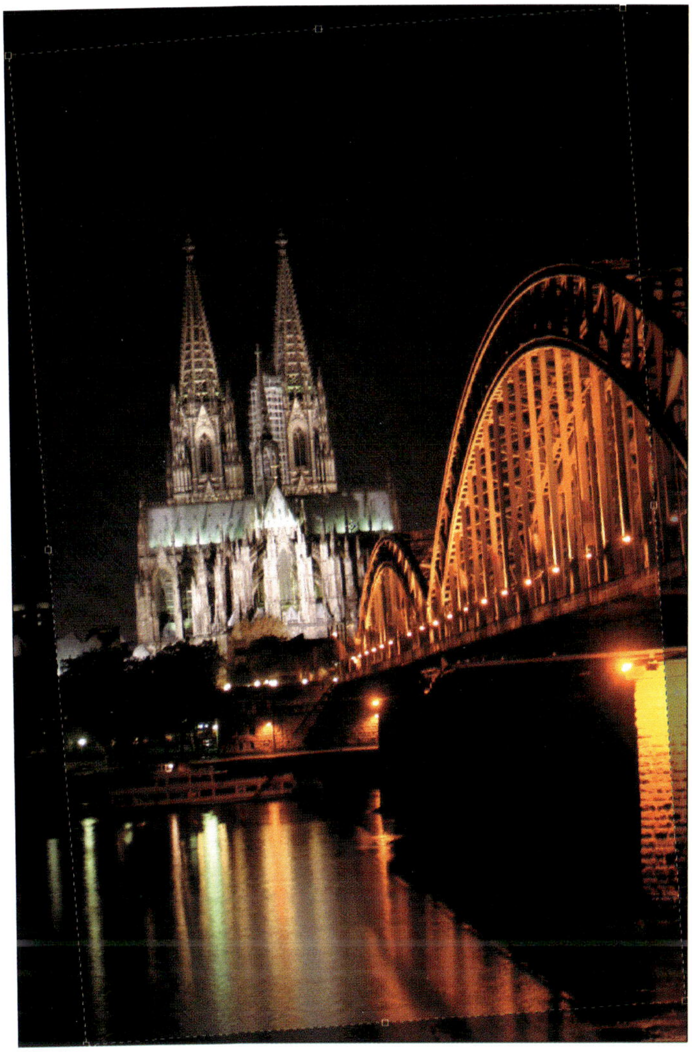

Figure 4.15 After you have rotated the crop box to your reference line, you can adjust all four corners so they are within the image area and the crop can be applied.

After you have your rotation established and your cropping corrected, you're ready to apply the crop. When you do so, the image will be automatically cropped and rotated in one step (Figure 4.16).

Elements 5 provides two automated tools designed to straighten an off-kilter image. The first is selected by choosing Image > Rotate > Straighten Image from the menu, and the second by choosing Image > Rotate > Straighten And Crop Image. Either can be useful in theory, but in our experience, these tools rarely provide exactly the desired straightening effect. In fact, they sometimes rotate an image significantly, when only a very minor straightening is required. Consequently, we cannot recommend using either of these tools.

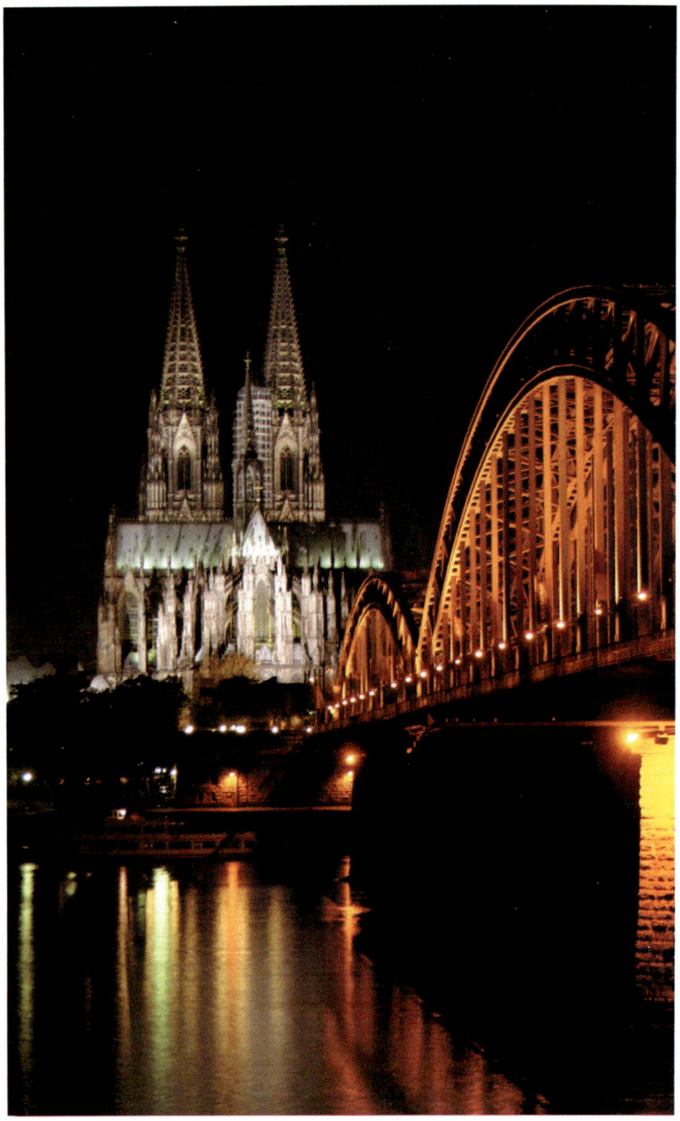

Figure 4.16 When the crop is applied after the crop box has been rotated, the image will be cropped and rotated in a single step.

Using the Custom Rotate Tool

Elements 5 provides an effective method for straightening images in small increments: the Custom Rotate tool. It is available by choosing Image > Rotate > Custom. When you select this tool, a dialog box opens, allowing you to enter the number of degrees of rotation to the Right or to the Left. This is quite straightforward, but Elements 5 does not provide any measuring tool that would let you determine an optimal number of degrees for rotation. Consequently, some guesswork and a trial-and-error technique is required (Figure 4.17).

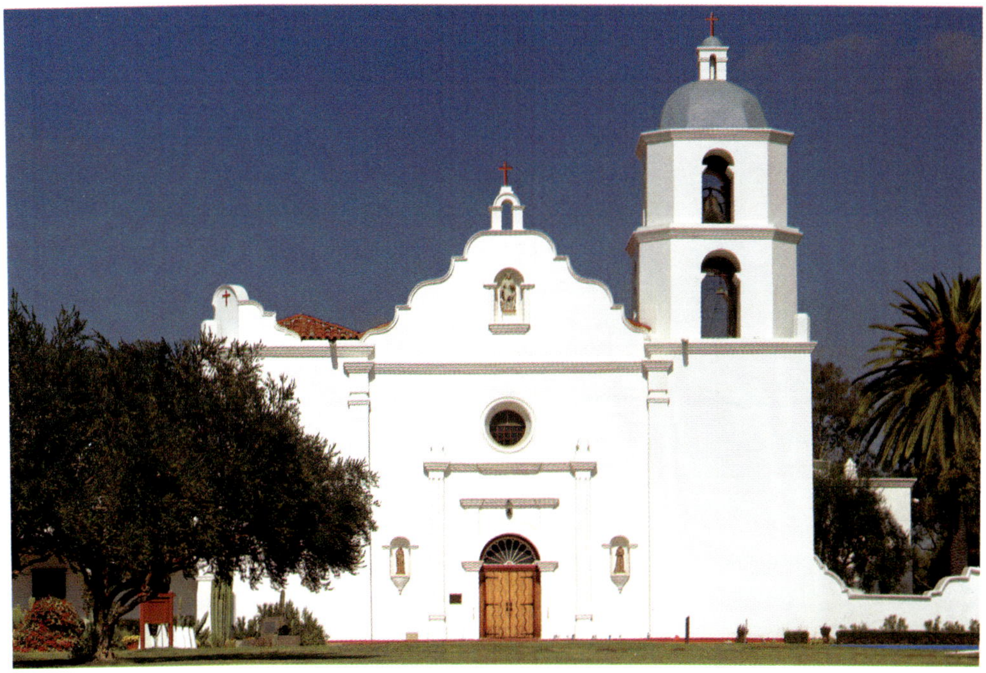

Figure 4.17 Especially when an image, such as this one, requires only minor straightening, the Custom Rotate tool can be useful.

To make it easier to judge the effect of any custom rotation that you will make, enable the Grid display by choosing View > Grid from the menu before selecting the Custom Rotate tool.

Unless you have an uncanny ability to estimate the number of degrees of rotation that is required to straighten any image, we suggest using the following step-by-step technique. Determine whether the image should be rotated to the right or the left. Enter a small increment, such as 0.3 degrees for images that do not require major rotation. (For images that are obviously very crooked, you might want to try a 1-degree increment.) Click OK to activate the rotation (Figure 4.18).

Note: If you are not satisfied with the amount of rotation that has been applied, be sure to use the Edit > Undo Rotate command to cancel it and then try again. Although you could simply continue to rotate in the desired direction by small increments to solve the problem, that will have an adverse effect on the image, because Elements will apply a calculation on the pixels during the rotation process. This will cause a small degree of quality loss. Although this loss in quality may not be very noticeable, repeated rotations could cause a cumulative affect to reduce the quality further and possibly to a more noticeable degree. Therefore, it is recommended that you undo the rotation and guess again. This ensures that a calculation on changing pixels occurs only once as opposed to multiple times.

If the first step has not achieved exactly the desired straightening effect, undo and try again. Use Custom Rotate and adjust the angle amount to the left or to the right, as appropriate, considering the current look of the image. You may need to make a few attempts to get it just right before you crop the image with the Crop tool to eliminate areas without pixels. Based on Peter's experience with this tool in various versions of Elements, you will definitely improve the accuracy of your estimates with some practice. Subsequently, you will need to do less experimenting with various degrees of rotation to achieve exactly the desired straightening effect.

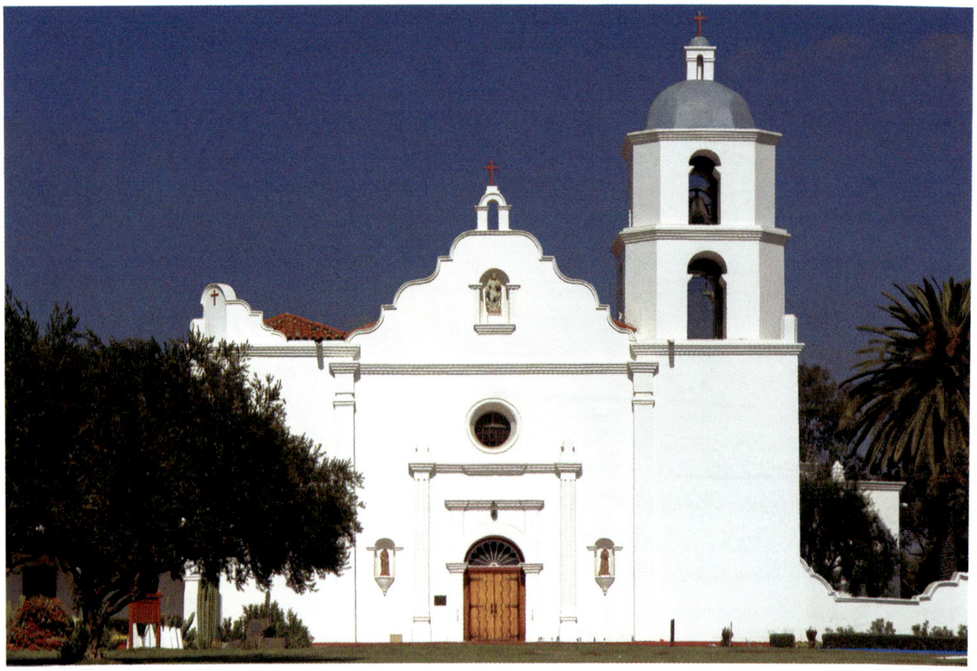

Figure 4.18 Applying a 0.3 degree rotation to the right, and then cropping with the Crop tool, has provided the desired effect—straight lines that appear straight instead of being skewed to the left.

Using the Straighten Tool

There is another method in Elements 5 that's designed for correcting crooked images: the Straighten tool. Select it from the Tools palette or just press the P key. Drag your cursor along a crooked edge within the image that should be perfectly horizontal, such as a horizon or the roof line of a building. After you release the mouse, Elements will automatically straighten the image (Figure 4.19) by ensuring that the line you identified is straight. When that's finished, crop the image as required.

Alternatively, you can allow Elements to do the cropping automatically. Simply select Crop To Remove Background from the Canvas Options drop-down list that appears whenever you select the Straighten tool. Two other options are available in the drop-down list: Grow Or Shrink Canvas To Fit and Crop To Original Size. The Grow Or Shrink Canvas To Fit option adds extra pixels to the image in order to maintain the rectangular image window dimensions needed after rotation is applied. As with extending the Crop tool outside the image window, the effect is the same. The background color swatch in the Tools palette determines the color of the additional pixels added to the image. The Crop To Original Size option has a similar effect. The difference is that the image will be cropped to a rectangular shape identical to the original dimensions of the image before the rotation was applied. Again, if any pixels are added in this process, they will be the same color as the background color swatch in the Tools palette.

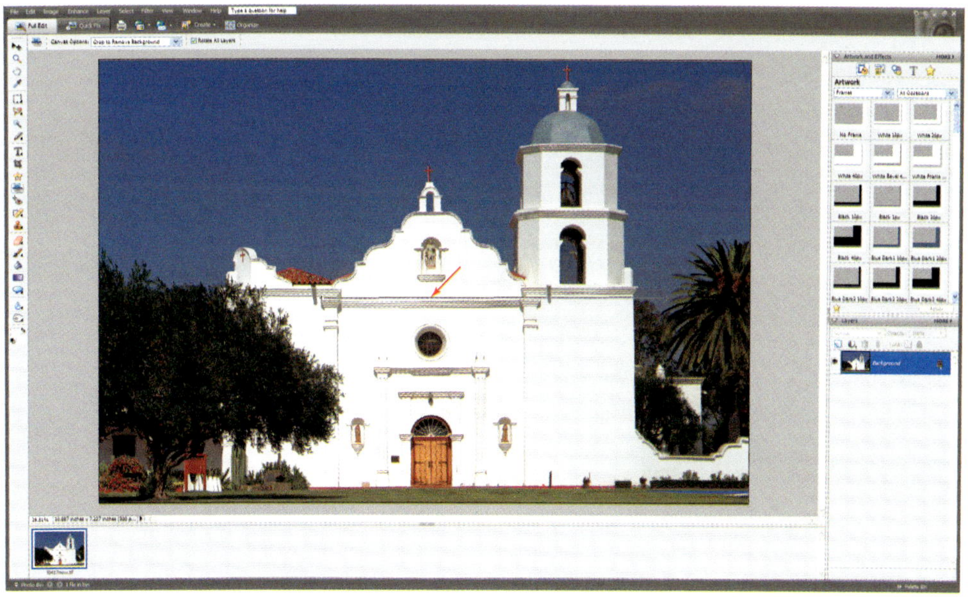

Figure 4.19 A simplified correction tool, Straighten can identify a crooked line or edge, such as the roof line above the circular window here. Elements will then straighten that line or edge, and it will also crop automatically if you have selected the Crop To Remove Background option. This tool is most appropriate with images that exhibit accurate perspective, so you may need to use the Correct Distortion filter before the straightening process.

The basic operation is not difficult, although the process takes some skill. You must draw the line precisely parallel to the subject line that you have identified. If you are not satisfied with the results, press Ctrl/F+Z to undo and start again. Chances are, you will find this method for straightening an image the easiest of the methods mentioned here in this chapter, and you may wonder why we waited to include this method last. If we presented this method first, you might have been tempted to skip trying the other methods. However, the advantage to understanding *all* the possible methods available is that you have a bigger bag of tricks. You never know when one method might prove to be more beneficial over another. And a diverse understanding of all possible methods provides you with the knowledge and tools for all possible situations.

Right-Side Up

Now that you've properly oriented your image and applied straightening and cropping to correct any problems, or to meet your aesthetic interpretation, you're ready to move on to basic tonal and color adjustments, the subject of the next chapter.

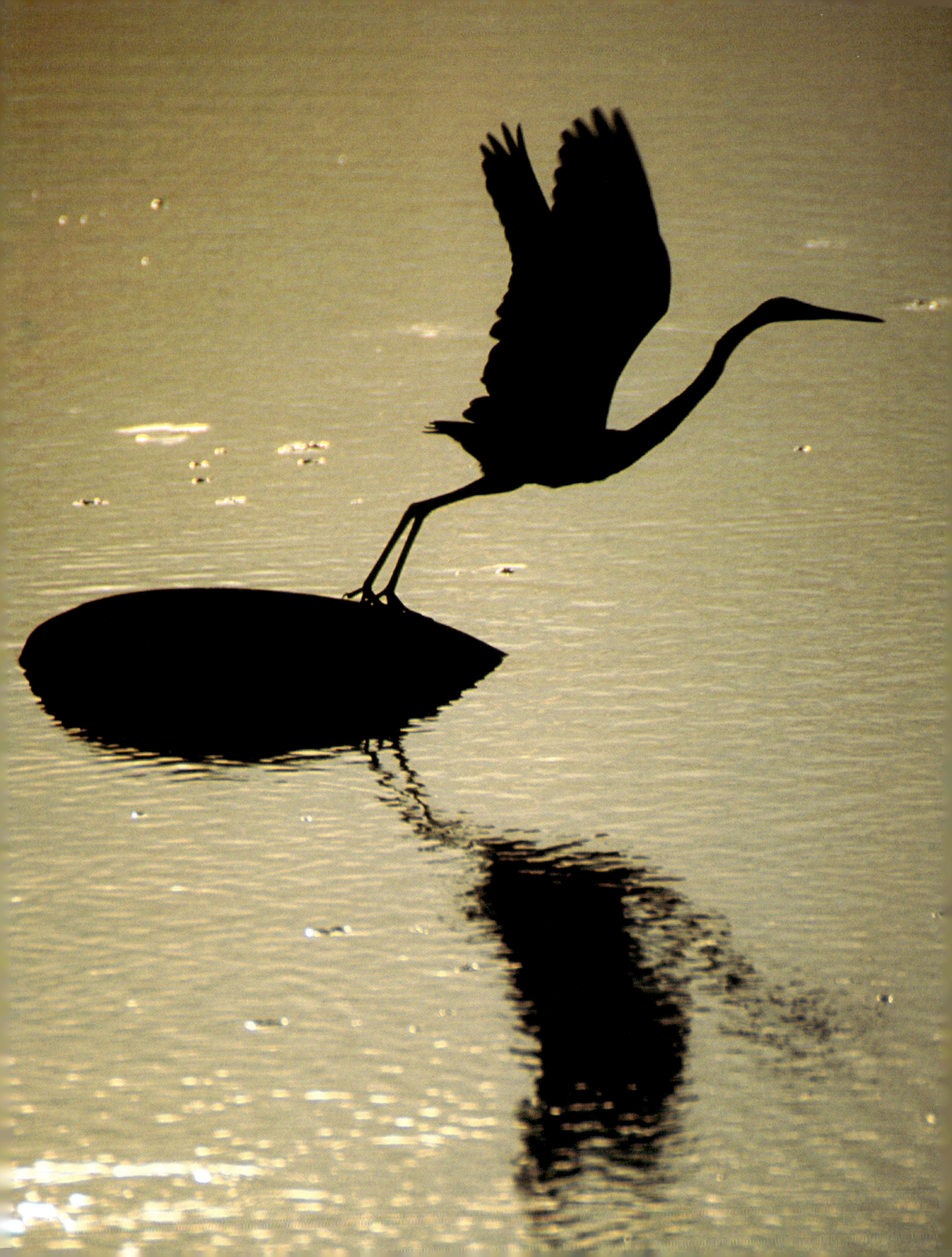

Tone and Color

As you start working on the actual adjustments to optimize your images in Elements 5, you'll want to start with basic tonal and color adjustments; these provide the foundation for building the final result. Having a firm understanding of how to apply these basic adjustments will ensure that you are working toward the best quality from the beginning. For many images, these may be the only adjustments you need. For other images, these adjustments represent the first step toward producing an image that matches the vision you had when you first clicked the shutter release.

5

Chapter Contents

Increasing Saturation for Evaluation
Prioritizing Adjustments
Making Tonal Adjustments
Making Color Adjustments
Using Quick Fix Adjustment Tools

Increasing Saturation for Evaluation

In Chapter 2, "Download and Sort," we presented the navigation tools and explained how you could use them to evaluate your images for sharpness and other image-quality considerations. As you get started with the basic tonal and color adjustments for photographic images, it is helpful to know about another method for evaluating your images: displaying full saturation (Figure 5.1). This method enables you to make better decisions about the specific adjustments needed and image-quality issues to keep an eye out for.

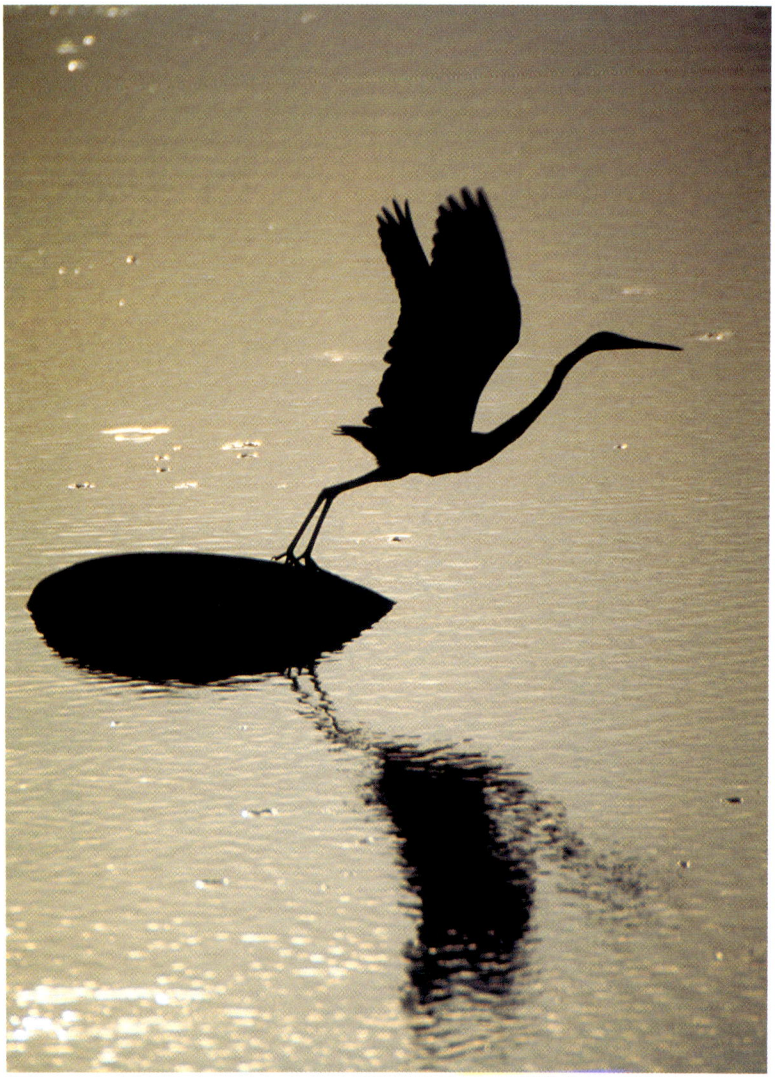

Figure 5.1 Carefully evaluating your image provides the opportunity to ensure that your adjustments result in the image you envisioned, even when tricky lighting conditions create a challenge to achieving the desired result. (Photo by Gabby Salazar)

If you have a difficult time evaluating the overall color in your images, temporarily boosting the saturation to its maximum value can provide a dramatic indication of exactly what colors exist in various areas. Besides exaggerating the colors that obviously exist within the image, this technique often reveals colors you weren't expecting to see. In particular, it can be a great tool for discovering subtle color casts in areas you thought were neutral.

To apply this adjustment, choose Enhance > Adjust Color > Adjust Hue/Saturation. This opens the Hue/Saturation dialog box (Figure 5.2), which will be addressed in great detail later in this chapter and in Chapter 8, "Advanced Color Adjustments." Move the Saturation slider all the way to the right, producing a value of +100. This boosts all colors in the image to their maximum saturation. Leave this dialog box open as you evaluate the image, moving the dialog aside if needed by clicking and dragging on its title bar.

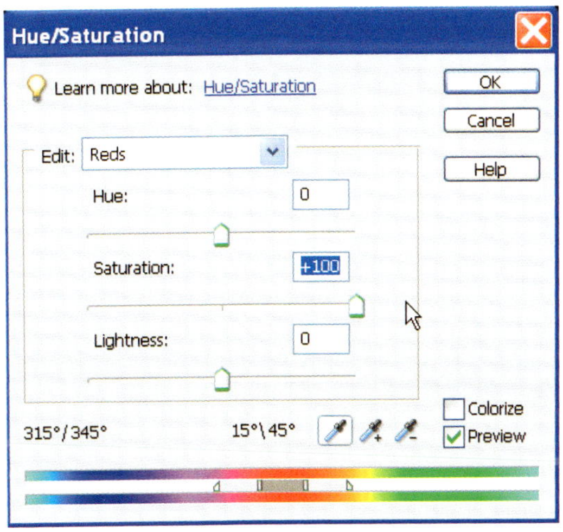

Figure 5.2 The Hue/Saturation dialog box allows you to adjust the saturation of all the hues in your image or of individual hues. To saturate the hues to their maximum potential, move the Saturation slider all the way to the right.

Review the full-saturation display of your image to get a sense of the colors in various areas (Figure 5.3). Pay particular attention to colors that you think don't belong where they are appearing. Don't worry that the colors temporarily look much worse. Instead, use this as an evaluative tool to decide what color corrections might be necessary later, and what color issues to keep in mind as you optimize your images. When you're finished evaluating the image, click Cancel to close the Hue/Saturation dialog box without applying an adjustment.

Prioritizing Adjustments

In any image-optimization workflow, it makes sense to perform the most basic adjustments first and then move on to more-advanced adjustments that allow you to exercise better control over your images. Taking this approach tends to simplify the process and allows you to gradually build to more-advanced adjustments as needed.

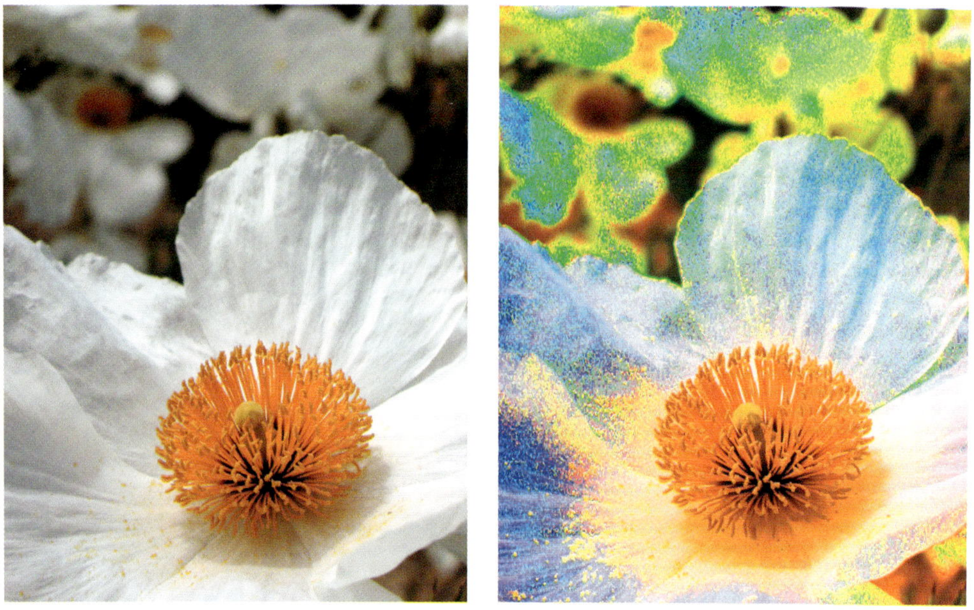

Figure 5.3 By temporarily increasing saturation to the maximum value, you can get a better idea of what color influences can be found in your image.

Some images may require only minor adjustment, and in those cases you need to employ only the basic tools. For other images you may need to pull every trick out of your bag to get the result you want. That doesn't mean you should be focusing on fixing problem images. In fact, we typically recommend working on only your very best images. The advanced methods, which we'll discuss later in this book, are still applicable to those images, allowing you to realize your true vision for them.

Starting the image-optimization workflow with the most basic adjustments also makes sense because that fits well with the typical process of learning to optimize your images. It is normal to start with the basics as you gradually start your trek up the learning curve. With a firm grasp on the basic adjustments that you'll want to apply, you can produce pleasing results for the vast majority of your images. As you progress to more-advanced techniques, your results will only improve, and you'll be able to better achieve your goals.

In this section and the following ones, we'll be talking about the basic tonal and color adjustments. We often refer to these as the *mini-lab* adjustments, because they represent about the degree of adjustment you could expect from a good film-processing lab. If the image was captured with proper exposure in the camera, these adjustments may be all you need. More likely, however, you'll want to move beyond these basic adjustments to produce even better results, as we'll discuss in later chapters.

The adjustments are presented here in what we consider to be the most logical order. However, that doesn't mean that this order is right for every image. Our general philosophy for performing adjustments is to solve the biggest problem first and then move on from there—in other words, prioritizing the adjustments based on the significance of each adjustment to the final result.

For most images, the tonal adjustment tends to be the most significant. Most digital cameras do an excellent job of capturing accurate color, and saturation tends to be good. Therefore, the standard order for us is tonal adjustment, color balance adjustment, and saturation adjustment.

Note: You should feel comfortable changing the order in which you apply adjustments to your images if the situation warrants it. Focus on solving the most significant problem with your image first and then working onward from there.

If you have an image for which the exposure was very good but the color is a bit off, you should feel perfectly comfortable making your color balance adjustment first before moving on to the tonal adjustments. Although the basic workflow presented in this chapter will work best for the majority of images, you should think of each adjustment as a modular piece of the full workflow. When the situation warrants, you shouldn't hesitate to change the order in which you perform the specific adjustments for your images.

Making Tonal Adjustments

The broad category of tonal adjustments includes any change in overall brightness or contrast within an image. Even more broadly, this category includes any adjustment that changes the luminosity values, without emphasis on changes to the colors. Tonal adjustments can most certainly affect colors—for example, darkening an image tends to enrich the colors, and brightening makes the colors appear less saturated. However, when making tonal adjustments, your focus is on the brightness and contrast, not the color.

Although you could use several methods to perform tonal adjustments, many of which will be covered later in this book, this chapter focuses on the most basic tonal adjustments.

Brightness/Contrast

The most basic tonal adjustment available in Elements 5 is the Brightness/Contrast adjustment (Enhance > Adjust Lighting > Brightness/Contrast). This dialog box contains only two sliders—one for Brightness and one for Contrast (Figure 5.4).

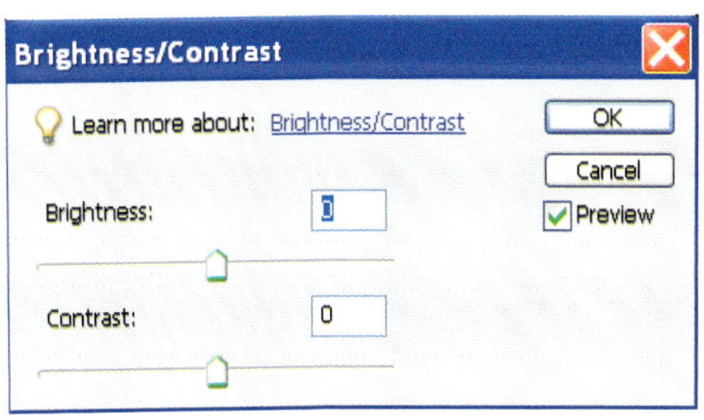

Figure 5.4 The Brightness/Contrast dialog box provides two simple sliders that allow you to easily perform tonal adjustments but doesn't provide the control necessary to produce the best results.

The Brightness/Contrast adjustment has a bit of a bad name among photographers. In many respects, this control provides the same general capabilities as other tonal adjustment options. Nothing is wrong with a basic brightness slider that allows you to adjust the tonality of your image, and this control is similar to other adjustments you'll look at later.

However, the Contrast slider in the Brightness/Contrast dialog box can be a bit of a problem. This is because it affects both the highlights and the shadows within your image to the same extent, brightening highlights to the same degree that it darkens shadows. This may not seem like a significant problem, but when you consider the importance of preserving highlight detail within your images, the limitations of this adjustment tool become clearer.

One of the advantages of other tonal adjustment methods—particularly Levels—is that, unlike the Brightness/Contrast adjustment, you are able to adjust black point (shadows) and white point (highlights) independently. In other words, you can increase the overall perceived contrast by sacrificing shadow detail, which isn't generally a problem, without sacrificing highlight detail. You can achieve the same degree of perceived contrast without producing highlight areas that look "wrong" because too much detail has been lost.

Another side effect of using the Brightness/Contrast control is that it can be difficult to produce pleasing contrast. Often, the choice seems to be between not enough contrast and an image that looks a bit harsh (Figure 5.5).

Having said all that, sometimes you will want to use the Brightness/Contrast dialog box. It is a good way to get started when you aren't yet familiar with the other options available to you. Also, at times simplicity may be important, either because you are trying to quickly prepare an image for sharing on the Web or via email or because you are having a difficult time using more-advanced controls on a given image. It is a convenient control to use when an image needs a simple contrast boost (Figure 5.6).

As you'll see throughout this book, we suggest that you perform all adjustments on a separate layer, rather than adjusting the pixel values in your image directly. *Adjustment layers* are special layers that don't contain pixel data, but instead hold instructions on how the actual pixels in the image should be changed in appearance. Therefore, the first step toward making a Brightness/Contrast adjustment (or any other adjustment for which an adjustment layer is available) is to make an adjustment layer. To do so, click the Create Adjustment Layer button at the top of the Layers palette). This is the button with a half-black and half-white circle icon on it. A list of available adjustment layers will then be displayed (Figure 5.7).

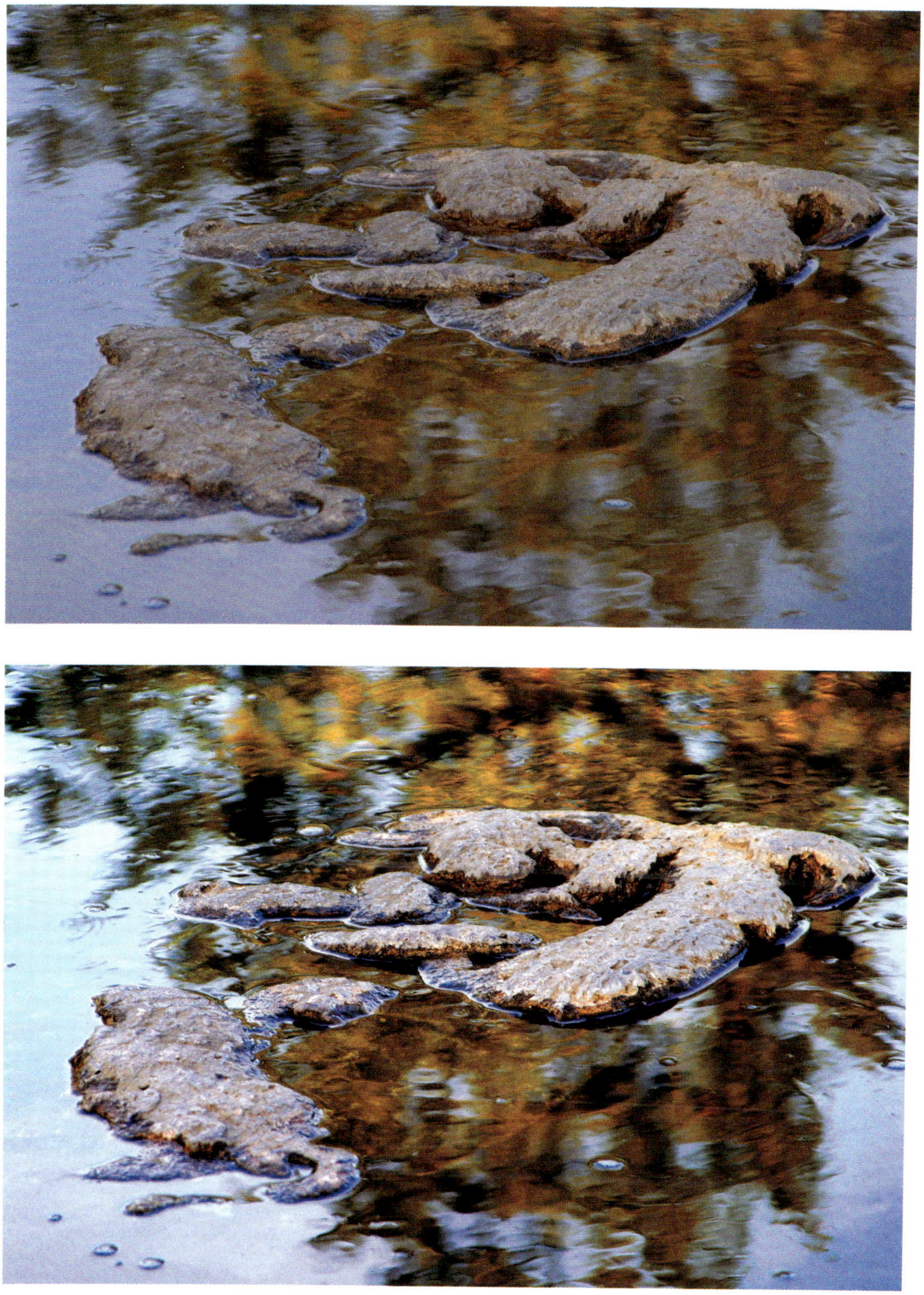

Figure 5.5 The Brightness/Contrast adjustment makes it easy to perform basic tonal adjustments on an image that looks flat (top). However, there is a considerable risk of producing images that have a little too much contrast (bottom) with too much detail sacrificed in highlights or shadows.

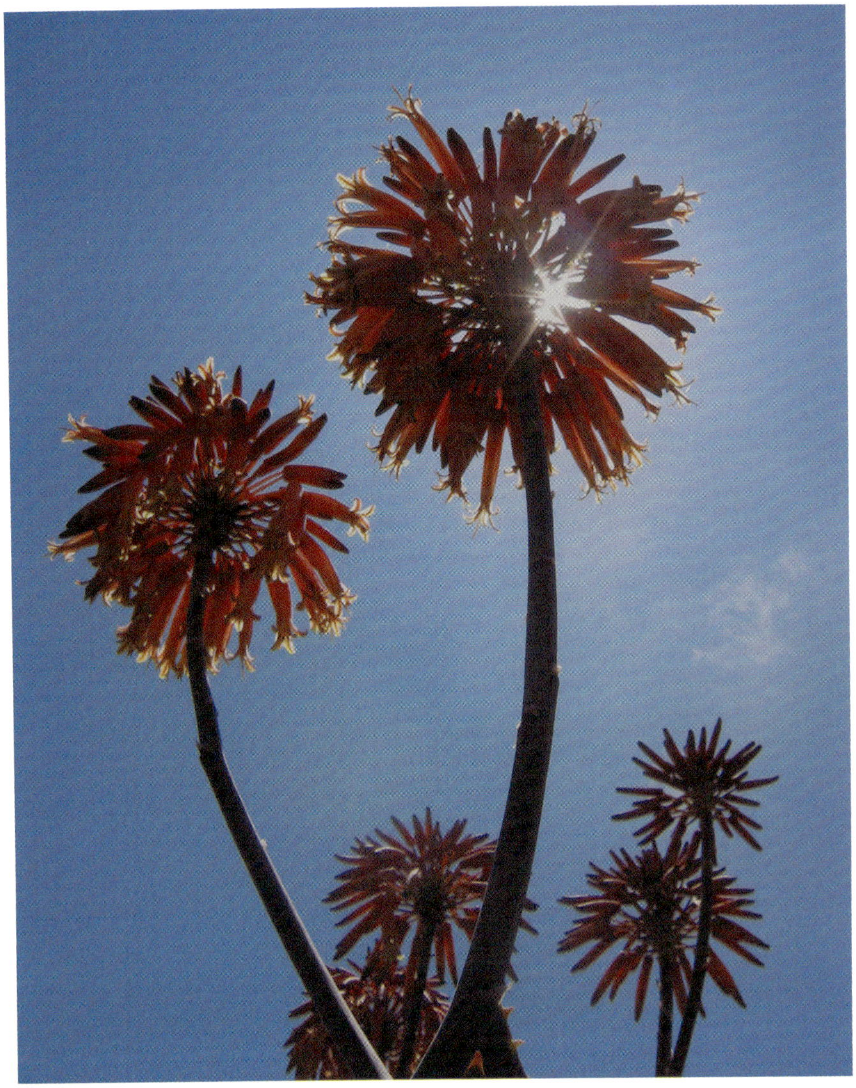

Figure 5.6 When an image requires a simple boost in contrast, the Brightness/Contrast adjustment may provide all the control you need to improve the image.

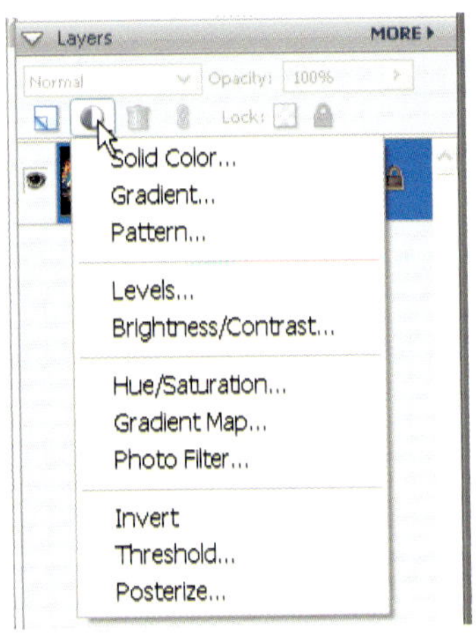

Figure 5.7 Click the Create Adjustment Layer button (the one with the half-black and half-white circle icon) to see a list of available adjustment layer types.

Note: Adjustment layers enable you to provide instructions on how an image should be modified without changing pixel values directly. Using these layers is the preferred method for adjusting your images. As you will notice, however, not all adjustment functions are available when you select Create Adjustment Layers in Elements.

Select the Brightness/Contrast item from the list of available adjustment layers, and the layer will be created. You'll see on the Layers palette that the adjustment layer is placed above the currently active layer. In this case, because you're making the first adjustment on this image, the only layer is the Background layer, so the adjustment layer goes above that. In addition to the new adjustment layer in the Layers palette, the Brightness/Contrast dialog box opens (Figure 5.8). You're immediately ready to start making adjustments to the image, comfortable that these adjustments are being handled by an adjustment layer that effectively behaves as a filter over your image, rather than causing changes to the underlying pixel values.

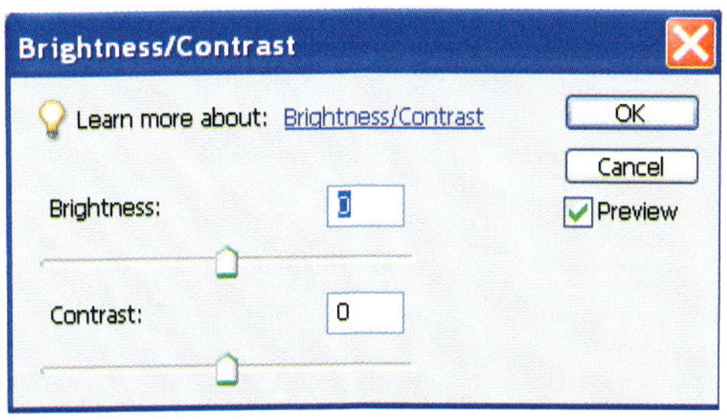

Figure 5.8 The Brightness/Contrast dialog box is displayed when you create a new Brightness/Contrast adjustment layer, allowing you to perform basic tonal adjustments on your image.

The recommended approach for using Brightness/Contrast is to start with the Contrast slider and then fine-tune with the Brightness slider (Figure 5.9). Because the Contrast adjustment has the potential to cause a significant loss of information within the image, establishing this value to optimize contrast without sacrificing significant detail is the most important consideration. The Brightness slider then becomes something of a fine-tuning control, allowing you to adjust the overall brightness without significant concern of causing a greater loss of detail in highlights or shadows. Make sure the Preview checkbox is selected so you can see the effect of every adjustment in your image as you move the sliders.

When you're finished fine-tuning the Brightness and Contrast sliders, click OK to apply the changes to this adjustment layer. You're now ready to evaluate the results of your adjustment (Figure 5.10). Although you were able to see the effects of your adjustments as you made them, sometimes it is difficult to make a good evaluation of the final result as you're making minor adjustments to the sliders. We therefore recommend after making an adjustment that you take an overall look at the image and evaluate it with and without the adjustment you've applied.

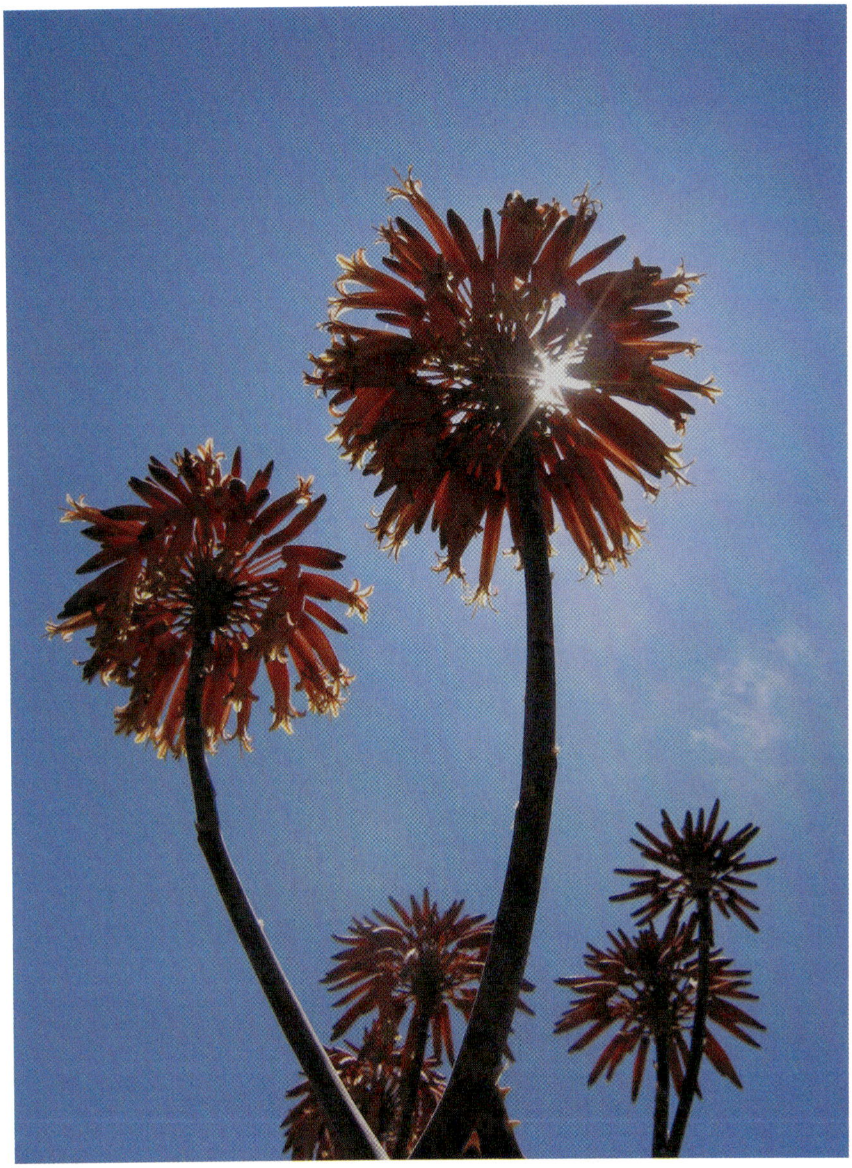

Figure 5.9 A good approach to using Brightness/Contrast is to adjust the Contrast slider to achieve the desired contrast within the image, and then fine-tune using the Brightness slider.

The easiest way to do this is to turn off the visibility of the Brightness/Contrast adjustment layer on the Layers palette. To do so, click the eye icon to the left of the layer. That allows you to hide or reveal the change you made to that adjustment layer. By toggling the visibility off and on, you can switch between "before" and "after" views of the adjustment. This gives you a greater perspective on the adjustment you've applied to the image, and this context often makes it much easier to make a critical evaluation of the results you've achieved. The hope, of course, is that you like the after version more than the before.

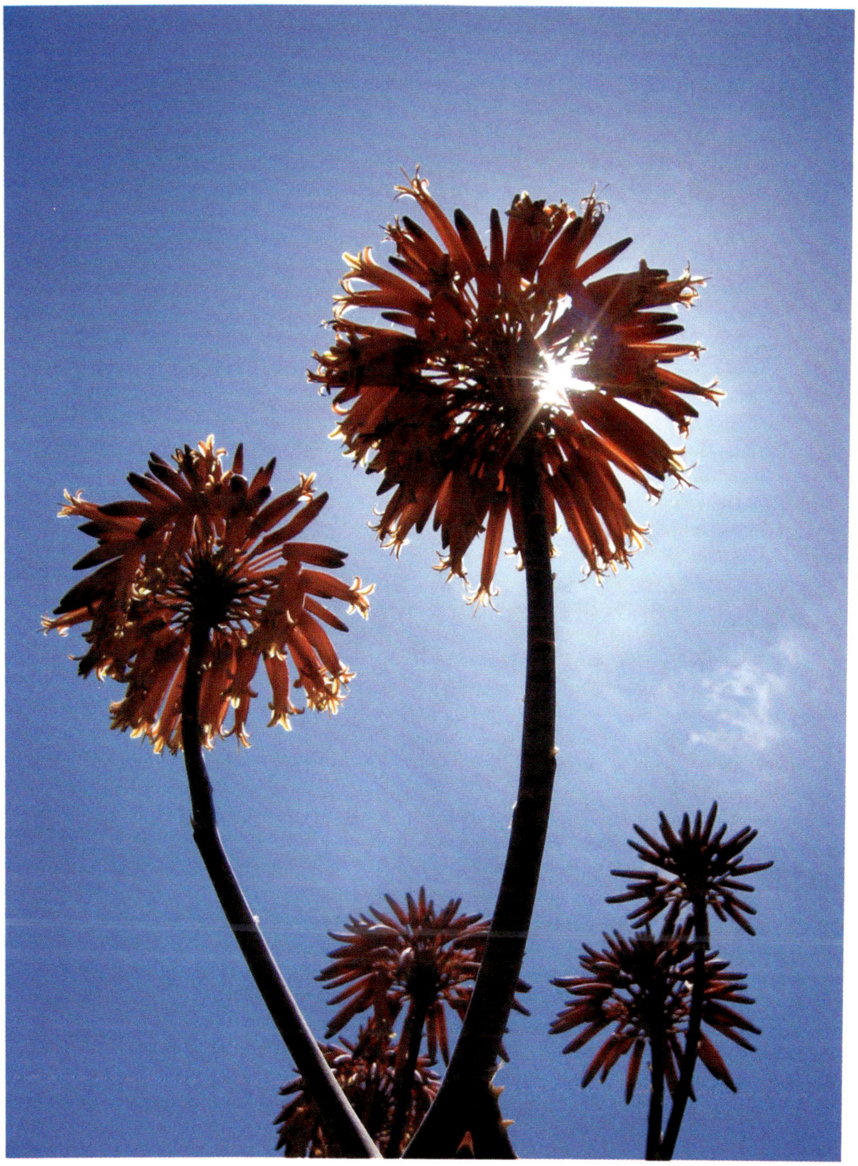

Figure 5.10 Although other adjustment tools provide greater control over the changes you make to your images, Brightness/Contrast does enable you to make good basic adjustments provided loss of highlight detail doesn't become a problem.

Convert 16-Bit Files

If you are working with a 16-bit image, Elements will not allow you to create adjustment layers or even a duplicate layer; if you try to do so, a box pops up indicating that this action cannot be performed on a 16-bit file and asking whether you want to convert it to an 8-bit image.

If you want to do so, click Convert Depth to convert that image to 8-bit. Although Elements does not support adjustment layers with 16-bit images, you can use most of the options under the Enhance item, but only directly on the pixels. We therefore recommend converting to 8-bit and using adjustment layers, except for situations where extreme adjustments are required.

If at any time you decide you aren't completely happy with the adjustment you've made, whether for the Brightness/Contrast adjustment layer you've created or any other adjustment layer you'll make later, revising the adjustment is remarkably easy. Simply double-click the thumbnail icon on the Layers palette for the adjustment layer you'd like to revise, and the dialog box will be displayed. The sliders and any other controls in the dialog box will be exactly where you left them the last time you clicked OK. You can then change the settings for any of the controls, revising your original adjustment. In fact, you can return to the adjustment layer as often as you like, making an infinite number of revisions, without any concern of cumulative damage to your image. That is because only the final settings count; earlier "versions" don't damage the image, because you are applying an adjustment without changing the underlying pixel values in your image.

Benefits of Adjustment Layers

Using adjustment layers rather than adjusting pixel values directly within your image has many benefits. Among the most significant benefits are the following:

- There is no cumulative loss of image quality when making multiple adjustments because you are effectively applying a filter over your image rather than changing the underlying pixel values.
- You can quickly see a "before" and "after" view of your image by turning off the visibility of any adjustment layer.
- You can revise the adjustment at any time by double-clicking the thumbnail icon for the adjustment layer on the Layers palette, and all the controls will be exactly as you left them last time you clicked OK in the dialog box for that adjustment layer.
- You can reduce the Opacity (in effect the visibility) of the adjustment layer as a quick way to reduce the effect without changing the actual settings for the adjustment layer.
- You can apply a layer mask to the adjustment layer to target the adjustment to specific areas, as we'll cover in Chapter 10, "Targeted Adjustments."
- You can delete any particular adjustment layer at any time, should you decide that you no longer want that adjustment (increased Saturation, for example).

Levels

The Levels adjustment provides much greater control over tonal adjustments for your images. In many respects, it can be thought of as providing the same overall functionality as Brightness/Contrast, but Levels provides the capability to adjust contrast by independently controlling shadows and highlights within your image. In addition, a separate adjustment for midtone is available.

Of course, this makes Levels sound remarkably easy, which isn't necessarily the conclusion you would draw after looking at the Levels dialog box (Figure 5.11). After you have a better understanding of the basic information presented in this dialog box and of the methods you'll want to utilize for basic tonal adjustments (and even color adjustments by working on individual color channels), you'll feel very comfortable using Levels and will be less likely to decide to revert to Brightness/Contrast.

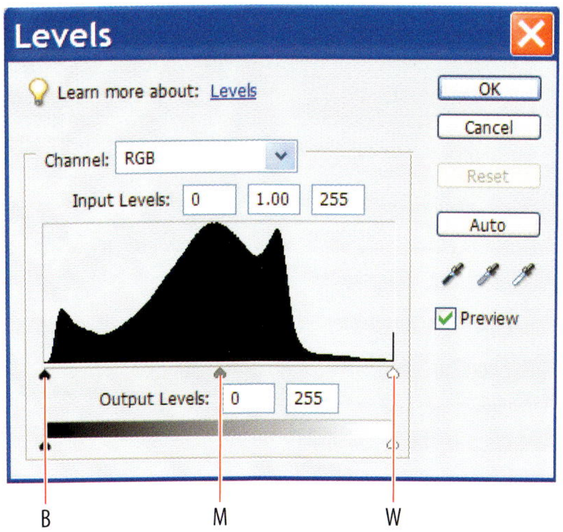

Figure 5.11 The Levels dialog box appears rather complicated—but after you understand how to utilize this control effectively, you won't feel intimidated. The key controls allow you to adjust the black point (B), middletone value (M), and white point (W).

The primary component of the Levels dialog box is a histogram display that charts the distribution of tonal values within your image. The tonal values are represented from black at the extreme left to white at the extreme right. This gradation of tonal values is shown as a gradient bar along the bottom of the histogram chart. The shape of the histogram chart tells you about the distribution of tonal values within the image. For example, histogram data that is shifted toward the left (Figure 5.12) indicates that the image is generally dark. However, that doesn't necessarily tell you anything about the quality of the image; it may simply be a dark scene. Similarly, a brighter image will have a histogram shifted toward the right.

Problem Signs

The key issues to watch out for on the histogram are clipping and gapping. *Clipping* is an indication that information has been lost in the highlights or shadows of your image. *Gapping* is represented by gaps in the histogram, and indicates tonal values that are not represented in your image.

Clipping is indicated on the histogram display by data running off the end of the chart. Clipping might be displayed in two ways. One is as a spike at one end of the chart. This is most commonly seen at the highlight end and is often caused by specular highlights within your image, such as reflections from water, glass, or metal. In other words, it isn't necessarily a major problem within the image, as we don't expect to see detail in such highlights.

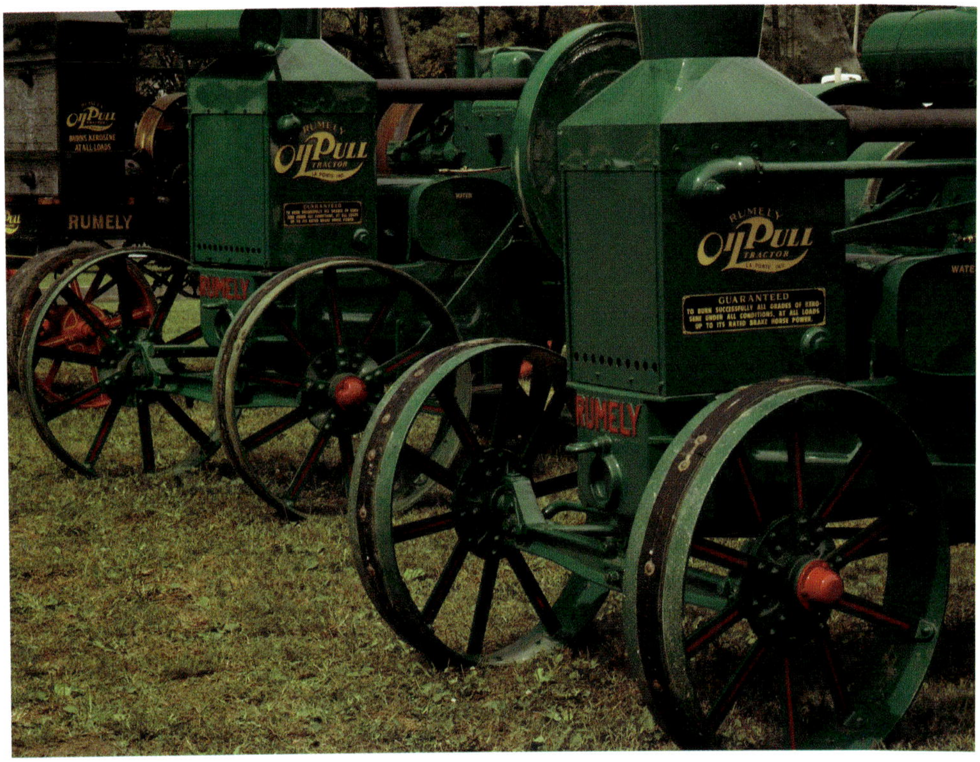

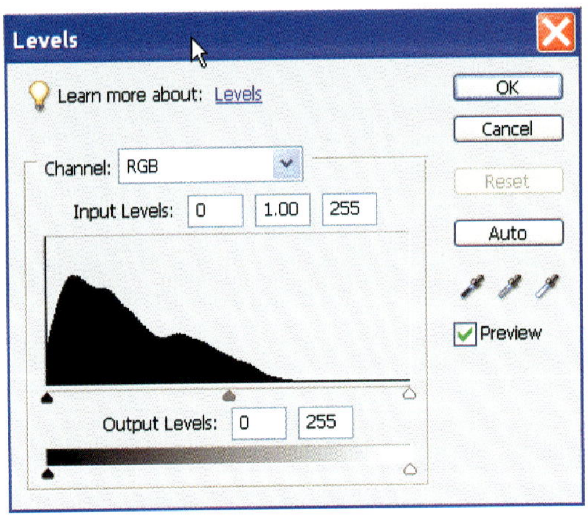

Figure 5.12 A histogram chart that is shifted to the left indicates that the image is relatively dark—but doesn't provide any real information about the quality of the image.

The other type of clipping is more likely to represent a problem within your image, especially if it occurs in the highlights. In this type, the data of the histogram gets cut off abruptly at the end of the chart, rather than ending gracefully before the chart ends (Figure 5.13). If you think of the histogram as representing a mountain range, ideally the mountains should gradually drop down to the flatland before the chart ends. If instead the mountains end suddenly in a cliff, detail is lost in the area that would have gradually lowered to the base of the chart. All pixels within the "missing" tonal values have been clipped to the minimum (black) or maximum (white) value at that end of the histogram chart.

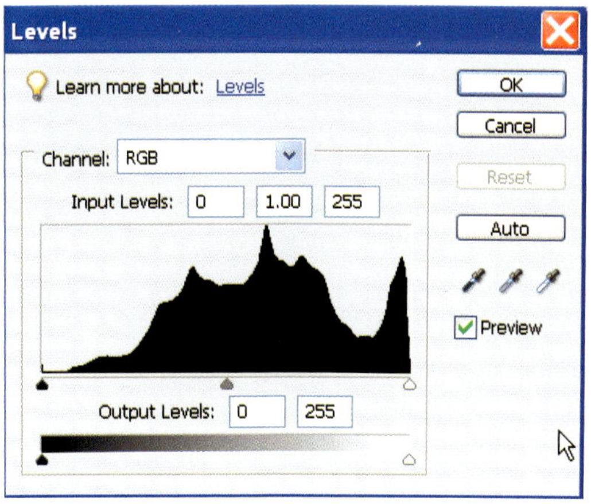

Figure 5.13 Clipping exhibited by an abrupt cutoff of tonal data at the highlight (right) end of the histogram chart indicates a potentially serious loss of detail in your image.

Ideally, your image shouldn't exhibit any clipping when you get started with your adjustments. If it does, it is generally preferred that the clipping occur in the shadows rather than the highlights, as we are usually more forgiving of lost shadow detail in a photographic image than blown highlights. However, you also want to be careful not to produce excessive clipping as you are adjusting contrast with Levels.

Another problem to be aware of is gapping in the histogram (Figure 5.14). You can think of the histogram chart as a bar chart made up of many narrow bars, so that the final result typically looks like a curving data display rather than one composed of individual bars. However, when gapping occurs, you start to see the individual bars that create the data display. Gapping indicates that certain tonal values are not represented by any pixels (or by very few pixels) in the image.

Note: Gaps in the histogram rarely occur for 16-bit files, because many more values are available than the 256 represented by the histogram display. 16-bit files have 65,536 tonal values per color channel available, compared to 256 values per channel for an 8-bit file. As a result, 16-bit files can lose a significant number of tonal values without obvious gapping or the posterization it can be indicative of. However, as noted earlier, Elements does not support adjustment layers with 16-bit files so we recommend converting to 8-bit and using adjustment layers unless extreme adjustments are required.

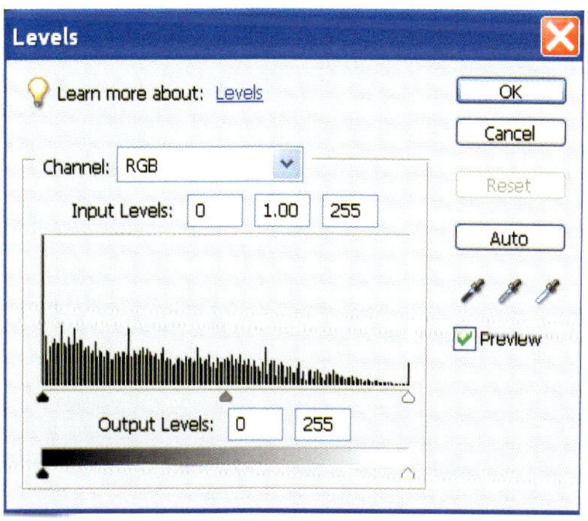

Figure 5.14 Gapping in the histogram indicates that all available tonal values are not represented in the image. When gapping becomes significant enough, the result is a loss of smooth gradations of tone and color in the image, referred to as posterization.

Gaps in the tonal values indicate that smooth and subtle transitions between tones and colors within the image may be compromised. Instead of making a gradual change from one value to another with 10 values in between, for example, the transition may be from one value to another without any transition values between them. This lack of smooth gradations is referred to as *posterization*.

However, gaps in a histogram are not an indication of a serious problem with your image. Minor gaps of only a few pixels wide, representing just a few tonal values, aren't likely to be visible with the human eye. In fact, it isn't until the gaps become relatively extreme (at least 10 tonal values) that they are likely to be visible in the final output. Although gaps certainly indicate a potential problem, they don't define image quality by themselves. If you have significant gapping in an image, use caution not to make extreme adjustments that may worsen the situation, and closely evaluate the final image to ensure that visible posterization doesn't exist.

Basic Levels Adjustments

With a basic understanding of the concepts behind Levels, you're ready to start making an adjustment. To do so, create a new adjustment layer for Levels by clicking the Create Adjustment Layer button on the Layers palette and selecting Levels. For most adjustments with Levels, there are only three controls you need to use. These are the black point, middle-tone, and white point sliders. All three are found directly below the histogram display in the Levels dialog box. The black point slider (for shadows) is at the far left, the white point slider (for highlights) at the far right, and the midtones slider in between the two. Together these controls allow you to adjust the overall contrast (with the black point and white point sliders) and brightness (with the midtones slider) of your image with excellent control.

As with the Brightness/Contrast control, we recommend establishing overall contrast before fine-tuning brightness. Therefore, start with the black point and white point sliders. These provide contrast adjustment while enabling you to vary the amount of adjustment being applied to the shadow and highlight areas of your image. You can, for example, sacrifice more detail in the shadows to improve overall contrast without losing significant highlight detail.

As a general rule, most images benefit from having the brightest pixel value set to white and the darkest pixel value set to black. Obviously plenty of exceptions exist, but it is a good basic rule. Because you know that the last data point at each end of the histogram chart represents the darkest and brightest pixels, you could make a basic adjustment by dragging the black point and white point sliders inward to the point where the data begins at each end of the histogram (Figure 5.15).

Of course, this is a somewhat arbitrary way to approach an image. Although it will indeed produce good results for most images, it isn't an ideal solution for every one. Photography is very much a visual pursuit, so it makes sense to perform a visual review of the image and decide whether you're happy with the results of the adjustment you've made. You may want to back off the adjustments slightly in some situations to minimize the risk of introducing excessive contrast. In other situations you may want to bring the sliders in just a bit farther to produce stronger contrast. It is up to you to determine the best adjustment for a particular image.

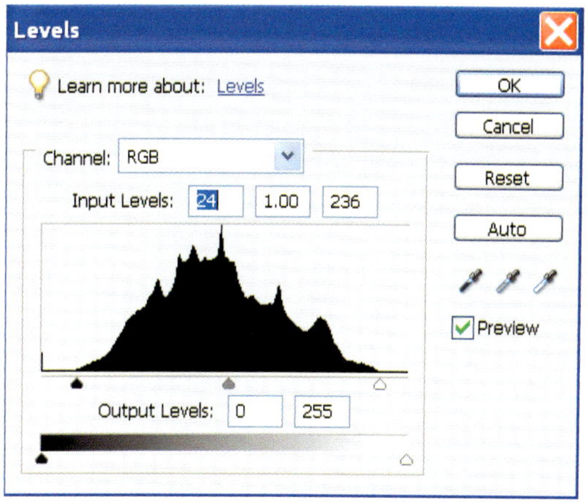

Figure 5.15 A good general approach to setting the black and white points within Levels is to bring the black point and white point sliders inward to the point where the data begins at each end of the histogram chart.

Note: If you're having trouble making appropriate adjustments, you can hold the Alt/Option key to change the Cancel button to a Reset button in most dialog boxes in Elements. If you then click the Reset button, all settings in the dialog box will return to their default values.

After you've established the black and white points for the image, effectively performing a well-controlled contrast adjustment, you are ready to adjust the middle-tone slider. This slider can be thought of as a brightness control. Moving the slider changes which pixel value within the image should be mapped to a middle-gray tonal value, but the result is a brightness shift. This adjustment doesn't have any rule of thumb you can follow in terms of positioning the slider at a particular point along the histogram chart, so you'll need to make a decision based on a visual review of the image.

After you've adjusted all three sliders, you've finished the basic tonal adjustment with Levels. Click OK, and the Levels dialog box will close. As with any other adjustment layer, if you change your mind about the adjustment at a later time, you can simply double-click the thumbnail icon for the Levels adjustment layer on the Layers palette; the dialog box will be displayed, with the sliders positioned exactly as you left them last time you clicked OK.

Note: The Levels dialog box also includes eyedroppers that allow you to click areas of your image to automatically set the black, white, and neutral (gray) values. However, these tools tend to require a hunt-and-peck approach that doesn't allow you to make very accurate adjustments, so we prefer not to use them.

Clipping Preview

Although a basic visual evaluation of your image while making adjustments with Levels is certainly effective, it can be even more helpful to use the clipping preview display available in Levels. This display allows you to see exactly where you are losing detail within your image as you adjust the black point and white point sliders. As a result, you can make a much more informed decision about the settings you'd like to use for these sliders.

When you start with an image that lacks strong contrast (Figure 5.16), and want to maximize the contrast without sacrificing detail in highlights or shadows, the clipping preview display allows you to see exactly where you'll lose detail based on your specific adjustment of the black point and white point sliders.

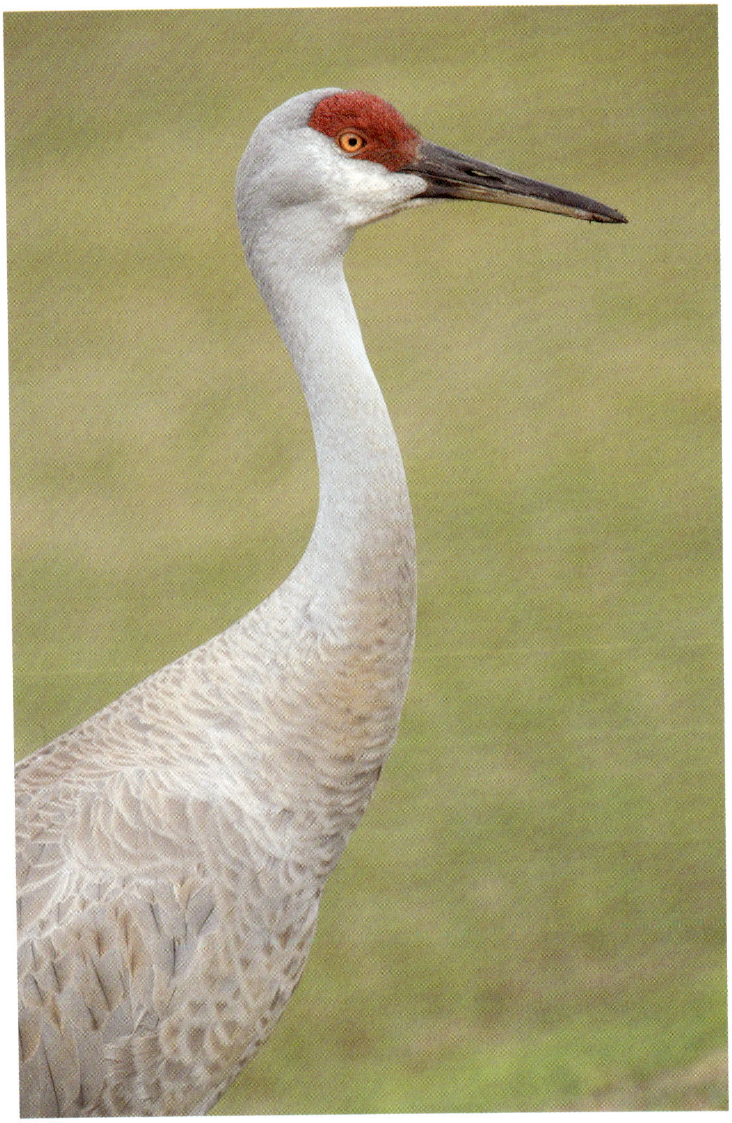

Figure 5.16 If you have an image such as this one that lacks adequate contrast, it is helpful to be able to maximize contrast without sacrificing highlight or shadow detail. The clipping preview feature of Levels provides exactly this solution.

We recommend adjusting the white point first, simply because highlight detail tends to be the more critical adjustment. If you've already created a Levels adjustment layer for the image you're working on, double-click the thumbnail icon for that layer on the Layers palette. Otherwise, create a new Levels adjustment layer.

To enable the clipping preview display, hold the Alt/Option key while you adjust the white point. Your image display will initially change to a completely (or almost completely) black display. This indicates that no pixel values (or very few) are clipped to white without making any adjustment. As you continue to hold the Alt/Option key, slide the white point slider to the left. You'll see more pixels showing up as you move the slider (Figure 5.17). As a general rule, it's best to adjust the white point until pixels just start showing up in the clipping preview. This is the point where you've maximized contrast and tonal range within the image, while sacrificing minimal highlight detail. Of course, the benefit of the clipping preview display is that you're able to make an informed decision about the amount of detail you are sacrificing to achieve the level of contrast you'd like to see, and that detail's location within the image.

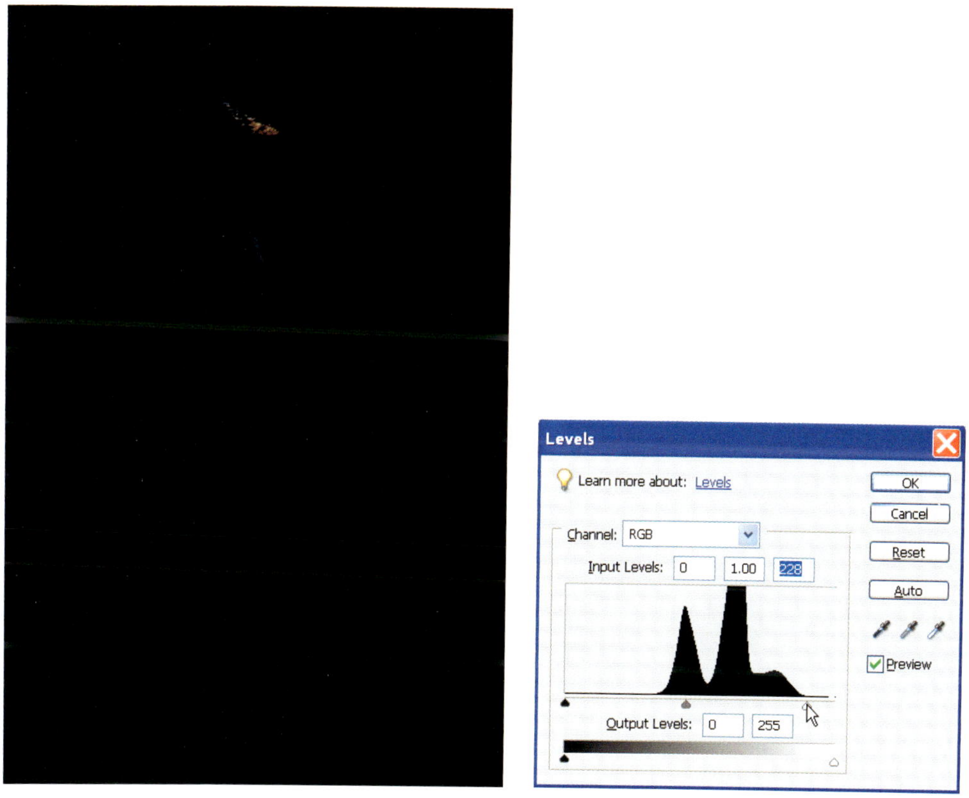

Figure 5.17 By holding down the Alt/Option key while adjusting the white point slider in Levels, you'll see a clipping preview showing you where in the image you'll lose highlight detail for a given adjustment.

Note: The color of the pixels that show up in the clipping preview display indicate the color channels that are losing detail within the image. The pixels won't appear as pure white or black in the image until the clipping preview shows those values. However, even if they aren't pure white or black, they are probably very close if any channels are clipping, so you can generally treat such values as though they were indeed white or black.

The process for setting the black point is nearly identical: hold the Alt/Option key while adjusting the black point slider, and you'll see a similar clipping preview display, except that now it will start completely (or almost completely) white, with pixels showing up to indicate where you're losing shadow detail (Figure 5.18). As discussed previously, you are generally willing to sacrifice more shadow detail as opposed to highlight detail to maximize contrast. The clipping preview allows you to make an informed decision about how much detail you're giving up with a particular adjustment and the location of that detail, so you can better determine the extent to which you can push the black point to produce the desired contrast level.

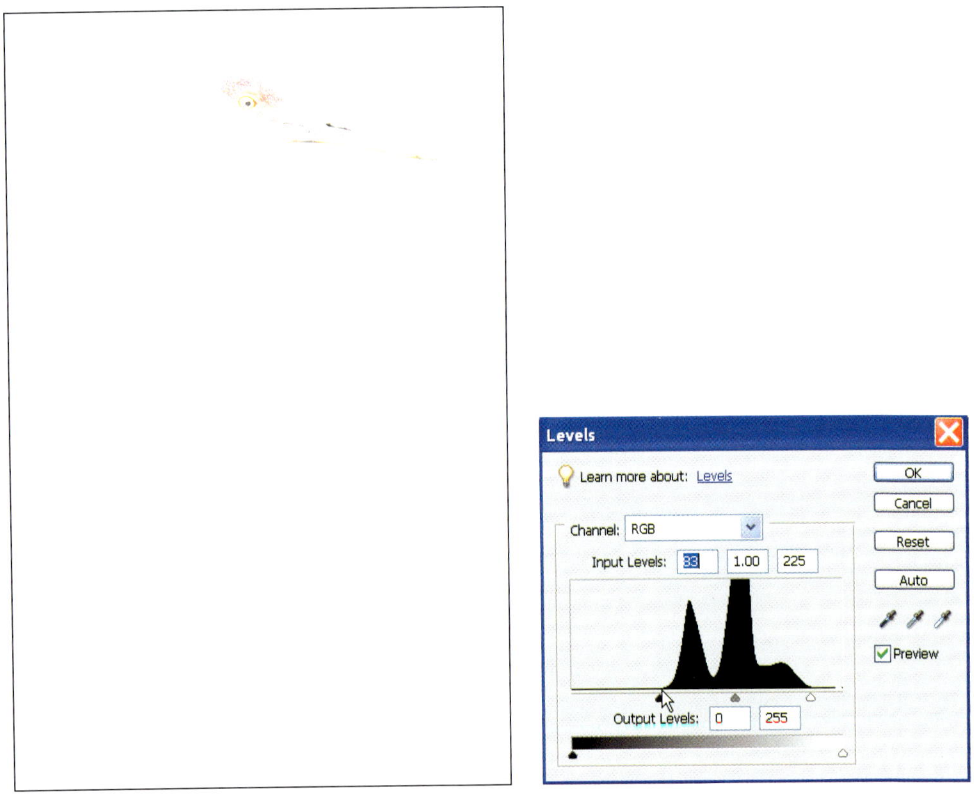

Figure 5.18 While holding down the Alt/Option key and adjusting the black point slider in Levels, the clipping preview shows where the image will lose shadow detail for a given adjustment.

After you've adjusted the black and white points with some guidance from the clipping preview, you're ready to adjust the middle-tone slider for overall brightness. Because this doesn't affect the extreme tonal values within the image, there isn't a clipping preview for the middle-tone slider. You'll need to rely on a visual evaluation of the image for this adjustment. Move this slider until the image looks visually pleasing, matching your creative intentions.

When you're finished with all three of these adjustments, using the clipping preview for the black and white points, you've produced an image with optimal contrast based on your willingness to sacrifice detail to achieve your goals (Figure 5.19).

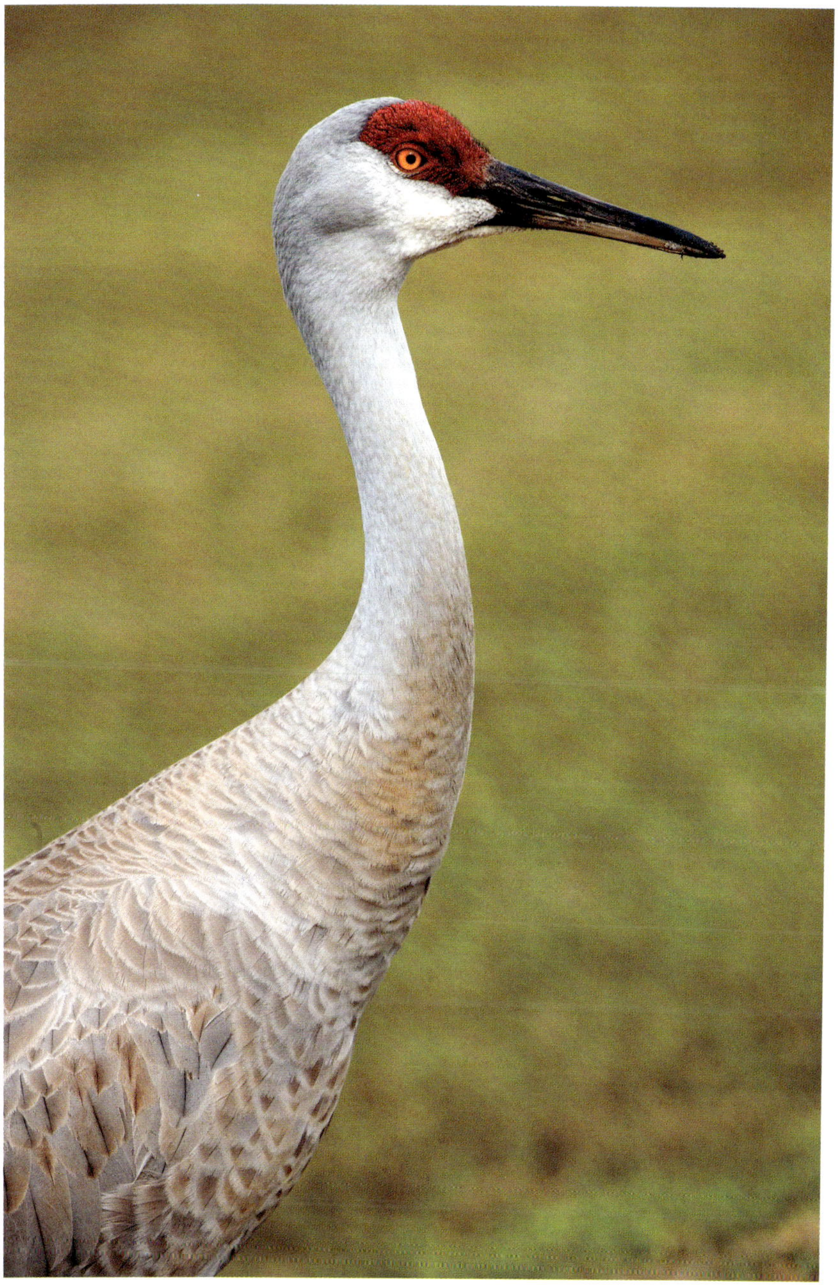

Figure 5.19 After you have adjusted the black and white points by using the clipping preview of Levels, and then fine-tuned the middle-tone slider to taste, the result is an image with optimal contrast and with detail lost only where you've decided it was worth sacrificing.

Making Color Adjustments

After you've optimized the overall tonality of your image, the next step is typically color adjustments. At the most basic level, these include adjusting the color balance to remove any undesired color cast or to introduce one that is desired, and adjusting the saturation of colors within the image to taste.

Color Balance

Color balance adjustments are most often thought of as ways to eliminate an undesirable color cast within an image. In many cases, the goal is to make areas that should be neutral in the image truly neutral. However, this can be a challenging goal to achieve. Just because something truly is neutral doesn't mean it should appear as perfectly neutral within your image. For example, if you place an 18% gray card in a scene during sunrise, you can be assured that the gray card won't appear gray. It will be influenced by the warm light of sunrise and will appear with a golden hue.

Instead of merely producing an "accurate" effect, we think the focus of a color balance adjustment should be to eliminate any color influence you don't like and to add a color influence that you prefer. The result needs to be close to reality to be accepted by those who will view your images, but you do have a fair amount of latitude. Focus on producing the best aesthetic results, and you'll be well on your way to accurate results as well.

Elements does not provide a Color Balance adjustment utility. However, several alternatives are available, including Color Variations (Enhance > Adjust Color > Color Variations); in our experience, this is the most effective alternative to a full color balance control utility. The Color Variations tool is not available for use with adjustment layers, so when you use it, you will be working directly on the pixels.

We therefore recommend that you make a duplicate copy of your image layer before making any Color Variations adjustments. You can easily duplicate a layer by right-clicking the background image in the Layers palette and choosing Duplicate Layer. In most cases, you will see a new layer appear with the name Background Copy. Make sure the copy layer is highlighted in the Layers palette to make it the active layer when you apply Color Variations changes to the image. By working on a duplicate layer, you simulate advantages that are similar to those that an adjustment layer can provide. For example, you can lower the Opacity to reduce the strength of the adjustment if you choose to do so. You also help to preserve the integrity of the pixels in the original background layer in case you should need to revert to the original version.

Note: To avoid directly modifying pixel values, you can use the Levels adjustment layer discussed earlier in this chapter.

The Color Variations dialog box (Figure 5.20) provides options for increasing or decreasing the amount or red, green, and blue in an image, You can specify whether you want to influence the midtones, shadows, or highlights with the adjustment. At the default level (with the pointer at the center of the Adjust Color Intensity scale) Color Variations produces a moderate increase, or decrease, of red, blue, or green, as you will note in the preview image available in the dialog box. Rarely will you need to set a higher intensity level, unless the color cast you need to remove is severe. We recommend experimenting with an Adjust Color Intensity Amount level of about half the default for making very subtle adjustments. If more is required, perhaps a stronger level of Increase Red to correct a blue color cast, simply click on the pertinent thumbnail (such as Increase Red) in order to apply the effect twice.

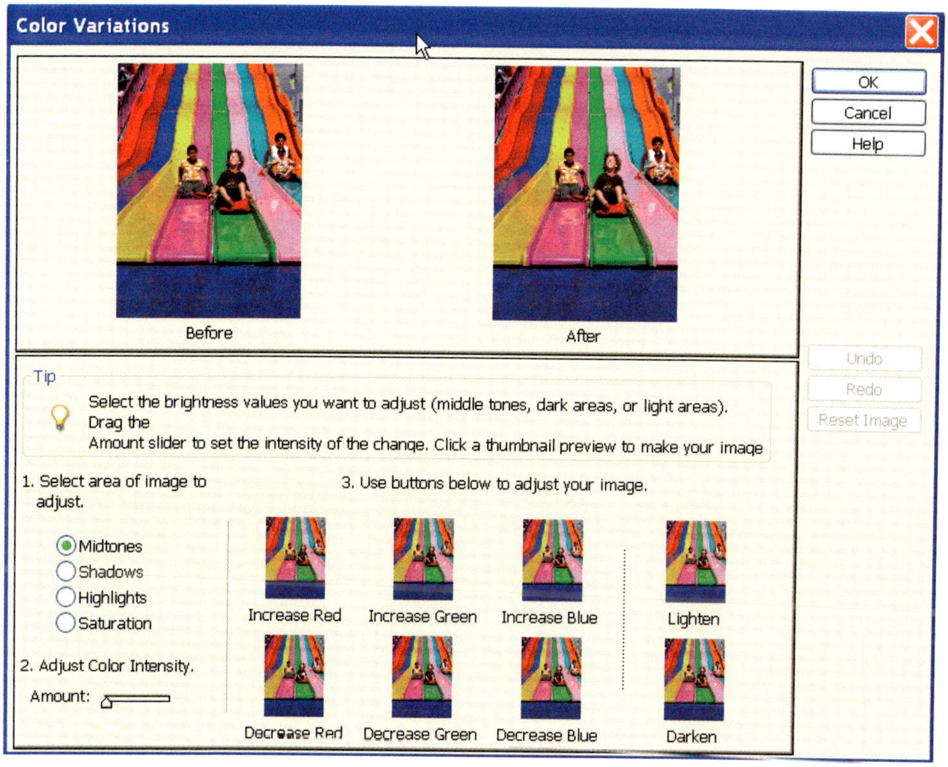

Figure 5.20 The Color Variations dialog box provides a variety of options for adjusting the levels of red, green, and blue in your images. Although this dialog box is certainly versatile, the preview image is small, so evaluating the effect of adjustments can be difficult.

As mentioned, it is important to keep in mind that when you make an adjustment with Color Variations, you are adjusting all pixel values within the image (if you did not make a duplicate copy of your image layer as suggested earlier). Of course, in later chapters you'll look at how to control the adjustments so they affect only certain areas of the image. For now, the key to understand is that by making a selection that should affect only red, green, or blue in Color Variations, you affect all pixels within the image; they will be shifted toward the color value that you choose to increase or decrease.

The primary disadvantage of using Color Variations is that the preview image is quite small. Consequently, it's difficult to accurately judge the effects of the various options. Some trial-and-error experimentation will be required with various images, to get a feel for the exact effect that the default level of intensity will produce.

If you find that experimentation to be tedious, you might want to try the automated Remove Color Cast tool (Enhance > Adjust Color > Remove Color Cast). This dialog box provides an eyedropper that you can click on an area of the image that should be gray, black, or white (Figure 5.21). After you do so, your image changes to reflect the effect that was produced. If that is not satisfactory, click Reset to cancel the change and try again, sampling a different area of the image that should be gray, black, or white. In some cases, this tool can be quite effective, as long as your image has an area that makes for an ideal target for color cast removal. Although we do not typically recommend using automated tools, Remove Color Cast is one of the exceptions because of the drawbacks of Color Variations and because Elements 5 does not provide a more advanced alternative.

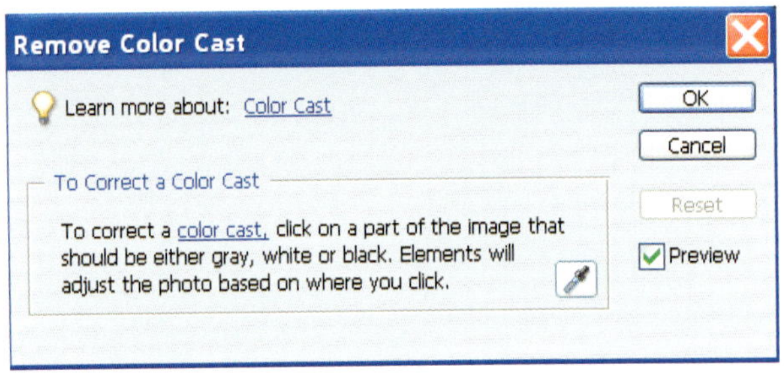

Figure 5.21 The Remove Color Cast utility is easy to use and can be effective if your image includes an area that should be perfectly black, white, or gray. Even then, the results may not be exactly as desired, so you may need to experiment by clicking on various other suitable targets, if those are available within an image.

Color balance correction is generally required with images that exhibit a color cast (Figure 5.22).

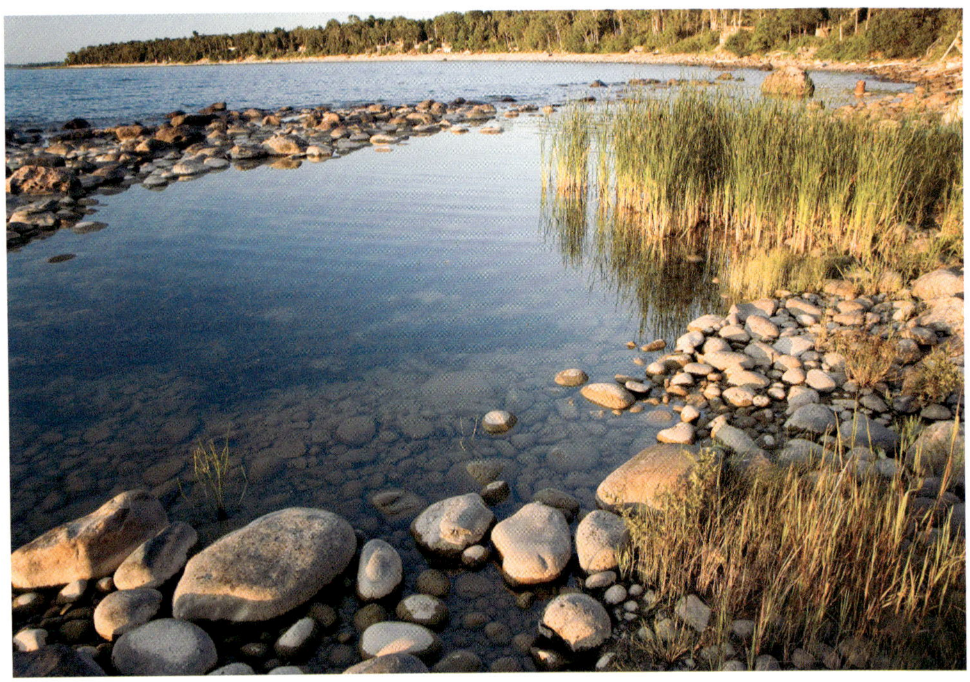

Figure 5.22 If you have an image with an undesirable color cast, such as magenta in this case, you will want to use one of the tools available in Elements 5 to solve the problem.

In that case, you may want to try both Color Variations (Figure 5.23) and Remove Color Cast (Figure 5.24). Of course, the latter is most useful with images that include some area that should be rendered as pure white, gray, or black. In addition to color cast correction, you will sometimes want to change the color balance for aesthetic reasons, perhaps adding a slight warming effect to a landscape or nature photo, for example. In general, most people respond more favorably to an image with a warm effect, perhaps because it reminds them of images made at sunset. For that type of adjustment, Color Variations is more useful because it allows you to add red or to decrease blue for a yellower balance; you might want to try both actions, in small increments, until you achieve just the desired effect.

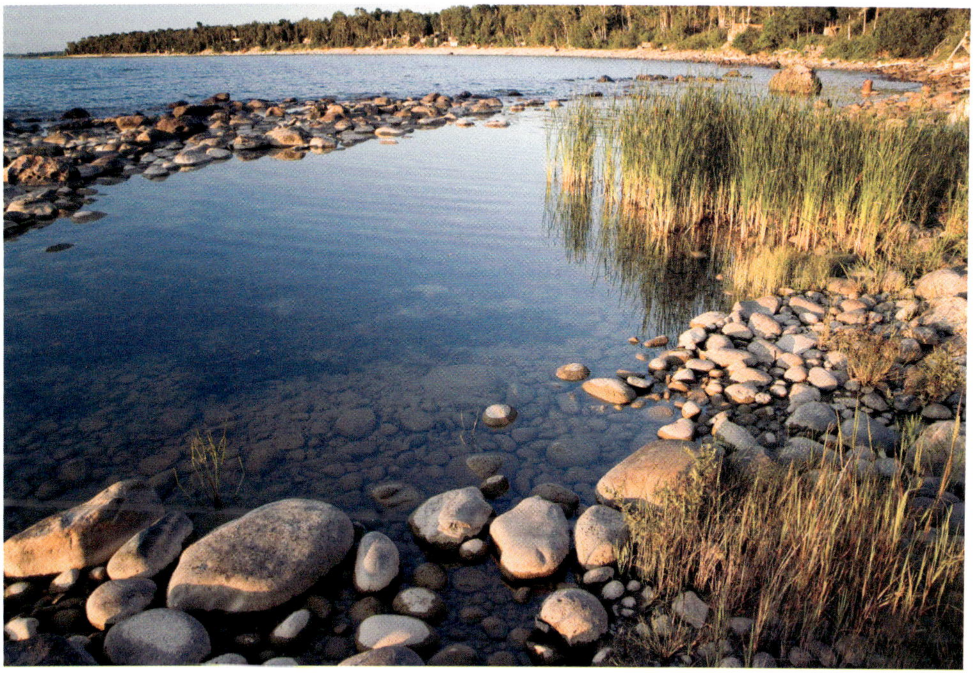

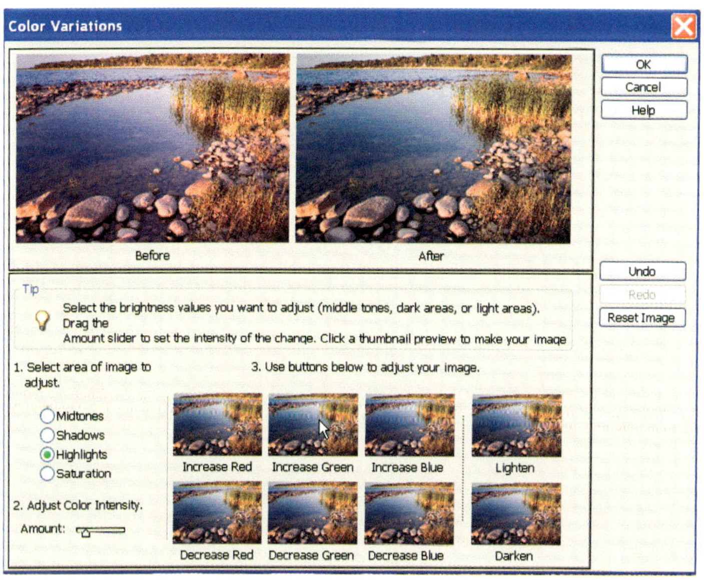

Figure 5.23 The magenta cast has been minimized using Color Variations, by adding Green (+10) to Shadows, Highlights, and Midtones for a relatively neutral image with more-accurate color.

Elements 5 provides other color correction tools under the Enhance menu, including Auto Color Correction and Auto Smart Fix. Both tools also adjust other parameters, including tonal values and contrast, for an overall "fix." We do not typically recommend such tools because they provide no user control whatsoever. Still, when you find an image with a color cast that is difficult to correct by using other methods, you may want to try Auto Color Correction (Figure 5.25), the more useful of the two fully automated options. Once again, be sure to create a duplicate layer before using this tool. If it does not produce ideal results, click the Reset button to cancel the changes, or lower the Opacity of the layer to moderate the color correction effect; naturally, you can also delete the duplicate layer if you want to eliminate all Auto Color Correction adjustments.

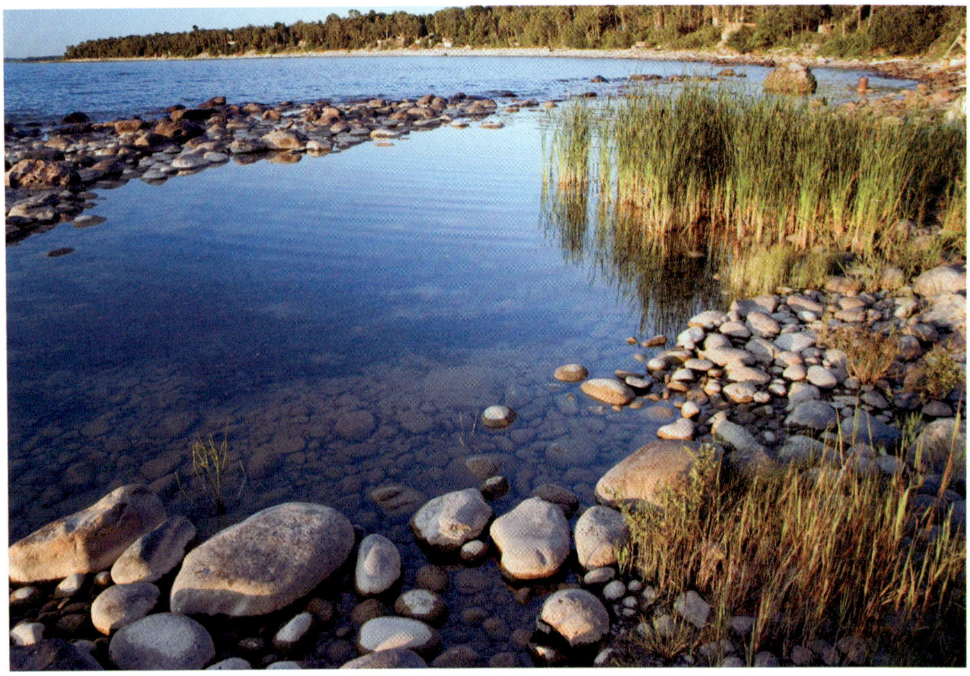

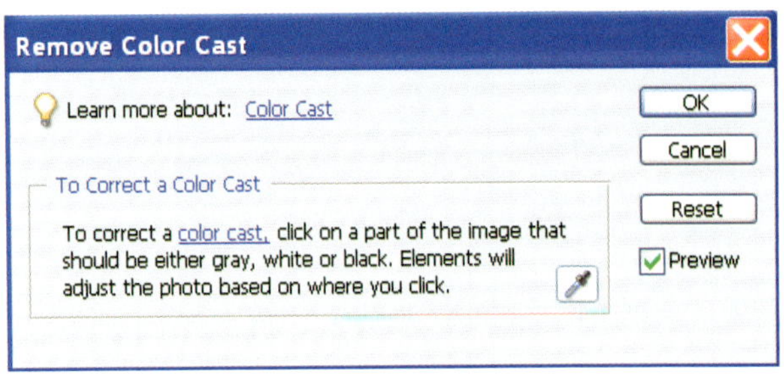

Figure 5.24 The Remove Color Cast utility was less effective with this image made at sunset, in spite of "sampling" various areas of rock that should theoretically be gray. The overall color balance is somewhat blue, although that could be corrected using Color Variations to reduce blue.

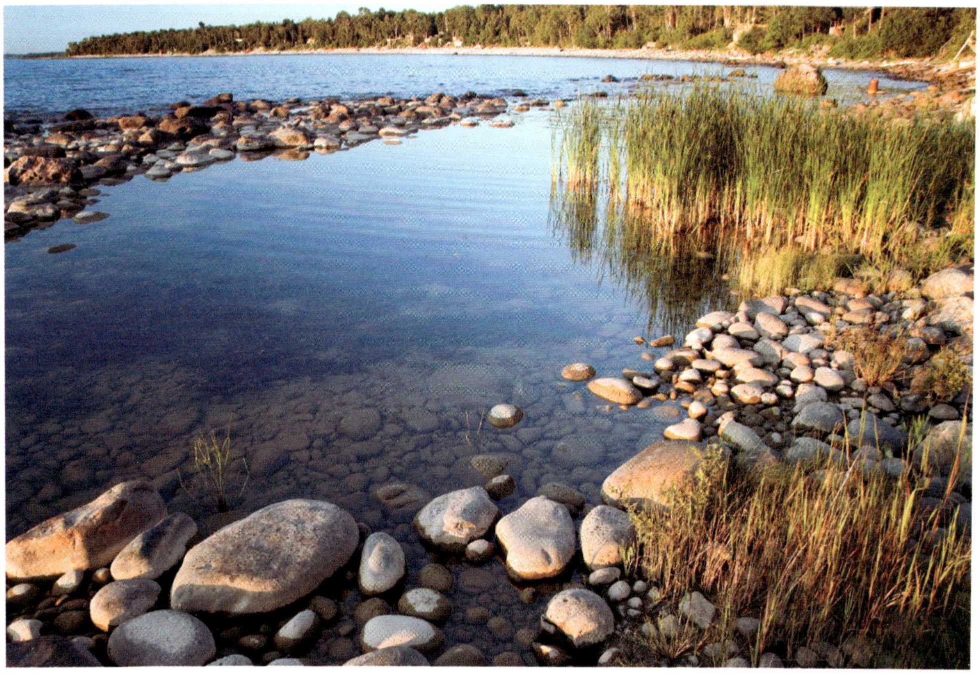

Figure 5.25 Although we do not usually recommend the use of automated tools such as Auto Color Correction, this tool can sometimes be useful. In this case, it corrected the blue cast left by the Remove Color Cast utility, although even more-accurate results would have been possible by using Color Variations.

Another utility similar to Remove Color Cast is called Adjust Color For Skin Tone (Enhance > Adjust Color > Adjust Color For Skin Tone). When selected, a dialog box opens that provides an eyedropper for clicking various areas of skin tones until achieving the desired color balance (Figure 5.26). This feature can be somewhat useful, especially if you sample various areas of skin tone from different people within one photo, until achieving the most pleasing effect.

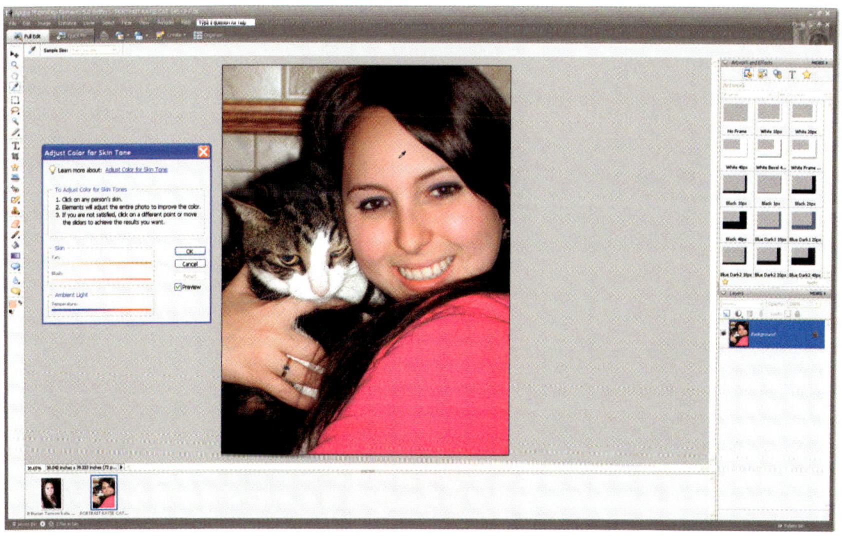

Figure 5.26 For images of people, the Adjust Color For Skin Tone utility can be useful because it provides a sampling option (eyedropper) that allows for experimenting with slightly different effects until finding one that is close to ideal.

Adjustment sliders available for Tan and Blush are designed to produce a more tanned look or a more pinkish skin tone, respectively; both aspects can also be reduced, of course. Experiment with the sliders if you wish, but use them sparingly because they can produce effects that do not appear natural. An Ambient Light Temperature slider is also available for shifting the color balance of the identified skin tones for a more cool (blue) or warm (red/yellow) effect. Again, this works best when used in small increments and requires a practiced eye that can recognize "ideal" skin tones.

Basic Saturation

After you've achieved appropriate overall tone and an accurate or visually pleasing color balance, the next consideration is the saturation of the colors within your image. This calls for a Hue/Saturation adjustment (Figure 5.27). Although this control allows you to perform a wide variety of adjustments, let's start with a basic saturation adjustment (though not as strong an adjustment as described at the beginning of this chapter when using Hue/Saturation for evaluating the image). In Chapter 8 we'll cover Hue/Saturation in even greater detail, but for now we'll keep it simple.

Start by creating a Hue/Saturation adjustment layer, in the same manner that you created the Levels or Brightness/Contrast adjustment layer covered earlier.

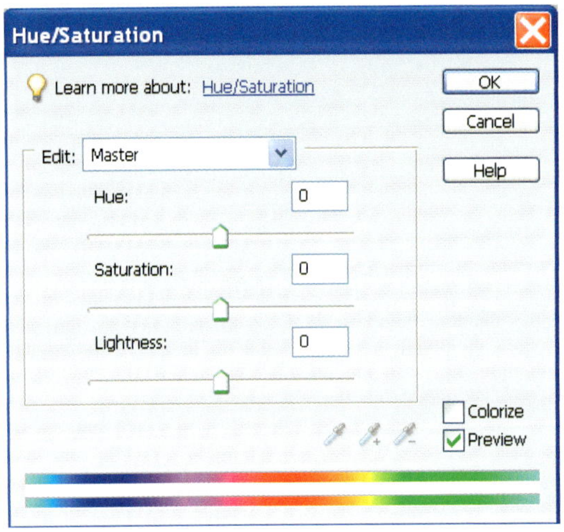

Figure 5.27 Hue/Saturation allows you to perform basic saturation adjustments, along with a variety of other adjustments covered in Chapter 8.

In general, photographers want to boost the saturation of the colors in their images, so the most common adjustment is to increase the Saturation value. However, you'll certainly find situations where you'll want to reduce saturation slightly. For example, if you are producing an image with a watercolor appearance, you'll want to tone down the colors slightly so they don't appear overpowering.

Although you can reduce saturation to any degree based on your preference for how the image should look, you should take more care when increasing saturation. An excessive amount of increase can create problems within the image. For starters, the colors may start to look artificial because they are too vibrant. Also, by shifting colors to their most saturated values, you are reducing the total number of possible values and therefore increasing the risk of posterization in the highly saturated areas of the image. As a general rule, use caution when increasing the Saturation slider to a value greater than +20. That doesn't mean you can't increase Saturation further, just that you should carefully review the image, at 100% magnification, to make sure you aren't introducing any problems in doing so.

Other than exercising some care in how much you increase saturation, making an adjustment is really as simple as deciding how strong you want the effect to be. If your image doesn't have very strong saturation (Figure 5.28), you can easily produce a more pleasing image by increasing the Saturation setting slightly with a Hue/Saturation adjustment.

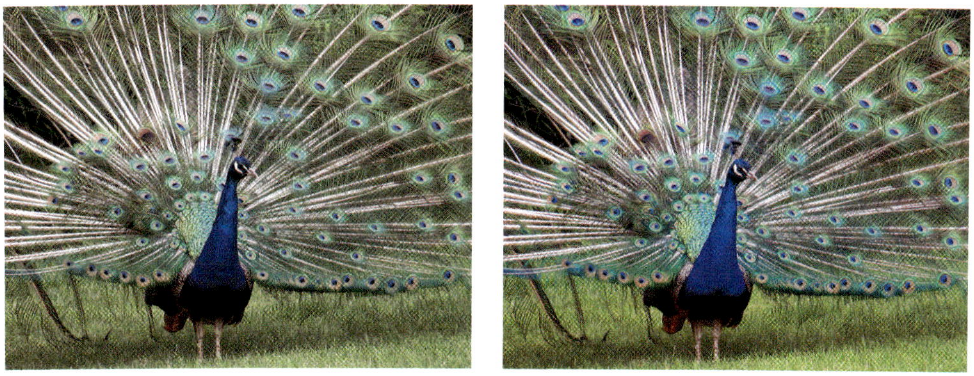

Figure 5.28 When an image has colors lacking in vibrancy, the perception is an image that is flat (left). Boosting the Saturation setting adds life to the image (right).

Provided you are cautious not to apply an excessive boost in saturation, a basic increase in Saturation with the Hue/Saturation adjustment is one of the more straightforward adjustments you'll make in a basic workflow for your images.

Using Quick Fix Adjustment Tools

In addition to the utilities already discussed and others to be covered in Chapter 8, Elements 5 offers other adjustment options in the Quick Fix section. Although all the same tools are also available under the Enhance menu, they are conveniently laid out in Quick Fix, in dialog boxes at the right side of the screen, under the heading General Fixes (Figure 5.29). However, it's important to note that these tools provide less user control than similar utilities available under Enhance.

Some of the General Fixes options are fully automated, including Red Eye Fix, Auto Levels and Auto Color, while others, such as Smart Fix and Auto Sharpen, provide some control, with a slider that simply allows you to increase the effect (although this also provides some user control with a slider that allows for increasing the overall effect of the tool). Others, such as Hue/Saturation, provide some control over the effect, with a slider that simply allows you to increase the effect. The problem with these tools is that they do not provide feedback as to the exact amount of an adjustment that you will make. In contrast, a utility such as the full Hue/Saturation dialog box allows you to set percentage increments for adjustments; you can then record those levels and use them later for images made at the same time and calling for the same level of adjustment.

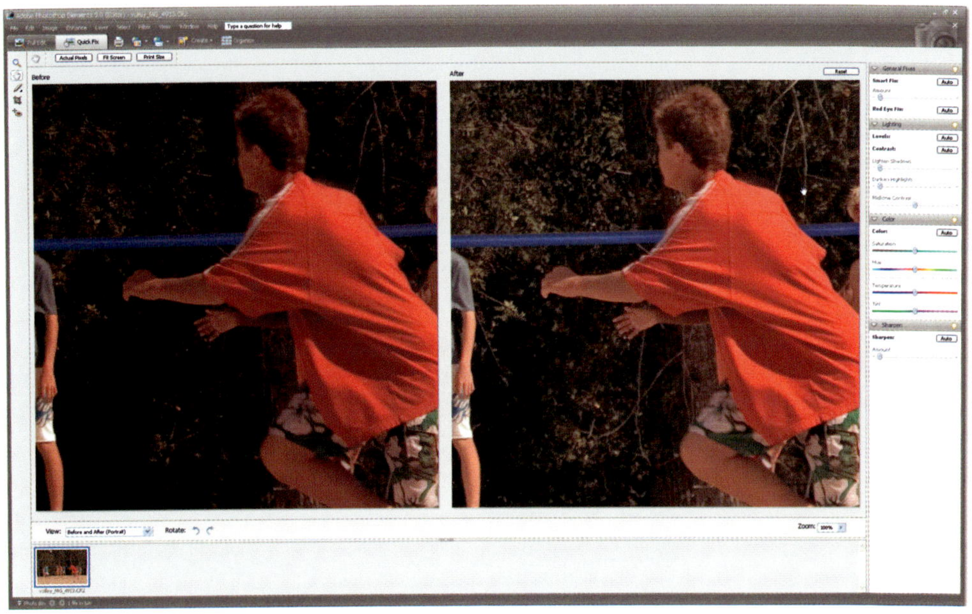

Figure 5.29 Quite a few image-adjusting options are provided in Quick Fix under General Fixes. These options are primarily intended for simplified improvement of snapshots rather than more "serious" images, because they do not offer the same level of user control as similar utilities provided under the Enhance menu.

Note: In Quick Fix, adjustment layers cannot be selected, so any image adjustments directly affect the pixels. Consequently, it's worth using the utilities in the Full Edit section instead, particularly those that support adjustment layers.

Although Elements 5 is often marketed with an emphasis on the "simple" Quick Fix options, these offer no real advantage to the serious imaging enthusiast. In fact, they provide less control or repeatability than the conventional utilities available under the Enhance menu. Frankly, the Enhance options are not really more complicated than the tools in General Fixes, although they may not be quite as intuitive. After reading this book, and some experimentation, you will be able to master all of the adjustment utilities for more-complete control over the exact look of your images. Consequently, we will not cover General Fixes further in this book.

Basically Done

After stepping through the adjustments covered in this chapter, you've completed the basic image-optimization workflow. For some of your photos, this will provide all the adjustment required, particularly if you started with an excellent capture right out of the camera. After completing this basic workflow, you're ready to move on to other adjustment options—some more advanced, others simply different—for even greater control over your more "difficult" images.

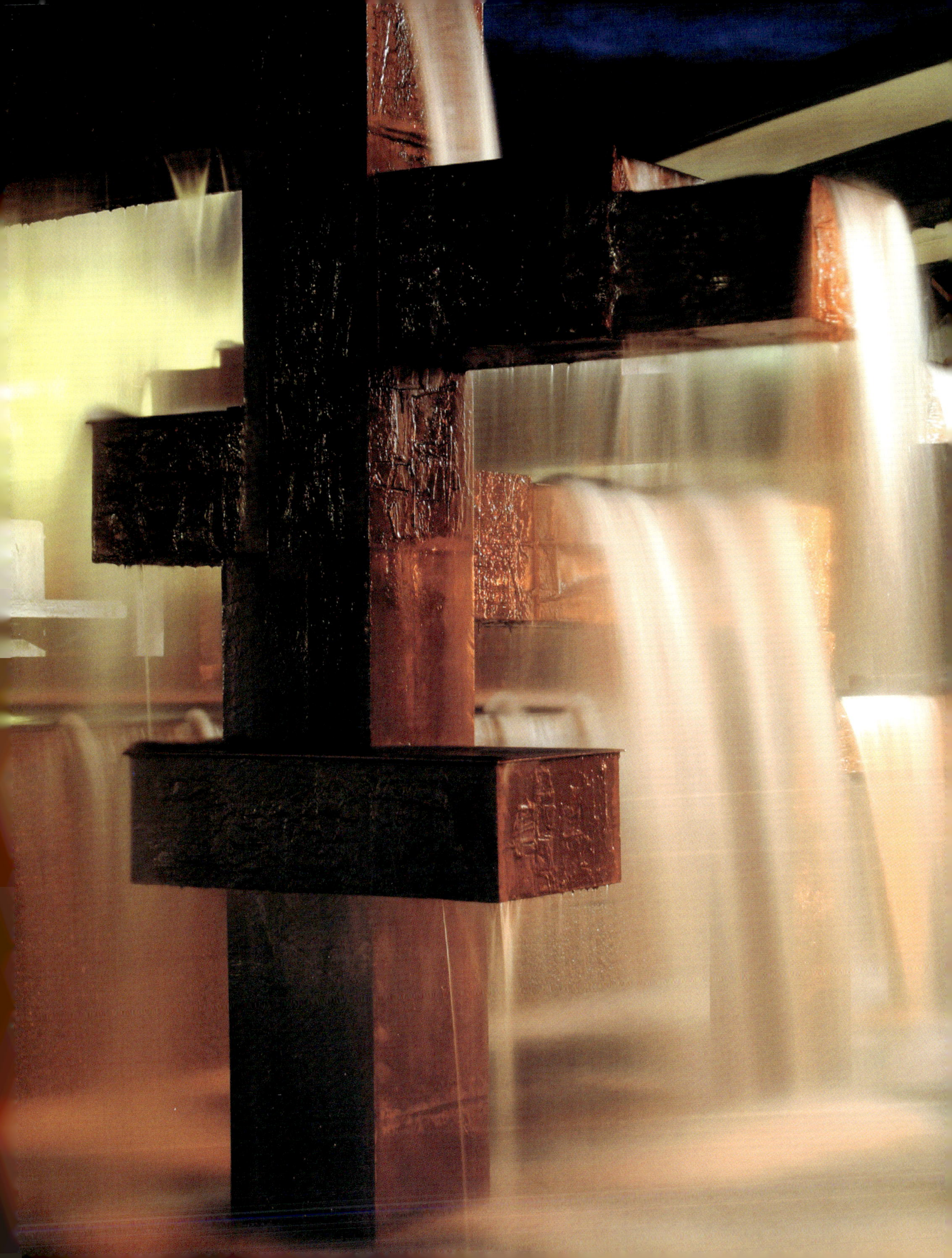

6 Image Cleanup

Chances are you'd like to perform some cleanup on most of your images. Whether it is just a matter of eliminating dust spots, or a more extensive removal of objects you wish hadn't been in the scene to begin with, you can use a variety or tools and techniques to remove unwanted elements from your images. In this chapter you'll take a look at the various tools Elements 5 provides to clean up and touch up specific areas of your images.

Chapter Contents

Cleanup Workflow
Clone Stamp
Healing Brush
Spot Healing Brush

Cleanup Workflow

Virtually every image will require some degree of cleanup work if you're going to get the best results. Cleanup may be required for digital captures because of dust on the sensor, for film scans because of dust or scratches, or for any image that includes an unwanted element such as a power line across the sky (Figure 6.1).

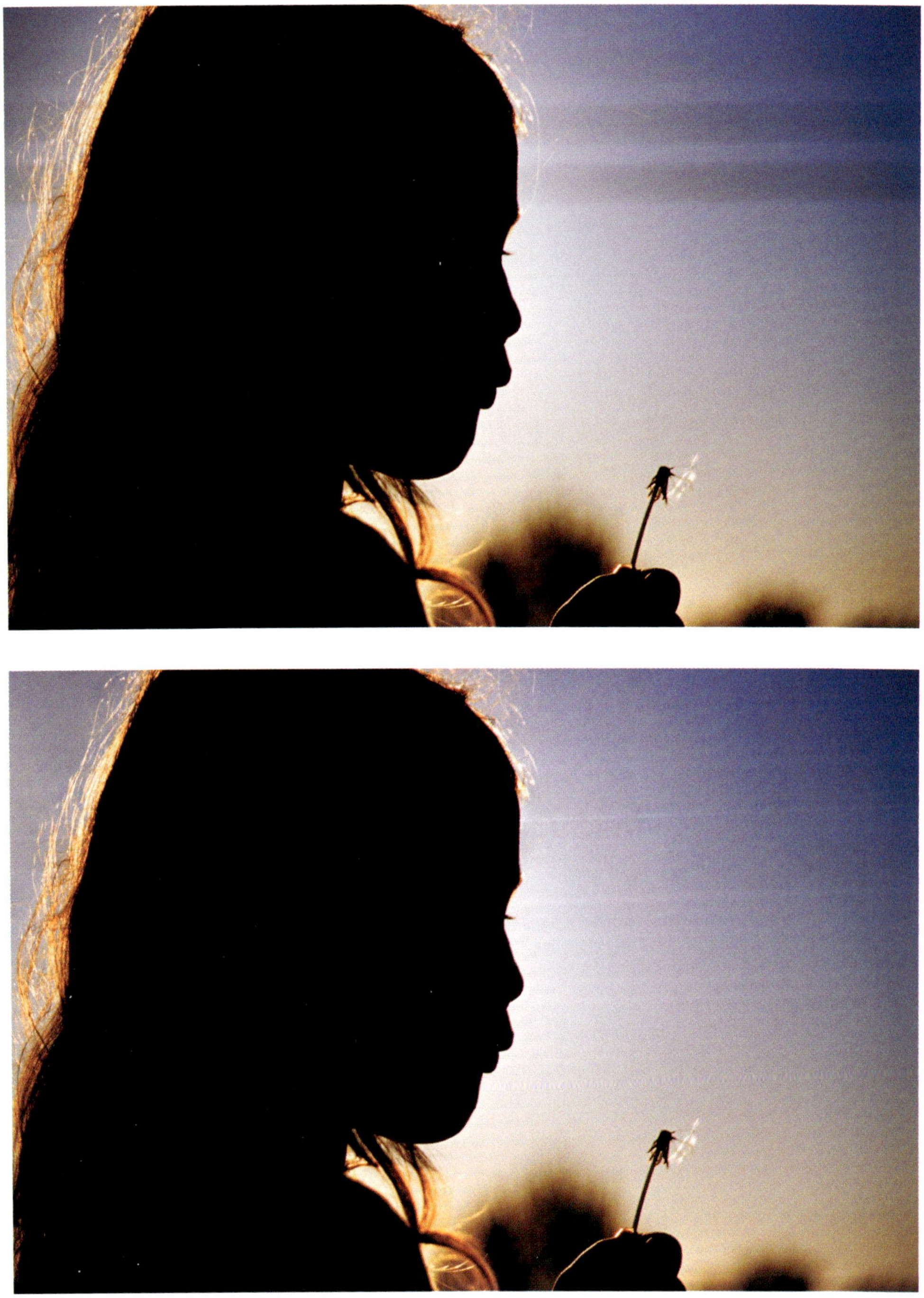

Figure 6.1 There are a variety of situations where you'll need to clean up areas of your image, such as the power lines in the top-right of this photo.

If cleanup is something you'll likely do for most images, the main question is when in your workflow you should perform that cleanup work. When you're using a layer-based approach to your workflow, it isn't critical to perform your cleanup at any particular stage. Even so, we suggest that you don't do it too early in the process of optimizing your images. Cleanup can be a very detail-oriented task and in many cases can require considerable time and effort. It doesn't make much sense to invest in the cleanup process until you're sure the image is worth the effort. Therefore, it makes sense to perform at least a basic optimization on an image before you start with cleanup.

In other words, the basic workflow presented in Chapter 5, "Tone and Color," should be completed, at a minimum, before you begin cleanup work. This will give you an opportunity to determine whether the image really warrants the effort often required for cleanup.

The following are the key tools you'll use for this cleanup process:

Clone Stamp This tool is most effective for cleaning up portions of your image when it is important to preserve the original texture with some precision. It allows you to copy pixels from one area of the image to another, to cover up pixels that represent problem areas. This is useful for most any image, and is commonly used for cleaning up dust spots or scratches or removing extraneous elements from a scene represented in a photo.

Healing Brush Use this when you need to replace the texture of a problem area in your image but want to maintain the existing tone and color. The Healing Brush works similarly to the Clone Stamp tool, except that it blends the copied pixels, preserving texture but blending tone and color to match the destination area. The Healing Brush is most often used for cleaning up blemishes in portraits, but it is also incredibly helpful for cleaning dust or scratches from any area of an image that contains smooth textures.

Spot Healing Brush The Spot Healing Brush is essentially an automated Healing Brush, allowing you to paint away defects without actually selecting a source of pixels to copy. It is helpful for cleaning up dust and scratches in areas of the image with smooth textures, if the area surrounding the defect represents good replacement values. It is an excellent tool for cleaning up dust in the sky, for example.

Clone Stamp

The most common tool for image cleanup is the Clone Stamp tool. This tool allows you to copy pixels from one area of your image to another, covering unwanted elements within the image with an appropriate replacement. This is much easier than trying to paint replacement pixels yourself, because you can select pixels that are a perfect match for the destination area from directly within the image.

Getting Started

Before you start using the Clone Stamp tool, you should configure the tool and your working environment so you're ready to work. As you can probably imagine by now, you should work with the Clone Stamp tool on a new layer, so you aren't actually replacing pixels within the image. Instead, you'll be copying pixels from within your image onto a new layer, so they cover up the pixels in the original that you don't want to have visible.

Start by selecting the Clone Stamp tool from the Tools palette or by pressing the S key. With the tool active, you're ready to start configuring it for the most effective use.

Set Up the Layers Palette

The first step is to create a new image layer to serve as the target for the pixels you'll copy with the Clone Stamp tool. Because the new layer will be placed directly above the currently active layer, first click on the Background image layer to select it. You want the new layer to be above the Background image layer but below all adjustment layers so the adjustments will affect cloned pixels to the same extent as the underlying image layer.

Note: You can work with the Clone Stamp tool in a variety of ways. We recommend utilizing a separate layer for cloned pixels because that will maximize flexibility and maintain the ability to fix any mistakes later.

To create a new layer, click the Create A New Layer button on the Layers palette. The new layer will have a name such as *Layer 1*, which won't really tell you a lot about the layer when you open the image later. We recommend renaming the layer, particularly because cloning often requires cleaning up small areas of an image, and the thumbnail for the layer on the Layers palette may make it appear that the layer is empty, leading you to delete it without realizing its importance. You can rename the layer by simply double-clicking the name of the layer. You can then type a new name, such as **Clone Stamp** or **Cleanup**, and press Enter/Return to apply the new name to the layer (Figure 6.2).

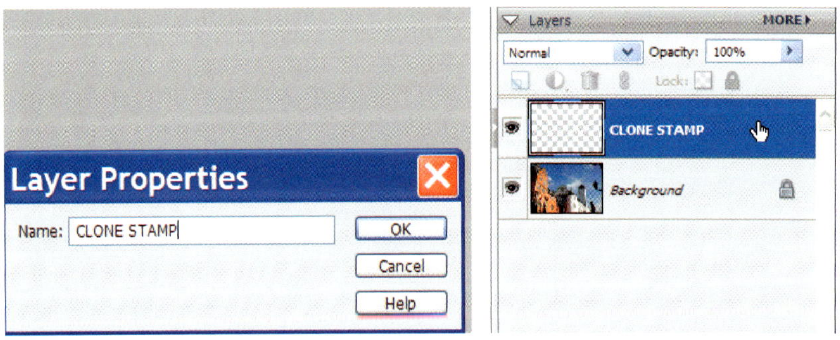

Figure 6.2 Giving the new layer for cloning a name such as *Clone Stamp* helps avoid confusion about what the layer is there for.

Because you'll be placing cloned pixels onto a separate layer, you'll want to take advantage of a feature (which you'll look at in a moment) that allows you to copy pixels from layers other than the active layer. However, you don't want to let the Clone Stamp tool "see" the effect of adjustment layers on the Layers palette, or they will affect the cloned pixels twice—once when you are copying the pixels, and again after the pixels are placed on the new layer (Figure 6.3).

Figure 6.3 If you don't turn off the visibility of adjustment layers while you're cloning onto a new layer, the pixels you copy won't match the surrounding area.

When you're using the Clone Stamp tool, in order to clone onto a separate layer without including the effects of other adjustments you've made, the only layers visible should be the Background image layer and your new Clone Stamp layer. You should turn off the visibility of all adjustment layers. When we say *adjustment layers* in this context, we're referring to any layer that changes the appearance of any area of the image. Although we haven't covered any of these other layers yet, there will be many such techniques discussed later in this book.

Note: You may be tempted to place the Clone Stamp layer above the adjustment layers so they won't affect cloned pixels twice. However, if you ever decide to change the settings in any adjustment layer, the pixels will no longer match properly.

To turn off the visibility of all but the Background and Clone Stamp layers, click the eye icon to the left of *all other layers* on the Layers palette. When the eye disappears from beside all other layers, those layers will no longer be visible. The Layers palette is properly configured for the Clone Stamp tool when the only eye icons you see are next to the Background image layer and your Clone Stamp layer (Figure 6.4).

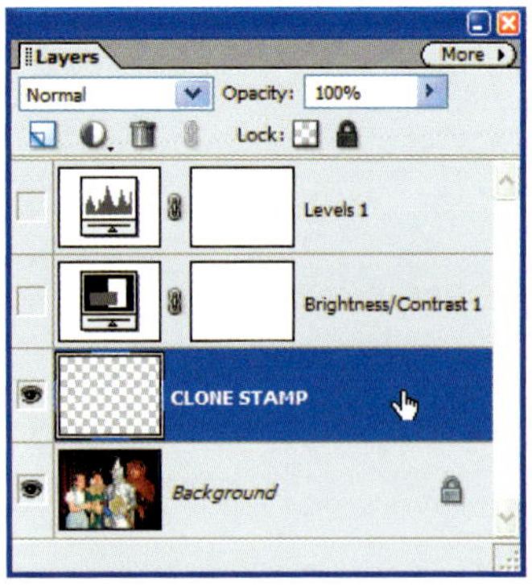

Figure 6.4 Your Layers palette is properly configured for using the Clone Stamp tool when only the Background image layer and Clone Stamp layer are visible.

Configure the Options Bar

When you select the Clone Stamp from the Tools palette, the Options bar near the top will include several settings you can establish for the Clone Stamp tool. Although these settings offer a variety of ways to configure the tool, the vast majority of the time you'll use the same ones. Therefore, after you've configured the Clone Stamp tool for the first time, you'll need to only glance at the Options bar to confirm that the settings are as they should be.

The first setting to consider is the brush presets item. This allows you to define the shape, size, and hardness of the brush (Figure 6.5). In most situations we recommend using a standard round brush when working with the Clone Stamp tool, though at times you may find a different shape useful. The second option item, Size, allows you to choose the brush size in terms of pixels by using the slider control. This is not particularly helpful, because you probably don't know how many pixels wide you want the brush to be. Instead, you'll set the size later by using the area you want to clean up for reference. This leaves only the hardness of the brush to be considered at this point.

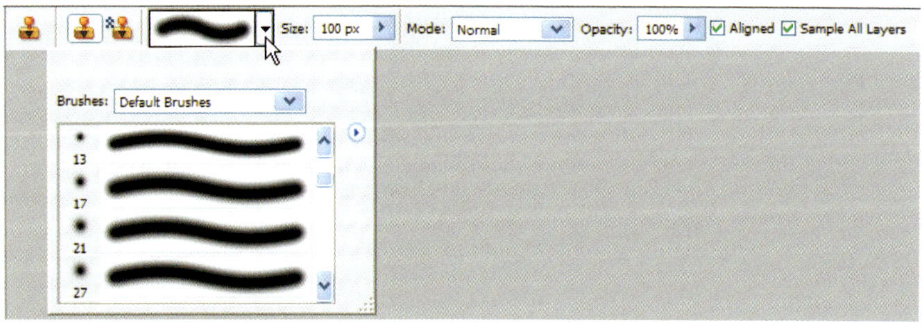

Figure 6.5 The brush presets item on the Options bar allows you to adjust the size and shape of a brush. You can select a hard brush or a soft brush; however, the ability to fine-tune hardness is not available. You can adjust that aspect by using a keyboard shortcut, a valuable amenity.

Note: To see the exact size of the brush you are using, make sure the Caps Lock key on your keyboard is *not* set.

Elements doesn't include an option to adjust hardness for any of the brush tools (including the Clone Stamp tool) on the Options bar. However, you can still adjust the hardness of the brush in 20% increments by holding the Shift key and pressing the left square bracket key ([) to reduce hardness, or the right square bracket key (]) to increase hardness. As you're using that control to adjust the Hardness setting, watch the brush sample icon on the Options bar changing to reflect the effect of the change that you have made.

You can select a hard- or soft-edged brush from the brush presets drop-down list; it's easy to tell the difference by looking at the thumbnail of the brush stroke preview in the brush drop-down palette. We cannot ever recommend using a Hard brush with the Clone Stamp tool, because it produces a result that is too obvious, with a harsh transition between the pixels you've cloned and surrounding pixels (Figure 6.6). A Soft Round brush works well when cloning in areas that don't have significant detail, such as when cleaning up dust spots in the sky. However, in areas with crisp texture, a soft-edged brush can leave obvious indications of your work, in the form of "soft" areas where the pixels are blended too much, outlining your brush strokes. In that type of situation, you might want to start with a Soft brush but increase hardness by 20% by using the shortcut keys referenced previously. However, you can certainly experiment with different Hardness settings (using the keyboard shortcut) to find the one that works best for any particular cloning task.

Figure 6.6 A hard-edged brush should never be used with the Clone Stamp tool because it leads to obvious transitions between cloned and surrounding pixels, such as the straight lines within the pattern here.

The next item on the Options bar is Mode, also called Effect Mode, which controls blending for the Clone Stamp tool. In other words, this control allows you to change the appearance of the pixels you're cloning as they are placed on the new layer, in a way that varies based on the mode chosen. As you can imagine, when you're trying to remove elements of an image by copying pixels from elsewhere within the image, you don't want the appearance of those pixels to change. You should therefore leave the Mode set to Normal when working with the Clone Stamp tool.

The Opacity control determines whether the pixels you copy with the Clone Stamp tool will be shown at full opacity, or whether they will be partially transparent. Normally, you'll want to completely replace the underlying pixels, so a 100% Opacity setting would be suitable. However, in some situations you may want to reduce the impact of an area of your image, without completely replacing the detail. For example, you may want to tone down some blemishes on a person's face without completely removing them. By using the Clone Stamp at a reduced Opacity (perhaps around 50%), you can partially block the underlying pixels to minimize their effect without completely removing them.

The Aligned checkbox controls how the source area is reset with each stroke of the Clone Stamp tool. With the Aligned checkbox selected, each time you release the mouse and then click again, the relationship between source and destination pixels you have defined remains unchanged. For example, if the source of pixels to be cloned is 50 pixels directly to the left of the destination area, each time you release the mouse and click elsewhere in the image, the source will be 50 pixels to the left of the new location. This is generally the preferred behavior, so as a general rule we recommend leaving the Aligned checkbox selected.

If you *deselect* the Aligned checkbox, after you have set a source of pixels within the image and you release the mouse and click again to start copying more pixels, the source will reset to the original point you established. This is helpful if you want to copy the same pixels repeatedly within the image, but it does increase the chance that the cloning will become obvious in the final image. If you're going to deselect the Aligned checkbox, take particular care to ensure that it doesn't become obvious you have copied the same pixels repeatedly within the image.

Finally, the Sample All Layers checkbox on the Options bar specifies whether the Clone Stamp tool will work on only the current layer, or whether it will be able to see all layers and copy the composite result of those pixels. In other words, when the box isn't selected, you can work on only a single layer; when it *is* selected, the Clone Stamp will copy pixels exactly as you see them in the image. Because you're cloning onto a separate layer, you'll definitely want to make sure the Sample All Layers checkbox is selected.

Cloning Pixels

After you've selected the Clone Stamp tool, configured your Layers palette to work on a separate layer, and established appropriate settings on the Options bar, you're ready to select a source area for the pixels and start cloning them onto a new layer.

Select an Appropriate Source

Selecting an appropriate source of pixels within your image is the most important skill to develop when working with the Clone Stamp tool. The source of pixels determines how well the pixels you copy match those around the destination area, which in turn determines how seamless the correction you're making will be. It takes some practice to be able to quickly select the best source area, in terms of color, tone, and texture. Hence, we encourage you to practice cloning things out of your image.

Note: To improve your skills with the Clone Stamp, give yourself an assignment with a test image. Remove something significant from the scene, trying to produce a result where nobody can tell that anything was removed from the image.

When selecting a source area within the image, you need to choose pixels that will blend in perfectly with the destination area in terms of tone, color, and texture (Figure 6.7). That doesn't mean the pixels you copy have to be an exact match, just that they need to fit in well with the surrounding pixels after you've copied them. As you're learning to use the Clone Stamp tool, take the time to carefully look at the image to find the best source of pixels to place in the area you're trying to clean up.

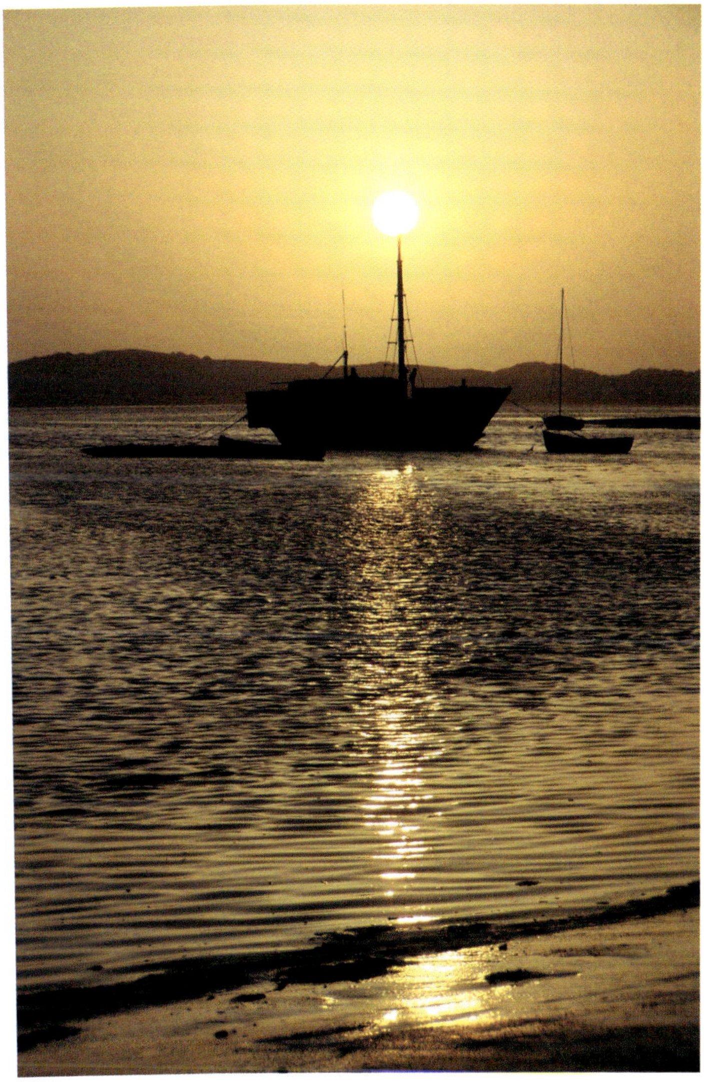

Figure 6.7 Choosing an appropriate source is critical when working with the Clone Stamp tool. Even areas that seem relatively uniform, such as a sky, will have subtle tonal variations as seen in this image. These variations need to be considered when selecting a source for cloning.

After you've chosen an appropriate source of pixels that you will use, hold the Alt/Option key and click on that source area. This will establish the position within the image where pixels will be copied from. Release the Alt/Option key and move your cursor to the destination area: the defect that you want to cover. Left-click, and the pixels that you have sampled will be copied onto the destination area. If the effect does not appear seamless, choose Edit > Undo Clone Stamp and start again, by sampling a slightly different area or changing the brush size or hardness if necessary.

Paint with the Clone Stamp

With the source of pixels for the Clone Stamp established, you're almost ready to start removing the first blemish in your image. However, before you do so, it is important to set the brush to an appropriate size (Figure 6.8).

As mentioned earlier, you can't set the brush size without knowing where you're going to clone—there is no single size that will always be appropriate. Instead, the brush should be a suitable size relative to the area you're trying to clean up (Figure 6.9). As a general rule, you want the brush to be no larger than the problem you're trying to solve; even if you plan to clean up a relatively large area, you may want to use a smaller brush and work small sections at a time.

Note: If you don't have the Preferences set to show brush size, you can't see the relative size of your brush for the Clone Stamp or other tools. To correct this, choose Edit > Preferences > Display & Cursors, and set the Painting Cursors option to Full Size Brush Tip.

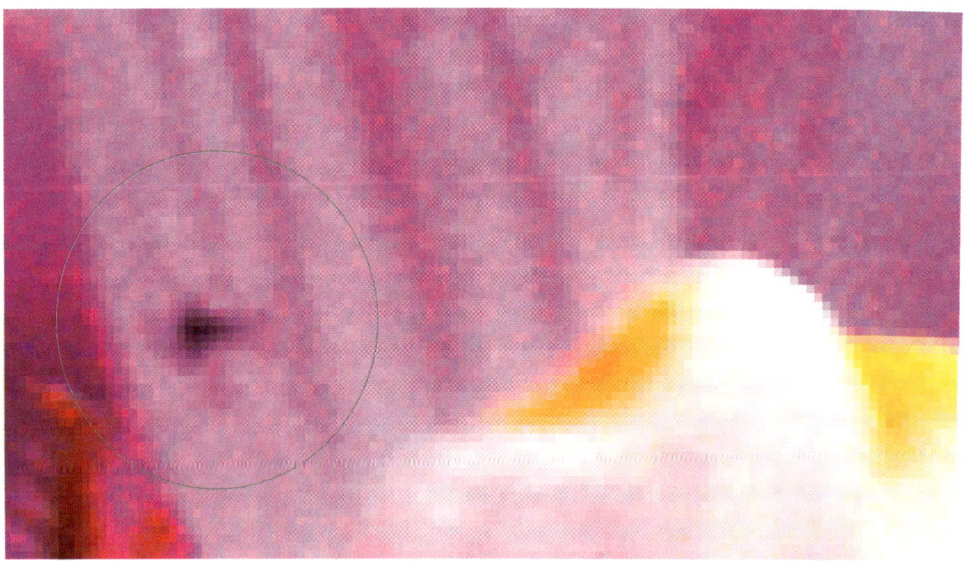

Figure 6.8 If you use a brush size that is larger than the area you are attempting to clean up with the Clone Stamp, you'll affect surrounding areas and increase the risk of having areas that have obviously been altered.

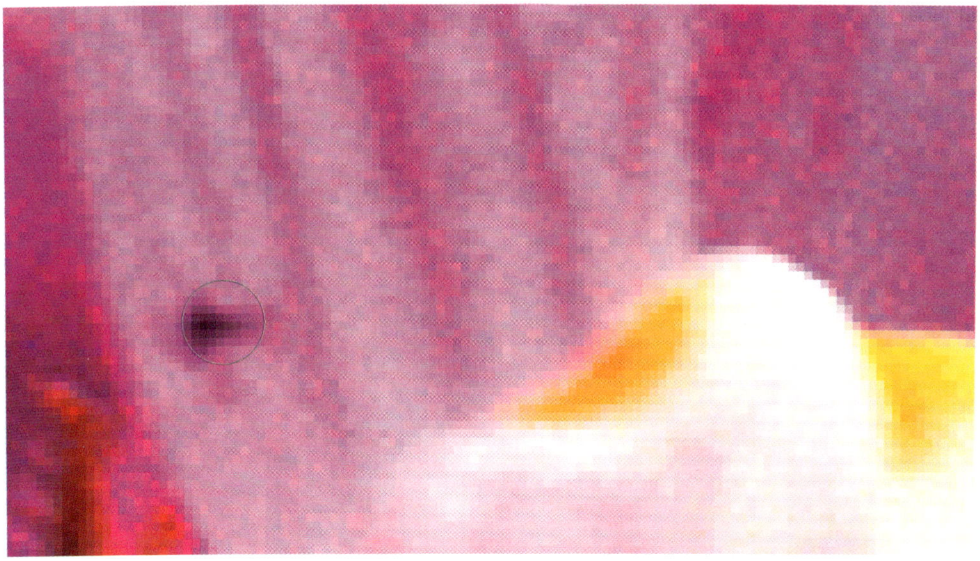

Figure 6.9 The brush size for the Clone Stamp should be no larger than the size of the area you're trying to clean, and often a bit smaller so you can carefully build up your corrections in that area.

To size the brush, place your mouse over the area you want to clean up and then use the left square bracket ([) to reduce the brush size and right square bracket (]) to increase the brush size, until the brush is an appropriate size. (Do not depress the Shift key for this control.) You can also right-click to find other brush size/hardness options and then press Enter/Return to dismiss the Brush palette from the screen.

Note: If you have set the proper Preferences setting to display cursors with brush size but still aren't seeing the correct display, make sure Caps Lock is not turned on. The Caps Lock key toggles between Brush Size and Precise options for your mouse pointers.

As you're working with the Clone Stamp tool, there are two basic ways you'll employ the brush. The first is to simply click on a target area to repair a small blemish. For example, for dust spots in the sky you should need to click only once on each dust spot. For larger areas, you will want to use a different technique: click and drag the brush slightly to repair sections at a time by "painting" the area. If you click repeatedly, you'll tend to build up an obvious pattern in the cleaned-up portion of your image. At the same time, you don't want to click and drag excessively, or you'll risk having too much repetition of patterns within the repaired area. Instead, use short brush strokes, clicking and dragging over small areas as you build up the correction.

Naturally, if you keep the same relationship between source and destination as you work with the Clone Stamp tool, you'll end up with less than optimal source pixels for certain destination areas. To prevent this problem, and also to avoid the risk of producing duplication within the image that is relatively easy to see, sample a new area of pixels frequently. In fact, it is best to select a new source every time you employ the

Clone Stamp tool, selecting a source area that is best suited for the specific area that you intend to fix at a given moment.

Note: Select a new source area for the Clone Stamp tool for every blemish you need to fix. This technique will help ensure the best match for those pixels while also reducing the risk of obvious duplication of shapes and textures within the image.

Producing effective cleanup results without any obvious indication that you've changed the image requires a certain amount of practice with the Clone Stamp tool. Start with relatively easy tasks, such as cleaning dust spots out of the sky, before you move on to more advanced efforts. With practice, you'll become proficient in selecting an ideal source area quickly and easily, enabling you to clean up an image seamlessly (Figure 6.10).

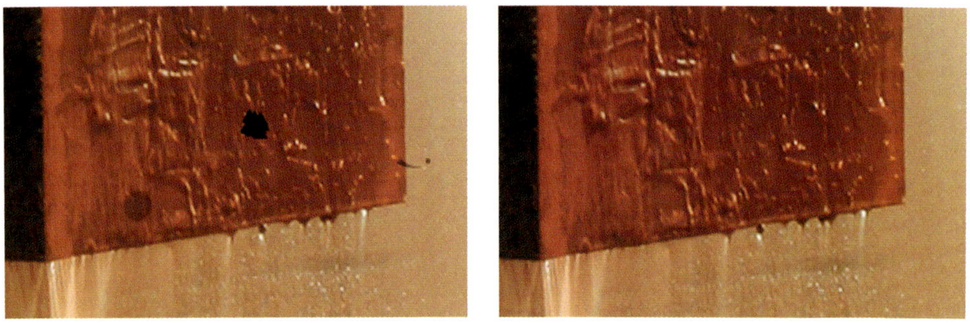

Figure 6.10 With some practice, you'll be able to clean up areas of your image with no evidence that any changes have been made, even in complicated areas.

After you're finished cleaning up your image with the Clone Stamp tool, you can turn the visibility of your adjustment layers back on so you can see their effects: click the box to the left of each thumbnail on the Layers palette so the eye icon appears again. Just remember to turn the visibility off again and click on the Clone Stamp layer to make it active if you need to perform additional work with the Clone Stamp.

Note: Remember, when you are cloning onto a separate layer, it is important to have the Sample All Layers checkbox (in the Options bar near the top of the screen) selected. In addition, be sure that the visibility of all adjustment layers is turned off, and that the Clone Stamp layer is active while you're working with this tool.

Fixing Cloning Mistakes

In many cases the Clone Stamp tool is used to correct "mistakes" in the image, though these weren't necessarily caused by mistakes made by the photographer. However, even when you're cleaning up problems in your image with the Clone Stamp tool, you may run into situations where the cloning is less than perfect. Fortunately, fixing mistakes is remarkably simple when you are working with the Clone Stamp tool on a separate layer, as recommended earlier in this chapter.

Note: The ability to simply erase pixels from the cloning layer when you make a mistake is one of the best reasons to work on a separate layer with the Clone Stamp tool.

First, be sure the Clone Stamp layer is the currently active layer; if it isn't, click its thumbnail on the Layers palette. Then select the Eraser tool from the Tools palette (the shortcut key is E). On the Options bar, select a brush with the same hardness as you were using with the Clone Stamp tool, and adjust the size of the brush as needed for the area you want to correct. Then simply "paint" over the image in the area where you want to erase the effects of your cloning. This will remove those pixels from the new layer you created, allowing the original pixels in the Background image layer to show through again (Figure 6.11). Now you can start the cloning process again, with a slightly different technique to prevent making the same mistake as you made previously.

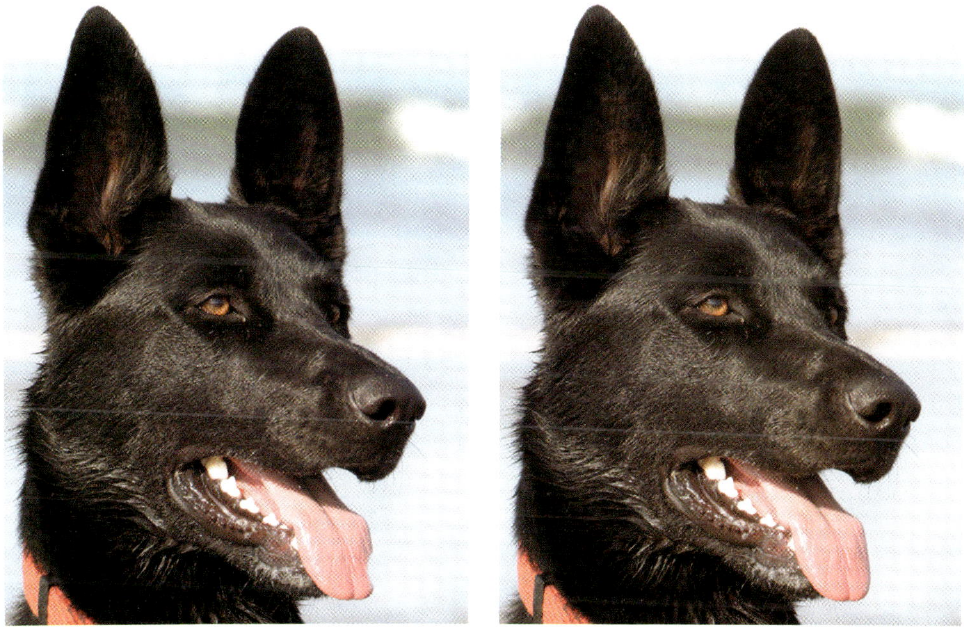

Figure 6.11 When cloning on a separate layer, it is easy to fix mistakes by using the Eraser tool to remove cloned pixels from your Clone Stamp layer. For example, while trying to clean up some clutter in the background, a portion of the dog's tongue was accidentally removed. Erasing pixels on the Clone Stamp layer quickly solves the problem.

Note: It is possible to undo a mistake by clicking a state on the History palette or by pressing Ctrl/⌘+Z. However, this doesn't provide a solution when you've closed the image in the meantime, or when you don't realize you've made a mistake until you've already done other cleanup work you want to keep.

Healing Brush

After you know how to use the Clone Stamp tool effectively, you pretty much already know how to use the Healing Brush as well. In fact, the Healing Brush is even easier to use than the Clone Stamp because you don't have to be as careful about the selection of a source area within the image. This is because the Healing Brush copies only texture, automatically adjusting the pixels you copy to a destination area so they match the overall tone and color of the surrounding area.

More specifically, the Healing Brush adjusts the overall tone based on the pixels just outside the painting area where the brush is applied. For example, if you are removing a dark scar on a pale facial area, the brush will obviously be painting over the dark scar. A tone calculation just under the brush (the dark scar) would not be desirable and is not employed by the algorithms that power the Healing Brush. Hence, the overall tone matching will be calculated based on the pale skin tones outside of the brush stroke, producing the desired effect.

This is an ideal tool for fixing many problems within your image because of the automatic blending it provides. For example, when cleaning dust spots in the sky, you don't have to worry about selecting a source area that matches perfectly in terms of tone and color. Instead, you need to find an area with only an appropriate texture, and the Healing Brush will do the rest.

Note: The Healing Brush is an even better tool than the Clone Stamp for cleaning dust in areas with smooth texture such as sky. It automatically blends pixels to produce a perfect match with minimal effort.

Getting Started

The first step is to configure the Healing Brush for proper use, with the same procedure that we recommended for the Clone Stamp tool. Create a new layer on the Layers palette; give it a name such as **Healing Brush** so you'll know what that layer is for. Turn off the visibility for any adjustment layers; then select the Healing Brush tool from the Tools palette (the shortcut key is J). With the tool active, you're ready to adjust the settings on the Options bar.

Note: The Healing Brush is found under the Spot Healing Brush on the Tools palette. You'll therefore need to click and hold the Spot Healing Brush button so you can select the Healing Brush from the pop-up menu. (Alternatively, you can right-click the tool to access a drop-down menu that allows you to select either of the Healing Brush tools.)

The brush size, as with the Clone Stamp, should be adjusted with the square bracket keys as you are preparing to work with the tool. However, the Hardness should be set for the maximum, using the Shift key and the] on your keyboard (Figure 6.12).

Because the Healing Brush is automatically blending the pixels you copy, using a soft-edged brush will only create more work for it. The Mode should be set to Normal to avoid unexpected results, and the Source should be set to Sampled.

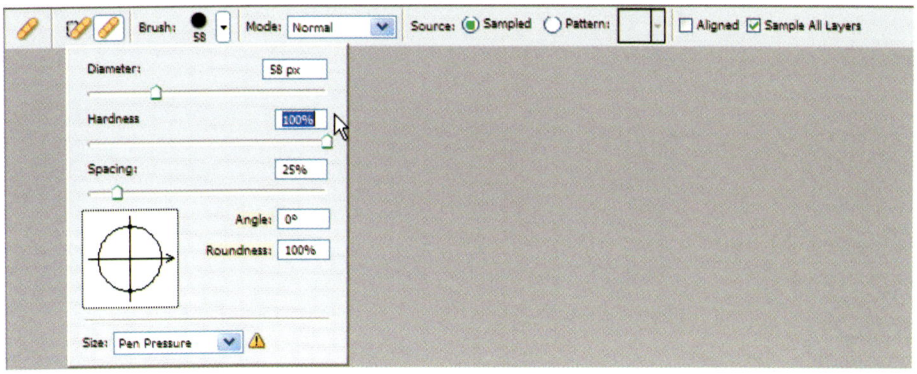

Figure 6.12 A hard-edged brush should be used for best results with the Healing Brush, because it automatically blends copied pixels.

Note: If you were to change the blending mode for the Healing Brush tool to Replace, it would behave exactly like the Clone Stamp tool.

As with the Clone Stamp tool, the Sample All Layers checkbox should be selected because you're working on a separate layer. However, you may not want to select the Aligned checkbox. Because the Healing Brush is used to repair problems by blending the source pixels into the destination, you don't need to be as careful about the source selection or about trying to avoid creating repeating patterns. In fact, it is often helpful to leave the Aligned checkbox unselected so you can select a source with a texture that will work well for a variety of areas within the image you need to clean up. For example, when touching up a portrait, you could select a single area of smooth skin texture as your source, and use that source for a variety of areas on the face.

Note: Although it is possible to use the same new layer for both Clone Stamp and Healing Brush work, it's preferable to use separate new layers for each of the two tasks in order to handle them independently.

Healing Pixels

After you've configured the settings for the Healing Brush, you're ready to start cleaning up your image. Again, this tool functions in exactly the same way as the Clone Stamp tool. Hold the Alt/Option key and click on a source area to sample (copy) pixels. Look for an area with the best texture for the area you wish to clean up. The pixels will automatically be adjusted to blend with the tone and color of that area. Then you can use a single click technique, or "paint" by clicking and dragging with small strokes, to clean up problem areas within the image (Figure 6.13).

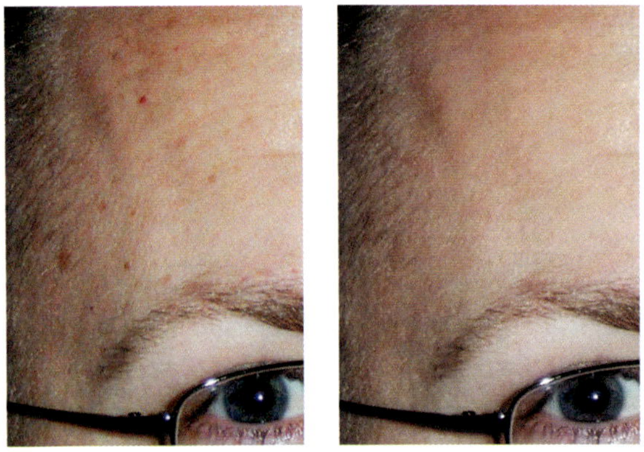

Figure 6.13 When working with the Healing Brush, use small strokes for each area you are trying to correct (left), building up each small correction until you have touched up the complete image (right).

When you first start working with the Healing Brush tool, you'll notice that as you hold down the mouse button, the pixels you're painting don't match the destination area. However, as soon as you release the mouse, the pixels will be adjusted to blend in, producing an excellent match in most cases, provided you've selected a source with appropriate texture.

Note: I recommend making small brush strokes with the Healing Brush, rather than attempting to clean up large areas at once. This is because the Healing Brush can take time to blend, and a larger area will require considerably more time.

If you are using the Healing Brush near a high-contrast edge, you may get some "blooming," in which the blend near that edge produces a mismatch of tone or color that bleeds into the area you're correcting. In that case, creating a selection around the area you want to clean up will constrain the blending so it won't look beyond the selection for pixel values to blend with. We'll cover the creation of selections in Chapter 9, "Making Selections."

Note: As with the Clone Stamp, it's worth working on a separate layer for the Healing Brush tool because that will allow you to easily correct problems even if you don't discover them until much later. Simply use the Eraser tool to erase any cleanup pixels on the Healing Brush layer that you'd like to remove.

Minimizing Healing

The Healing Brush does an excellent job of blending pixels in the area you are cleaning up, but sometimes the effect will be too strong. When you're trying to clean up dust spots in the sky, the blending works remarkably well, allowing you to perform the same basic task as you would with the Clone Stamp tool but without being as careful about the source of pixels. When using the Healing Brush, you really need to worry about only the texture of the source area.

One of the most common examples used for the Healing Brush is to remove wrinkles from a person's face. However, if you completely remove those wrinkles, the person won't look the same, and chances are they won't like the difference. (This is a typical case of the effect being too strong.) Although many people would like to take a few years off their face, the Healing Brush doesn't provide a way to reduce the strength of the effect as you're working. The blending it performs is done at full strength and will therefore completely replace the area you use it on.

Because you're working with the Healing Brush on a separate layer, however, you can control the strength of the adjustment. By reducing the Opacity setting for the layer you're putting the Healing Brush pixels onto, you can reduce the impact of the adjustment. At the default Opacity setting of 100%, the Healing Brush pixels will completely cover up the underlying pixels. As you reduce this setting, the underlying pixels will be able to show through to some extent, minimizing the effect of the Healing Brush.

By reducing the Opacity setting for the layer, you can produce a more realistic correction for your image (Figure 6.14). Instead of completely removing a person's wrinkles, you can tone them down so they won't be as obvious. Instead of making the person look like they had extensive plastic surgery, for example, you can make them look like they were photographed under more flattering lighting. Each situation will call for a different Opacity setting for the Healing Brush, but in general you'll want to start experimenting with a value of about 50% and fine-tune from there. (The tool for adjusting opacity is at the top of the Layers dialog box.)

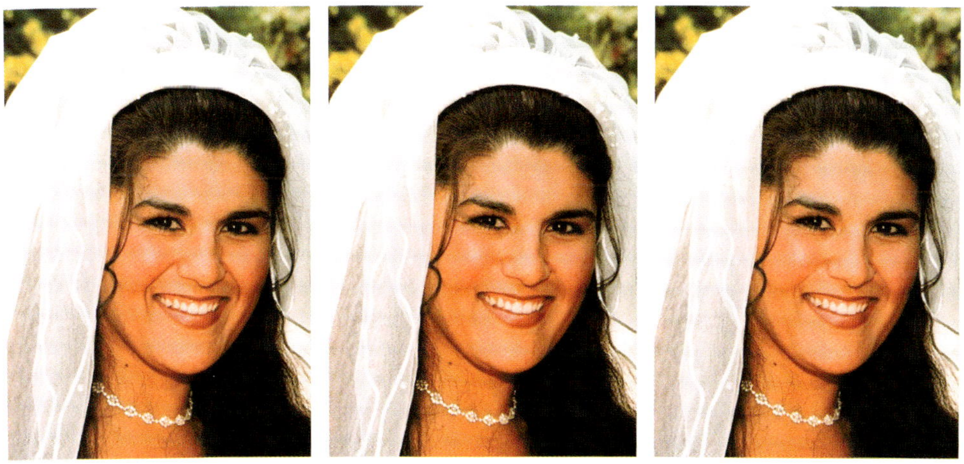

Figure 6.14 When you want to reduce laugh lines or wrinkles in an image (left), but using the Healing Brush causes an unnaturally strong effect (center), you can reduce the Opacity of the Healing Brush layer on the Layers palette. This produces a more realistic correction, creating the effect of more flattering light while maintaining the character of the subject (right).

Spot Healing Brush

This tool provides the same blending corrections of the Healing Brush, but without the need to select a source area from within the image. In other words, you do not need to sample pixels.

Although the Spot Healing Brush does not allow you to choose a source area within your image, this tool works well when the "problem" area is surrounded by pixels that represent an appropriate match. (That's because the tool automatically samples or copies nearby pixels.) Any time you have a blemish surrounded by an appropriate texture for repair, the Spot Healing Brush is an excellent tool for the correction.

Using the Spot Healing Brush is remarkably easy. Simply select it from the Tools palette and then click or paint over the blemishes you'd like to repair (Figure 6.15). Initially a partially transparent overlay will be displayed, showing you the area that will be affected by the Spot Healing Brush. When you release the mouse, the area you painted over will be automatically adjusted.

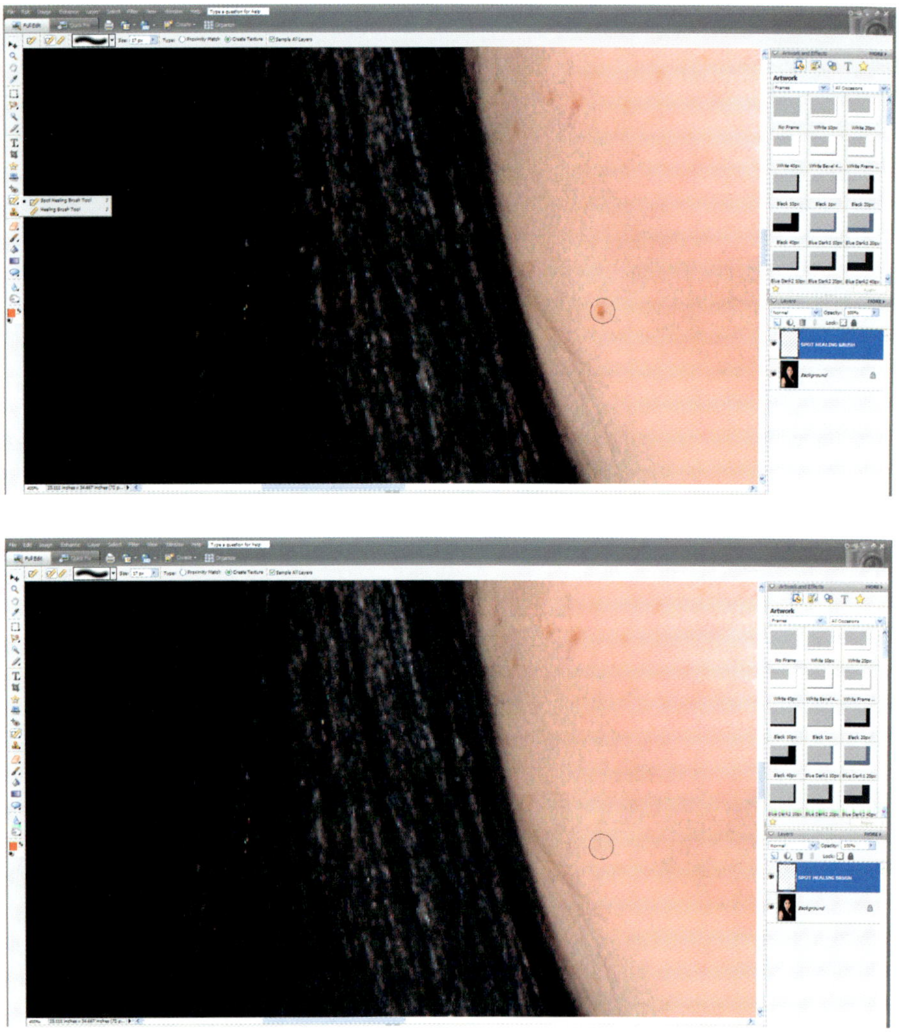

Figure 6.15 With the Spot Healing Brush, all you need to do is paint the area you want to correct (top), and Photoshop Elements 5 will do the rest (bottom).

The Options bar for the Spot Healing Brush includes very few controls. The only setting you'll need to consider (other than brush size, which should be adjusted using the left and right square bracket keys) is the Type option. We recommend choosing the Proximity match option; when you do so, the Spot Healing Brush tool will look to the pixels surrounding the "problem" area to find textures that should be blended during the repair. However, in some situations this won't provide a good match, such as when contrasting tones or colors are near the area to be repaired. In that case, choose the Create Texture item instead. This will cause the Spot Healing Brush to look within the area that you have fixed and attempt to produce an appropriate texture based on the pixel values within that area.

Although the Spot Healing Brush isn't a perfect solution for all situations, it does provide a simple way to work when you're just cleaning basic blemishes within your image.

A Clean Image

At this point in your workflow you have completed basic tonal and color adjustments and have cleaned up various blemishes, resulting in a clean image with good overall tone and color. You should now be relatively happy with the results that you have achieved. However, you may also be feeling that you'd like to take more control over the image, fine-tuning adjustments to affect certain areas. This calls for advanced adjustments, often targeted at particular areas of the image, which will be the subject of the next part of this book.

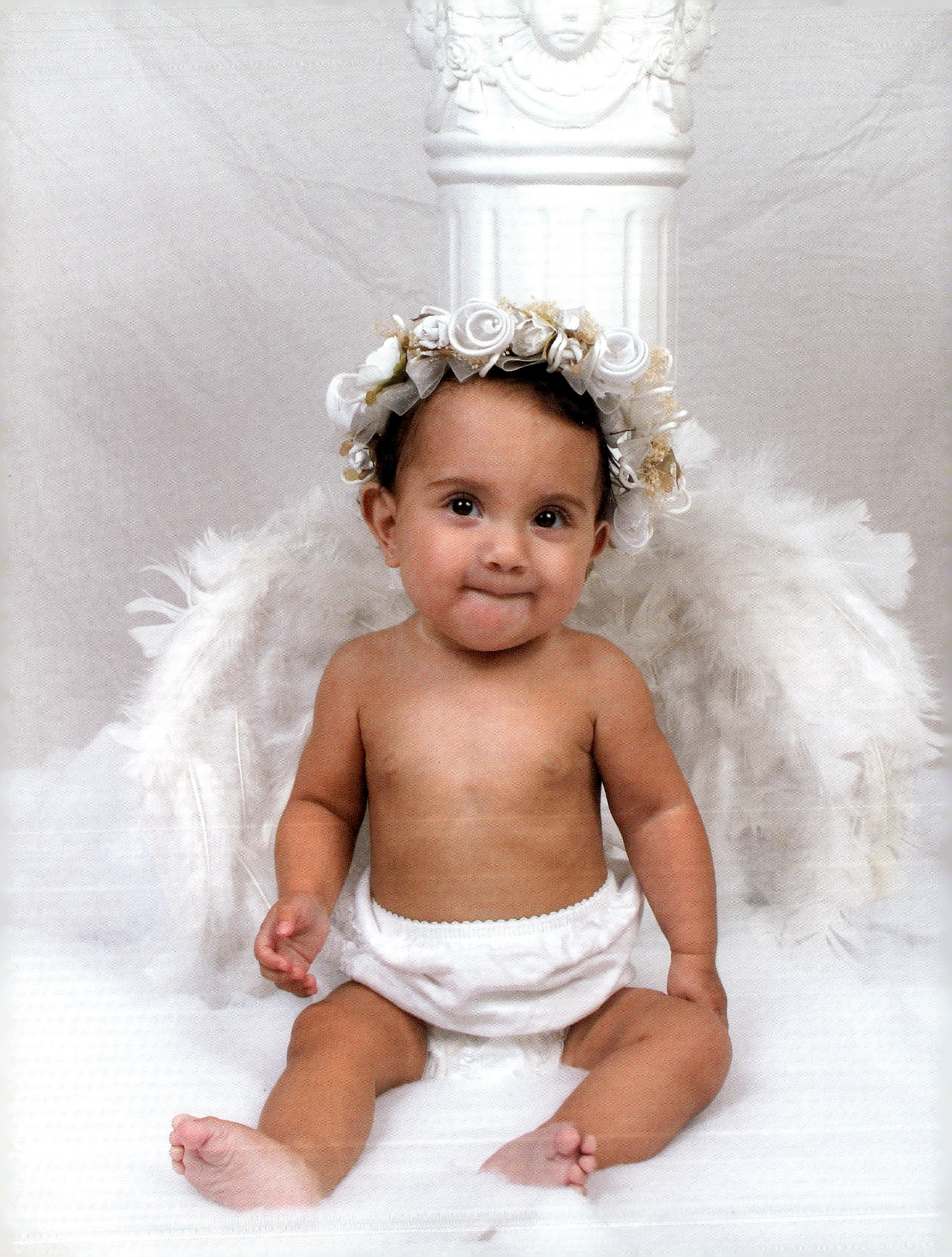

III

Advanced Adjustments

Producing the very best image in a digital workflow requires considerable control in the adjustment process. Previous chapters have helped you organize and perform basic optimization on your images. Now it is time to roll up your sleeves and focus on getting exactly the results you envision. This includes making more-advanced adjustments than were covered in previous chapters, as well as targeting adjustments to specific areas of your images.

Chapter 7 **Advanced Tonal Adjustments**
Chapter 8 **Advanced Color Adjustments**
Chapter 9 **Making Selections**
Chapter 10 **Targeted Adjustments**
Chapter 11 **Creative Adjustments**

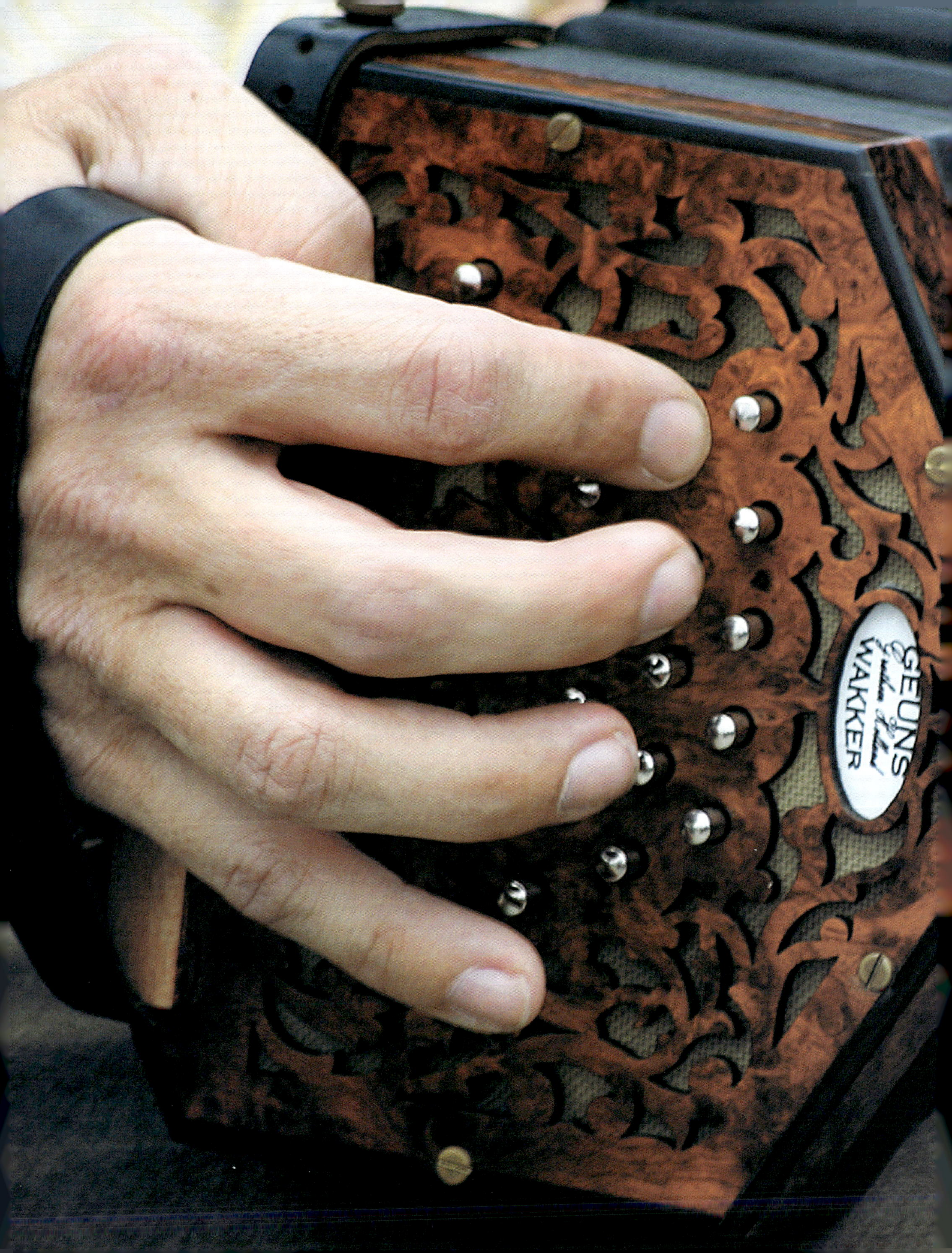
GEUNS
WAKKER

Advanced Tonal Adjustments

7

Performing tonal adjustments seems like a relatively simple task, because you are focused on perfecting only two straightforward qualities of your image: the brightness and the contrast. However, you can use a variety of additional techniques to produce tonal adjustments within your images. This chapter will focus on helping you exercise greater control over those adjustments.

Chapter Contents

Shadows/Highlights
Adjust Color Curves
Selective Adjustments

Shadows/Highlights

An improper exposure can result in an image that has dark, murky shadows or extremely bright highlight areas with little visible detail. The Shadows/Highlights tool allows you to recover detail that is obscured by dark shadows or very bright highlights caused by excessive contrast (Figure 7.1). This tool is surprisingly easy and intuitive to use, and it offers an effective method for adjusting areas of your image based on their tonal value. More specifically, it represents a good way to perform at least an initial recovery of image detail that you might have thought was lost for good.

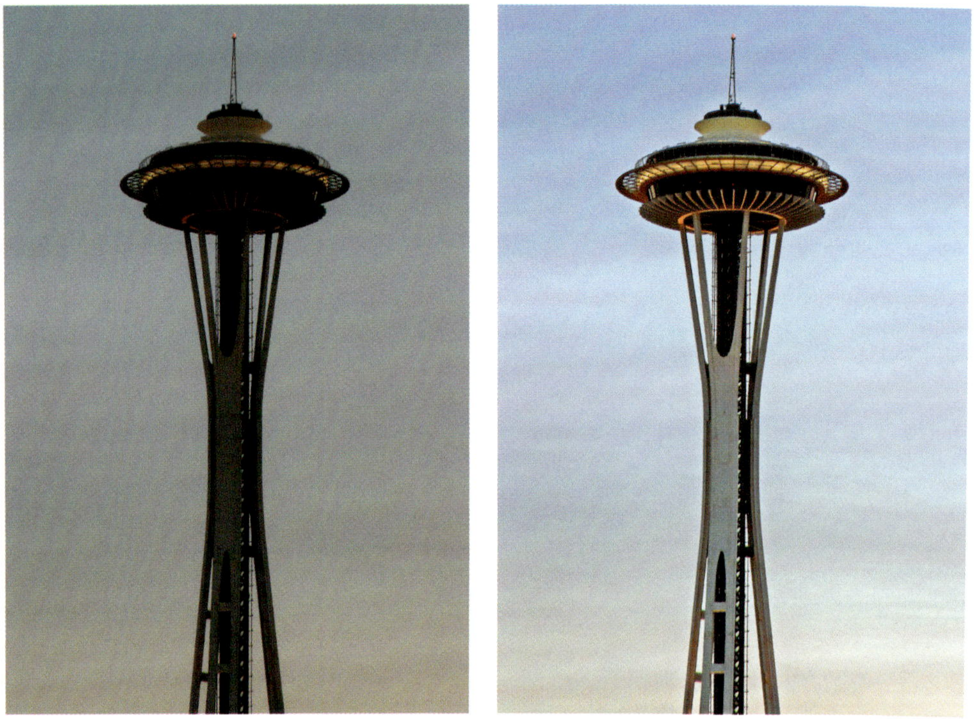

Figure 7.1 The Shadows/Highlights tool provides a way to salvage images that have lost detail in excessively dark shadows or excessively bright highlights.

You might use Shadows/Highlights when your image was taken with the light source behind the subject being brighter than the light source in front of the subject. We've all seen photos of someone standing with the sun brightly shining behind them. In a situation of this type, the camera's light metering system is affected by the very bright background, which results in an image whose subject is too dark. In a portrait, for example, the person's face may be dark, with details difficult to discern.

The Shadows/Highlights tool is a quick and easy way to lighten all the dark areas within an image. In this example, that would reveal details in the person's face and would also tone down the overall contrast in the image. This adjustment typically fits at this point in the workflow because you would have likely already tried other tonal adjustment methods, particularly Levels, and found they did not extract adequate shadow detail.

Because you can't apply the Shadows/Highlights tool to an adjustment layer, we recommend duplicating your Background layer as the first step. To do so, click the thumbnail for the Background layer and drag it to the Create A New Layer icon at the top of the Layers dialog box (Figure 7.2). With the duplicate image layer active, choose Enhance > Adjust Lighting > Shadows/Highlights.

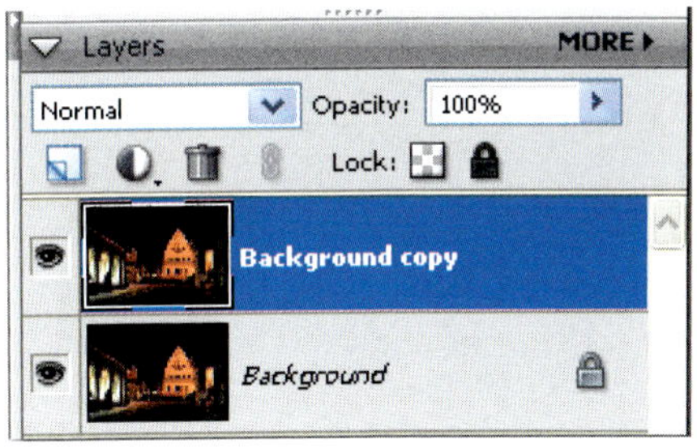

Figure 7.2 Because you can't use Shadows/Highlights on an adjustment layer, create a duplicate of the Background layer to work on.

The Shadows/Highlights tool automatically applies some shadow lightening (25%) to every image, whether or not that is required. Typically, that is not the desired correction required by a particular image. But the dialog box offers three sliders that let you take full control: Lighten Shadows, Darken Highlights, and Midtone Contrast (Figure 7.3).

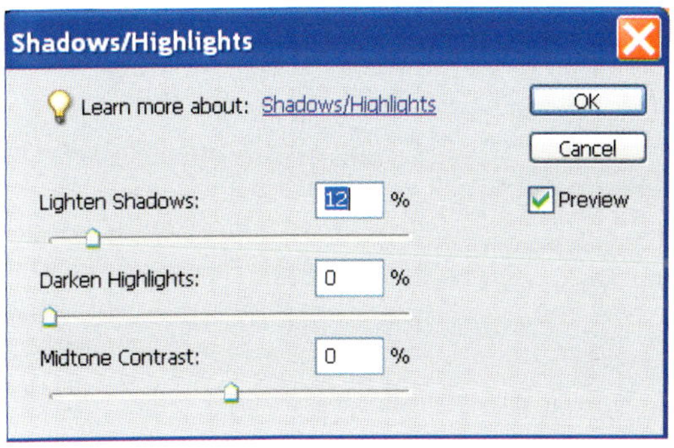

Figure 7.3 The Shadows/Highlights dialog box enables you to adjust three distinct sliders; you can recover shadow detail, highlight detail, and adjust (typically, increase) midtone contrast.

In effect, you can think of the Lighten Shadows slider as allowing you to decide how much to lighten the darkest areas of your image, and the Darken Highlights slider as providing a similar ability to darken the brightest areas. Your first reaction may be that doing either will simply reduce contrast and produce a muddy image. However, keep in mind that this adjustment is designed for correcting contrast that is too high or for extracting more detail from the darkest and brightest areas of your image. As you make shadow or highlight adjustments (or both) in high-contrast images that would benefit from both corrections, take a conservative approach. In other words, take care not to overcorrect, which could create an image that is excessively flat or that has an artificial appearance (Figure 7.4). When used conservatively, with a modest amount of adjustment, the result is an effective increase in detail without a problematic loss of contrast.

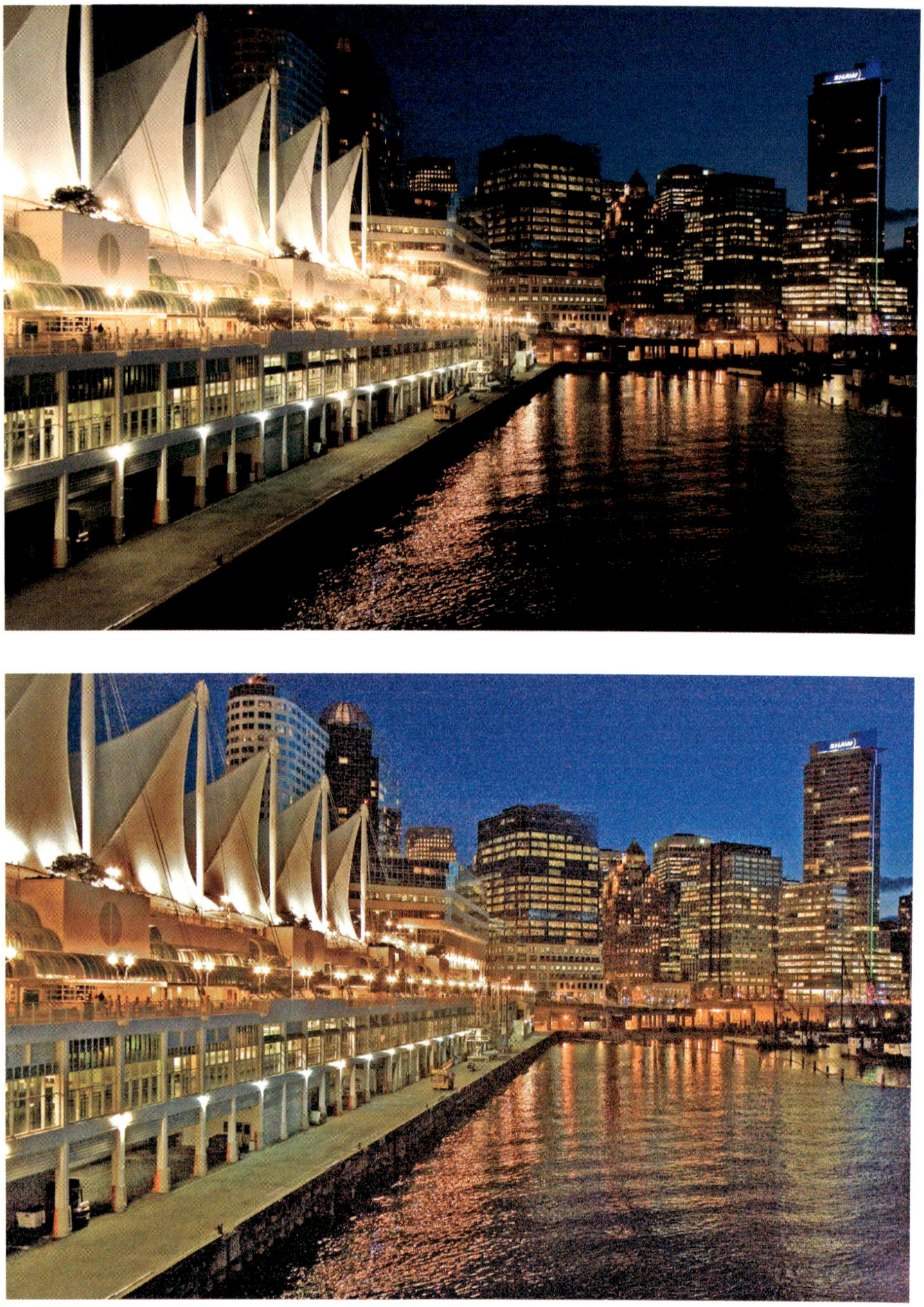

Figure 7.4 Extreme adjustments with the Shadows/Highlights tool will result in images with an artificial appearance, although you could use this to create a new artistic interpretation of your image.

Using the Shadows/Highlights tool is a simple matter of adjusting the sliders to extract the desired level of detail in the image. This process is intuitive because you can see the effect that a specific amount of adjustment makes to your images (Figure 7.5). The default level of shadow lightening is not ideal for most images, so make your own settings, taking care to avoid an excessively flat or artificial appearance (as shown earlier in Figure 7.4).

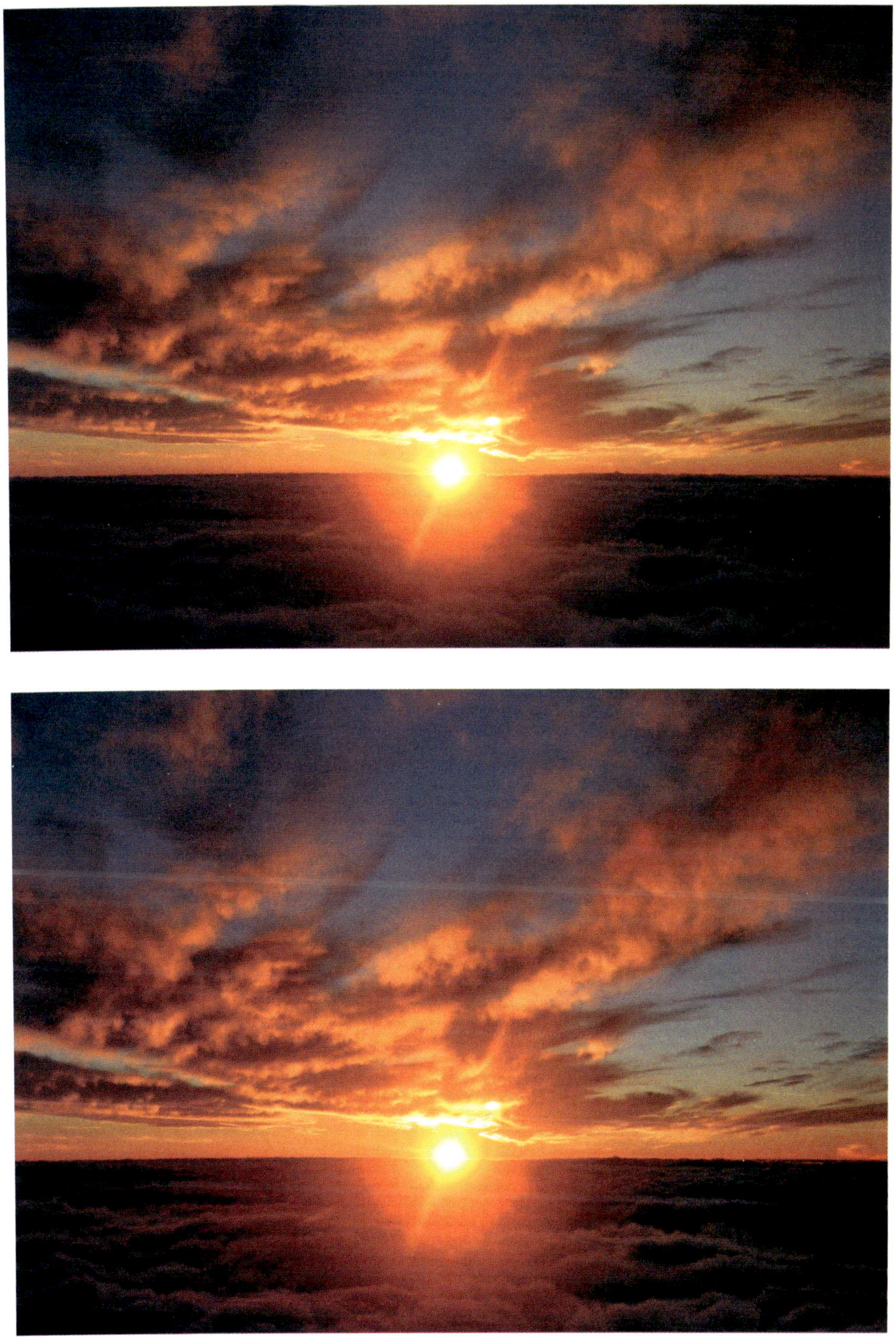

Figure 7.5 The sliders adjust the strength of your adjustments for Shadows and Highlights. In this image, detail has been enhanced in the clouds with a Lighten Shadows adjustment.

As you can imagine, no software solution can work miracles. In other words, the Shadows/Highlights tool can darken excessively bright areas, but it cannot create detail that was not captured when the image was made (Figure 7.6). Hence, this tool is not an alternative to making a correct exposure when taking a photo or when scanning a slide or negative to make a digital image file. Some images will require the application of both the Darken Highlights and Lighten Shadows sliders for the most technically accurate or the most visually pleasing results (Figure 7.7). Experiment with various levels for both until you find the combination that produces the desired results. Although this can be a bit time-consuming with difficult images made under extremely high-contrast lighting, the process is intuitive and not at all complicated.

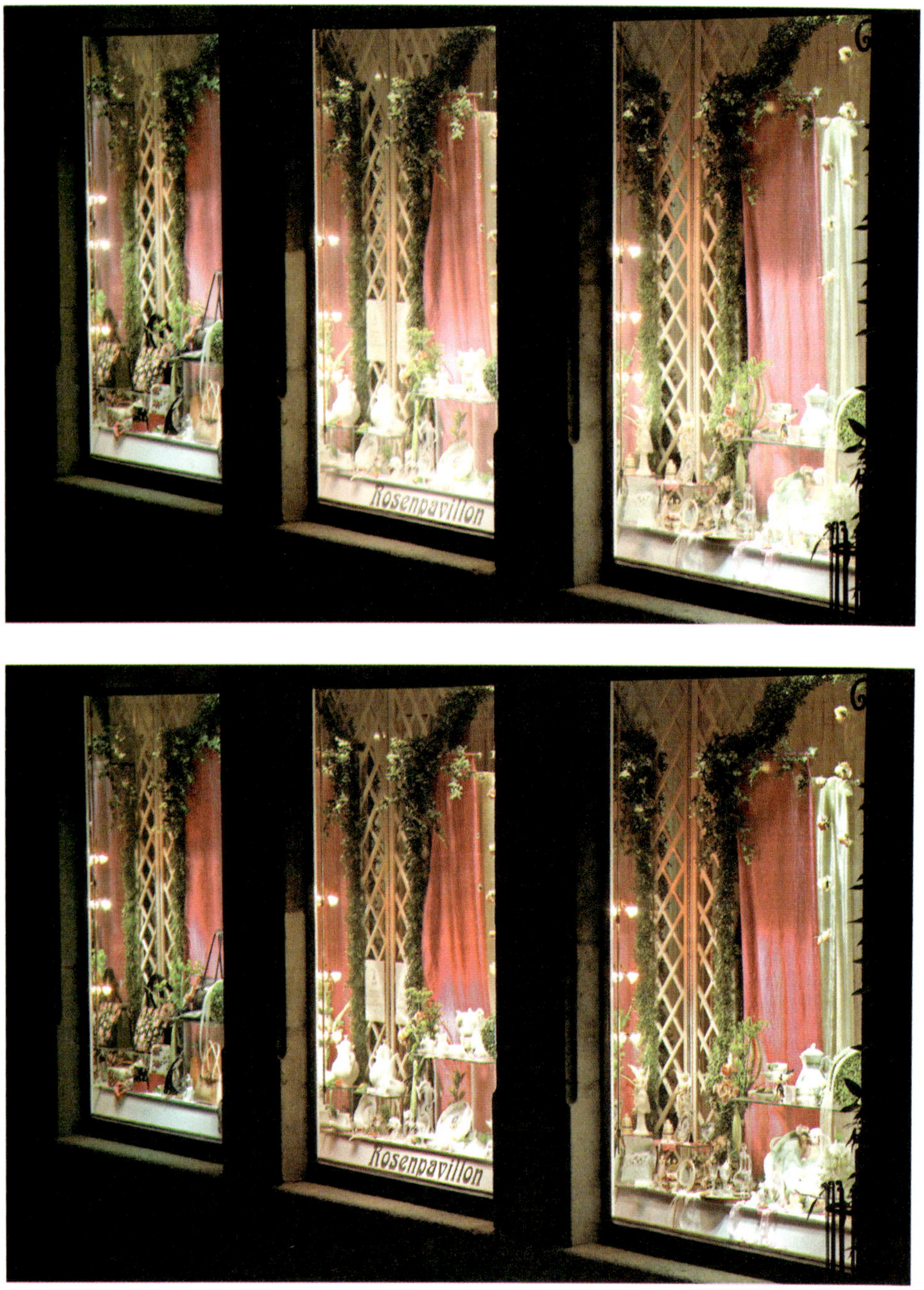

Figure 7.6 The Darken Highlights tool can be useful for toning down extremely bright areas. Although this will recover detail in *some* highlight areas, no software can provide detail that was not captured when the image was made, due to overexposure in this instance.

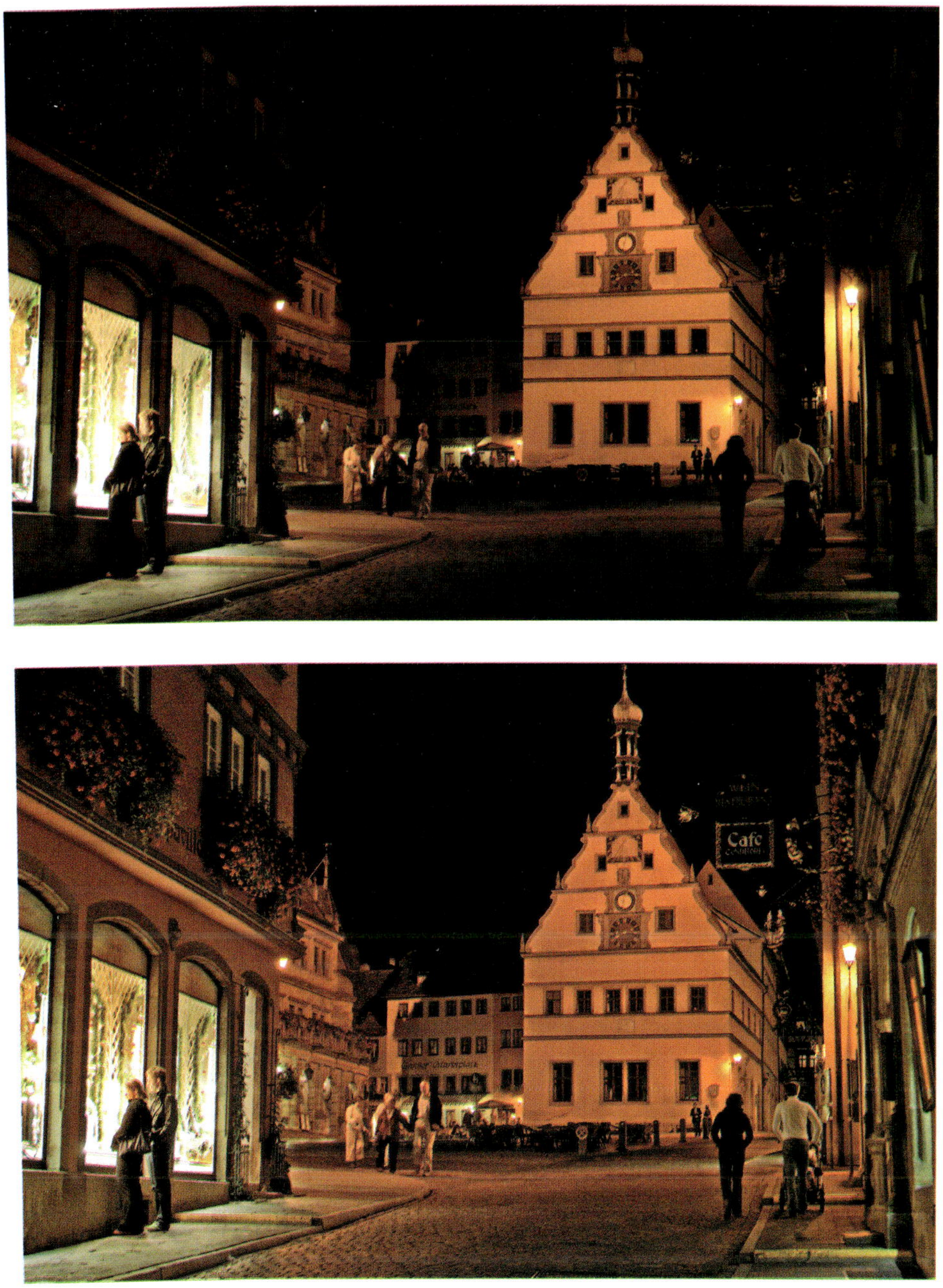

Figure 7.7 Some high-contrast images benefit from the application of both the Darken Highlights and Lighten Shadows tools; you can also boost the midtone contrast. The exact amount of each adjustment depends on the effects you want to achieve for creative reasons.

Whether you decide to brighten shadows or darken highlights (or both) in order to extract more detail, the process can result in an overall reduction in image contrast. That's why Adobe provides the Midtone Contrast slider. This tool allows you to apply compensation by adjusting contrast for just the middle-tone values within the image, leaving the shadow and highlight areas you've already adjusted relatively unchanged (Figure 7.8). No specific level of contrast is ideal for every image, but as a rule of thumb, try increasing the value by about 10%. Some images might benefit from a decrease in midtone contrast; a –10% level is a good starting point while experimenting.

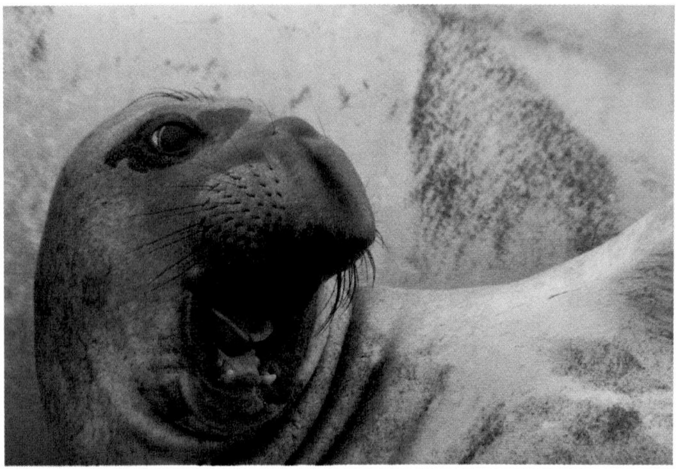

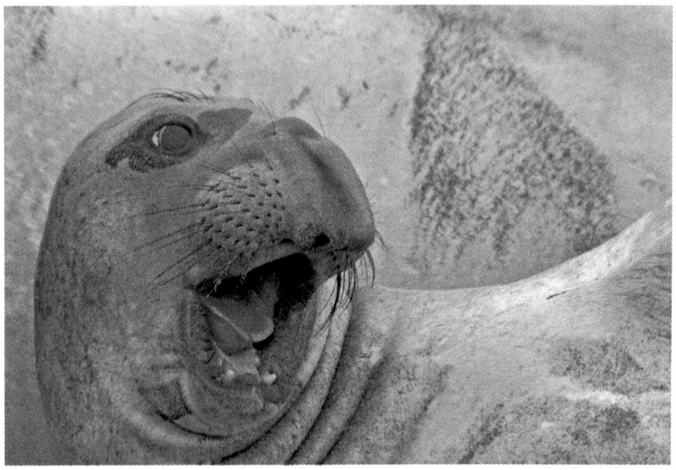

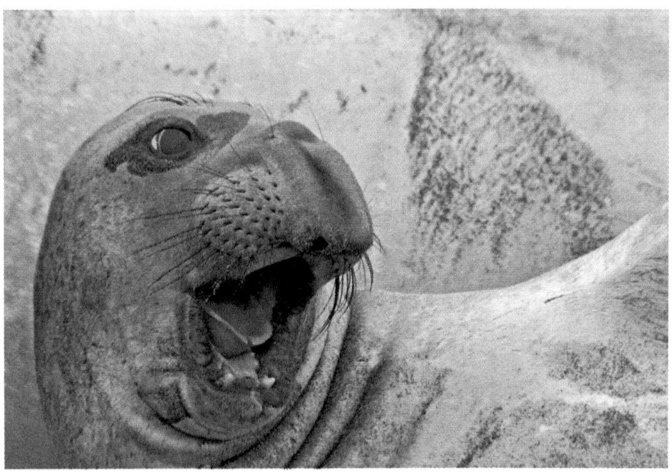

Figure 7.8 The Midtone Contrast slider allows you to compensate for the general loss of contrast that typically occurs with a Shadows/Highlights adjustment. In this series, we have lightened shadow detail (center) and then modified midtone contrast (right) for a more natural effect.

Note too that in Quick Fix, Elements 5 offers a nearly identical tool with the same three sliders: Lighten Shadows, Darken Highlights, and Midtone Contrast. This tool is available under the Lighting submenu in the General Fixes dialog box (Figure 7.9). However, in Quick Fix you can't work on a separate layer; consequently, we recommend working in the Full Edit section of Elements 5 for shadow/highlight detail recovery. Note too that in Quick Fix, this tool's slider scales do not show percentages to denote the precise amount of adjustment that you have made with each of the three controls. That omission is not a real problem, but it does make it difficult to apply the same level of adjustment to a series of similar images made at the same time and requiring the same amount of correction.

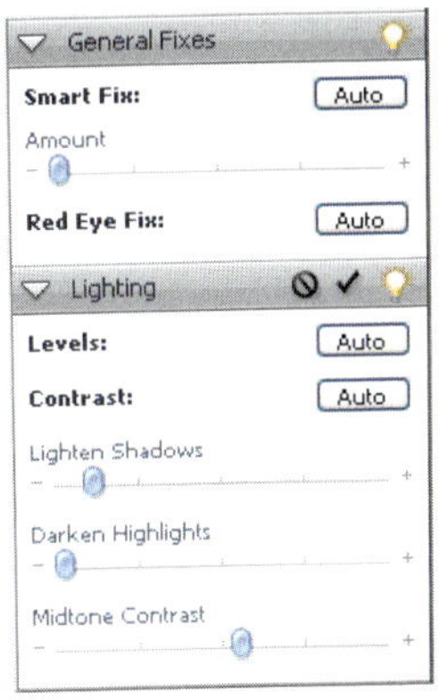

Figure 7.9 The Midtone Contrast slider in the Lighting submenu in Quick Fix allows you to compensate for the general loss of contrast that typically occurs with a Lighten Shadows or a Darken Highlights adjustment.

Adjust Color Curves

Adjust Color Curves is a new feature in Elements 5. To access this tool, select Enhance > Adjust Color >Adjust Color Curves. When you first open Adjust Color Curves, you'll note that it includes six thumbnails of your image, each designating a different adjustment option. Five are for adjusting tonal values, and one is for producing a special effect. The following settings are available:

- Increase Midtones (in other words, increase midtone brightness)
- Lighten Shadows
- Backlight (in other words, lighten areas that are dark in a backlit photo)
- Increase Contrast (specifically, for midtones)
- Darken Highlights
- Solarize

Note: Despite the name, Adjust Color Curves is primarily a tonal adjustment, not a color adjustment tool. We're not sure why the term *color* is included in its name or why it appears in the Adjust Color menu.

The final option is primarily intended for a special effect. Although it does adjust tones and contrast, it replicates the solarized effect that was possible when making prints in a photography darkroom. When you first open Adjust Color Curves, the Increase Midtones option is already active, as indicated by the border around the first thumbnail. Elements has applied a predefined level of adjustment (brightening midtones). If that provides the effect you want, click OK. Elements will apply the correction to your image file, and the dialog box will then close. Naturally, you can click any of the other thumbnails instead to make another type of correction, again at a predefined level of adjustment.

Note: We recommend using Adjust Color Curves with layers. Before opening this tool, create a new layer by dragging the Background image layer onto the Create A New Layer button on the Layers palette.

Select the Advanced Options by clicking the triangle next to this item. Four slider scales appear: Adjust Highlights (toward darker or brighter), Midtone Brightness (lighter or darker), Midtone Contrast (greater or lower), and Adjust Shadows (lighter or darker), as shown in Figure 7.10. The slider is initially located in the center of each scale, and you can move it to the left or to the right of center to modify the level of adjustment for any of the four parameters. As you make changes, the "curve" also changes to reflect the modifications to your image, but you have no actual control over the curve. In other words, you cannot drag the curve to modify tonal values. Frankly, the curve may be of some value to those who have developed great expertise in Photoshop and are skilled at curve interpretation, as discussed in Tim's book, *Photoshop CS2 Workflow* (Sybex, 2005). However, this kind of expertise takes a lot of time and practice, and the Adjust Color Curves tool is an excellent starting point toward understanding the concepts for this method or form of image adjustments.

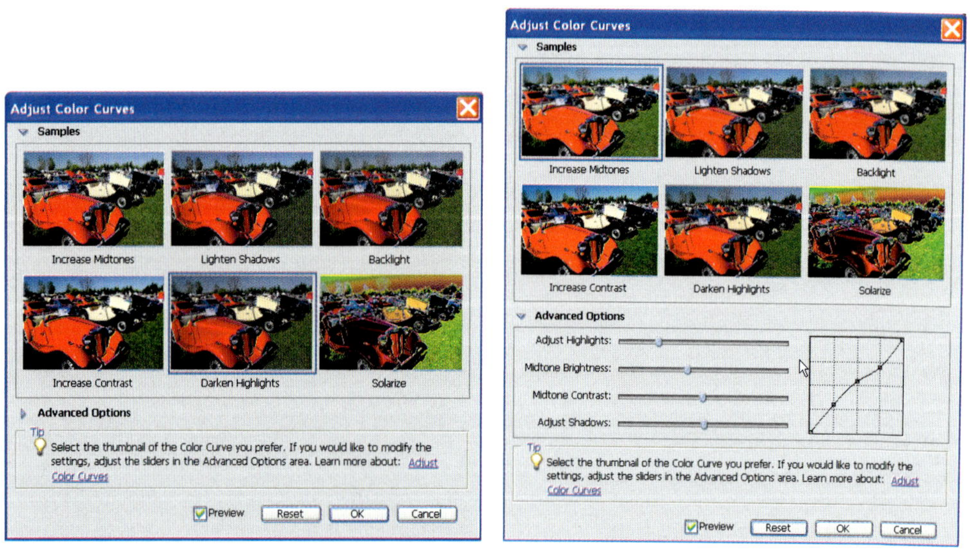

Figure 7.10 The Adjust Color Curves tool provides automated "fixes" with five preset adjustments as well as an option to solarize, which is a special effect. Select the Advanced Options, however, and you get much greater versatility, with extensive user control over the level of adjustment for four distinct parameters.

Using the Advanced Options is really quite intuitive because any change you make is reflected in your image when you stop moving the slider. That "update" does take a split second for completion; changes do not occur while your cursor is on the slider control. We recommend making changes in small increments and checking the results to see whether you are satisfied. Keep making small changes until your image reflects the desired effect.

As you have probably realized, some of these options are similar to the Shadows/Highlights tool or the options available under Lighting in QuickFix. But there is a significant difference in Adjust Color Curves that can be a real benefit: the option of moving the slider in either direction.

That ability provides greater versatility because you can both lighten and darken highlight areas and shadow areas (Figure 7.11). These two images exhibit exaggerated levels of adjustment, of course, and illustrate the entirely different effects that are possible with Adjust Color Curves. By comparison, when using the other Shadows/Highlights tools, you can only darken highlight areas and lighten shadow areas. The same applies to Midtone Contrast. In Adjust Color Curves, you can set either a higher level or a lower level of contrast. In the other utilities, only an *increase* in midtone contrast is possible. And as a bonus, Adjust Color Curves provides an entirely new tool that allows you to adjust only midtone brightness.

Granted, you can achieve some of the same effects by using Levels as discussed in Chapter 5, "Tone and Color." For example, when using Levels you can adjust the midtone value in either direction; that's similar to adjusting the central slider in Levels to lighten or darken midtones. In fact, we recommend applying Levels first; that's why we discussed that tool earlier in this book. Just like Shadows/Highlights, we recommend you consider Adjust Color Curves as a fine-tuning tool and not as a primary tool for tonal adjustment. Start by adjusting highlights, shadows, or midtones—only to the extent actually required, of course—and conclude by fine-tuning midtone contrast to maintain a snappy, pleasing effect but without excessive contrast.

Note: For a quick comparison between the original image and the adjusted image, deselect the Preview checkbox at the bottom of the Adjust Color Curves dialog box and then select the checkbox to toggle the preview on again.

Selective Adjustments

Up to this point, the tools in this chapter have allowed you to target adjustments to a particular area of the image, but that targeting has been based on tonal values for the pixels, not their "geographic" location within the image. Now let's consider two distinct methods of fine-tuning tonality (darkness or lightness) of specific areas of the image, regardless of their tonal values.

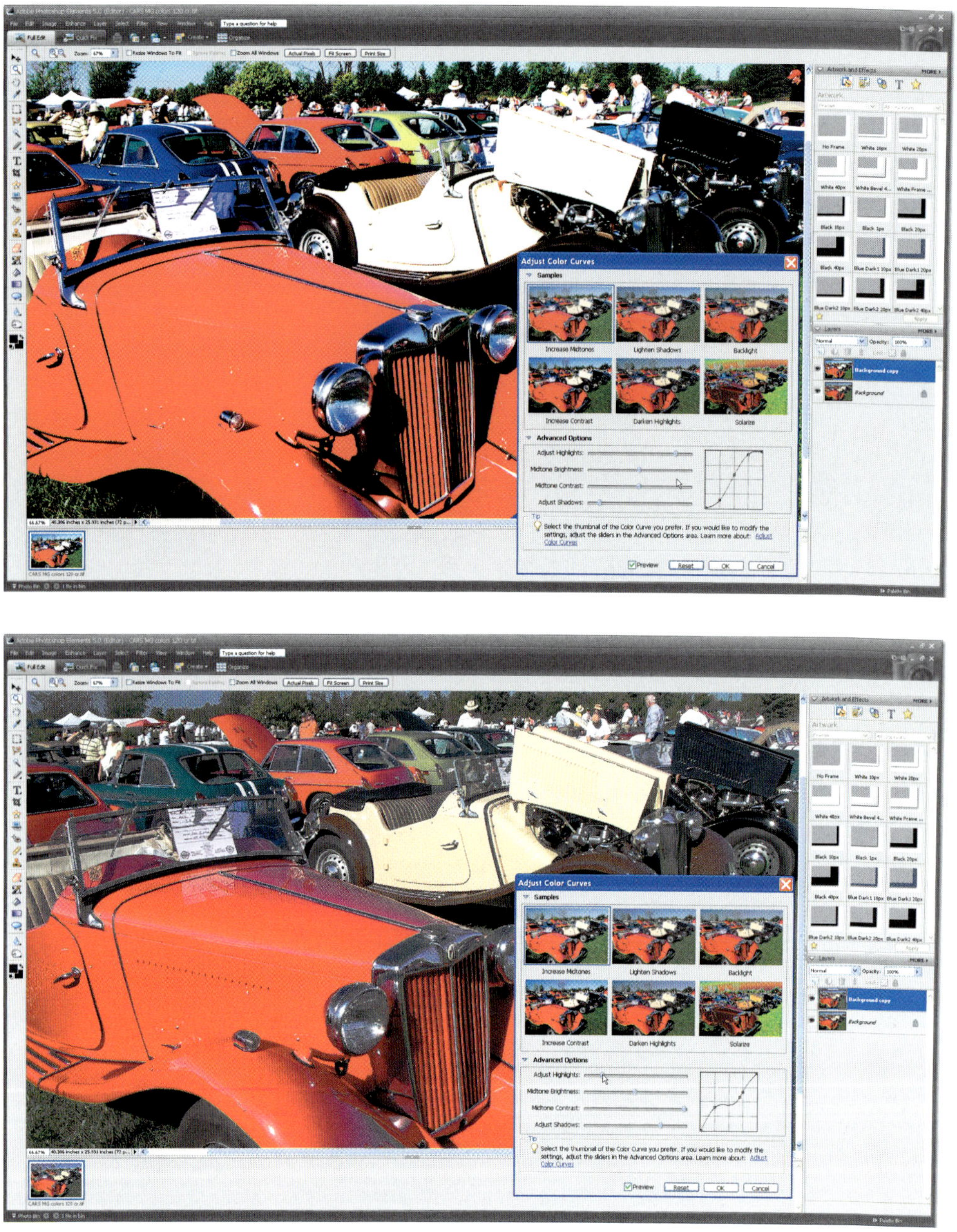

Figure 7.11 Adjust Color Curves provides greater versatility than Shadows/Highlights by providing one extra tool, Midtone Brightness, which can be set for a higher or lower level. Adjust Color Curves also provides the capability to adjust highlights, shadows, and midtone contrast in either direction—toward lightening *and* darkening, as illustrated in an exaggerated manner in these images.

To understand why you might want to do so, consider this example. Let's say you made a portrait photo on a sunny day of two friends wearing baseball caps, framed against a colorful mural on a building in the background. Because the bills of their caps cast a shadow over their faces, those important areas are quite dark. In addition, a small portion of extremely bright sky is included in the image, which is distracting. You decide to improve the photo by lightening their faces and darkening the small section of sky, without affecting other highlight or shadow areas in the image. You can achieve this with a targeted tonality adjustment.

Elements provides a Dodge tool and a Burn tool, covered later in this chapter, that you can use for lightening or darkening a specific area. This dodging and burning concept was borrowed from the wet darkroom. When using an enlarger in a darkroom, you can use various instruments to block light from specific areas of an image. Blocking light to small areas during exposure is referred to as *dodging*, and it results in the blocked areas being lighter in a print than they otherwise would have been. *Burning* is the opposite: blocking light from *most* of the image in order to concentrate light on a specific part. Consequently, that part of the print would be darker.

We'll discuss how to use the Dodge and Burn tools later in this chapter, but first we'll walk you through a more sophisticated method for dodging and burning: painting with light. You can use this technique for the same purpose: to lighten a specific area or to darken a specific area. However, the "painting with light" technique provides greater flexibility and a technical benefit—it does not require you to apply the effect directly to an image layer.

Setting Up

As you know by now, any adjustment you apply to an image should be done on a *separate* layer. Hence, the first step here is to create a new layer to paint on so you can apply selective lightening and darkening to the image. However, you want the layer you create to have special properties. Therefore, Alt/Option+click the Create A New Layer button in the Layers palette to open the New Layer dialog box so you can adjust the settings for the layer as it is created.

To help stay organized, we recommend giving the layer a name such as *Dodge & Burn* (although you will not actually be using the Dodge or the Burn tool for this technique). However, you can enter any name that will help you remember why this layer was added.

The most important setting here, and the key to the whole technique, is the Mode setting (Figure 7.12). This sets the blending mode for this layer, which affects how the pixels on this layer will interact with underlying pixels to produce the final effect. We recommend selecting the Overlay option from the Mode drop-down list, because it results in a relatively strong effect and slightly increases contrast. However, you could also use Soft Light if you prefer, which produces a more subtle effect. If you want to change your mind later or experiment with the Mode options, you can find the same list of options at the top of the Layers palette. Just be sure to have the correct layer active (or selected) when changing layer modes.

After you set the blending mode, a checkbox below Mode appears. We recommend selecting this box so the layer will be filled with 50% gray, which is the neutral color for the Overlay and Soft Light blending modes. In other words, with these particular blending mode settings, filling the layer with 50% gray won't cause any change in the image, but will make it easier to see where you've applied dodging and burning.

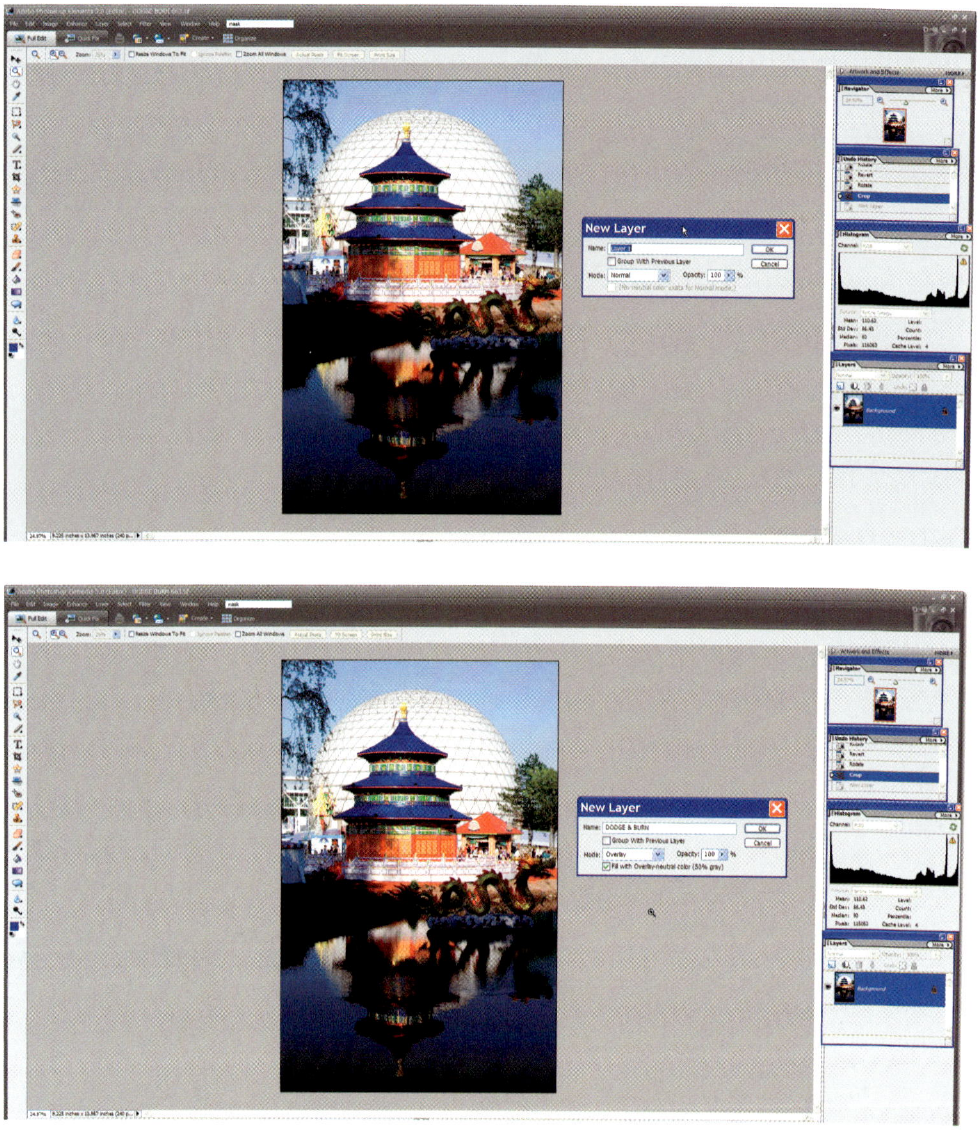

Figure 7.12 Alt/Option+click the Create A New Layer button to open the New Layer dialog box. After establishing the appropriate settings for dodging and burning, you can click OK to create the layer.

Click the OK button in the New Layer dialog box, and the layer will be created based on the settings you've established.

Now you're ready to configure the Brush tool, which will be used to paint with light, applying selective lightening and darkening to the image. Start by selecting the Brush tool from the Tools palette or by pressing the B on your keyboard. Then press D to set the colors on the color boxes (the bottom item in the Tools palette) to their default values of black foreground and white background (Figure 7.13). You can also click the small icon below the bottom-left corner of the color boxes to set these defaults. Note that you can switch the foreground and background colors by pressing X as you're working, allowing you to easily switch between black and white (or alternatively, click the small bending arrow icon in the upper-right corner of the color boxes).

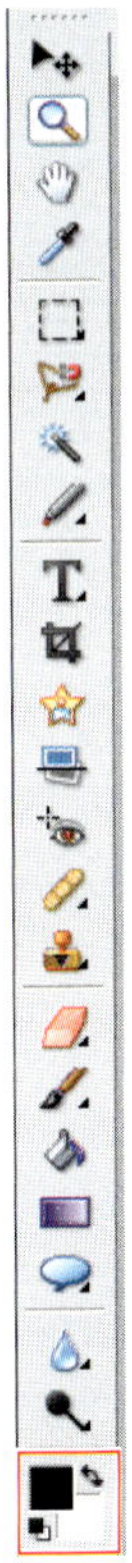

Figure 7.13 Pressing D resets the colors to their defaults of black and white.

On the Options bar, select a Soft Round brush. Alternatively, you can hold Ctrl/⌘ and press the left square bracket key ([) to reduce hardness completely. The Mode on the Options bar should be set to Normal, because you want the brush itself to behave normally and changes to be applied only by the layer itself.

> **Note:** It is important that the Brush be set to Normal blending mode and the layer you're painting on be set to Overlay or Soft Light.

The Brush's Opacity option should be set to between 10% and 20%. You can set this value quickly by using keyboard shortcuts: press 1 for 10%, 2 for 20%, and so on. If you want to set the value to something in between, such as 15%, just press 1 and 5 in relatively rapid succession. You'll likely want to readjust the Opacity setting, which controls the strength of the dodging and burning, as you're working on the image (Figure 7.14).

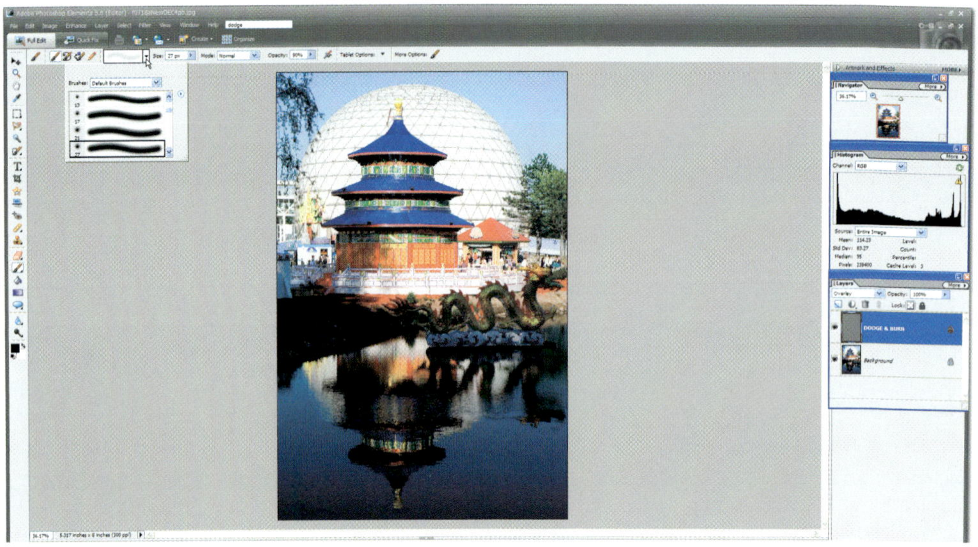

Figure 7.14 On the Options bar, select a soft-edged brush with a reduced Opacity setting for dodging and burning.

Note: If you're using a tablet, you can also use pen pressure of the stylus to determine the Opacity setting when dodging and burning with this method.

Painting with Light

With your new layer and the Brush tool properly configured, you're ready to start dodging and burning. Paint with black to darken (burn) portions of your image, and switch to white when you want to lighten (dodge) other areas. Because you will be painting at a reduced opacity, the result will be relatively modest. If necessary, you can paint over areas multiple times to build up an effect. However, the best effect is usually subtle. When someone looks at the final image, they shouldn't get the impression that you were using dodging and burning techniques. However, when you turn off the visibility of the Dodge & Burn layer that you created, you'll see a difference between the images (Figure 7.15).

It is important to understand the behavior of the Brush tool when working at a reduced opacity for this "painting with light" technique for dodging and burning. As long as you hold down the mouse button, the effect will not accumulate no matter how many times the mouse passes over a particular area. However, if you release the mouse and start painting again, the effect will be uneven if you partially overlap areas you've previously painted. Therefore, it is important that you click and hold the mouse button while painting until you've covered the entire area you want to adjust. Then release the mouse and start painting again in additional areas you'd like to change.

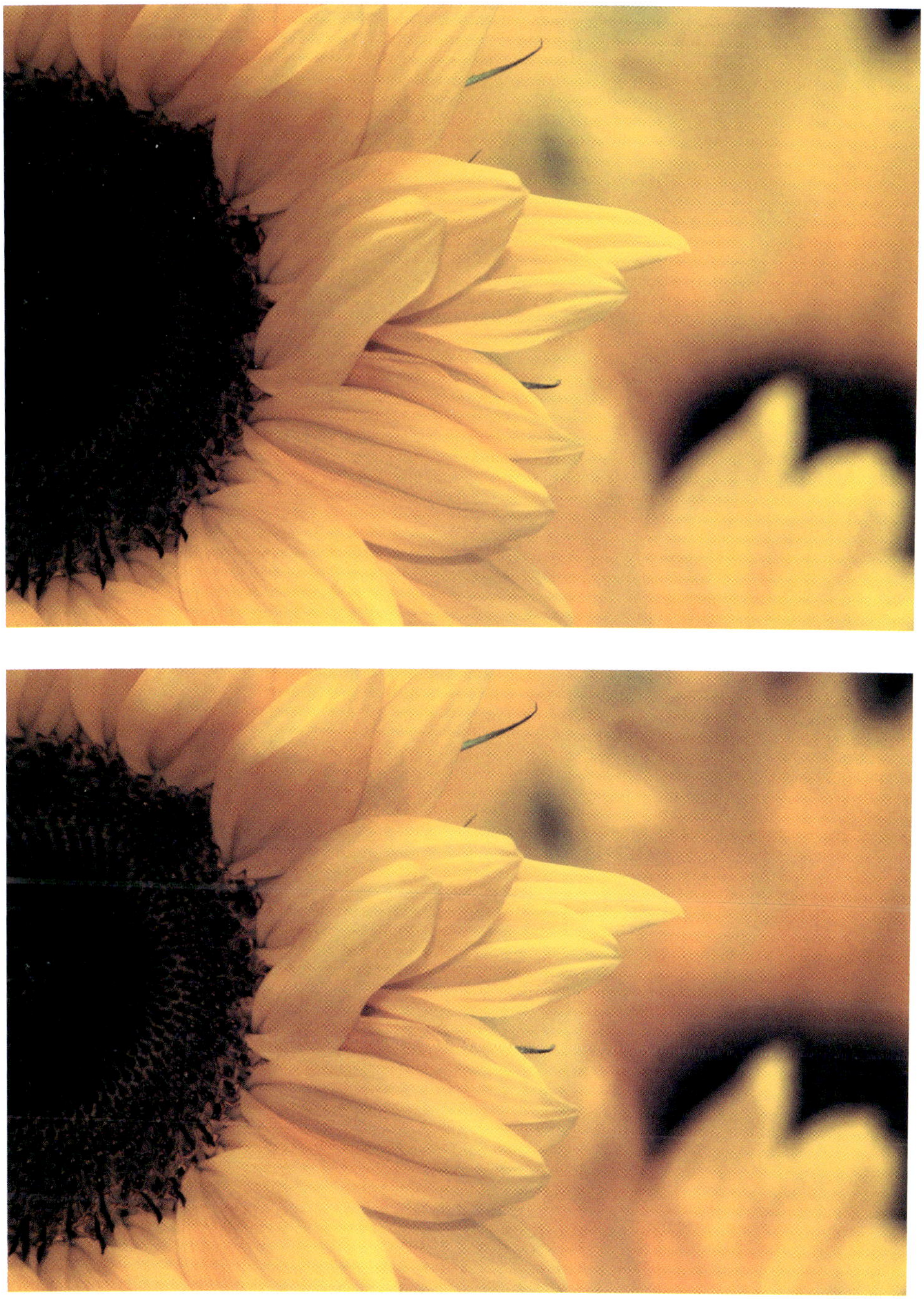

Figure 7.15 The best effect from dodging and burning is one that isn't an obvious modification but one that produces a more pleasing final result. Here the center of the sunflower has been lightened to show more detail, and various dodging and burning has been applied to the flower petals to increase contrast.

Dodging and burning is one of our favorite techniques in Elements because the "painting with light" technique can bring out details in various areas of the image or simply emphasize particular elements. So much of the image optimization process seems mathematical, including adjusting sliders and other controls to apply formulas to an image. This "painting with light" process of dodging and burning is different, allowing you to work directly on the image. As a result, it feels more artistic than other methods and enables you to take great control over tonal adjustments.

Dodge and Burn Tools

We'll now cover the options that Adobe provides specifically for selectively lightening or darkening an area: the Dodge and Burn tools. You can find them by right-clicking the Sponge tool in the Tools palette. Employing the most basic method, you could select the Dodge tool and drag it over areas that you want to lighten. Switch to the Burn tool and drag that over areas you want to darken. This simplistic technique will work, but we cannot recommend it because the effect will be applied directly to an image layer. In addition, it does not offer quite the flexibility of the alternative method presented in the previous section.

Instead, start by duplicating the image by right-clicking the Background layer and choosing Duplicate Layer. This will allow you to work on a copy instead of the original background layer. Name the duplicate layer **Dodge & Burn Tools** and start by practicing with lightening a dark area of an image. Select the Dodge tool, and check the controls that are available on the Options bar. Choose a soft-tipped brush and a suitable Size for the image area that you intend to lighten. From the Range option, select Midtones or Shadows depending on the tonality of the area that needs some lightening. (When dodging, you probably would not select Highlights, the final Range option.)

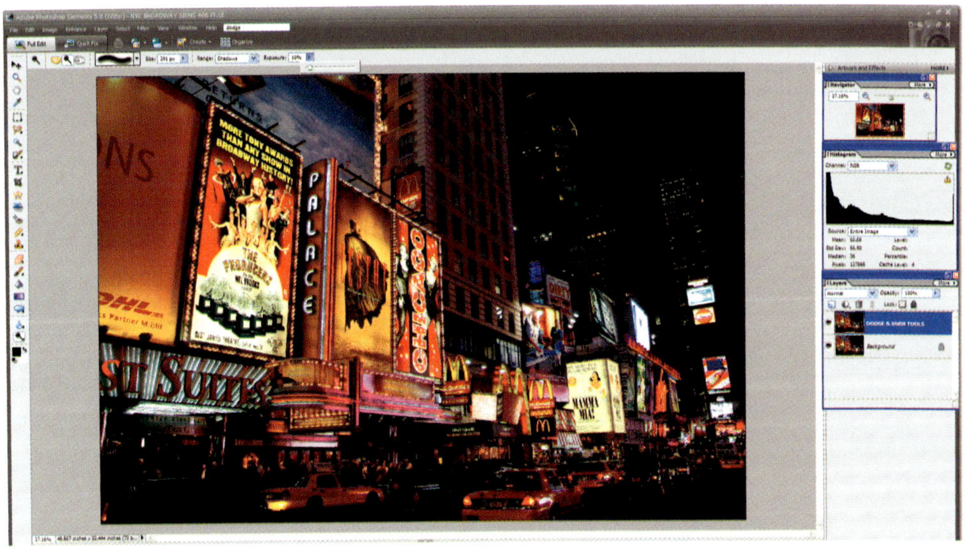

The default level for Exposure is 50% and produces an obvious lightening effect on dark shadow areas. We recommend setting this to a much lower level, as low as 20% or even 10%, for a particularly subtle effect. After you've finished setting these options, begin dragging the Dodge tool over the area that needs to be lightened. Drag several times over the same area until the lightening effect is adequate. You can undo the modification any time by choosing Edit > Undo or by pressing the undo shortcut, Ctrl/⌘+Z.

Now, experiment with the Burn tool on the same duplicate layer in order to darken an excessively bright area of your image (Figure 7.16). (If your practice image does not exhibit that problem, open a new image and duplicate the Background layer as explained earlier in this section.) You can use the Burn tool in the same manner as the Dodge tool, but you'll select Highlights or Midtones from the Range option. Then, drag the tool over the area that needs to be modified. Before doing so, reduce the Exposure level from the default 50% in order to produce moderate darkening; experiment with a 20% level. Remember, you can increase the effect of this tool by dragging it over the area several times.

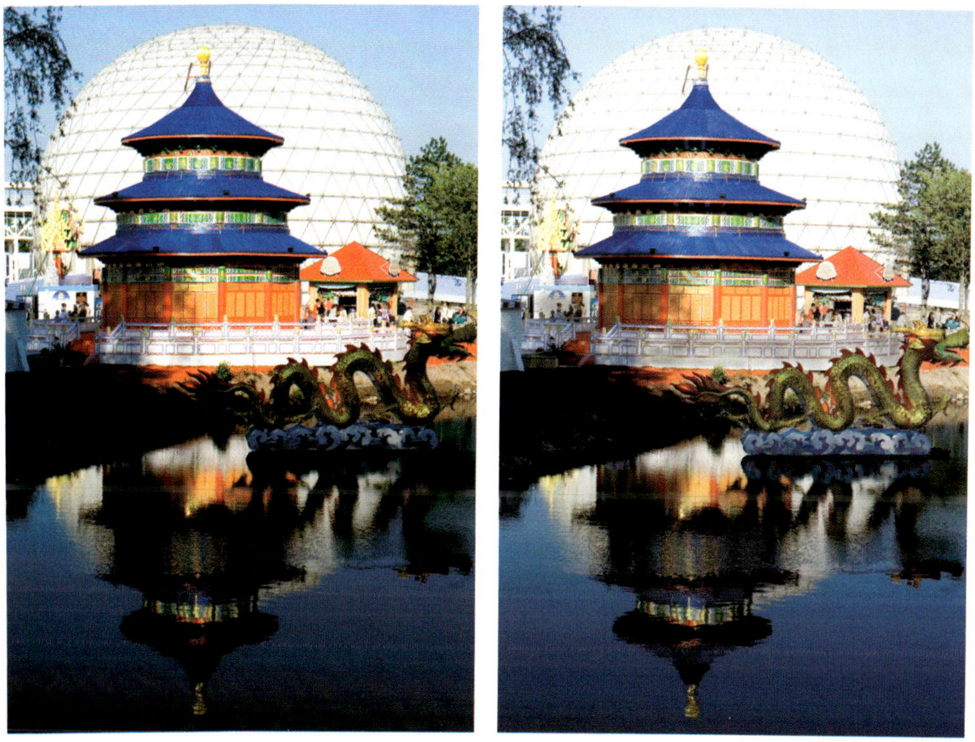

Figure 7.16 This image (left) is an ideal candidate for dodging and burning because it exhibits both dark shadow areas and some excessively bright highlight areas. Here (right) the dragon has been lightened, and the railing in the center of the photo has been darkened. Because the modifications are subtle, the image still looks natural.

Note: When you need to drag the Dodge or Burn tool over an area several times for a stronger lightening or darkening effect, release the mouse button occasionally instead of painting the area for a long time. By doing so, you will be able to undo incrementally—since the last time you released the mouse button—instead of undoing everything since you started the dodging or burning on an area.

Correcting Mistakes

Of course, now and then you may be less than satisfied after you complete extensive dodging and burning adjustments on an image. Fortunately, because you applied the changes on a separate layer, it is easy to fix mistakes even if it is too late to simply undo one or more steps.

You have two basic ways to correct significant mistakes. The easiest is to select the Eraser tool (from the Tools palette) and a soft-edged brush and then erase the areas you don't like (Figure 7.17). Because you're working on a separate layer, all that you will erase are the pixels you painted onto your Dodge & Burn layer.

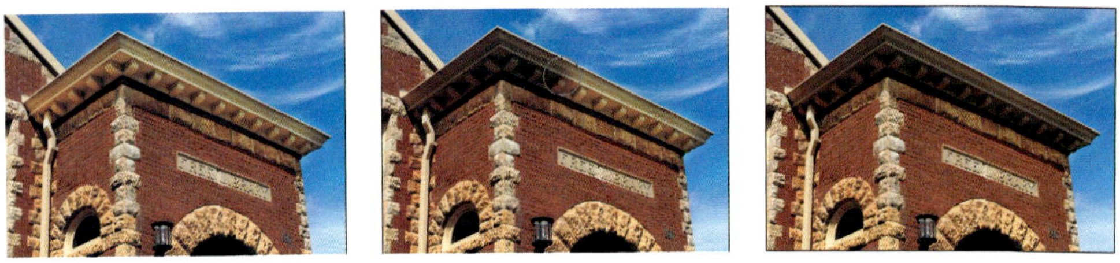

Figure 7.17 You can use the Eraser tool on the Dodge & Burn layer to quickly erase mistakes you made when painting on that layer. For example, here the roof line was overlightened (left), and the Eraser tool is being used (middle) to remove that effect from the Dodge & Burn layer (right).

Using the Eraser works well, but the disadvantage is that the middle gray pixels that fill the layer will also be erased. This isn't a major problem, but it does make it more difficult to see where you've painted at a reduced opacity if you look at the layer by itself. The checkerboard pattern representing transparent pixels left after erasing doesn't provide good contrast for viewing the partially transparent pixels painted for the dodging and burning effect (Figure 7.18).

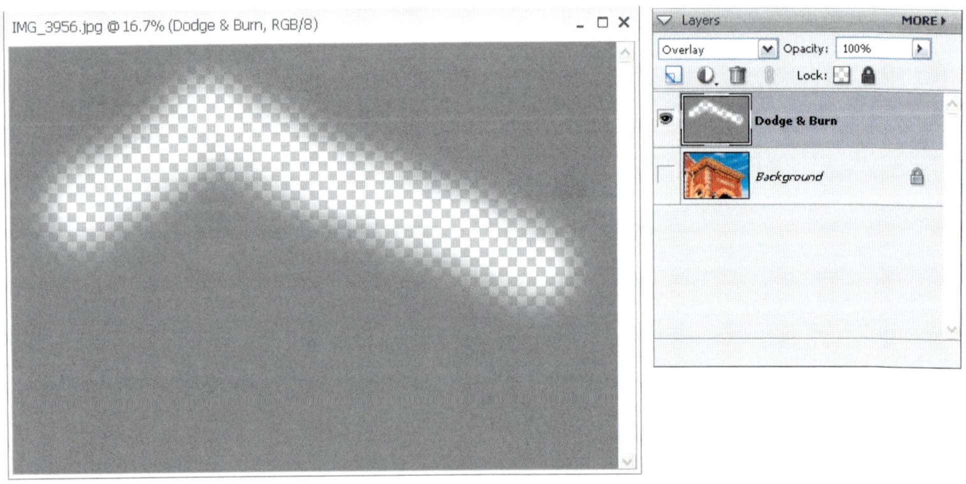

Figure 7.18 When you erase on the Dodge & Burn layer, you'll leave transparent pixels behind (shown as a checkerboard pattern). These transparent pixels, much like 50% gray pixels, won't have any effect on the underlying image.

To avoid this problem, though with a slightly more complicated process, you can instead paint with 50% gray to remove the effect of any dodging and burning in particular areas of your image. To start, click the foreground color from the Tools palette to access the Color Picker. Set the Hue (labeled H) and Saturation (labeled S) to 0, and set the Brightness to 50. Click OK; then change the Opacity for the Brush tool on the Options bar to 100%, and paint over the image in areas where you want to remove the dodging and burning effect. When you're finished, you can reset the colors to the defaults and adjust the Opacity as desired to continue dodging and burning in other areas of your image.

Fine-Tuned Tonality

By utilizing tools that allow you to exercise greater control over tonal adjustments, you can produce a result that is much closer to your original vision. This represents just one more step in the workflow toward a perfect final image. With tonal adjustments perfected for the overall image, you're ready to move on to more-detailed color adjustments.

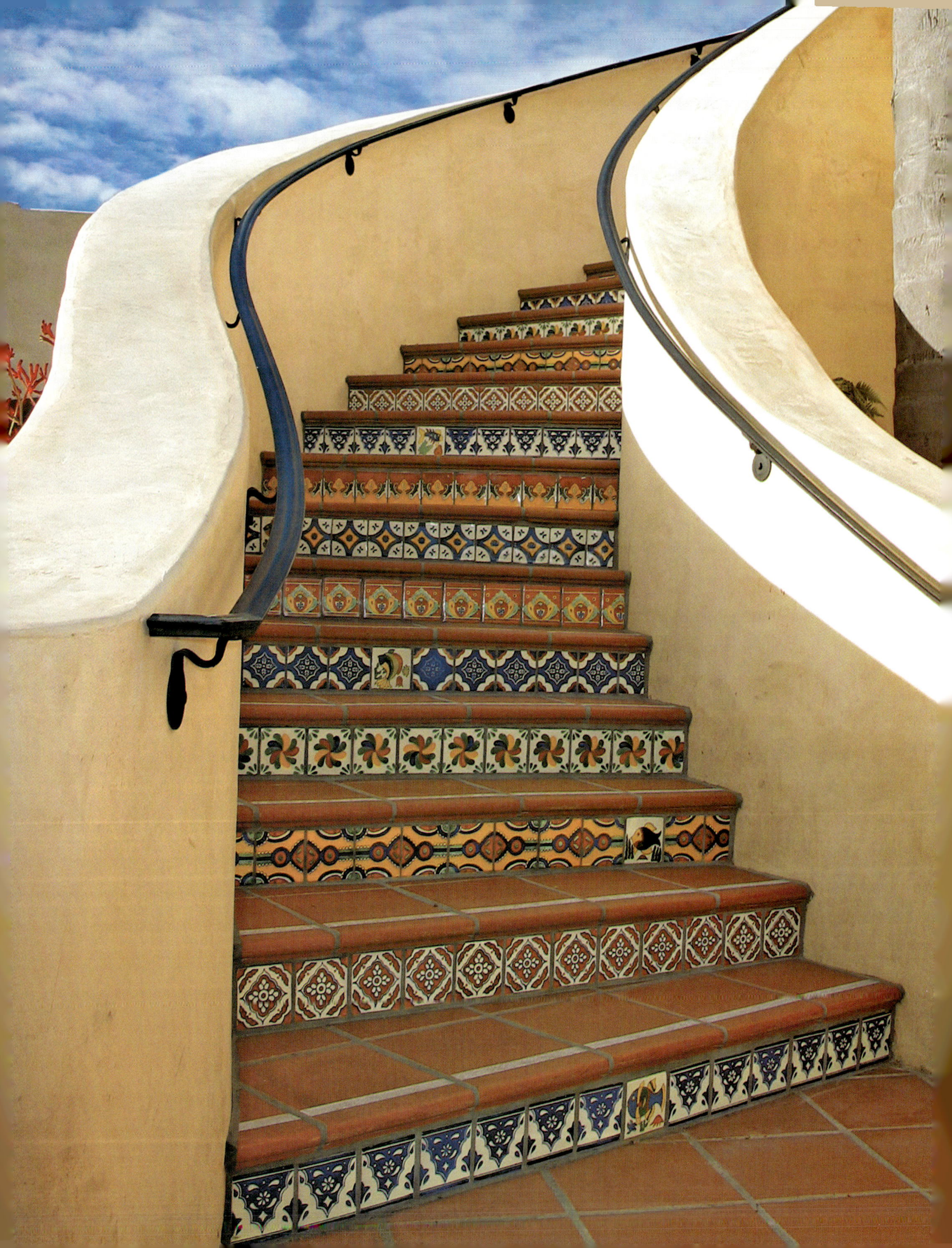

Advanced Color Adjustments

Getting the color just right in an image is a major goal for photographers. For many, it borders on being an obsession. But when it comes to getting the best results in a photographic image, a little obsession can be useful. Taking the color in your images to the next level requires a collection of techniques that allow you to better control the colors in a relatively targeted way. In this chapter you'll look at those techniques by using the tools available in Elements 5.

8

Chapter Contents

Hue/Saturation
Color Casts
Targeted Color Painting
Targeted Saturation Painting

Hue/Saturation

In Chapter 5, "Tone and Color," we made an overall saturation adjustment by using a Hue/Saturation adjustment layer and using the Master (default) option in the Edit drop-down list available with this tool. However, Hue/Saturation includes considerably more power than that basic adjustment. In fact, it allows you to target specific color ranges within your image to apply fine-tuning to various areas as needed (Figure 8.1). As you're becoming more detailed in your workflow process, you can put Hue/Saturation to greater use to fine-tune various colors.

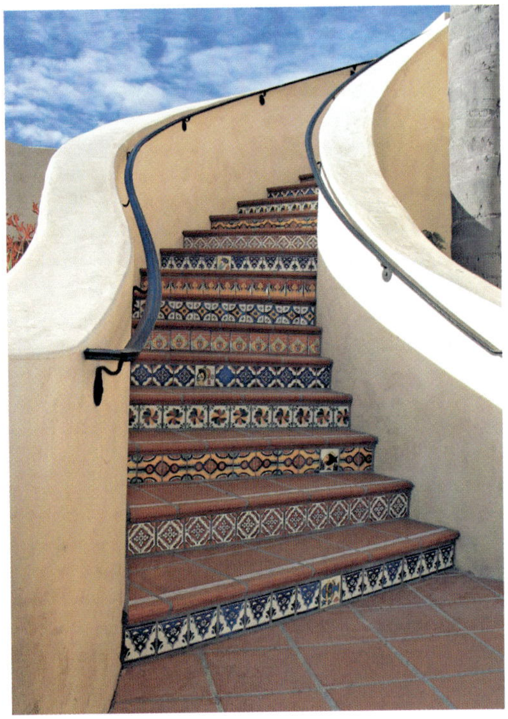

Figure 8.1 When color is critical to the story of a photo, being able to fine-tune the color to perfection is critical. Advanced color adjustments provide this control over the colors in your photos. (Photo by Alice Cahill, www.alicecahill.com)

Using Preset Color Ranges

The most basic way to target a specific range of colors with the Hue/Saturation adjustment is to select a color option from the Edit drop-down list at the top of the Hue/Saturation dialog box (Figure 8.2). Doing so will limit the adjustments you make with the Hue, Saturation, and Lightness sliders to affect only the color range that you select: Reds, Yellows, Greens, Cyans, Blues, or Magentas. By using the Master option, you can make individual adjustments for each of the available color ranges in addition to an overall change that affects all colors in the image.

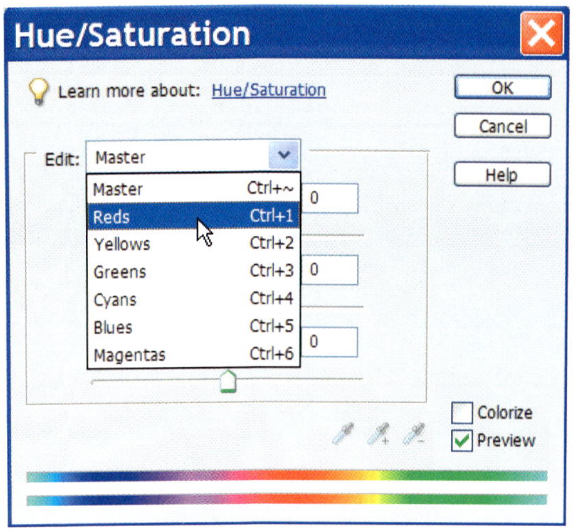

Figure 8.2 You can choose an item from the Edit list in Hue/Saturation to adjust a specific preset range of colors in the image.

For example, if an image exhibits a pleasing color balance but a magenta color influence is still causing a problem (Figure 8.3), you can select Magentas from the Edit drop-down; then, simply reduce the saturation in that color only. In the image shown in Figure 8.3, the saturation adjustment was –44. That reduction brought the magenta areas of the image toward neutral. A 100% reduction in magenta saturation would have turned any magenta area to a pure gray. You aren't limited, however, to just reducing saturation for a specific color to remove its influence. You can make any adjustment—minus or plus—within Hue/Saturation and have it targeted to a specific range of colors.

Note: Be sure to check other areas of your image for possible unwanted side effects whenever you are targeting a specific color range for adjustment.

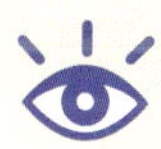

The only problem with this approach is that Adobe's idea of which colors should be included within a given color range might not necessarily match your definition of that range or your goals for the image. Fortunately, you can customize any range of colors to produce exactly the effect you want.

Customizing Ranges

The horizontal color gradient bars at the bottom of the Hue/Saturation dialog box are linear representations of a color wheel. The top gradient represents the range of possible "before" values for the colors in your image, and the bottom one represents the "after" values. When you select a color range from the Edit drop-down list, markers appear between the gradients to indicate the colors in the image that will be affected by any adjustment you make (Figure 8.4).

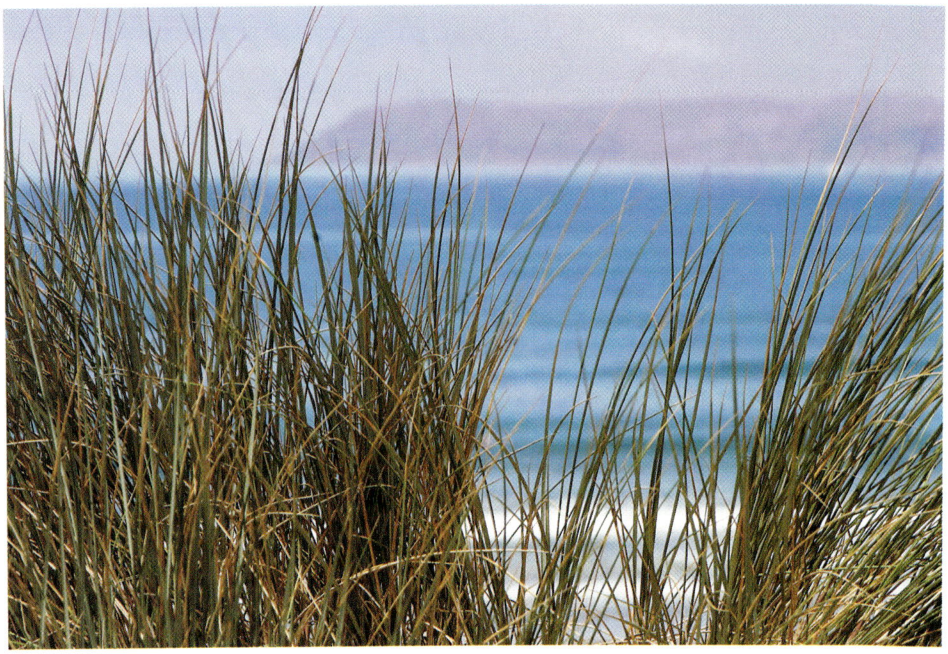

Before

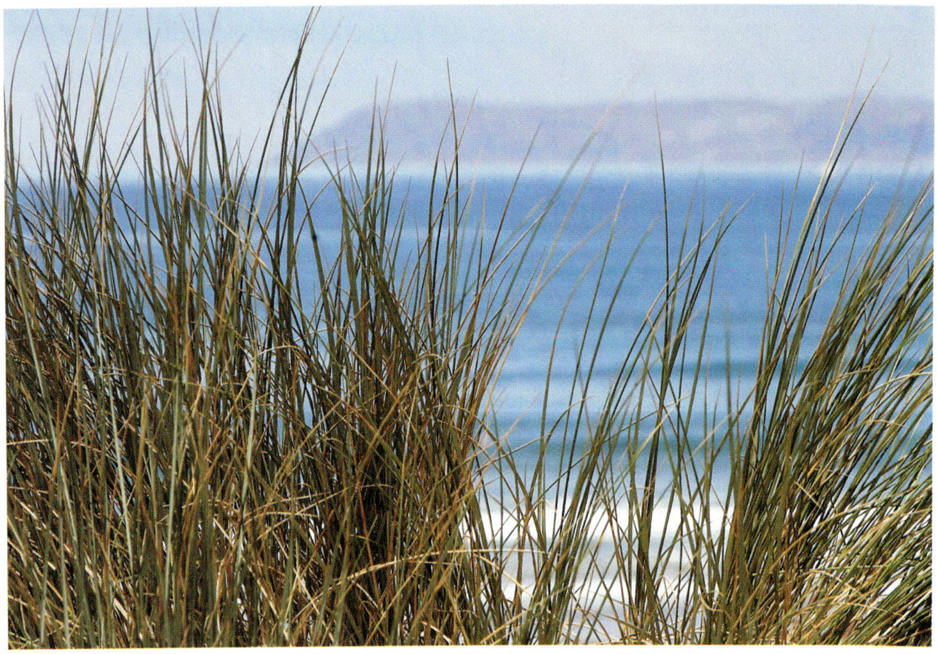

After

Figure 8.3 When an image has an otherwise good color balance but a single problem color, such as magenta in this image, a targeted saturation adjustment provides a solution.

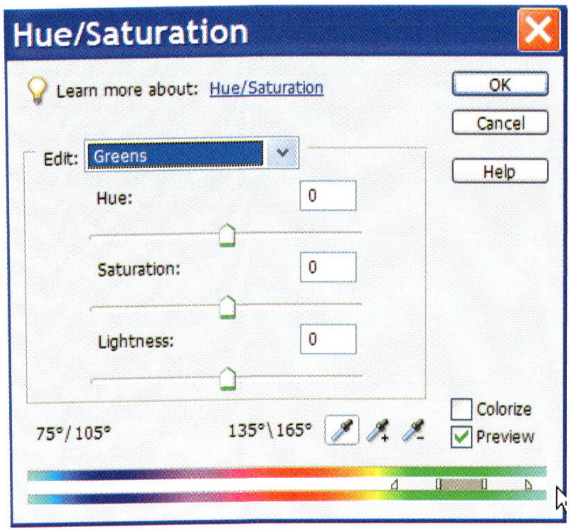

Figure 8.4 When you select a range of colors from the Edit drop-down list in Hue/Saturation, that range is indicated by markers between the color gradients at the bottom of the dialog box.

The vertical bars indicate the range of colors to be adjusted. Colors falling between these bars will be completely affected by any adjustments you make. The trapezoid sliders represent the blending of the adjustment. The range of colors between the bar and the trapezoid will have an effect that tapers off, with a stronger adjustment for colors near the bar and a diminishing adjustment near the trapezoid. The distance between the bar and the trapezoid determines how gradual (or abrupt) the transition between affected and unaffected colors will be.

Note: When you change the range of colors for one of the preset ranges, the name may change automatically based on the new range you have defined.

You can change the color range to be adjusted by simply dragging any of the vertical bars or trapezoids to define a new range. However, identifying an appropriate range of colors just by looking at the color gradient can be a challenge. Instead, try starting with an exaggerated adjustment so it will be easier to see the range of colors you've defined within the image. We typically reduce the saturation completely so the range is obvious within the image, but you could also increase saturation completely or shift the hue, depending on what will help that range stand out in your image (Figure 8.5).

When you start to adjust the range of colors, keep the trapezoids pulled in close to the vertical bars in order to see an abrupt difference between included and excluded colors. The vertical bars and trapezoids don't move together, so you may need to shift a trapezoid whenever you move the corresponding bar. After you have positioned both vertical bars so they define the basic color range in the image as accurately as possible, move the trapezoids away from the bars as needed to produce a transition for the adjustment you'll apply. The amount of transition required will depend on how defined the color separation is in your image and on how gradually you want your adjustment to fade away at the edge of the color areas to be affected.

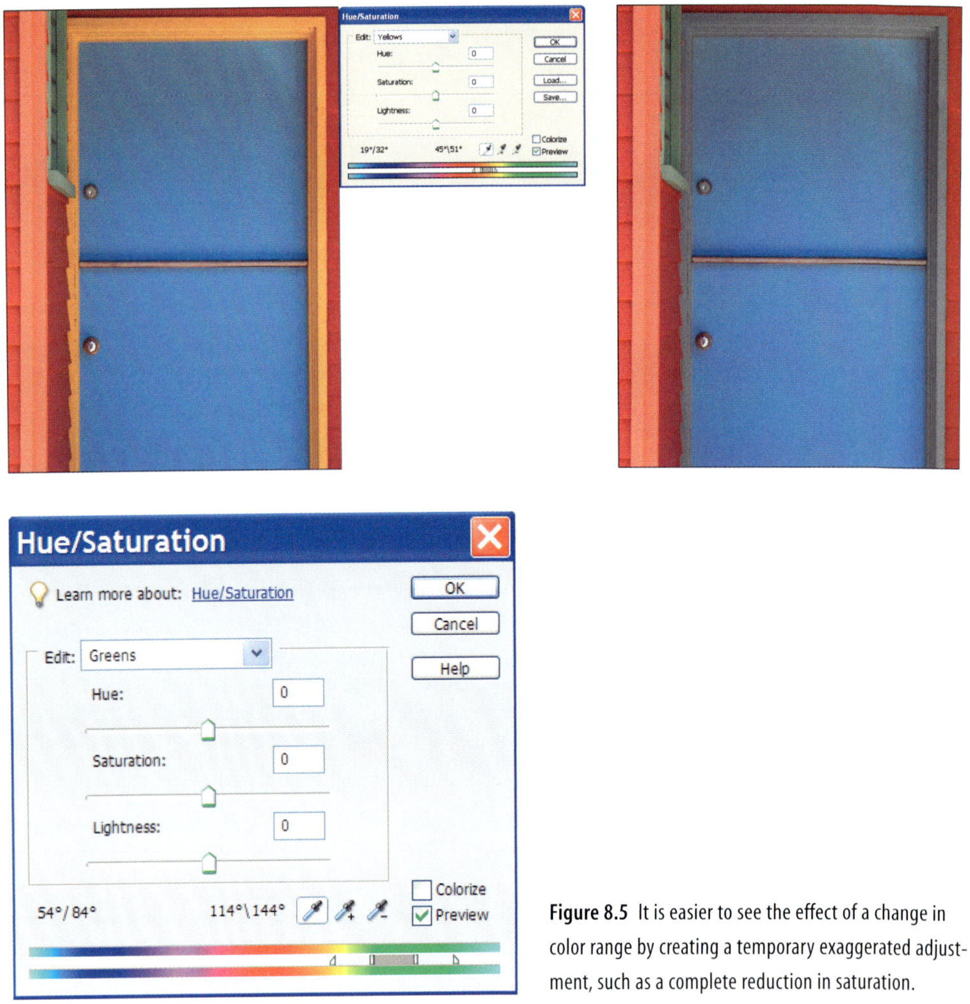

Figure 8.5 It is easier to see the effect of a change in color range by creating a temporary exaggerated adjustment, such as a complete reduction in saturation.

Eyedroppers for Color Range

In addition to the method discussed here, you can also use the eyedroppers in the Hue/Saturation dialog box to define the range of colors you want to adjust. After you select one of the colors from the Edit drop-down list, the eyedroppers become available, with the Eyedropper tool selected by default. Simply click an area of the image that contains the color you want to adjust, and that value becomes the center of the range of colors to be affected.

You can then switch to the Add To Sample eyedropper and click additional colors that you want included in the range. This expands the range of colors being adjusted. Keep in mind that the result will be a single contiguous range of colors. For example, if you start by clicking a blue value and then click a red value, the final range of colors will span from the blues through the magentas and all the way to the reds.

Eyedroppers for Color Range *Continued*

If you have defined a range of colors that is too broad, simply select the Subtract From Sample eyedropper and click the color values you want to exclude from the range. Again, you cannot exclude a color from the middle of a range, so anything you subtract will define a boundary of the contiguous range of colors you'll be affecting.

Although this method can be helpful at times, it often leaves you clicking around the image to find the right pixel to define the appropriate range of colors. We therefore recommend that if you use this method to start defining the range of colors you want to adjust, you should use the direct adjustment method we've discussed in this section to fine-tune the result.

After you've perfectly defined the range of colors, you can undo any exaggerated adjustment (such as a complete desaturation) that you made to help define the range and then make the actual adjustment you want to apply to that range. In Chapter 5 we discussed using only Saturation adjustments for an image. However, when you have targeted a specific range of colors within an image, you are not restricted to adjusting only the saturation in order to create or maintain a realistic-looking photo. You can use the Hue slider to adjust the basic color of the specific range you're adjusting, and you may even want to use the Lightness slider (which adds white or black to the color you're adjusting) to modify the tonality of that range. By using all three sliders, you can fine-tune a specific range of colors to produce the desired results.

Defining Inverse Ranges

At times you may find yourself wanting to adjust the opposite of a given preset range of colors in your image. For example, you may want to boost everything except the shades of blue and cyan found in the sky, so you can improve the vibrancy of colors in a landscape without producing an artificial-looking sky.

To create this range of colors, you essentially need to wrap one vertical bar and trapezoid slider around to the opposite end of the color gradient so you can produce a larger range of colors. To do so, drag the vertical bar off the end of the gradient; it will then show up at the opposite end (Figure 8.6). Drag the vertical bar inward (Figure 8.7), and then adjust the position of both vertical bars so the space between them (where the trapezoids are) defines the range of colors you want to exclude from the adjustment. As in the previous section, it is helpful to have an exaggerated adjustment—such as a complete reduction in saturation (Figure 8.8)—active while you adjust the color range so you can see the effect in the image (Figure 8.9).

After defining the range of colors to include everything except the colors you want to exclude from the adjustment, you can fine-tune the position of the trapezoids to set a blending for the adjustment. Then adjust the sliders as needed to produce the desired effect in the image.

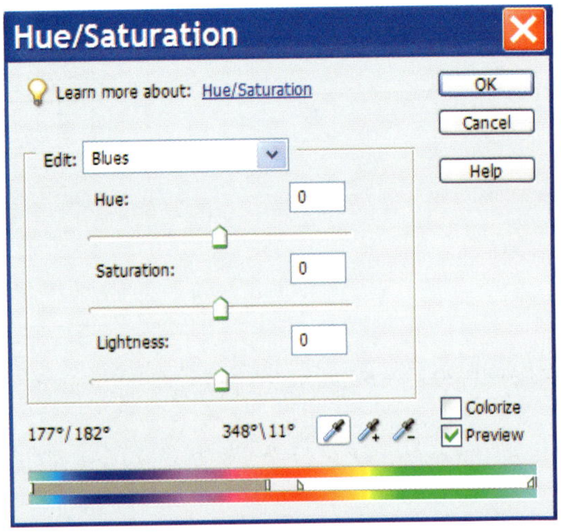

Figure 8.6 When you want to define a range of colors that includes everything except a small range, you'll likely need to drag one vertical bar all the way off the range to place it at the opposite end of the color gradient. For example, here we want to increase saturation of all colors except red, because red is already heavily saturated.

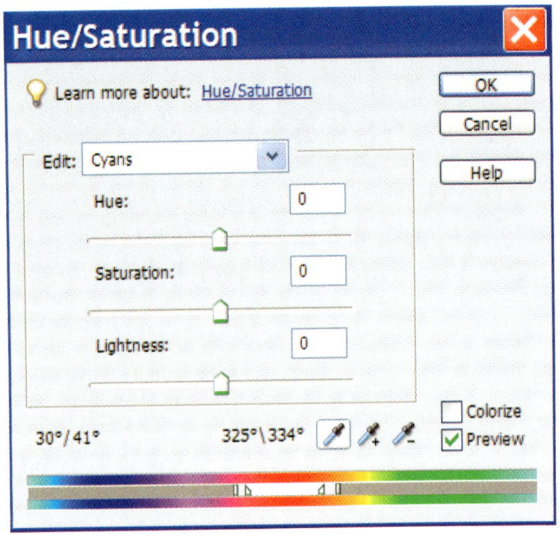

Figure 8.7 After bringing the slider to the opposite end of the color gradient, adjust it to the appropriate position for the color range you want to define.

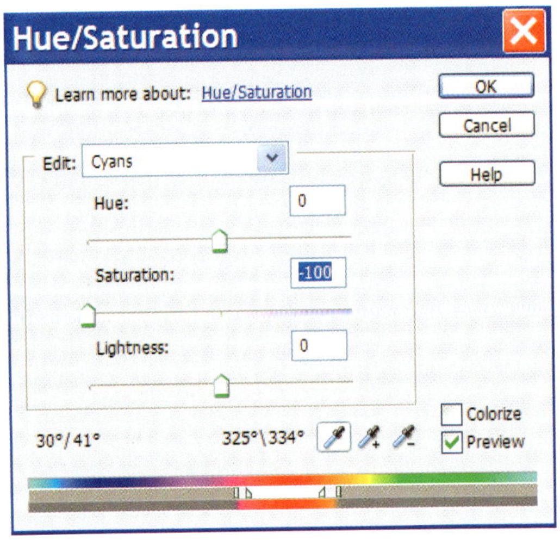

Figure 8.8 This shows a complete reduction in saturation.

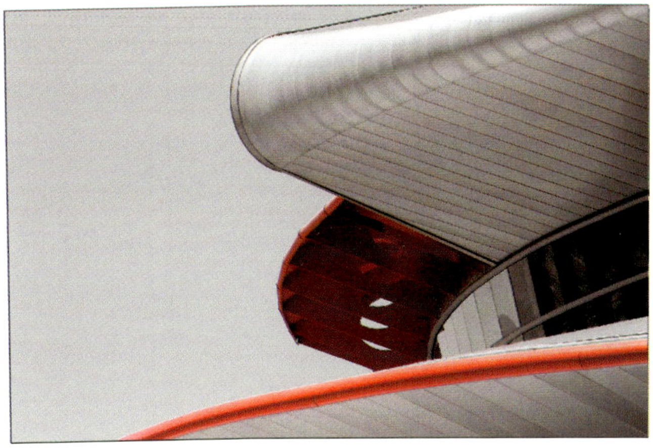

Figure 8.9 An exaggerated adjustment will make it easier to fine-tune the range of colors you want to include in the final adjustment.

We encourage you to experiment with the possibilities that are available with full control over the saturation of individual colors. For example, consider desaturating all colors except red in an image. The result will be a photo that is black-and-white in most respects, except that any red elements remain in color (Figure 8.10). This usually works best when your photo contains one red element and not several, although that is a subjective judgment.

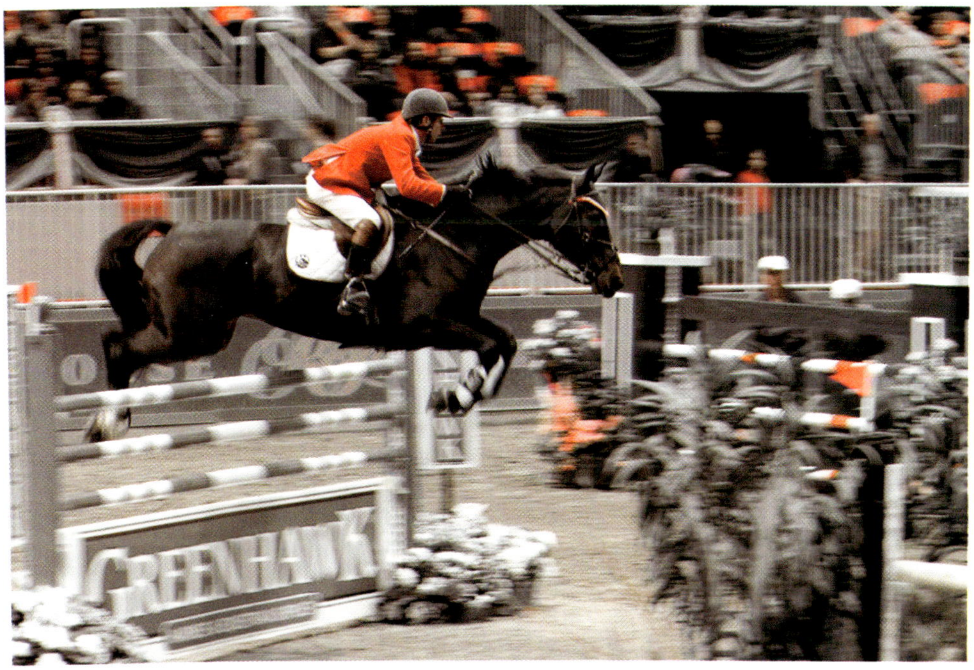

Figure 8.10 For a photo that is black-and-white in all respects except for a single color, desaturate all other colors by 100%.

And take advantage of the layer mask technique discussed in Chapter 10, "Targeted Adjustments," for more-targeted control. While working with Hue/Saturation and using an adjustment layer, desaturate all colors in the image by 100% for a black-and-white image. Click OK to accept that change. Afterward, select the Brush tool, and use Set Background Color tool to select black. Begin painting on the adjustment layer with black, but paint over only one specific element that was red in your color photo (Figure 8.11). This technique hides the adjustment layer in the parts of the image that you select, allowing the red to show through; it's particularly useful where you want to "colorize" only a single part of the image and not all the red elements, for example.

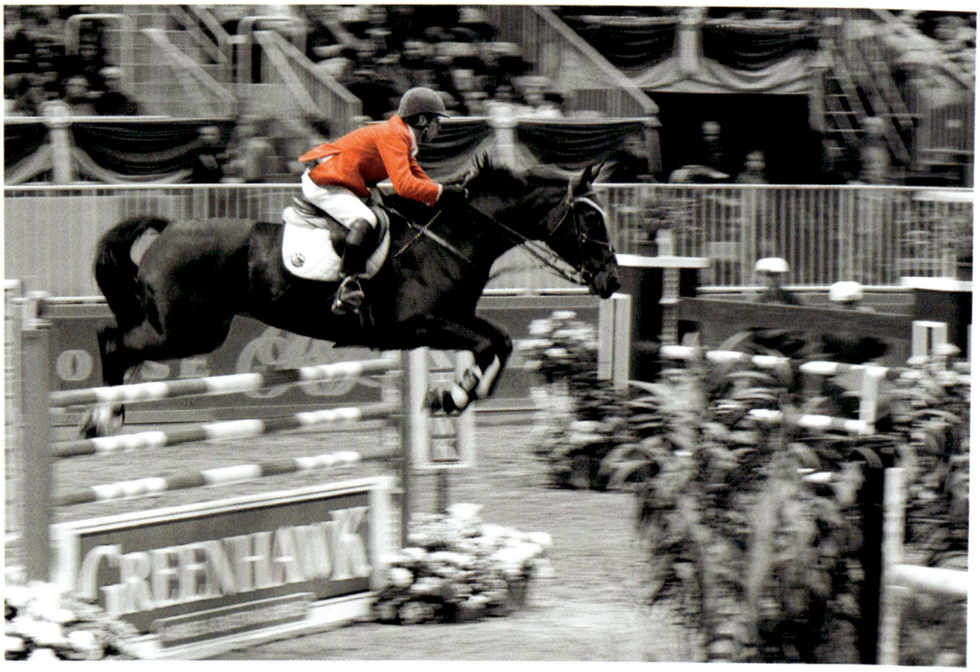

Figure 8.11 Taking a more targeted approach is sometimes a preferable technique. You can use a black brush on an adjustment layer to provide greater control over the specific element that will be colorized.

If you make a mistake—painting beyond the intended area—simply press X on your keyboard; the brush will change from black to white and will act as an "eraser" of the colorizing effect. Use that to undo a previous brush stroke. This feature is possible because painting with white allows the adjustment layer to be visible again. After the mistake is corrected, press X to revert to the black brush and continue the colorizing process. Naturally, you can use both techniques on any color, not merely red.

Color Casts

In Chapter 5, we discussed the concept of color casts and some of the basic tools you can use to eliminate them: Color Variations, Remove Color Cast, and Adjust Color For Skin Tone. And earlier in this chapter, we discussed how to use Hue/Saturation for a similar purpose.

So far, we have assumed that a color cast is undesirable (such as the magenta cast in the "before" photo in Figure 8.3) and that you want to get rid of it. In truth, sometimes you may want to add a color cast to an image, such as adding a warming (red/yellow) effect to a landscape photo (Figure 8.12). In the following sections, we will present a couple of more advanced methods you can use to add or remove a color cast.

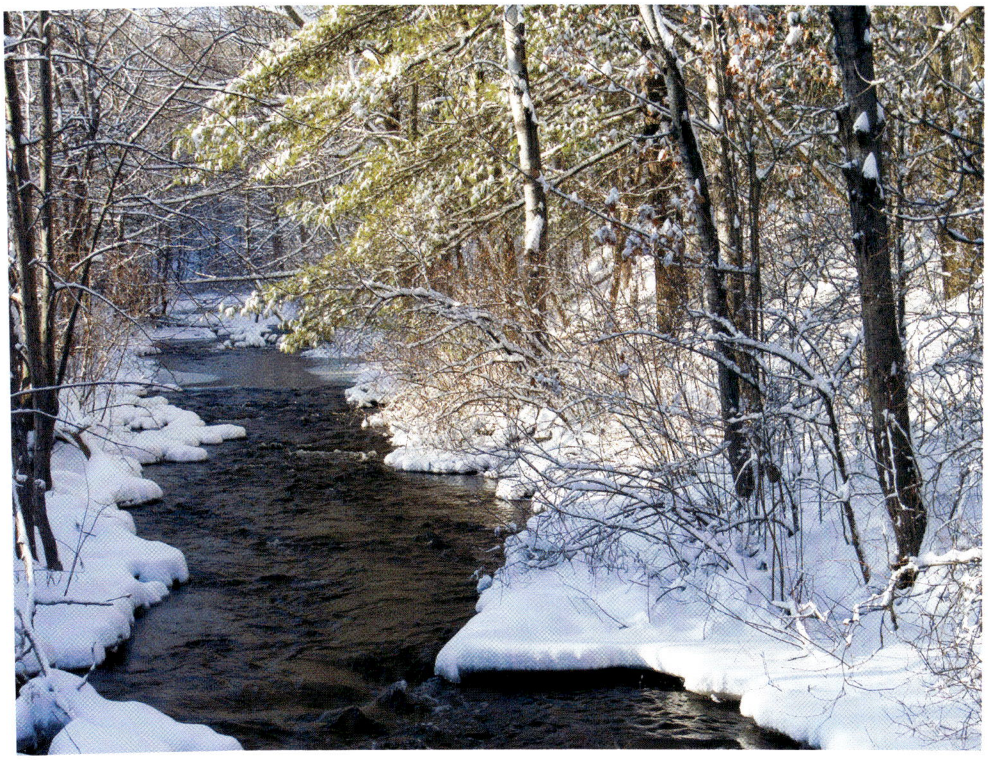

Before

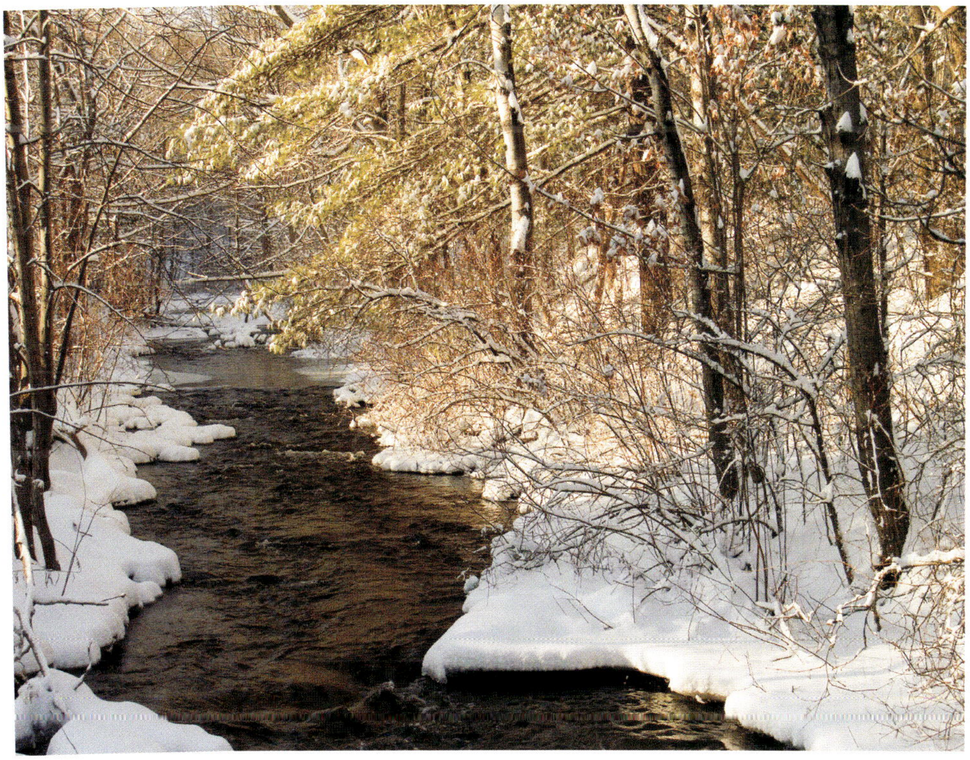

After

Figure 8.12 Although the first image is accurate in terms of the slightly "cool" color balance of the scene when the photo was made, the second image is more pleasing or inviting because of the addition of a "warming" effect.

Solid Color

At first glance the Solid Color adjustment layer probably doesn't seem all that useful because the color you add with it completely hides your image. However, you can use it effectively to add a desired color cast to an image or to compensate for an undesirable cast.

When you look at your image, you should have a pretty good idea of what color cast you want it to have (Figure 8.13). Adding a color cast is simply a matter of knowing the color of the cast you'd like to apply. For removing a color cast, the selected color will need to be the opposite of the cast that is influencing the image. Fortunately, by setting up the adjustment layer properly, you can select a color while observing the change in the image, making it easier to find just the right color.

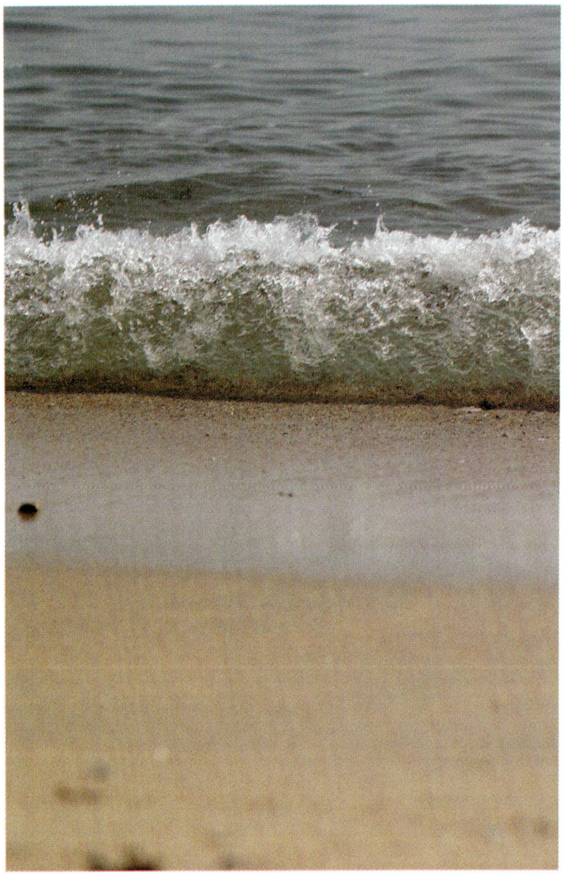

Figure 8.13 When you're going to use a Solid Color adjustment layer, you should be able to determine the color you'd like to add to the image to achieve a desired effect. For example, we have decided to add a warm cast to this image.

To start the process of adding a color cast, add a Solid Color adjustment layer on the Layers palette. Immediately after doing so, click OK in the Color Picker dialog box that appears. Your image will then disappear and be replaced by a solid color. Don't worry about what the color is—you just want to configure the adjustment layer so you can preview the effect in the image. First, change the blending mode from the default of Normal (at the top of the Layers palette) to Color. That will produce a layer that lets you alter only the color of the underlying layer without changing tonality or texture. In other words, none of the detail in the photo will be altered; only the color appearance will change.

Then reduce the Opacity to about 20% to reduce the effect of the color shift being applied. You'll be able to fine-tune the specific percentage that produces the desired effect, but for now you just want a moderate effect while selecting the color (Figure 8.14).

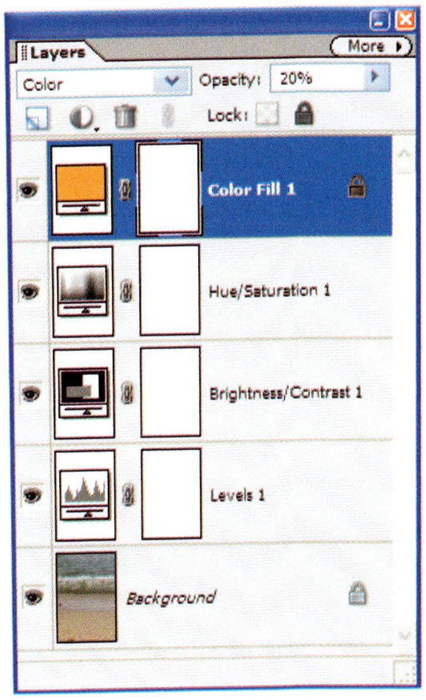

Figure 8.14 When you are using a Solid Color adjustment layer to apply or compensate for a color cast, first create the adjustment layer and click OK; then change the blending mode to Color and the Opacity to about 20%.

With the adjustment layer properly configured as discussed, double-click the thumbnail for the Solid Color adjustment layer on the Layers palette. This opens the Color Picker box, allowing you to select the color you'd like to add (Figure 8.15).

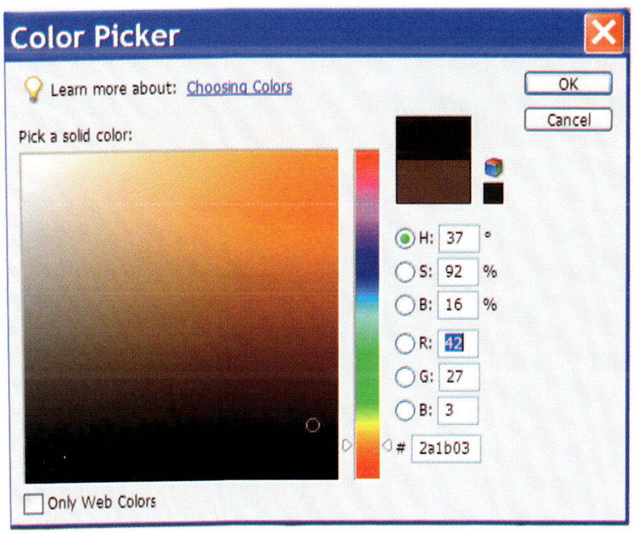

Figure 8.15 You can use the Color Picker to select the color you'd like to use with the Solid Color adjustment layer.

Note: The color swatch in the Color Picker dialog box will divide into two colors after you choose a new color. The bottom half of the swatch will reflect the old color, and the top half of the swatch will reflect the new color you have selected.

Because of the way you have configured the adjustment layer, the image will update to show you a preview of the effect whenever you select a color. With the Hue (abbreviated as H) option selected in the Color Picker, click along the vertical (multicolored) color bar to select a basic color. Then click the larger color box (under Pick A Solid Color) to define the specific saturation and brightness. Based on the preview in the image, fine-tune your color selection by clicking various areas within the Color Picker until you achieve the desired result. Keep in mind that you'll be able to tweak the strength of the adjustment afterward with the Opacity of the adjustment layer. After you've found the right color, click OK.

Finally, adjust the Opacity setting for the adjustment layer to dial in the desired strength (Figure 8.16). As a rule of thumb, try experimenting with a value of about 10 to 20 percent. Keep in mind that you'll often want to reduce the Opacity to less than you think is necessary to avoid an artificial appearance in the image. We also recommend reviewing the "before" and "after" versions of the image by toggling the visibility of the adjustment layer on and off (by clicking the eye icon to the left of the adjustment layer thumbnail on the Layers palette).

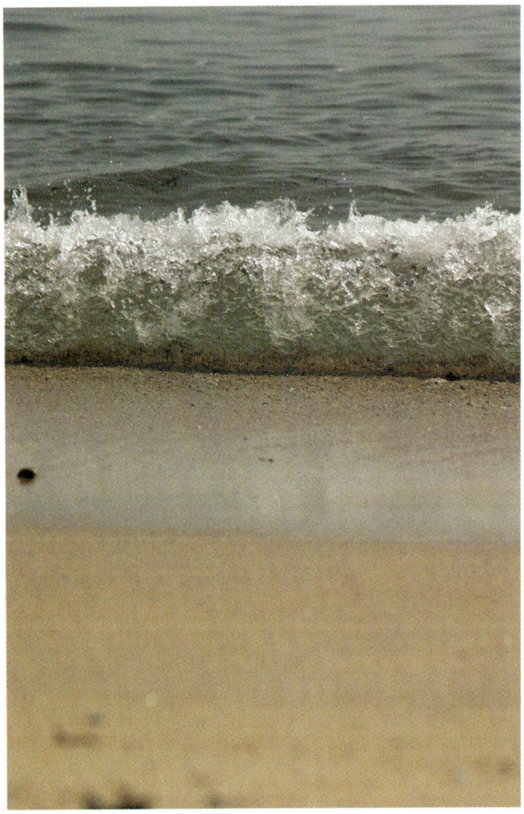

Figure 8.16 With the color selected, adjust the Opacity of the Solid Color adjustment layer to produce the desired effect.

Average Color Removal

When you're trying to *remove* a color cast from an image, trying to find just the right color for the Solid Color adjustment layer can be a challenge. Often, simply compensating for the average color in the image will provide a simple way to remove an undesirable color cast (Figure 8.17).

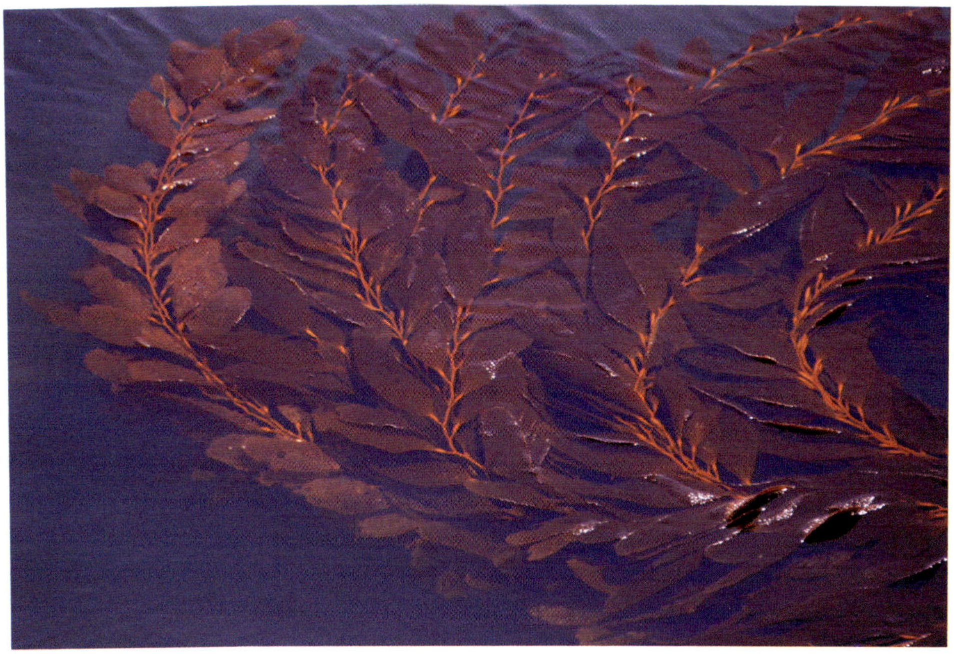

Figure 8.17 The average color removal technique is an excellent way to correct strong color casts in an image.

The first step to using this method is to create a duplicate copy of the Background layer. The simplest way is to drag the thumbnail for the Background image layer on the Layers palette to the Create A New Layer button. (Alternatively, click the Background layer to make sure it's the active layer, and press Ctrl/⌘+J.) You then want to figure out what the average color is in the image. That is the color you will select for this duplicate layer, which will in turn provide information about the color cast influencing the image. To find the average color, simply click the Background Copy layer to make sure it is the active layer, and choose Filter > Blur > Average from the menu. The result will be a solid color on this layer representing the average color value for all pixels within the image (Figure 8.18).

Because this color is the average of all pixels, it approximately represents the color cast for the image. To compensate for this color cast, you first need to invert it by choosing Filter > Adjustments > Invert (or pressing Ctrl/⌘+I). This will "reverse" the color so it represents the opposite of the color cast identified by the Average blur.

Next, change the blending mode (at the top of the Layers palette) from the default Normal to Color so this duplicate image layer can affect only the color of the underlying image (Figure 8.19). Then adjust the Opacity slider for this image layer to adjust the strength of the effect so that it compensates for the color cast in the image (Figure 8.20). The final value will depend on how strong the color cast was to begin with, but start with a value of around 50% and work your way (most likely downward) from there.

Figure 8.18 Applying the Average Blur filter to the Background Copy layer results in a layer where all pixels have the same color value.

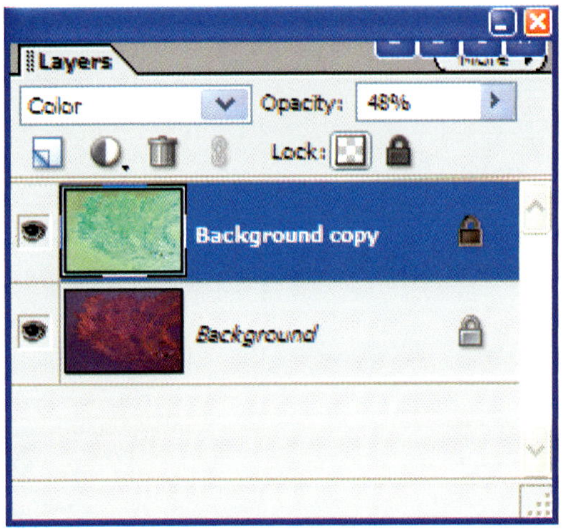

Figure 8.19 After inverting the Background Copy layer, change the blending mode to Color and adjust the Opacity as needed.

Note: When you're finished applying the average color removal effect, you may need to apply additional adjustments to compensate for the loss of saturation and contrast that can result. The Hue/Saturation and the Levels tools, both available for use with adjustment layers, are useful choices for that final fine-tuning.

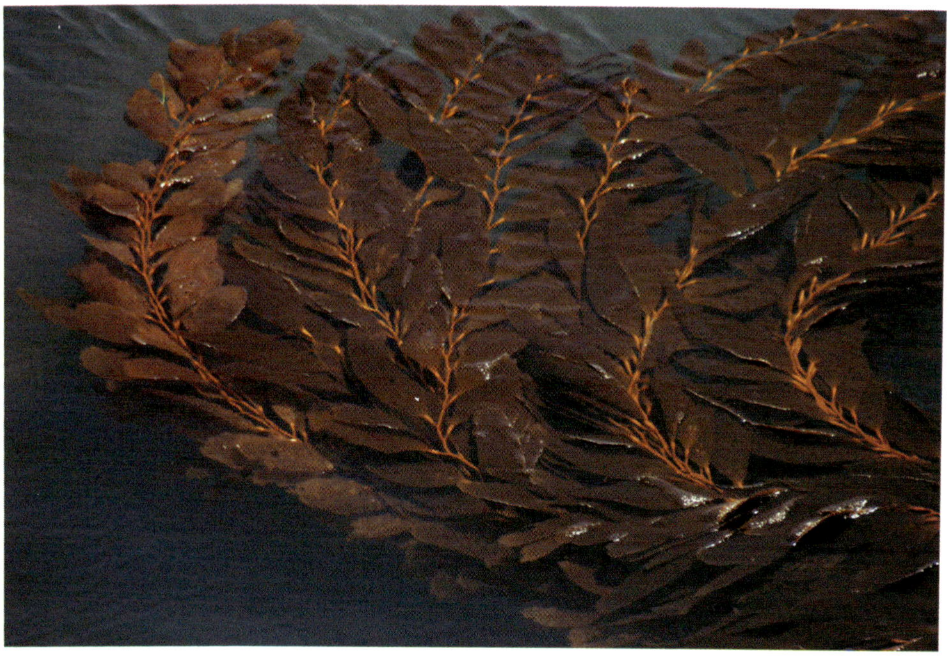

Figure 8.20 With the color cast successfully removed, you may need to boost saturation or contrast to compensate for the "averaging out" of much of the color within the image.

Targeted Color Painting

When you really want to take control over a color fix in your photo, sometimes it is best to paint the color right into the image. This provides an opportunity to be precise about the location within the image to be affected, painting color exactly where you need it. Of course, you don't want to simply paint with a solid color over the pixels of your image. Using proper settings, you can paint with color so that the only effect is a change in color in the target areas, without any loss of texture or detail.

This method is particularly useful for spot fixing color contamination within an image (Figure 8.21). For example, if an object was near the front of the lens when a photo was taken, it will add a translucent color wash to the scene. Photographers often use such an effect intentionally, but when it is accidental, it can lead to a color problem. Many situations can introduce color contamination without damaging the texture of the underlying areas of the image, and fortunately you can easily fix such problems.

As you can well imagine by now, you shouldn't paint your color adjustment directly onto the Background image layer. Create a new empty layer (by clicking the Create A New Layer icon in the Layers palette); this will be the layer to which you can apply the painting. Rename this layer; we usually use *Color Fix* for this type of adjustment, but any name that helps you remember why you added this layer is suitable.

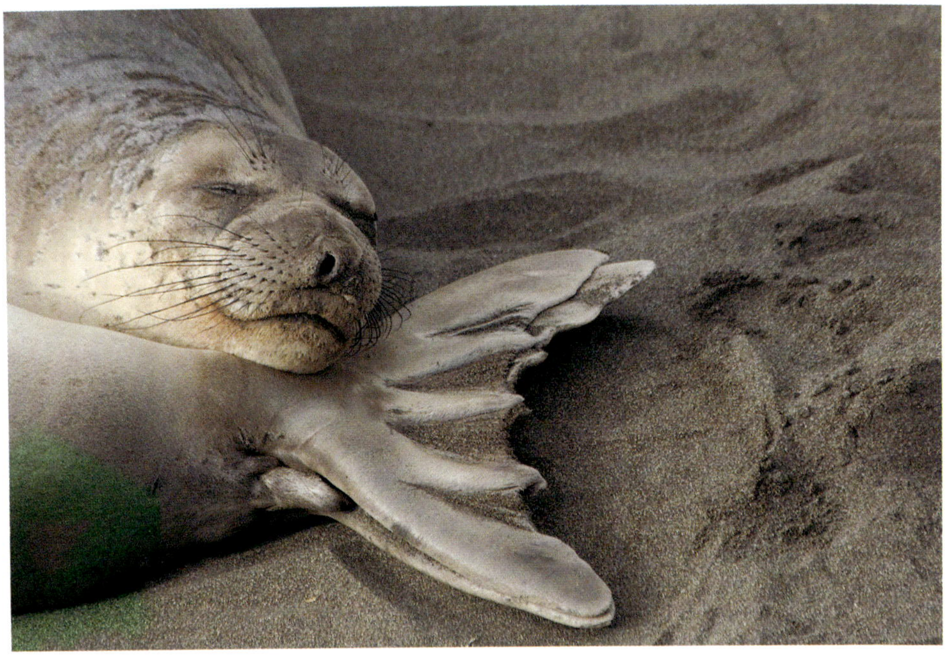

Figure 8.21 Targeted color painting is an excellent technique for fixing isolated color contamination in an image when only the color has been affected but the underlying texture remains, such as the green wash in the bottom-left of this image.

The key setting for this layer is the blending mode. Because you want to adjust only the color of the underlying image layer, you should change the blending mode (at the top of the Layers palette) from the default Normal to Color. That step will limit the effect of anything painted on this layer so it applies to only the hue and saturation (the overall color) of pixels below, without changing their texture or tonality.

Note: You can also use the Hue blending mode for this technique, which will limit the change to only the basic color value without changing the saturation or brightness of the underlying pixels.

With the layer configured as suggested previously, the next step is to choose and configure the Brush tool. Click the Brush tool on the Tools palette or press B. On the Options bar that appears at the top of the screen, select a soft-edged brush and set Opacity to 100%. Now use the Eyedropper tool to select the color you'll be painting with. The Eyedropper tool is useful because it allows you to select a color from directly within the image and not some arbitrary color.

Note: You can also select a color from the Color Picker, the bottom item in the Tools palette, if there isn't an appropriate color within the image.

Before proceeding, be sure to set the Eyedropper tool options to use the 3 By 3 Average setting for sampling. To do so, select the Eyedropper tool from the Tools palette. While it is active, right-click the image area and choose 3 By 3 Average from the pop-up menu that appears (or alternatively, select this option from the Sample Size drop-down menu on the Options bar). By averaging several values (nine in this case), this option ensures that you will get a color that is more likely to match the surrounding area and that you won't end up with an inappropriate color because you happened to click an arbitrary pixel in an area that didn't match, such as when there is noise in the image.

Now, select the Brush tool as mentioned earlier. While the Brush tool is active, you can also use the Eyedropper tool; there is no need to switch tools. Simply hold the Alt/Option key, and you'll temporarily get the Eyedropper tool. While still holding the Alt/Option key, click the image at a point containing the color you'd like to use, and that color will be set as the foreground color (Figure 8.22).

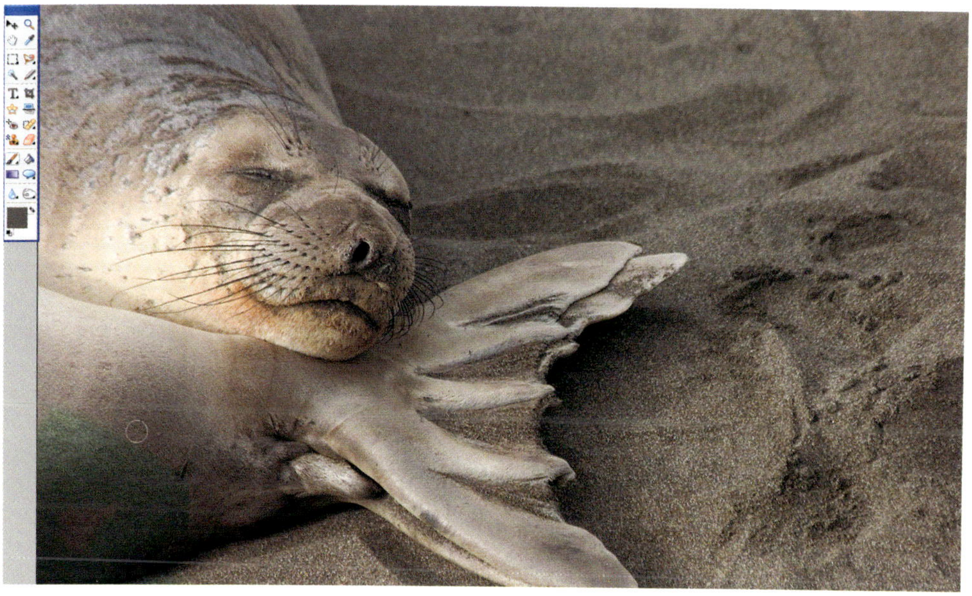

Figure 8.22 By Alt/Option+clicking an appropriate area of the image, you can set the foreground color to the color of the pixel area you clicked on. This color can be used for painting in the color correction.

Take Full Advantage of the Eyedropper

The versatile Eyedropper tool has three main settings. The most commonly used is Point Sample, in which the exact color under the eyedropper is sampled when the tool is clicked. The 3 By 3 Average looks at a larger 3×3 pixel range and selects an average color from these pixels. You can obtain an even larger average result with the 5 By 5 Average option. After using one of the Average settings, remember to reset the Eyedropper tool back to Point Sample. Otherwise, the next time you go to sample a precise color with the Eyedropper tool, the color result will not be an exact match to the area you've clicked on.

Continues

Take Full Advantage of the Eyedropper *Continued*

Whenever a brush-like tool is active, holding down the Alt/Option key toggles to the Eyedropper tool to allow quick access for selecting colors without physically switching back and forth between tools. The cursor gives visual clues as to which tool is active. When a Brush tool is active and you press the Alt/Option key, the cursor changes to an eyedropper. When the Clone Stamp or Healing Brush tools are active, the Alt/Option key turns the cursor into a target to signify that a sample can be taken for cloning purposes. The only exception to these visual clues occurs if the Caps Lock key on your keyboard is toggled on. This causes most cursors to become a generic precision cursor, which can make it hard to distinguish which tool is active. If you come across this behavior, suspect the Caps Lock key on your keyboard as the culprit. Press the Caps Lock key to toggle it off, and the normal cursor behavior will return, allowing you to be more aware of which tool you are using.

By painting over the area of the image that exhibits the color problem, you will change the color without affecting the overall tonality or texture of the area (Figure 8.23). You can therefore fix minor color contamination quite easily, selecting colors from directly within the image so you'll know they will look appropriate.

Note: If you want to apply a minor compensation for a color problem, rather than completely replacing colors, you can reduce the Opacity for the Color Fix layer.

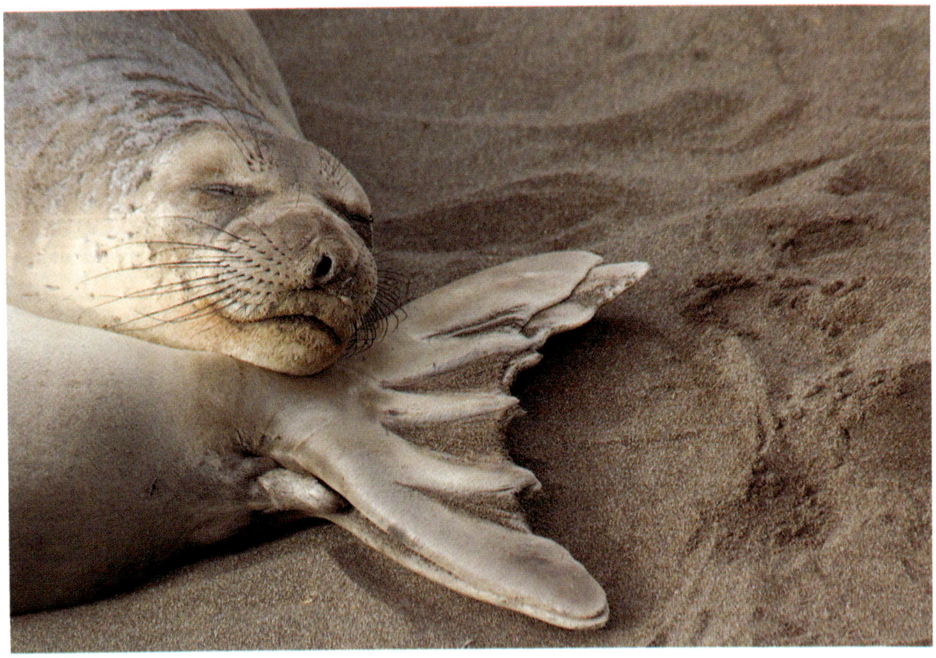

Figure 8.23 Painting the appropriate color with the Color blend mode on the layer will correct the color contamination without altering the tonality of the underlying pixels.

Targeted Saturation Painting

Similar to the technique described in the previous section, it is also possible to paint saturation adjustments to targeted areas of the image. You can use the Sponge tool in Elements to do this, but that tool requires you to paint directly on an image layer, or on a duplicate layer that doubles the file size unnecessarily. Instead, you can ignore the Sponge tool and paint targeted saturation adjustments on a new empty layer by using the Brush tool.

Start by creating a new image layer (click the Create A New Layer icon at the top of the Layers palette). Change the blending mode for this layer from the default Normal to Saturation. You may also want to rename the layer to something such as *Saturation Paint* so you'll always remember why the layer was added (Figure 8.24). Then choose the Brush tool, pick a soft-edged brush, and set the Opacity to 100%.

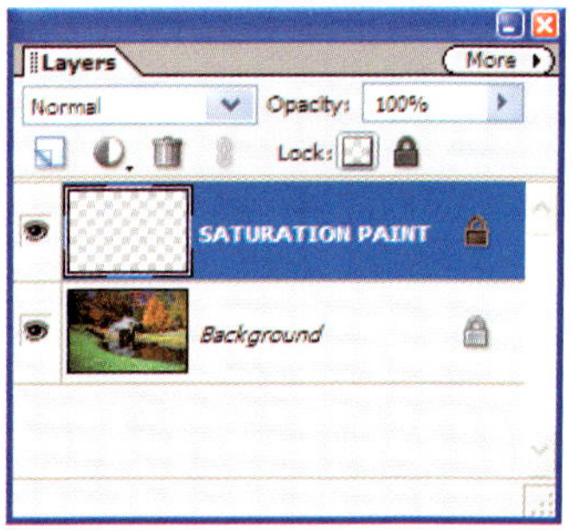

Figure 8.24 To paint saturation adjustments onto your image, create a new layer; give it a name such as *Saturation Paint*, and change the blending mode to Saturation.

The next step is to select a color to paint with by clicking the foreground color of the Color Picker, that's found at the bottom of the Tools palette. (Be sure to select Set The Foreground Color and not Set The Background Color.) Because you'll be painting on a layer that is set to the Saturation blending mode, you need to concern yourself with only the saturation level of the color you select. Therefore, you can click the Saturation (S) option in the Color Picker dialog box and use the small vertical gradient bar to select the saturation level you want to use (Figure 8.25).

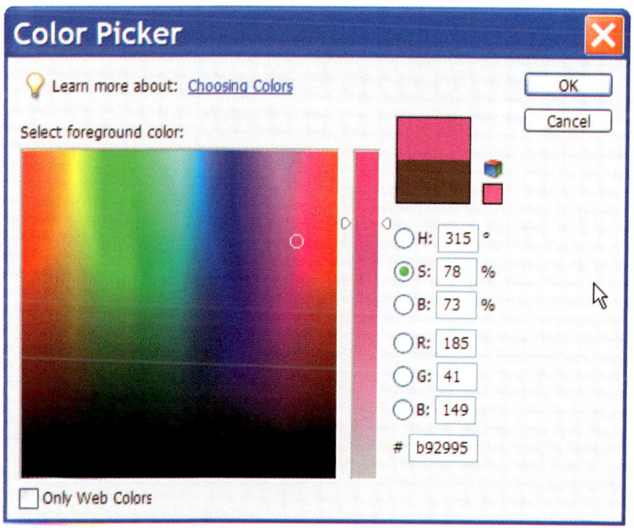

Figure 8.25 Use the Color Picker to select an appropriate saturation level (the actual color doesn't matter) for painting an adjustment on your image.

Note: Remember to return the Color Picker to the default view by clicking Hue (H) the next time the Color Picker is accessed.

Another alternative to selecting a specific saturation level is to simply choose a fully saturated color if you plan to increase saturation, or a completely desaturated color if you want to decrease saturation. You can then adjust the Opacity setting for the Brush tool on the Options bar to vary the strength of the adjustment. We recommend starting with a value of about 50% if you find you want to tone down the effect and then fine-tune the value from there based on the results you're getting. Just keep this in mind: When painting at a reduced opacity, you should hold the mouse down as you paint over the entire area that you want to adjust before releasing the mouse. Otherwise, you may paint over some areas more than once, causing an uneven adjustment to the image.

With the color properly selected, you can simply paint on the image to apply saturation adjustments in a selective way (Figure 8.26). When you need to vary the effect you're applying, simply choose a color with a different saturation level in the Color Picker or adjust the Opacity setting for the Brush tool on the Options bar.

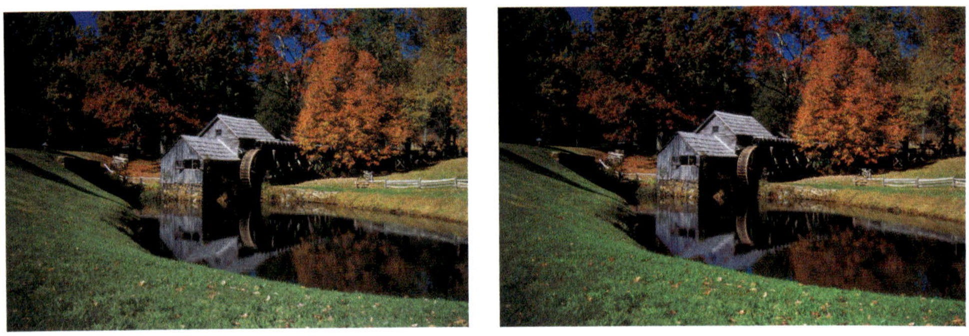

Figure 8.26 Painting with a color at a particular saturation level onto a separate layer set to the Saturation blending mode allows you to perform targeted adjustments to saturation within the image. In this image the green of the grass in the foreground was made more vibrant without oversaturating the green of the trees in the background. (Photo by Gabby Salazar)

Note: This method is a great alternative to eliminate red-eye in photographs of people if the Red Eye Removal tool yields less than ideal results. Simply use a neutral color such as black or white when painting on the Saturation Paint layer.

Ready to Get Selective

The techniques presented in this chapter will help you apply more-precise color adjustments to your images as you progress through the workflow from basic to more-advanced modifications. These color adjustments offer more control than standard tools, and in some cases they allow you to target the adjustments to specific color ranges within an image. In the next chapter you'll begin the process of producing targeted adjustments based on the location of pixels within the image rather than their tonal or color value.

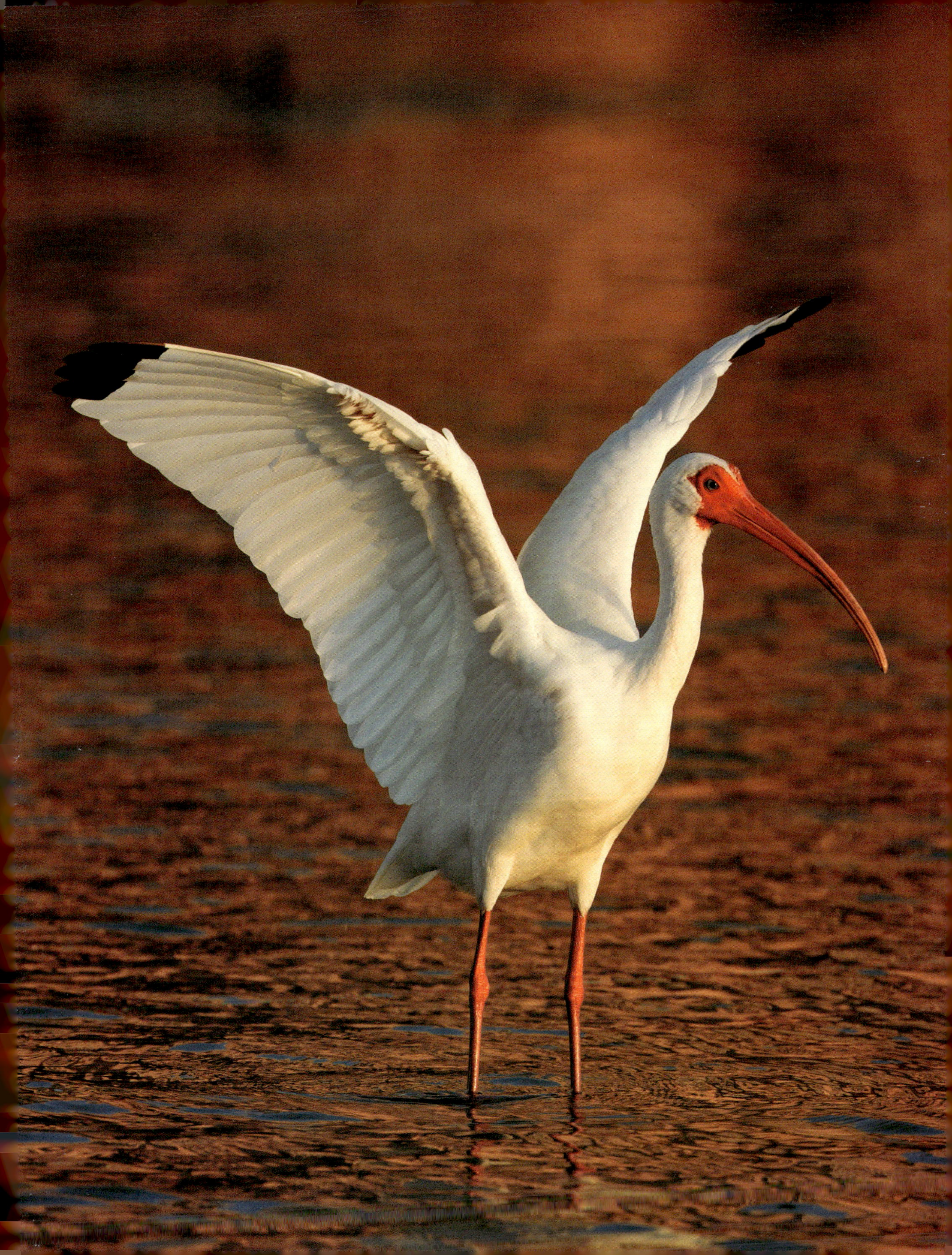

Making Selections

This chapter marks a turning point in the control you will be able to exercise over your images. In previous chapters, the adjustments you made either applied to the entire image or could be targeted in only relatively limited ways. Selections *allow you to take full control over your images by enabling you to make adjustments to specific areas and to produce an image that is exactly what you envision. The first step in exercising this control is to create the selections that define the areas you'd like to adjust within your image.*

9

Chapter Contents

Understanding the Selection Tools
Using the Threshold Technique
Modifying Selections
Saving and Loading Selections

Understanding the Selection Tools

Photoshop Elements 5 includes built-in tools for creating selections, most of which can be found on the Tools palette. Understanding these selection tools is the key to getting started with targeted adjustments, and this understanding will provide a strong foundation for the other selection methods we'll discuss later in this chapter. Creating a selection is the first step toward adjusting specific areas of your images (Figure 9.1).

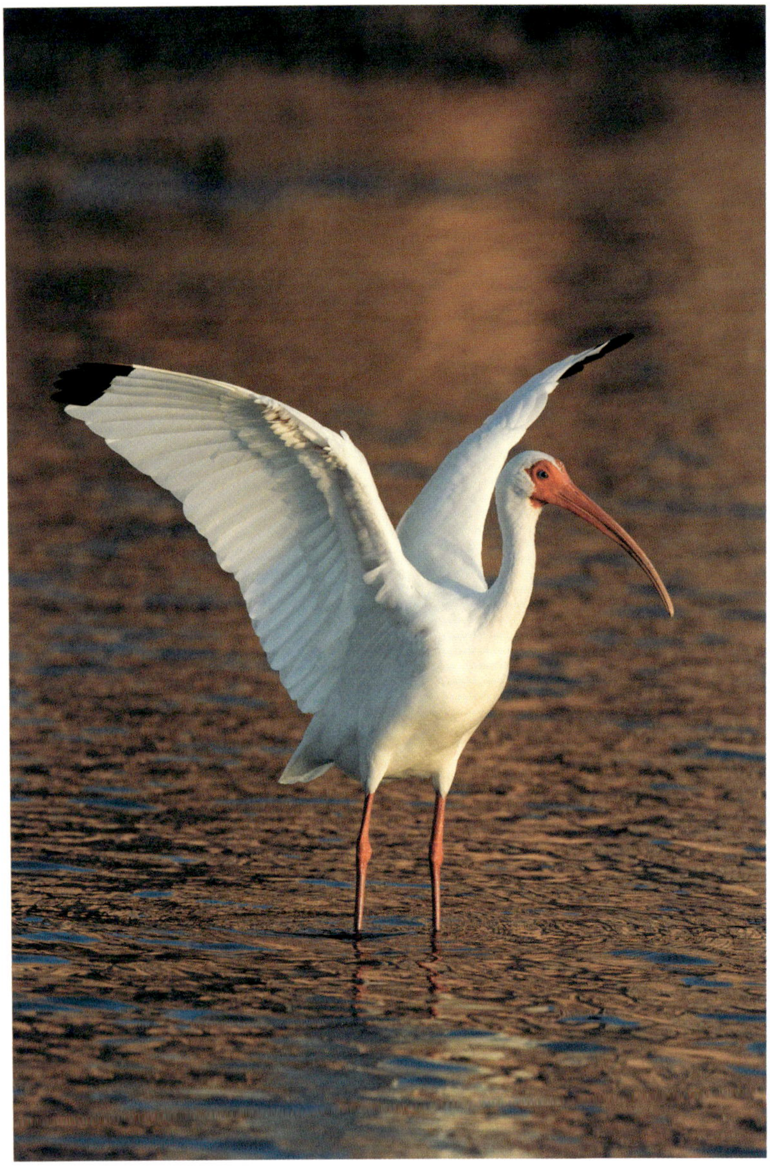

Figure 9.1 When you want to create adjustments targeted to a particular area of the image, a selection is the first step. For example, if you wanted to increase contrast in the background of this image without creating excessive contrast in the bird, you'd first create a selection that defines the background. (Photo by Arthur Morris, www.birdsasart.com)

Marquee

The Marquee tools are the most basic selection tools, which is another way of saying they are the least powerful. In fact, when it comes to making targeted adjustments to your images, these tools are frankly not up to the job. But because the Marquee tools are relatively simple in their operation, starting with them helps lay the groundwork for selections in general.

Elements offers two Marquee tools: Rectangular Marquee and Elliptical Marquee. Select the one you want by clicking and holding the current Marquee tool on the Tools palette (Figure 9.2); you can then choose the desired tool from the fly-out menu. You can also press M on your keyboard to toggle between the Rectangular Marquee tool and the Elliptical Marquee tool. The two tools work in the same way, with the only difference being the general shape of the selection created. Obviously, the Rectangular Marquee tool creates a rectangular shape, and the Elliptical Marquee tool creates an elliptical shape.

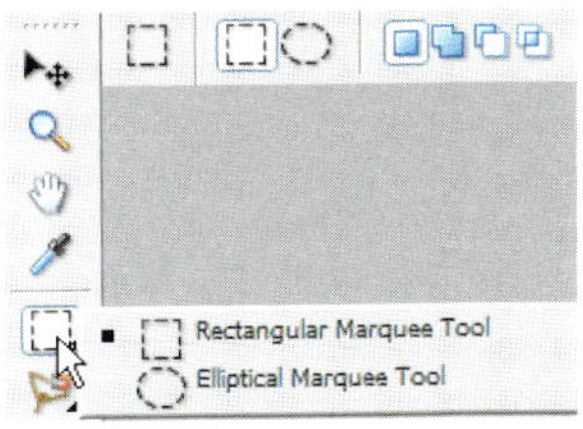

Figure 9.2 You can select either of the two Marquee tools, as desired, from the fly-out menu.

To create a selection with the Rectangular Marquee or Elliptical Marquee tool, first imagine a rectangle or ellipse bounding the area you would like to select in your image. Move the mouse pointer to any one of the corners or points of that imaginary rectangle or ellipse, and then click and drag to the point diagonally opposite your starting point. As you're dragging, Elements will create a dashed rectangle or dashed ellipse. When you release the mouse, that shape becomes the selection, outlined by the "marching ants" display defining the border of the selection, or *active area* (Figure 9.3). All pixels inside the border are selected, and you can manipulate them with any Elements tool without affecting other image areas. When making an elliptical selection as opposed to a rectangular one, you can keep your selection on a more precise target if you imagine a clock and start at somewhere between 10 and 11 o'clock (upper-left corner of the selection area) and drag toward 4 and 5 o'clock (lower-right corner).

In addition, while you're dragging to define the selection, you can use several modifier keys to change the behavior of the tool. Press and hold the Shift key to constrain the selection to a perfect square or a perfect circle. If you press and hold the Alt/Option key after you've started creating the selection, the selection will be centered on your starting point (Figure 9.4). Holding both keys will cause both effects to apply. Keep in mind that you must press these modifier keys after you start creating the selection or you won't get the expected behavior. That's understandable, because these shortcut keys also enable the Add To Selection and Subtract From Selection options (discussed later in the "Selection Modes" section).

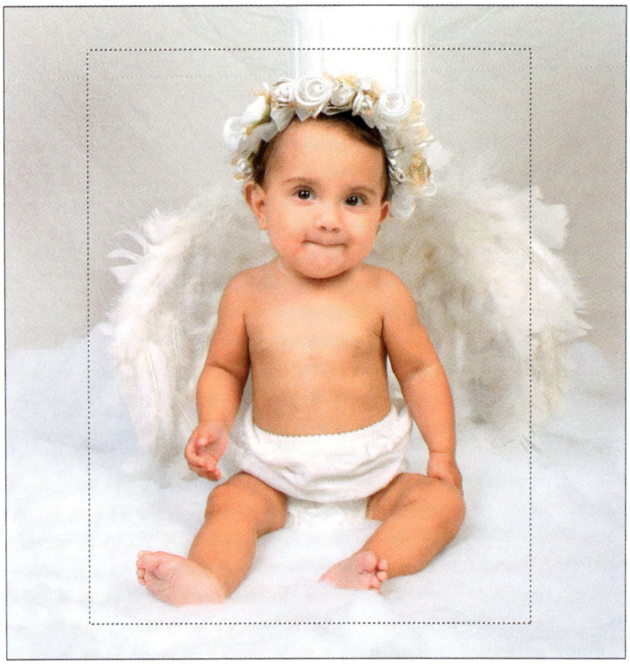

Figure 9.3 When you drag a rectangle or ellipse with the Rectangular Marquee tool, the selection defined by that bounding area will be created on your image. (Photo by Chris Greene, ImageWest Photography)

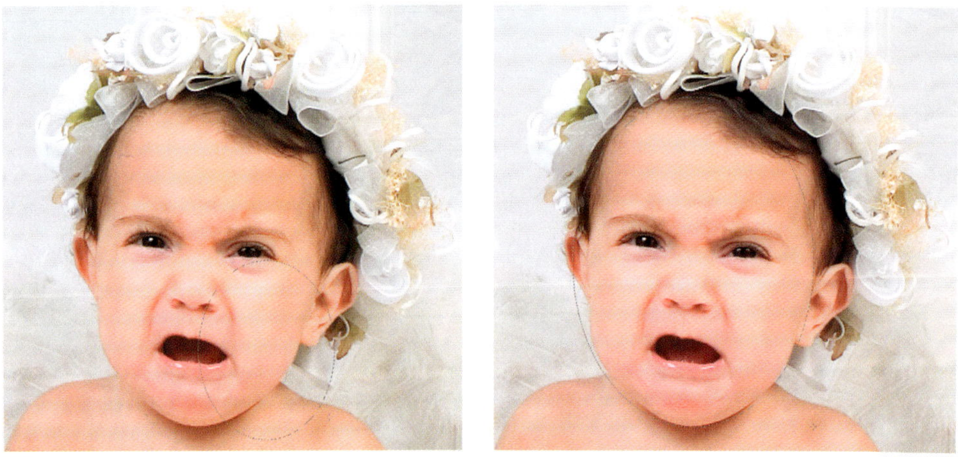

Figure 9.4 Usually the Marquee tools create a selection that has a corner on your starting point (left), which in this case was near the nose of the baby. Holding the Alt/Option key will cause the selection to be centered on your starting point (right). (Photo by Chris Greene, ImageWest Photography)

You can also change the position of the selection as you're drawing it with one of the Marquee tools. After you've started dragging to define the selection, press and hold the spacebar. This will activate the Hand tool functionality temporarily, but because you're in the middle of creating a selection, it will allow you to move the selection, rather than the image (Figure 9.5). After the selection is made, the spacebar goes back to allowing you to move the currently active image layer, not the selection. It might help to practice this technique to get the hang of it. Press Ctrl/⌘+D to deselect the selection when you want to try again.

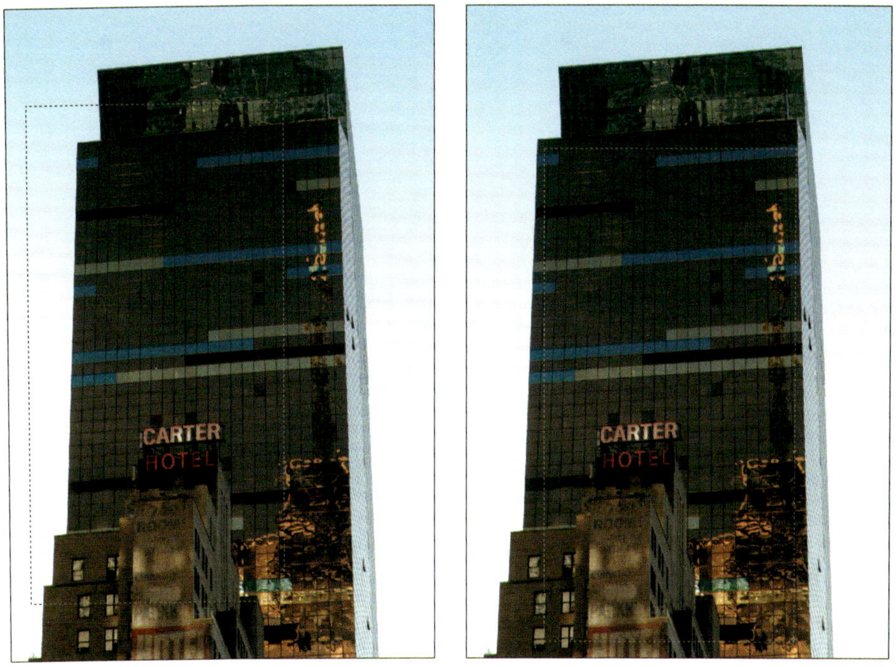

Figure 9.5 Holding the spacebar allows you to drag to move the selection while you're in the process of creating it with one of the Marquee tools.

When the Marquee tool is active, the Options bar above the image area contains controls that you can use if desired (Figure 9.6). We'll postpone discussing some of these options to the next section, because they affect all selection tools.

For the Feather setting, we recommend using a value of 0 px (zero pixels) so that no feathering is applied. We'll explain how to apply feathering when you start making targeted adjustments in Chapter 10, "Targeted Adjustments."

For the Rectangular Marquee and Elliptical Marquee tools, a Mode drop-down list is also available. You'll usually want to use the Normal option, because it allows total flexibility in the dimensions of your selection. However, at times you may want to constrain your selection to a specific size or aspect ratio. Fixed Aspect Ratio and Fixed Size are helpful when you want to crop an image to a specific size, vignette an image, or mask out an image with a fixed shape and size.

Specifically, the Fixed Aspect Ratio mode allows you to set a specific relationship between width and height in the selection you'll create. When you choose this mode, the Width and Height text boxes on the Options bar become active, and you can enter values for each. This won't limit you to a specific selection size, only a fixed *relationship* between width and height. (That's why the boxes allow you to enter only numerals and not specify centimeters or inches.) As you drag the mouse after your initial click, no matter what direction you drag, the general shape of the selection will be fixed, with your mouse movement affecting only the size of the selection.

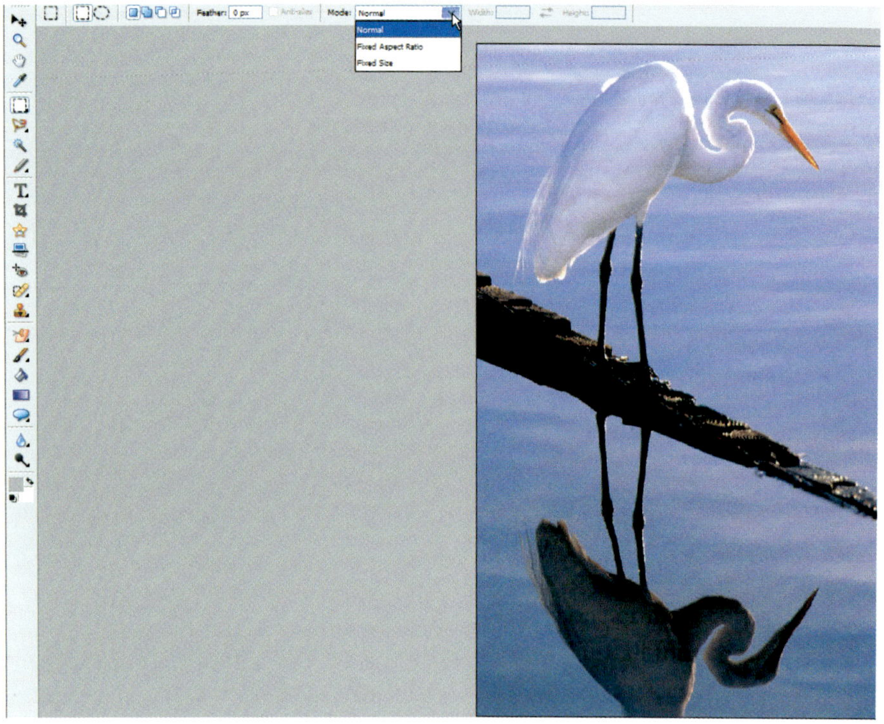

Figure 9.6 The Options bar includes settings for the Marquee tools.

Switch to the Fixed Size mode to create a selection of a specific size in the Width and Height text boxes that become available (Figure 9.7). Enter values for both dimensions, using *px* for pixels, *in* for inches, or *cm* or *mm* for metric measurements. For example, to create a selection that is exactly 8″×10″, set the Width to **8 in** and the Height to **10 in**. When you click the image, a selection of exactly those dimensions will be created, with the spot you clicked defining the top-left corner of the selection area. If you click and drag, you can't change the shape of the selection, but you can change the starting position of the selection.

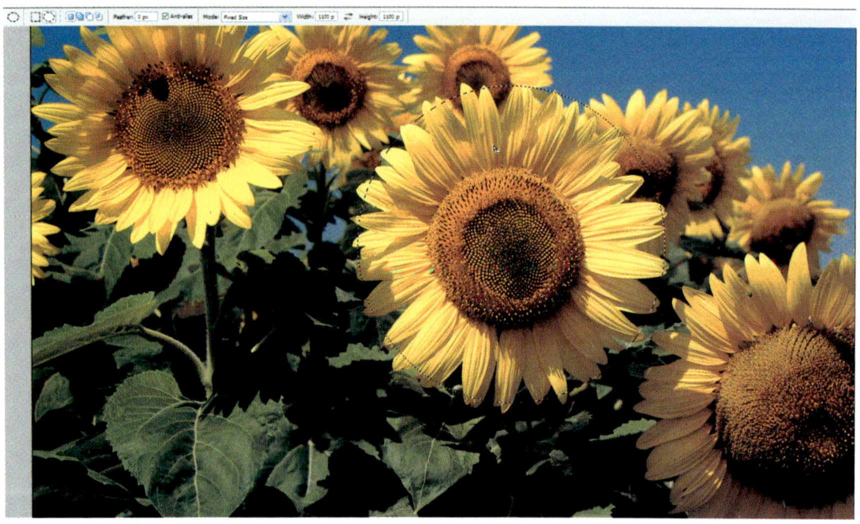

Figure 9.7 The Fixed Size mode allows you to specify a size for the selection when using either Marquee tool.

When you're using the Elliptical Marquee tool (but not the Rectangular Marquee tool), an Anti-alias checkbox (visible in Figure 9.7) becomes active. If you select this option, the edges of the selection will be smoothed so they don't have a jagged appearance. This is a particular concern for curved edges or diagonal lines, which is why Adobe provides that option for the Elliptical Marquee tool.

Selection Modes

After becoming familiar with how the two Marquee tools operate, you can start making more-complicated selections by adding pixels to or subtracting pixels from a selection. Start by using one of the Marquee tools to create a basic selection.

Note: The buttons discussed in this section can be applied to any of the selection tools available in Elements 5 (not only the Marquee tools).

Then, to the left of the Feather option on the Options bar, you'll find four buttons that allow you to modify the behavior of these (and other) selection tools:

- The first button, New Selection, causes the current Marquee tool to behave in the "normal" manner, creating a new selection whenever you use the tool. This is the option we typically keep active at all times, using shortcut keys to access the other options.
- The second button is Add To Selection. With this option chosen, the new selection will be added to the existing selection whenever you use a selection tool in Elements to surround pixels (Figure 9.8). For example, if you use the Rectangular Marquee tool to create a rectangular area, you could then turn that into a more complicated polygon shape by dragging to create additional selection areas. You can also hold the Shift key to access the Add To Selection option regardless of the current state of the tool.

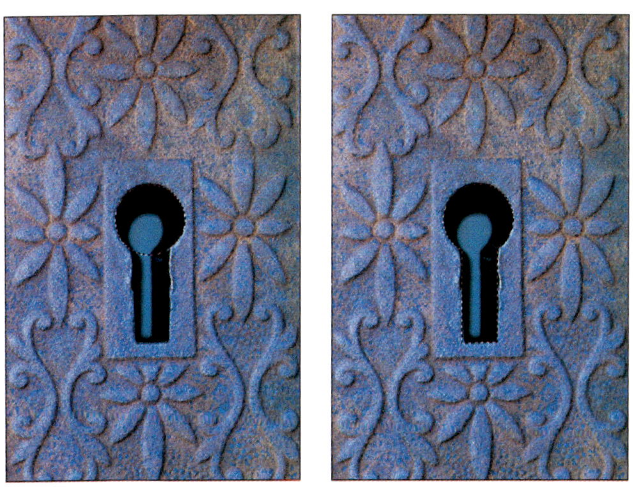

Figure 9.8 The Add To Selection button allows you to build up selections in multiple steps. In this case, we used the Elliptical Marquee tool to make the initial elliptical selection (left). Then, we used Add To Selection with the Rectangular Marquee tool to complete the selection shape (right). (Photo by Alice Cahill, www.alicecahill.com)

- The third button in the set is Subtract From Selection, which allows you to subtract pixels from an existing selection. When you click this button, Elements will omit the surrounded pixels from the existing selection that you made (Figure 9.9). For example, if you start with a circular selection created with the Elliptical Marquee tool and then draw another circle inside this selection after clicking the Subtract From Selection button, the result will be a "doughnut" selection. You can access this option by holding the Alt/Option key when using any selection tool.

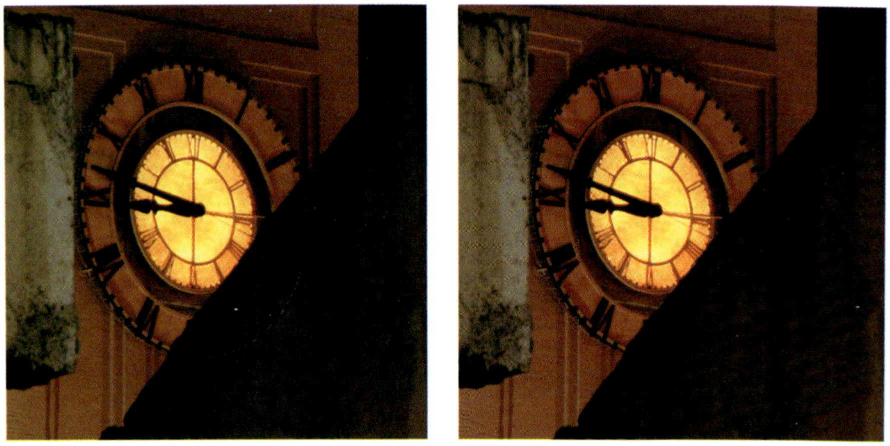

Figure 9.9 The Subtract From Selection button allows you to remove portions of an existing selection. In this case, we used the Elliptical Marquee tool to make the initial elliptical selection (left). Then we used the Subtract From Selection option with the Polygonal Lasso tool to subtract the straight edge area away from the initial selection shape (right).

Note: The add and subtract buttons are helpful, and you'll use them extensively as you build complicated selections that require a fair amount of fine-tuning, as you'll see later in this chapter.

- The last button of the four is one you'll use less frequently but that can be helpful in certain situations. This is the Intersect With Selection button. When this option is chosen, creating a new marquee when you have an existing marquee will result in a selection of only the pixels in the areas where the two marquees overlap. You can also access this functionality by holding the Shift and Alt/Option keys when using a selection tool.

Lasso

Also available from the Tools palette, the Lasso tool group contains three distinct tools that we'll discuss individually: Lasso, Polygonal Lasso, and Magnetic Lasso. The Lasso tool provides maximum flexibility, because it allows you to draw a custom shape around the pixels you want to select. And again, "marching ants" will define the active selection; you can then manipulate that area without affecting the other parts of the image.

Activate the Lasso by choosing it from the Tools palette or pressing L. Zoom in closely on the relevant part of the image so you can clearly see the edge of the area you want to select. Carefully position your mouse along that edge; then click and hold the mouse button. Drag the mouse along the edge so you're effectively tracing that edge to define your selection (Figure 9.10). Take the time to be as precise as you can so the selection you create will be as accurate as possible.

Note: For all of the Lasso selection tools, you can use the keyboard shortcuts discussed in Chapter 2, "Download and Sort," to zoom in and out while you are in the process of creating the selection. Also keep in mind that pressing the spacebar while still holding down the mouse button during the selection process will temporarily toggle to the Hand tool; that will allow you to move around in the image area while creating your selection.

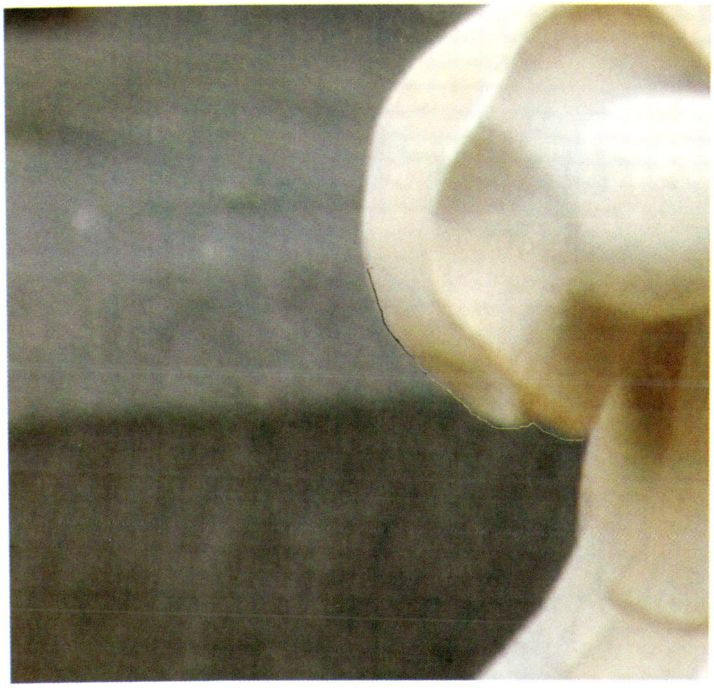

Figure 9.10 Use the Lasso tool to trace along the edge of the object you want to select in your image.

The Options bar for the Lasso tool contains the same four modifier buttons mentioned when discussing the Marquee tools: New Selection, Add To Selection, Subtract From Selection, and Intersect With Selection. They work in the same manner, allowing you to refine a selection by adding or subtracting pixels from an existing selection or to create a selection from the intersection of an existing and new selection. Also on the Options bar for the Lasso tool are the Feather and Anti-alias options. As mentioned previously, we recommend leaving Feather set to 0 px and Anti-alias selected.

When you are working with the Lasso tool on a zoomed portion of an image, you may find that the area you are trying to select extends outside the document window. In that case, as you near the edge of the document window, press and hold the spacebar. This will temporarily allow you to use the Hand tool so you can drag the image to change the area you are viewing. After moving the image, release the spacebar, and you can continue dragging the mouse to extend the selection. Remember to maintain a steady pressure on the mouse button while pressing and releasing the spacebar.

When you've looped around the entire area you want to select, drag the mouse to your original starting point and release the mouse button to finish the selection (Figure 9.11). If you don't finish at the same point you started, Elements will automatically complete your selection by extending a straight line from the point where you release the mouse button to your original starting point.

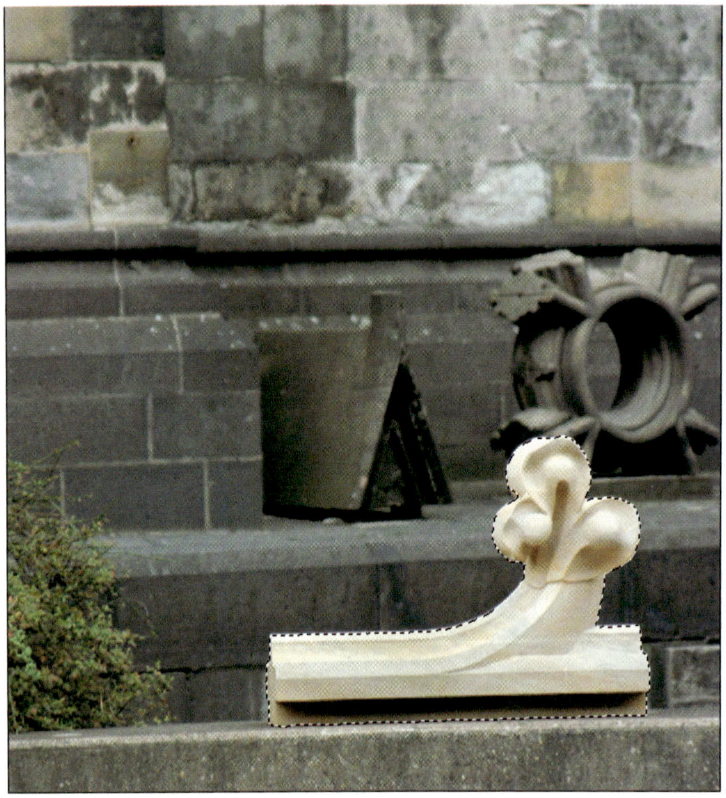

Figure 9.11 The Lasso tool allows you to produce a perfect customized selection with a bit of effort.

Working with the Lasso tool can require a steady hand and a bit of practice. It isn't always the fastest or easiest way to create a selection, but it does offer exceptional flexibility.

Polygonal Lasso

Another tool, the Polygonal Lasso, allows you to create selections composed of perfectly straight lines. To choose the Polygonal Lasso tool, click and hold the Lasso tool button on the Tools palette and then choose Polygonal Lasso Tool from the fly-out menu. You can also press L to activate the current Lasso tool, and then press L to cycle through the Lassos until you get to the Polygonal Lasso.

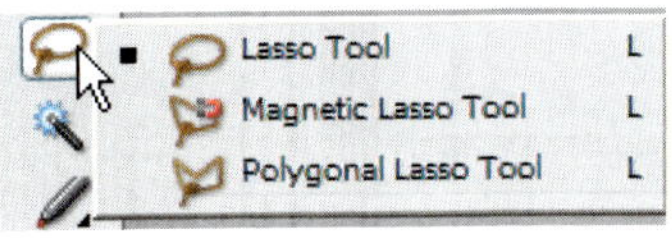

By using the Polygonal Lasso tool, you can create a selection with straight edges by "connecting the dots" with a series of anchor points. Start by clicking along the edge of the object that you want to select in your image. This will create the first anchor point at that position, with a line connecting that anchor point to your cursor (Figure 9.12). Wherever you move the mouse, the line will follow. Position the mouse so the line perfectly aligns with the edge of the object you're selecting and click again to create an additional anchor point. Continue clicking individual points to define the outer edge of the selection.

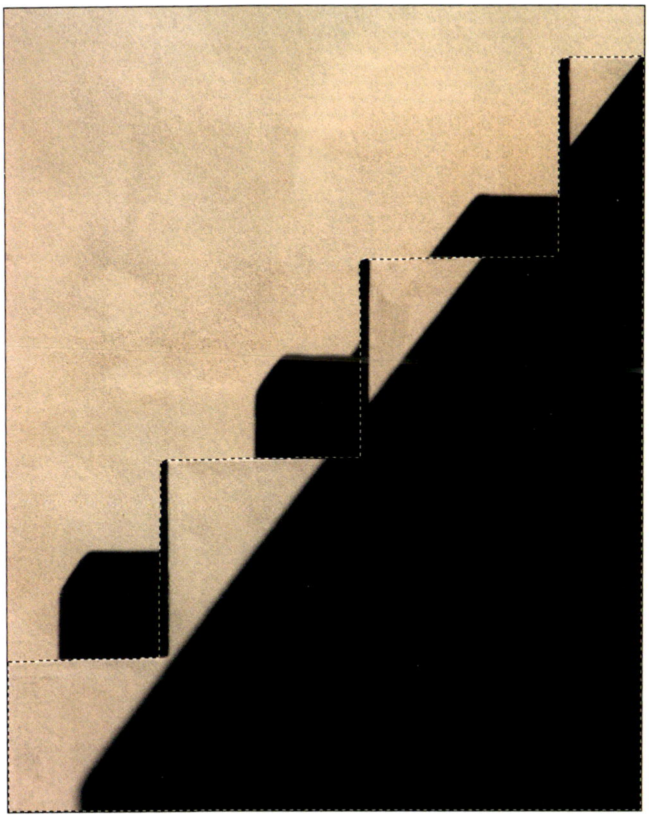

Figure 9.12 The Polygonal Lasso tool allows you to create anchor points that will be connected by straight lines to produce the final selection.

The standard set of four modifier buttons (New Selection, Add To Selection, Subtract From Selection, and Intersect With Selection) are available on the Options bar for the Polygonal Lasso tool, as are the Feather and Anti-alias options. In the case of the Polygonal Lasso, Anti-alias will affect both diagonal lines and the junction of two lines at an anchor point.

Although it is possible to create a "curved" line by placing many anchor points close together, you don't need to go to that extreme. If you reach a place where you can't really use a straight edge effectively (Figure 9.13), press and hold Alt/Option to temporarily switch to the regular Lasso tool, allowing you to click and drag to draw a portion of the selection edge freehand. When you want to return to the straight edges of the Polygonal Lasso tool, simply release the Alt/Option key, and you'll be back to placing anchor points to define straight edges within the selection. You can switch back and forth between the tools in this manner as frequently as needed.

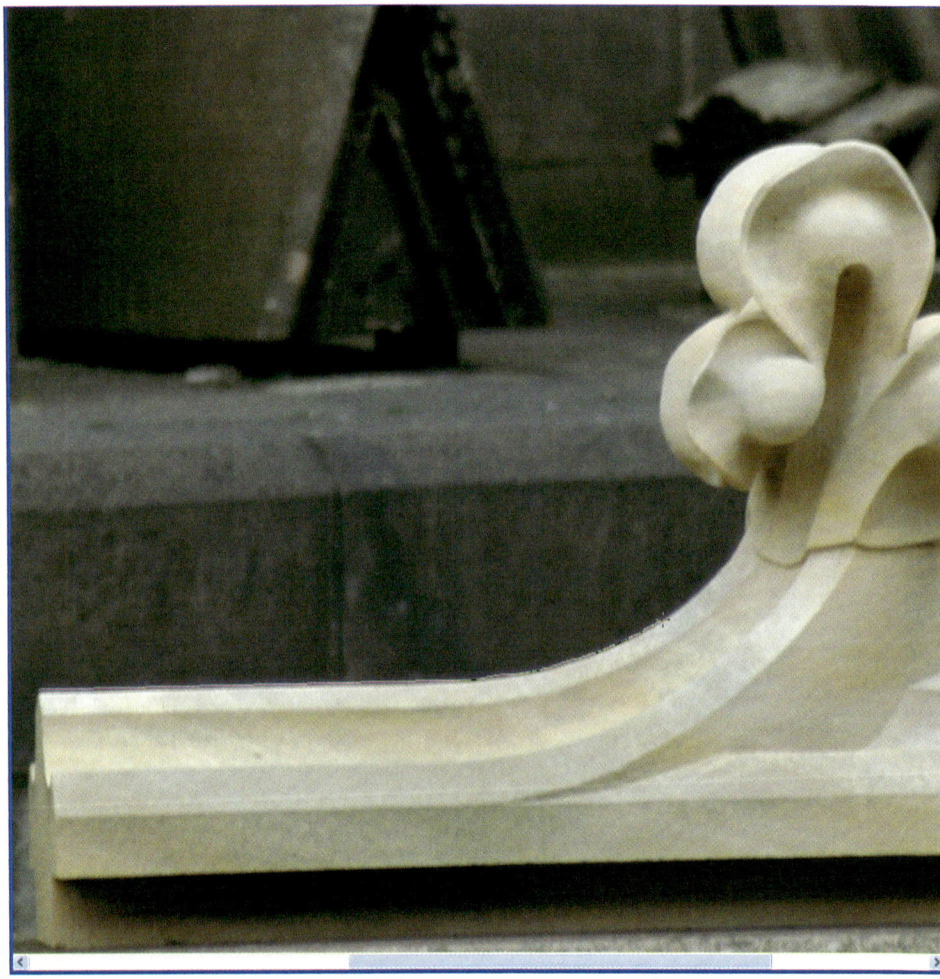

Figure 9.13 In this image, we used the Polygonal Lasso tool on the straight portion of the selection in progress; then we pressed the Alt/Option key to continue with a free-form selection.

As you're defining anchor points with the Polygonal Lasso tool, you may find that you want a particular edge to be perfectly horizontal or vertical. You can constrain the line created from one anchor point to the next by holding the Shift key before you click the new anchor point. Doing so will limit the current line between anchor points to a straight line in 45-degree increments. However, this option works only if you press and hold the Shift key after you've started creating the selection.

If you've placed an anchor point in an incorrect position, you can press Backspace or Delete to remove the previous anchor point. Each time you press the key, you'll delete the prior anchor point, all the way back to the initial anchor. If you decide you just want to cancel the current selection in progress and start over, press the Esc key; the selection will be cancelled and all anchor points removed.

To finalize a selection with the Polygonal Lasso tool, return the mouse pointer to the original anchor point. A small circle will then be added to the cursor, indicating you can click to close the selection shape. If you can't find the original anchor point, double-click in the image and the selection will be closed in a straight line from the point you double-click to the original anchor point.

Magnetic Lasso

The final Lasso option, Magnetic Lasso, is quite different from the other two and in some ways acts like a brush tool. Although it bears some resemblance to the other Lasso tools, it has a certain amount of automation built into it that makes it special. And although its name might make it sound like a tool for selecting metallic objects from your images, it's actually designed to assist you in selecting objects along their edges based on contrast at those edges. Similar to the Polygonal Lasso tool, the Magnetic Lasso tool defines a selection by placing anchor points. However, whereas you place those points manually with the Polygonal Lasso tool, the Magnetic Lasso places anchor points automatically based on edge contrast.

As with the Polygonal Lasso tool, you can find the Magnetic Lasso tool under the regular Lasso on the Tools palette. Click and hold the mouse on the Lasso tool to open the fly-out menu, and choose Magnetic Lasso. You can also press L to activate the current Lasso tool, and then press L to switch tools until activating the Magnetic Lasso.

Besides the standard set of four modifier buttons, the Feather setting, and the Anti-alias checkbox, the Options bar contains some special controls when the Magnetic Lasso tool is active. The first is the Width control; as you "paint" with the Magnetic Lasso tool, the Width setting determines the size of the area in which you'd like Elements to search for contrast. You could enter a value in pixels to determine the size of the edge width for the Magnetic Lasso, but obviously this is a rather arbitrary decision. Instead, simply place your mouse pointer along the edge where you'll start making the selection, and use the left bracket ([) or right bracket (]) key to reduce or enlarge the size of the edge width, respectively. You want the Width setting to be small enough that the strongest area of contrast within the sample area will be the edge you're trying to select, but large enough that you don't have to be overly precise in dragging the mouse pointer along that edge.

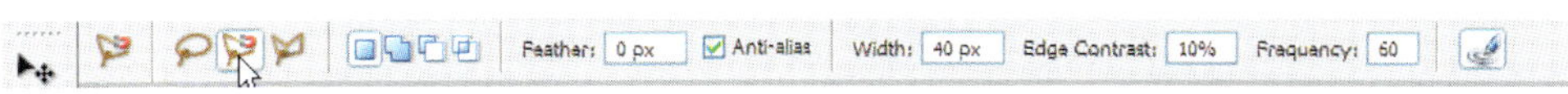

The Edge Contrast setting determines how much contrast the Magnetic Lasso should look for. For high-contrast edges, you can use a higher setting and you won't need to be as precise as you move the mouse along that contrast edge. For low-contrast edges, you should use a lower setting but be more precise in dragging the mouse along the edge you're trying to select. We generally find that a 10% value for Edge Contrast works well in most situations, and the difference in behavior is so slight with different values that we don't recommend changing it.

The Frequency setting determines how often anchor points will be placed as you drag the mouse pointer over the edge. A higher Frequency value will cause anchor points to be placed quickly in close proximity to each other; a lower value will cause them to be placed farther apart. Higher settings are best for well-defined edges, whereas lower settings tend to work well for more-nebulous edges. A value of 60 is suitable as a starting point, but you'll want to revise that number based on whether the anchor points are being placed at an appropriate rate. It is generally better to have a higher frequency with more anchor points rather than a lower frequency, so the shape of the selection will better match the edge of the object you're trying to select.

The final setting on the Options bar when using Magnetic Lasso is a Pen Pressure checkbox. This setting applies only if you are using a tablet. With the box selected, varying the pressure you apply to the stylus (pen) will affect the edge width. Pressing harder will cause the Width setting to decrease, as though the pressure is focusing the edge width onto a smaller area. Less pressure will cause the edge width to enlarge, so the Magnetic Lasso will look for contrast across a broader area.

With the Options bar settings established, you're ready to start creating a selection with the Magnetic Lasso tool. Position the cursor over the contrast edge you want to select, and click the mouse button once to place the initial anchor point. Then drag the mouse along the edge of the object you are trying to select. Elements will automatically place anchor points at the area of highest contrast within the radius (Width), with spacing based on the Frequency setting (Figure 9.14). If you get to an area of the image where contrast isn't adequate for the Magnetic Lasso to accurately place an anchor point, you can click the mouse to manually place an anchor point.

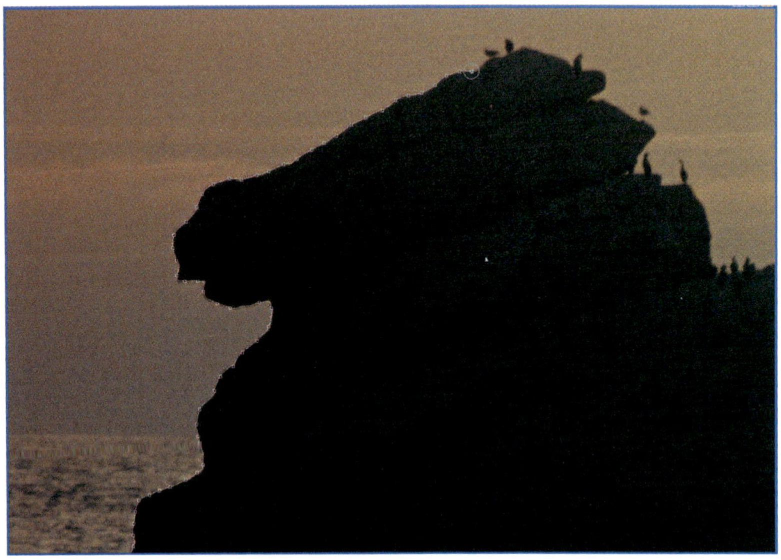

Figure 9.14 As you move the mouse along the edge of the object you're selecting, the Magnetic Lasso tool will automatically place anchor points at the place of highest contrast within the edge width.

At times you'll find the Magnetic Lasso doesn't do a very good job of placing anchor points where you want them and will place them in an inappropriate place. When that happens, you'll need to delete anchor points before trying again in the problem area of the image. First, move the cursor back to the last place where you want an anchor point. Then press the Backspace or Delete key once for each anchor you want to remove. They will be removed starting with the most recently created point. You can then adjust the Width with the square bracket keys, or change other settings on the Options bar, and drag again along the edge. If you can't find settings that work well for a particular area, place the anchor points manually by clicking the mouse.

If you need to create a straight-line edge along part of the selection, Alt/Option+click at an anchor point. This will add an anchor but will do so as though you were using the Polygonal Lasso tool, so a line will connect that anchor point to your cursor. Simply move the mouse to the next location where you'd like to place an anchor point, and click. The Polygonal Lasso behavior will continue until you Alt/Option+click to place an additional anchor point, at which point you'll return to the Magnetic Lasso tool.

To access the regular Lasso tool while working with the Magnetic Lasso, press and hold the Alt/Option key as you click and drag the mouse along the edge you want to define by drawing freehand. Click the mouse again without the Alt/Option key to return to the Magnetic Lasso.

If you decide you want to cancel the selection in progress, simply press the Esc key; all anchor points will be removed and there will be no active selection (unless there was a selection active before you started using the Magnetic Lasso).

The Magnetic Lasso tool is powerful, but it isn't perfect. Although it's quite competent in making selections based on contrast in the area that you identify, it won't create a perfect selection in most cases. However, because the basic selection is suitable in the vast majority of situations, this is an effective tool that will save you tremendous time. Think of it as a tool for creating a rough selection that you'll want to modify by using one of the options discussed; as such, it is a time-saver in terms of the overall process of creating the perfect selection.

Selection Brush

Elements offers a unique tool for creating selections by painting, called the Selection Brush tool. Many users find it easier to paint over the part of the image they want to select, rather than tracing around the edge to define the active area. This tool is designed for exactly that purpose.

Note: Under the Selection Brush tool is the Magic Selection Brush tool, which we'll discuss in the next section.

To get started, choose the Selection Brush tool from the Tools palette or press A. Then simply paint over the image to define the area you want to select. As you paint, the border of the area you paint will be marked by the marquee of a selection (Figure 9.15). You can adjust the size and type of brush with the tools available in the Options bar. As a shortcut to brush size, press the left bracket key ([) to reduce the brush size or the right bracket key (]) to increase the brush size.

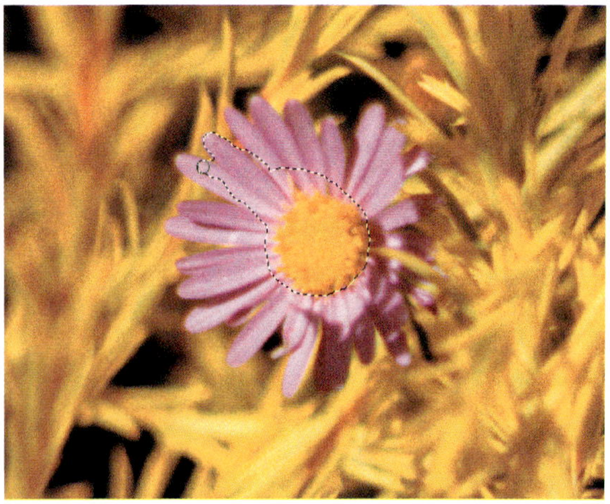

Figure 9.15 The Selection Brush tool in Elements allows you to paint the selection onto your image in order to define an active area.

Note too that there is a Hardness setting on the Options bar when the Selection Brush tool is active. This allows you to feather the selection as you create it. However, we recommend using a 100% Hardness setting in most cases and then applying feathering, as discussed in the next chapter.

The Mode drop-down list allows you to change the behavior of the Selection Brush from the default (Selection) to Mask. When you choose Mask mode, you will not be creating a marquee of the areas selected while painting. Instead, as you work with the Selection Brush you will be *masking*: specifying image areas that should not be selected by covering them with a color overlay (Figure 9.16). You can select any color from the Overlay Color option on the Options bar. Choose a color that's entirely different from the color of the subject so your painting effect will be obvious.

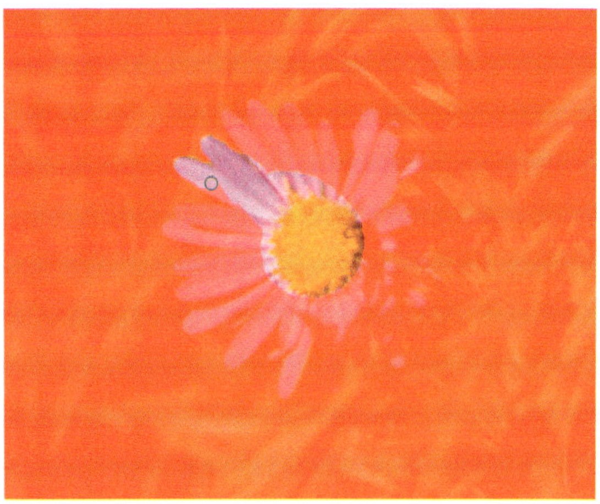

Figure 9.16 Besides using the Selection Brush tool to paint a selection marquee, you can also use it to paint a mask that covers nonselected areas by choosing the Mask option from the Mode drop-down list on the Options bar.

Whether you're using the Selection mode or the Mask mode, you can reverse the behavior of the tool (removing from the selection in Selection mode or adding to the selection in Mask mode) by holding the Alt/Option key as you paint.

Compared to the Marquee tools, the Selection Brush tool makes it more convenient to designate image areas to be selected, and you also get the bonus of a convenient masking option. Although you're painting over the area to be selected, you must use the same precision as tracing along an edge with other tools. Still, most users find that painting up to the edges requires less effort than tracing. In our experience, this painting process works best with the image magnified. Start with a large brush to designate a large section within the intended area. Switch to a smaller brush to select or mask precisely along the periphery of the area that you want to designate.

Magic Selection Brush

Right-click the Selection Brush in the Tools palette and you'll find the second option, Magic Selection Brush; you can also choose it by pressing F. This tool allows you to draw lines or dots to select part of an image. For example, you might select a specific object within the photo that's too dark or too drab and needs correction with Levels, Hue/Saturation, or another Elements tool. When you release the mouse button, the area you have designated should be automatically selected. This technique does not call for any precision. In fact, a single brush stroke along the object of interest may be all that is required.

This tool uses color and contrast data to analyze the image to determine the object you have designated. Sometimes it works incredibly well, especially when you use it to identify a distinct subject against a background of an entirely different color and texture with lots of contrast between the two elements. In that example, it should easily select just the subject area you intended.

Although the Magic Selection Brush sounds like magic, we do not recommend it because this tool is not always successful in identifying exactly the desired subject within a photo. Sometimes it will succeed and at other times it will fail. Although a few options are useful for problem solving, the Magic Wand tool discussed in the next section is a more useful alternative. When you select that tool, additional controls are available on the Options bar for greater precision in selecting exactly the image area that should be active.

Magic Wand

The Magic Wand tool was intended to create a selection with a single click of the mouse. When it succeeds, this tool seems truly magical. When too many clicks are required, it can be a bit frustrating. The trick is knowing what type of image is best suited for the Magic Wand tool and how to configure the Options bar controls for the best result.

This tool functions by sampling the pixel(s) that you click and then comparing other surrounding pixels to see whether they are a close-enough match. If they are, those additional pixels are included in the selection. Here's a simplified example of how that actually works or *should* work when all goes well. Imagine a photo of a mural on a smooth wall with distinct red, white, blue, and green sections. Click the Magic Wand on a blue area, and that will be selected and delineated by "marching ants." You can now manipulate this active area without affecting any other parts of the image.

Before setting the options for the Magic Wand tool, it is important to check a setting on the Options bar for the Eyedropper tool. Although these tools don't seem related, the Magic Wand tool uses the Sample Size setting from the Eyedropper tool to determine the actual value to use in evaluating pixels for inclusion in the selection. Choose the Eyedropper tool from the Tools palette, and choose an option from the Sample Size drop-down list on the Options bar. If you select Point Sample, only a single pixel will be used as the basis for pixel comparison by the Magic Wand tool. This can certainly provide precision, but it also introduces potential errors. For example, you could click a dust spot or a pixel with variation caused by grain or noise, and the resulting selection wouldn't match what you were intending to create. For this reason, we do not recommend using the Point Sample option.

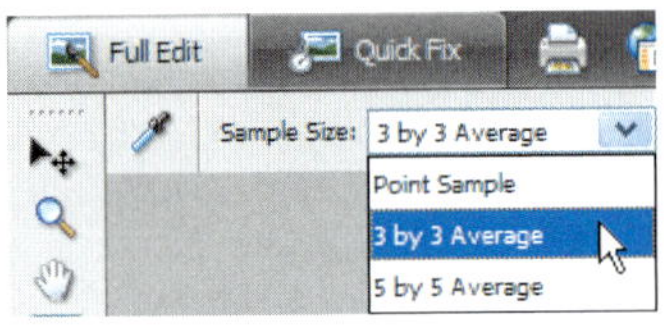

The 3 By 3 Average and 5 By 5 Average options, as their names indicate, sample a grid of pixels (a total of 9 or 25 pixels, respectively) surrounding the one you click and average their values. This average value is then used as the basis of the Magic Wand tool selection. Averaging helps to compensate for any local variation among pixels. We recommend the 3 By 3 Average setting, because it provides a suitable balance of precision and accuracy for most images. The 5 By 5 Average setting has a higher risk of averaging the pixel values to the point that the result isn't as accurate based on the pixel area you clicked.

After establishing the Sample Size setting, choose the Magic Wand tool from the Tools palette by clicking it or pressing W. The key to using the Magic Wand tool effectively is selecting the most suitable Tolerance level in the pertinent item on the Options bar. This setting determines how far apart pixel values can be and still be considered a match (Figure 9.17). With a low setting, pixels must be very close to the value of the pixel you clicked to be included in the selection. That leads to a risk that too few pixels will be identified. With a high setting, even pixels with very different values can be included in the selection, causing unrelated objects to be selected.

The Magic Wand tool is obviously best suited for images that have broad areas of similar tone and color you want to select. In addition to the mural mentioned earlier, another fine example is an area of open sky with no clouds. Because the pixels in the sky already have similar values, a relatively low Tolerance setting should be appropriate. You might start with a Tolerance value of 16 when experimenting.

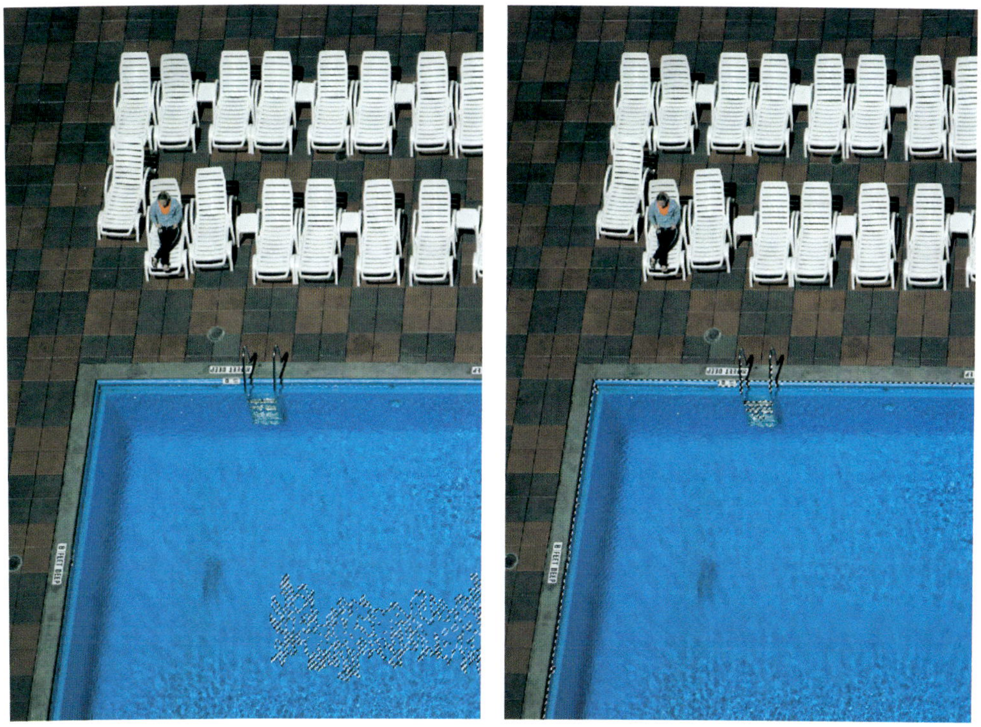

Figure 9.17 The Tolerance setting determines whether few (left) or many (right) pixels will be included in a selection.

Click the area of the image you want to select, such as a blue sky (Figure 9.18). You may find that the entire sky area was not selected, usually because of differences in the shade of blue; a very dark or very pale section of sky may have been ignored. In that case, set a higher tolerance level. Double-click the sky area to apply the higher tolerance to the new selection. If too few pixels are selected, choose Select > Deselect from the menu (alternatively press Ctrl/⌘+D). Set an even higher tolerance level and try again. Eventually you will find a Tolerance setting that produces the desired effect.

Sometimes you'll find that the Magic Wand selects too many pixels, including pixels from areas you didn't want to select. Using our blue sky example (Figure 9.19), perhaps this tool might select blue parts of the flag that's against the sky if the Tolerance level had been set too high. In that case choose Select > Deselect, set a lower Tolerance level, and click on the sky area to apply the new selection. You could also take advantage of the Subtract from Selection feature. With the Magic Wand active, right-click on the area that should not have been selected: the blue part of the flag in this example. This feature is also available as a button on the Options bar. Subtracting will select fewer pixels, reducing the selected area. This technique may require several clicks to achieve exactly the desired result. As discussed shortly, another feature is also available, Add To Selection, for increasing the selected area to include additional portions.

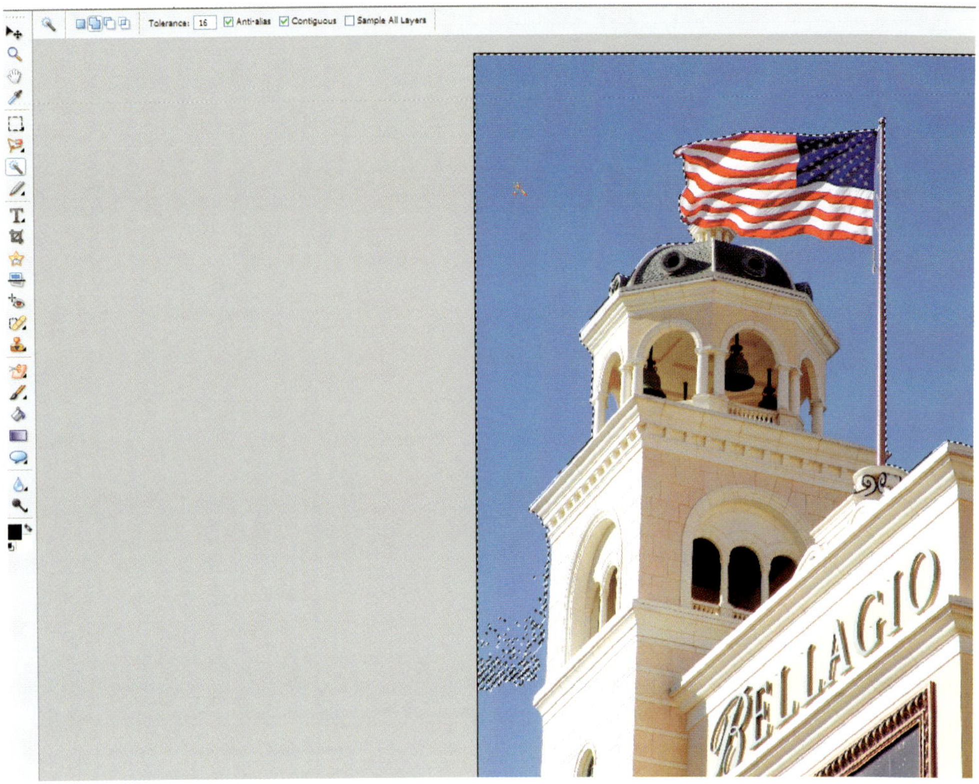

Figure 9.18 In some cases, an entire blue sky is automatically selected by the Magic Wand tool when using a Tolerance value of 16. For other images, such as this one, a higher tolerance level or another technique is required to achieve the desired effect.

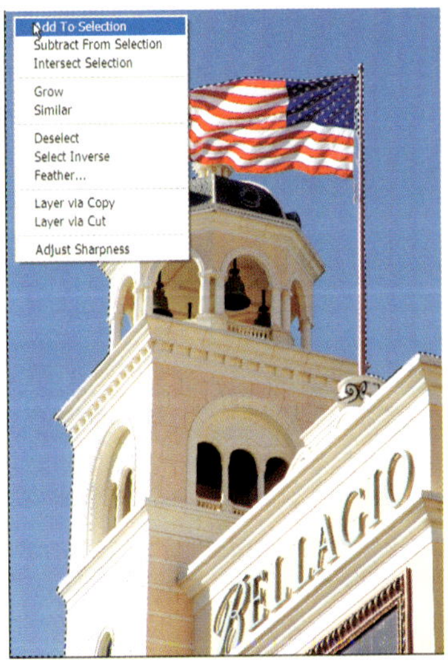

Figure 9.19 Because the sky in this image is not interrupted by branches or other intricate details, a full selection was easily achieved by increasing the Tolerance value from 16 to 24. The same effect could have been produced with a single click, using another feature, Add To Selection.

As a rule of thumb, consider doubling the Tolerance setting when a higher value is needed and halving it when a lower value is needed. Then narrow the value down by working between the established "border" values. For example, if 16 is too low, try 32.

If 32 is still too low, try 64. If that is too much, go back to a 48 for Tolerance (halfway between 32 and 64); continue "meeting in the middle" until you find an appropriate value.

Of course, you could spend a lot of time chasing the right Tolerance value. We recommend taking a tempered approach, trying to find a *suitable* value without spending too much time finding the *perfect* value.

If you can't find a suitable value relatively quickly, opt for a Tolerance setting that is a bit lower than needed. Then use the Add To Selection option to build up the final selection. That's available as a button on the Options bar or by right-clicking the image and choosing Add To Selection. Whenever the Tolerance level that you set is close to accurate, a few clicks with Add to Selection, or Subtract From Selection when that step is required, should produce the desired effect.

Note: It is better to start with a Tolerance value for the Magic Wand that results in a selection that encompasses less than the area you are trying to select and then build up the selection with the Add To Selection option.

It is important to keep in mind that when you add pixels to or subtract pixels from a selection by using the appropriate options with the Magic Wand tool, the selection is modified based on the pixel you click the second time. The natural tendency when adding to a selection with the Magic Wand tool is to Shift+click an area that isn't selected to add it to the selection. However, this will often cause areas you don't want to have selected to be added, based on the new sample point you clicked. You may need to Shift+click inside the existing selection, but at a different location than you originally clicked, to add the appropriate range of pixels to the selection. Also, keep in mind that you can adjust the Tolerance setting between mouse clicks when using the Add To Selection or Subtract From Selection buttons, giving you even greater control. Each time you click with the Magic Wand tool, pixels throughout the image are evaluated based on the Tolerance setting, regardless of whether the pixels are already selected.

Although the tolerance level is the pivotal setting for the Magic Wand tool, you'll want to consider other settings on the Options bar. The Anti-alias checkbox serves the same purpose as it does with the other selection tools discussed previously in this chapter, and I recommend leaving it selected.

The Contiguous option affects which pixels are evaluated. When you click a pixel with the Magic Wand, Elements looks outward from that pixel to find matching pixels. If it meets a pixel that doesn't match closely enough based on the Tolerance setting, that pixel creates a border. Pixels outside the areas defined by that border won't be considered (Figure 9.20). In other words, all pixels in the final selection will be contiguous, or neighboring each other.

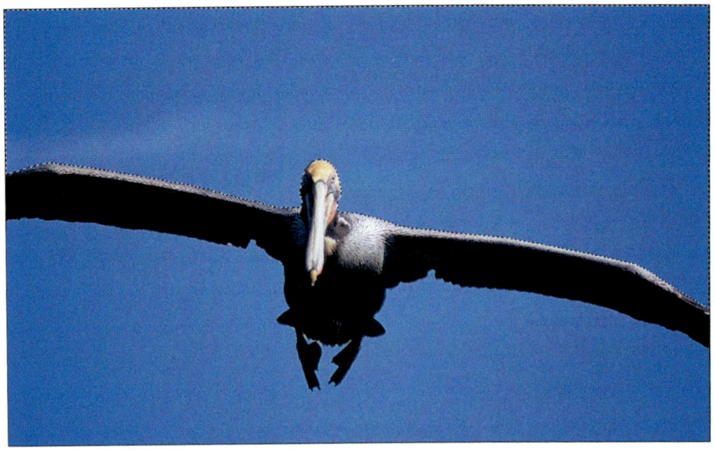

Figure 9.20 With the Contiguous option selected, pixels that are separated from the area of matching pixels won't be included in the selection.

With many images, you'll need to select similar areas that are *noncontiguous*. For example, you may want to select the sky in an image, but parts of the sky are blocked by trees, or by a bird as in Figure 9.20. Turning off the Contiguous option causes Elements to evaluate every pixel based on the pixel you click with the Magic Wand tool (Figure 9.21)

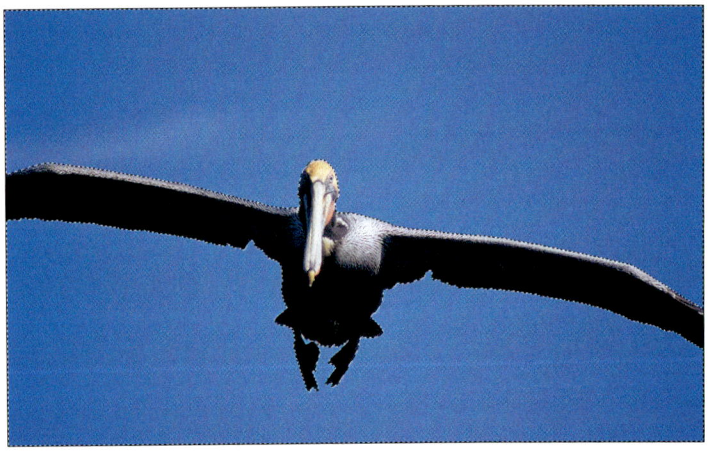

Figure 9.21 With the Contiguous checkbox deselected, all areas that match the pixel you clicked with the Magic Wand will be included in the selection.

The final item on the Options bar, Sample All Layers, allows you to specify whether Elements will evaluate pixel values based on all layers in the image or on only the currently active layer. Because you're viewing the image based on all visible layers, it usually makes sense to keep this option turned on. In fact, you can use this setting to make the Magic Wand tool more effective by creating a temporary adjustment layer that accentuates the difference between areas you do want to select and those you don't.

The Magic Wand tool is best for selecting areas of an image that have similar tone, texture, and color. If the area you are trying to select contains too much variation, evaluate the image to see whether you can easily select the opposite of what you really want. For example, if you want to select the foreground of an image, it might be easier to select the sky and then invert the selection by pressing Ctrl+Shift+I / ⌘+Shift+I.

Using the Threshold Technique

The selection methods covered so far in this chapter are quite straightforward and intuitive, but you can also use another trick to create selections. The Threshold technique is not a multipurpose tool for creating selections, but it can be useful with certain types of images.

In some situations, you'll want to select all the pixels in your image based on tonal value. Perhaps you'll want to select all the highlights, because you intend to tone them down a bit. Or you may want only the shadow areas because you want to work on those to extract a bit more detail. In either case, you can achieve the desired selection by duplicating the image and using the Threshold command to alter the layer based on tonal values.

Start by duplicating the image layer. We recommend reducing the Opacity of this new layer to about 50%, to make the next step easier to accomplish accurately (Figure 9.22).

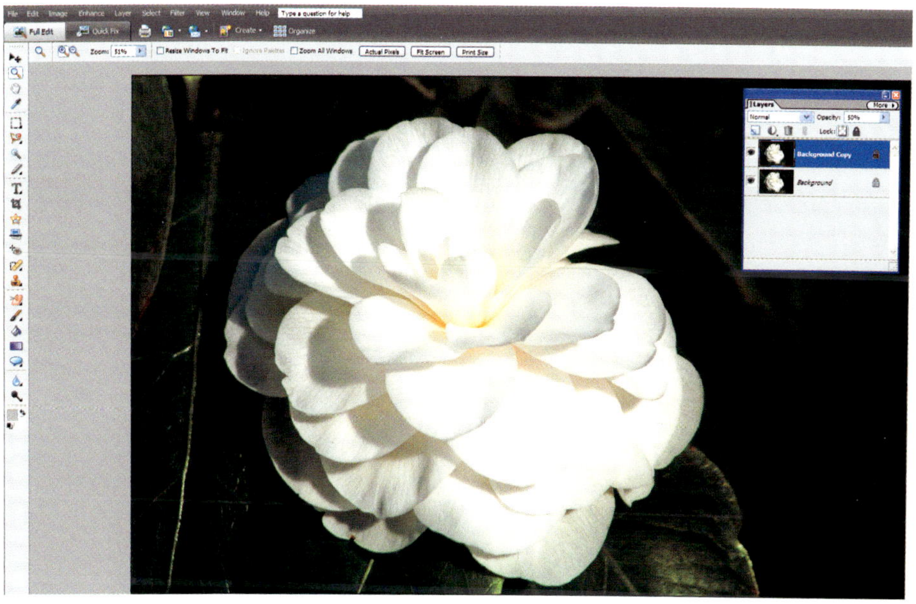

Figure 9.22 The first step in the threshold selection technique is to create a duplicate of your layer and reduce Opacity to about 50%.

Then run the Threshold functionality by choosing Filter > Adjustments > Threshold. The Threshold dialog box has only one value to adjust, which you can manipulate by using the slider. The value you set will determine the tonal value at which the pixels will be split. Elements will make any pixels at or greater than that value white, and any pixels less than that value black. Adjust the setting so the split between black and white occurs over the border of the area you want to select (Figure 9.23). Because you reduced the Opacity setting for this layer, you can see through it to help you determine the best value. When you have the value set, click OK.

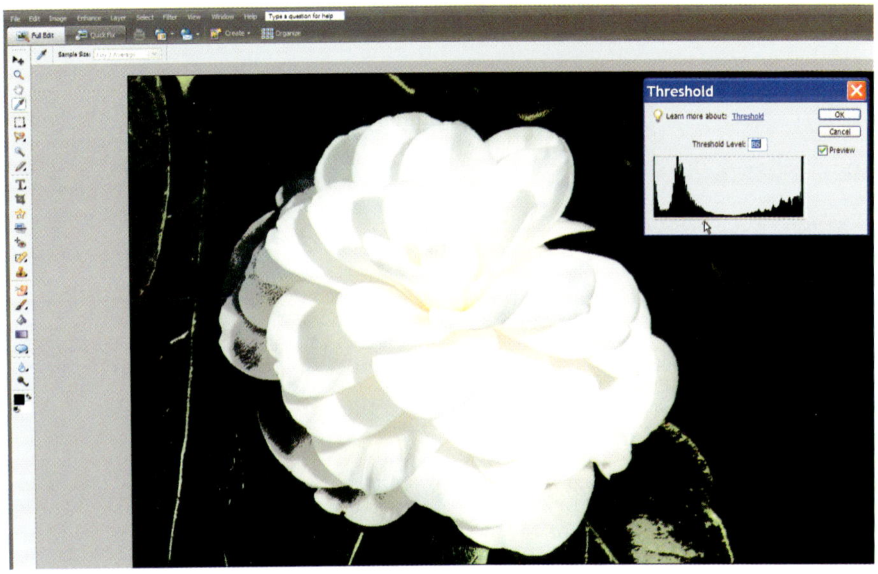

Figure 9.23 Adjust the Threshold setting to separate the area you want to select from the area that you don't.

Return the Opacity for this layer to 100% so it will be fully opaque. If you know certain areas shouldn't be included in the range to be selected, you can paint on those areas to clean up this template for the selection. For example, if black pixels are scattered around an otherwise white sky, you can paint with white to clean them up. Next, use the Magic Wand tool with the Contiguous option turned off, and click the area of the image you want to select. This will create a selection based on the specific tonal range you defined using Threshold (Figure 9.24). Chances are this won't produce an absolutely ideal selection, but it will quickly get you started with a good basic selection that you can modify as required for perfection.

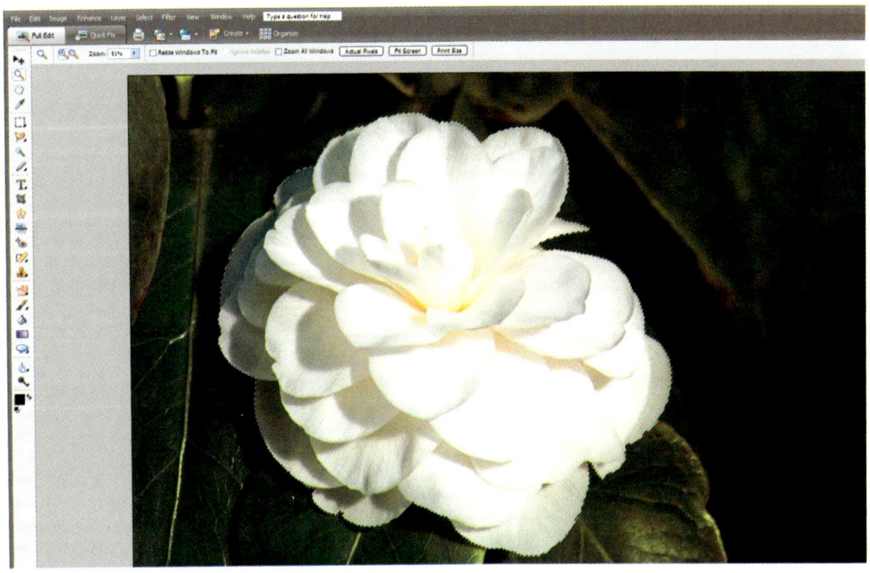

Figure 9.24 The result of the threshold selection technique is a selection that is easy to create. Threshold produces a suitable selection when the image demonstrates obvious tonal separation.

Modifying Selections

Using the appropriate tools to delineate an active area is an important start, but often you'll need to modify a selection slightly. A variety of Modify options are available, enabling you to change the size and shape of a selection after you have created it.

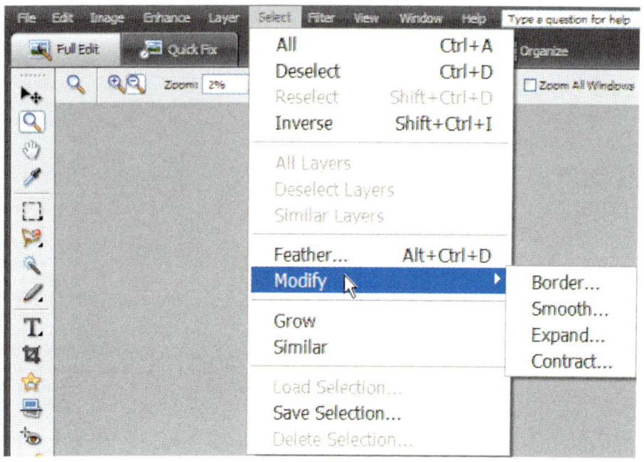

If you choose Select > Modify, you'll see four options for altering the selection:

- The Border option (Select > Modify > Border) allows you to change the selection so it includes only an area along the border of what had been selected. You can define how many pixels wide you want this final selection to be, and they will be split on either side of the existing selection (Figure 9.25). This can be helpful if you need to apply a blur around just the edge of a subject in a photo, for example.
- The Smooth option (Select > Modify > Smooth) smooths out rough edges or tiny flaws of a selection. You define a radius size in pixels, and Elements examines the selection and smooths it out accordingly. If you have jagged lines in a selection, smoothing will solve the problem. This option is also helpful when random small specks aren't included in a selection. For example, dust or grain in the sky can cause scattered individual pixels to be excluded from the selection. Using the Smooth option adds these areas to the existing selection (Figure 9.26). Be careful when using this on selections of fine detail; it can cause the selection to smooth out to the point that the details are no longer selected accurately.

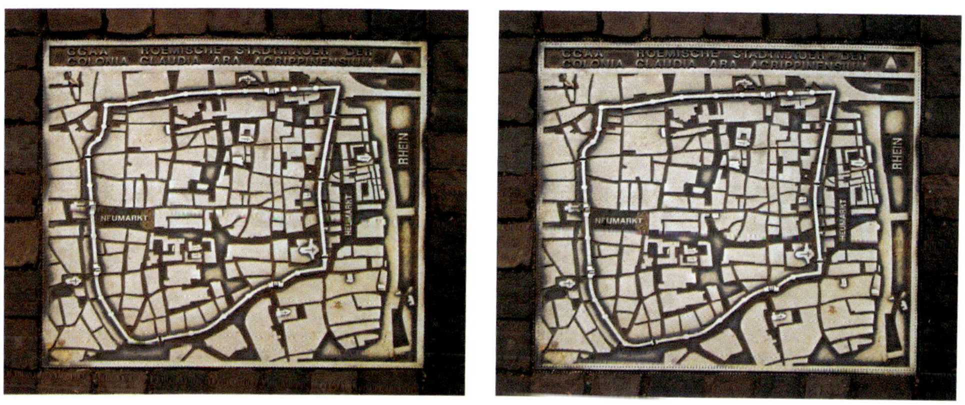

Figure 9.25 The Select > Modify > Border command produces a selection that defines the border of the original marquee.

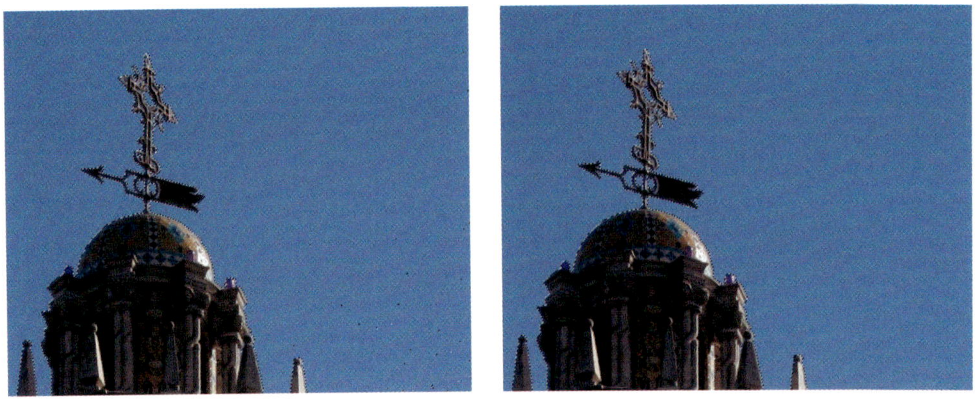

Figure 9.26 The Select > Modify > Smooth option is a great way to clean up a selection that left tiny areas excluded.

- The Expand (Select > Modify > Expand) option allows you to enlarge the selection by a set number of pixels and it respects the outer edge of your images. If a portion of the selection is along the outer border of the document, the selection won't be adjusted in that area.
- Conversely, the Contract (Select > Modify > Contract) option allows you to reduce the size of the selection by a set number of pixels and also respects the image edges.

The Grow and Similar options found on the Select menu also have similar behavior. The Grow option uses the Tolerance setting of the Magic Wand tool to expand the selection based on similar color values, but only contiguous pixels will be selected. The Similar option does the same thing, except that it selects noncontiguous pixels.

So far we have primarily discussed creating selections without a feathered edge. A feathered selection has a gradual transition between pixels that are and are not selected, so any adjustments made will also taper off. You can feather the edge of a selection by choosing Select > Feather from the menu. However, we prefer not to use this option, because it requires an arbitrary decision about the number of pixels the selection should be feathered by. Instead, we'll apply a Gaussian blur to the final result of the selection, which is typically a mask on an image or adjustment layer, as you'll see in Chapter 10.

Saving and Loading Selections

After you've created a selection, you'll probably want to save it for future use, just in case. In our opinion, any selection that required more than 10 seconds to create should be saved, even if you don't think you'll use it again. The selection is then saved as part of the image file, so you can always reload the selection in the future if needed.

Note: Not all image file formats allow you to save selections, because they don't all allow you to save alpha channels. If you're going to save a selection, it should be part of your master image file saved as a Photoshop PSD or TIFF image file.

To save a selection, choose Select > Save Selection from the menu. Although you can save selections in different documents with the same dimensions, we recommend saving them within the current document. Therefore, leave the Document setting to the default value, which will be the name of the current document. The Save Selection drop-down should be set to New so the selection will be saved as it is. If an existing selection has been saved, you can also choose that selection from the Save Selection drop-down, and merge the current selection with the previously saved selection. We do not recommend this option because it merges two separate selections together, so they can't be used separately in the future.

The Name is the key setting (and generally the only one you'll need to change) in the Save Selection dialog box (Figure 9.27). Be sure to save the selection with a descriptive name that will make sense to you in the future when you need to load a selection.

If you are using the New option from the Save Selection drop-down list, the Operation section of the dialog will have only a single option to create a new channel. Otherwise, you'll have the same options as you have for each selection tool to create a new saved selection (Replace): Add To Selection, Subtract From Selection, or Intersect With Selection.

When you click OK, the selection will be saved as an alpha channel.

Note: Saved selections aren't truly saved until you save the image that you stored them in. If you save a selection but then close the image without saving it, the selection won't be saved.

In the future, you can load the selection by choosing Select > Load Selection from the menu and choosing the name from the drop-down (Figure 9.28).

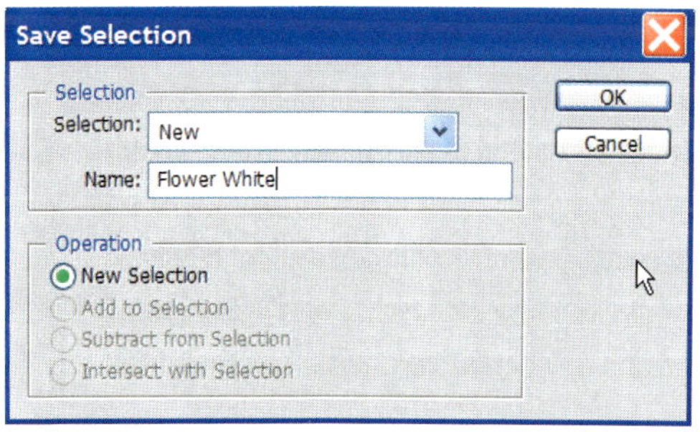

Figure 9.27 When saving a selection, give it a name that identifies it clearly so you'll be able to select it from a list later.

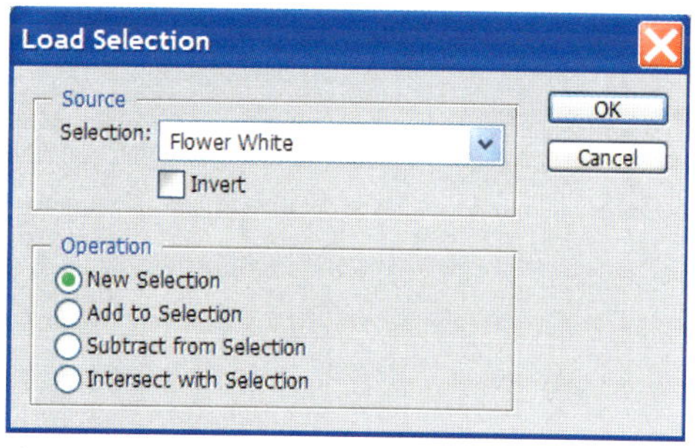

Figure 9.28 You can recall any saved selection by choosing it from the Load Selection dialog box.

Putting Selections to Use

By themselves, of course, selections don't do a thing. They just sit there like so many "marching ants" on your image. However, as mentioned earlier, when pixels are selected, they become the active area in an image; any manipulation will affect only those pixels. That means you can target adjustments to a particular area and protect other areas from being altered. Master the art of building perfect selections, and you've built the foundation for exercising absolute control over every pixel in your images, as you'll see in the next chapter.

Targeted Adjustments

Up to this point, each task in the image-optimization workflow has been leading up to the topics covered in this chapter. When working on an image, we tend to view the initial steps of the workflow as laying the foundation for the final and most important adjustments. Being able to exercise control over specific areas of an image—making adjustments specifically to those "active" areas—provides greater freedom, as mentioned briefly in Chapter 9, "Making Selections." It means you are limited only by your own imagination when it comes to producing the image you are trying to achieve. In this chapter, we'll cover the concepts and techniques that will allow you to produce an image that matches your vision.

10

Chapter Contents

Introducing Masking
Masking from a Selection
Masking by Painting

Introducing Masking

Targeted adjustments for your images utilize a method called *masking*, which enables you to define the specific areas of an image that should be affected by a certain adjustment. In Chapters 5 to 8, we discussed adjustments that apply to the entire image or apply selectively to specific tonal or color ranges. Masking an adjustment layer allows you to choose which areas of the image you would like to affect. For example, you might decide to increase the saturation in your subject but not the background. Or perhaps you'd like to lighten the subject but darken the background so that your subject stands out more prominently. In both examples, using a targeted adjustment (Figure 10.1) enables you to do just that.

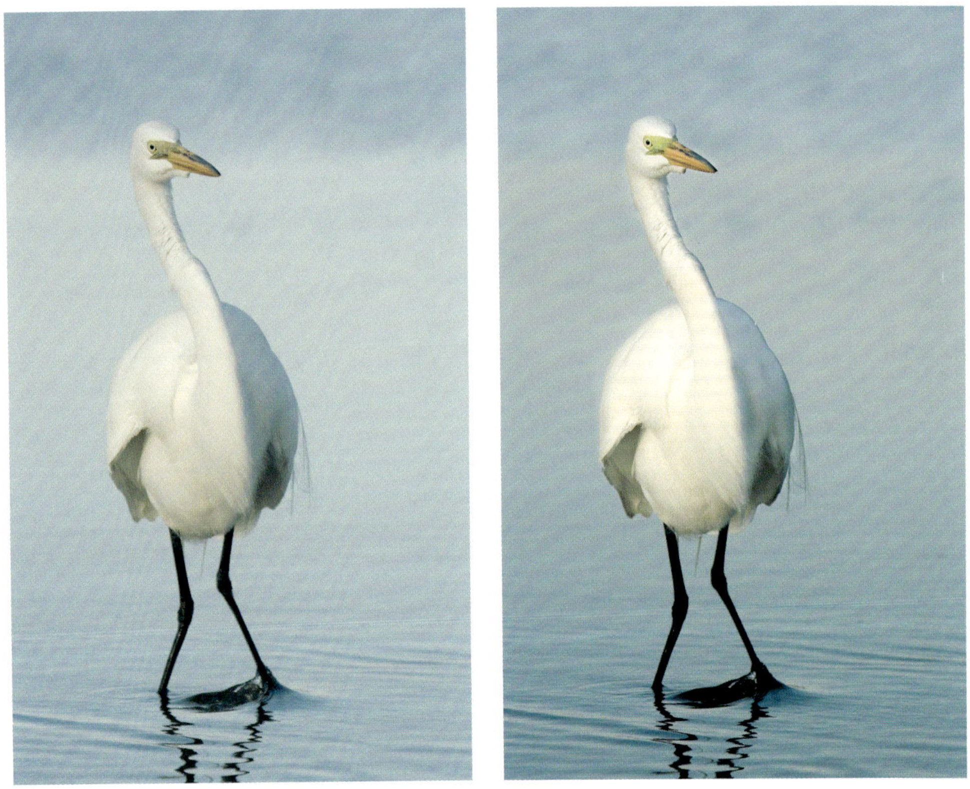

Figure 10.1 By making targeted adjustments, we were able to darken the background and brighten the Great Egret.(Photos by Ellen Anon, www.sunbearphoto.com)

You may have noticed that each adjustment layer contains a white box when you first create it (Figure 10.2). This white box is called a *layer mask*. You use the layer mask to control which parts of the image are affected by the changes you make in that particular layer. The layer mask is the same shape as your image. The white area of the layer mask corresponds to a part of your image that will show the effect of that particular adjustment layer. The black part of the layer mask indicates a part of your image that will not be affected by the adjustment. By default the layer mask is white and will show the adjustment on the entire image. By making parts of the layer mask black, you can block the modification effect from those areas of your image.

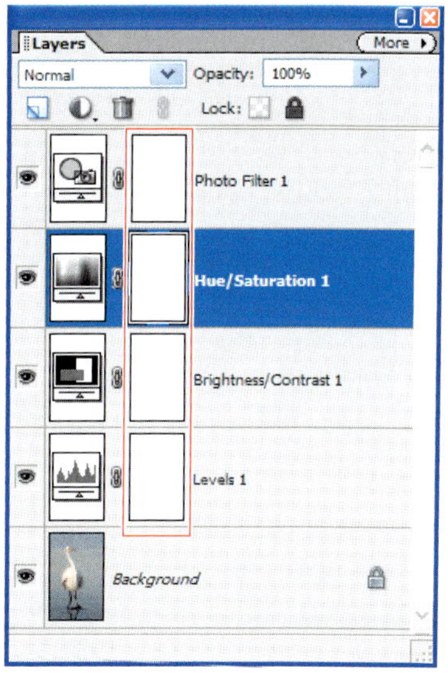

Figure 10.2 Every layer automatically has a layer mask. (Photo by Ellen Anon, www.sunbearphoto.com)

You can create a mask to block portions of an image in two ways. You can start from a selection, or you can paint on a mask to define the areas you want to block or to reveal. We'll cover both in the next two sections.

Note: Most people use the terms *hiding* and *revealing* for masking, but we prefer to discuss them as *blocking* and *revealing*. It can be useful to associate blocking with *black*. In his workshops, Tim often reiterates a useful concept: "Black blocks. . . white reveals."

Masking from a Selection

Creating a mask-based adjustment layer on a selection is not complicated. In Chapter 9, you learned how to create selections with a variety of tools and techniques. The most challenging part of using a selection as the basis of a mask is creating a suitable selection in the first place.

Select an image and create an appropriate selection of an area that you want to lighten, for example. You can then use the selection as the basis of an adjustment layer that will affect only the area you've selected. Make sure the selection is active—in other words, that the "marching ants" are visible. Then choose Layer > New Adjustment Layer, and select the type of adjustment you'd like to make: Hue/Saturation perhaps, to enrich the colors in the specified area. Make the desired adjustment. Because a selection is active, Photoshop Elements 5 assumes that you want to mask the image based on the current selection and creates the mask accordingly. The area that you select will remain white on the layer mask, but the rest of the layer mask will be black. Consequently, the modification that you make—to color saturation in this example—will apply only to the area that you selected when creating the adjustment layer (Figure 10.3).

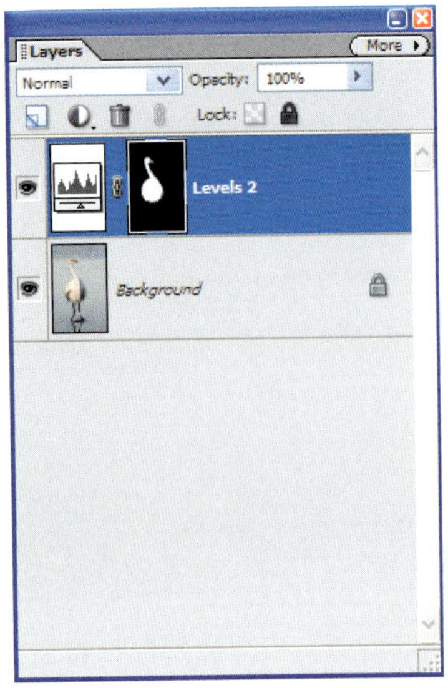

Figure 10.3 When you create a new adjustment layer with an active area, the layer mask will automatically reflect the selection. (Photo by Ellen Anon, www.sunbearphoto.com)

For reasons mentioned in Chapter 9, we do not recommend feathering the selection you create. Instead, later in this chapter, we'll show you how to apply the same effect as feathering, by blurring the mask after it has been created. This method will provide an opportunity to change the effect based on a preview of the result.

To become familiar with targeted adjustments, experiment with extreme modifications by using a Hue/Saturation adjustment layer. The concepts you learn will apply to all types of adjustment layers After you get comfortable with the mechanism of layer masks, you'll be able to apply them with ease to make subtle adjustments of all types.

Note: When viewing a layer mask, remember that black blocks and white reveals.

When creating a targeted adjustment, it can also be helpful to see what the image looked like before and after you created the mask. To toggle the mask on and off, hold the Shift key and click the mask thumbnail. A red X appears on the mask thumbnail when the mask is disabled (Figure 10.4).

At this point you have a basic targeted adjustment. However, a harsh transition may occur between the parts of the image that are affected by the adjustment and those that are not affected. That can make for a "cut-out" and unnatural appearance. To produce a more realistic effect, you need a more gradual transition between the affected and unaffected areas. Elements allows you to feather the selection, but that would call for a decision, in advance, as to the number of pixels you should select for feathering.

Instead, we recommend producing the same effect *after* creating the mask and while observing a preview: blurring the edge slightly to make it appear more natural. This will smooth the transition between areas that are blocked and areas that are revealed, producing a more gradual and realistic transition.

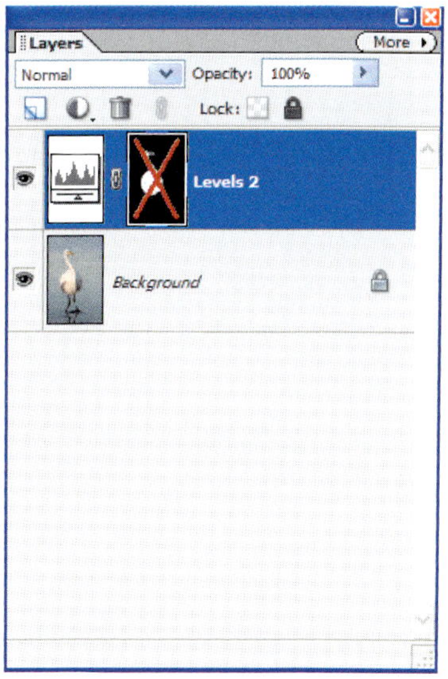

Figure 10.4 By holding the Shift key, you can toggle the mask on and off. (Photo by Ellen Anon, www.sunbearphoto.com)

First, make sure you have the adjustment layer selected. The layer mask will automatically be selected. Choose Filter > Blur > Gaussian Blur from the menu. While observing the effect on your image, select an appropriate blur setting (Figure 10.5). For objects with a relatively crisp edge, a value of 1 or 2 pixels often works well. For subjects with a "fuzzier" edge, you may need to blur with a higher pixel value. By applying a blur after creating the mask, you're able to determine the best setting for that specific situation.

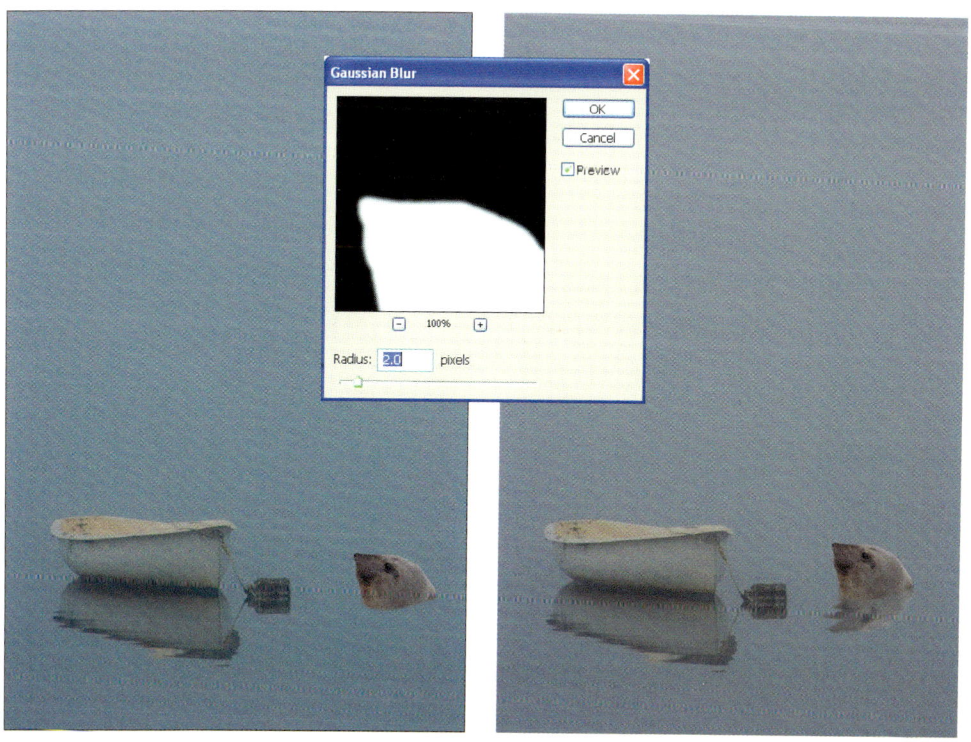

Figure 10.5 Applying a Gaussian Blur to the layer mask allows you to create a custom feathered edge that looks more natural.

Note: Note too that the pixel value chosen in the Gaussian Blur dialog box is often affected by image resolution. If you're working with a large, high-resolution image, for example, you will need to use a higher blur value than for a small image file that you're preparing for Web use. For an extremely large file, we suggest starting with a value of 2 and increasing it slightly if you find that necessary.

Masking by Painting

Creating a mask from a selection is simple, but at times it is best to *paint* the mask instead. As you've already seen, areas that are black on a mask are blocked so they are not affected by the adjustments you make; areas that are white are revealed so they are affected by any modification. Therefore, you can simply paint on the mask with black to block, or paint with white to reveal the effect as desired.

When would you want to use the painting technique? We find that it's most useful when you want to adjust an image area that is defined by relatively nebulous edges. Painting can also be convenient when you need to modify a mask after creating it from a selection or when creating a selection to start from is a challenge. In those situations, painting to define the mask provides the best solution.

To create a mask with painting, make sure you don't already have an active selection. Then create an adjustment layer. Again, we recommend making an exaggerated adjustment so it's easy to see exactly where in the image the adjustment layer will apply. To modify the mask for the adjustment layer, select the Brush tool, press D on your keyboard to set the colors to their defaults of black and white, and then press X as needed to switch foreground and background colors. Paint with black over the image to block the effect of the adjustment in specific areas of the image; paint with white to reveal the adjustment (Figure 10.6). You're not actually painting directly on the image, of course, but on the layer mask. You can think of this as erasing that can easily be undone. Paint in black to effectively erase pixels, but then paint in white to reveal those pixels again.

Note: We usually use a soft brush when painting an adjustment layer mask. That way the effect blends in gradually, and we may not have to use the Gaussian blur technique (discussed earlier) to feather the edges of the mask.

Note: You can always start with a selection to produce a basic layer mask and then paint on that mask to adjust it.

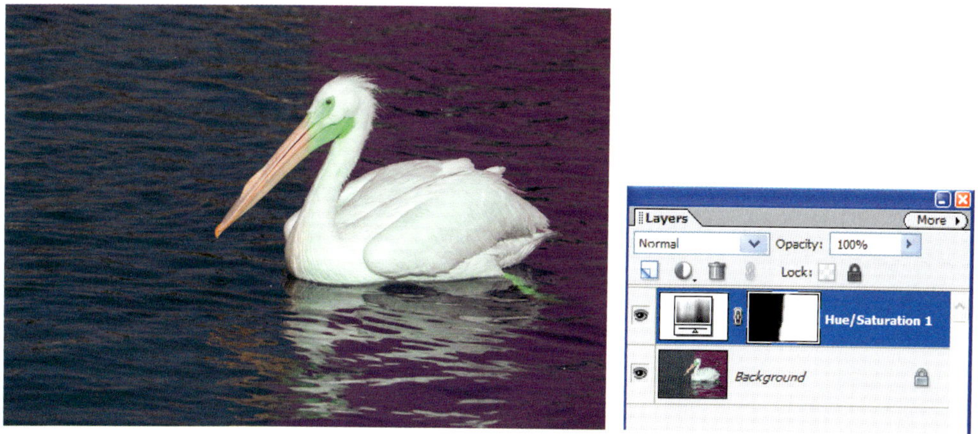

Figure 10.6 By making an exaggerated adjustment, such as the hue modification made here, it's easy to see that you can think of black as erasing while thinking of white as "unerasing" the effect. (Photos by Ellen Anon, www.sunbearphoto.com)

If you'd like to see what the layer mask looks like, hold the Alt/Option key as you click the layer mask thumbnail. This toggles the mask to be displayed as a black-and-white image for a more graphic display of the exact shape of the mask (Figure 10.7). This is a great way to determine whether there are areas you missed in the mask; if so, simply fix those by painting on the mask. Then hold down the Alt/Option key as you click the layer mask thumbnail once more to toggle back to the image view again.

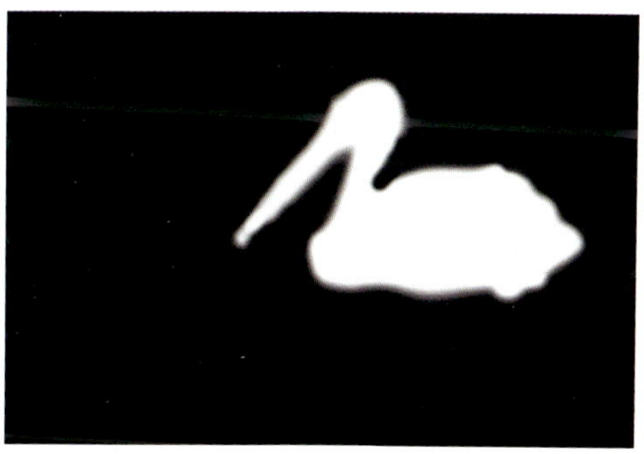

Figure 10.7 When you Alt/Option+click a layer mask thumbnail, you can see the black-and-white representation of that mask. (Photo by Ellen Anon, www.sunbearphoto.com)

If you later decide you need to further revise the adjustment layer mask, simply click the adjustment layer to make it active and paint as needed to change the areas where the adjustment is blocked or revealed. If you've already applied the Gaussian blur to the layer mask for the adjustment layer, reduce the brush's hardness setting. That will allow you to produce a soft edge with a smooth transition between areas that are and are not affected by the adjustment layer.

At times you'll want the adjustment layer to apply to a very small area of your image, but that area won't be conducive to making a selection. In such situations, it may seem that the only solution is to paint with black throughout most of the image, avoiding only the area that you want to modify. However, it's quicker to completely fill the initially white adjustment layer mask with black so it doesn't apply to any of the image; then, paint with white in the small area where you want the adjustment to be revealed.

To try this technique after creating the new adjustment layer, choose Edit > Fill Layer from the menu, choose Black from the Use drop-down list, and click OK. This fills the layer mask with black, blocking the effect of the adjustment from the entire image. You can then use the Brush tool with the foreground color set to white to paint the adjustment in the small areas where you'd like it to be applied.

Note: You can also use Alt/Option+Delete to fill a layer mask with the foreground color and Ctrl/⌘+Delete to fill a layer mask with the background color.

Alternative Methods of Placing Pixels

So far you've seen how you can paint with black or white on an adjustment layer mask to target specific areas where the adjustment should be blocked or revealed. However, it is helpful to keep in mind that you can use any method at all to place pixels onto a layer mask. As long as the mask is active (still selected) on the Layers palette, any painting will be applied to the layer mask rather than the image itself.

For example, let's say you'd like to only partially block or reveal the effects of an adjustment layer. In that case, paint on the layer mask with a shade of gray. This will cause the effect of the adjustment to be partially blocked or revealed to the extent that the shade of gray you use is nearly black or white, respectively. You could also paint at a reduced opacity to produce a similar effect. And, as we mentioned previously, you can paint with a soft-edged brush to produce a gradual transition between the areas that are and are not affected by the adjustment layer. At other times you may need to paint with a hard-edged brush to make a more distinct transition.

Note: You can use any method or tool that allows you to place pixels on a layer to place pixels onto a layer mask, so be creative when you're trying to solve a particular problem with a mask.

If you have created a targeted adjustment and want to make another adjustment to the same part of the image, Ctrl/⌘+click the layer mask; that will create a selection based on the mask. With the selection active, create a new adjustment layer. The new adjustment layer mask will reflect the same selection. That way you can easily make multiple adjustments to a portion of your image.

Applying a Gradient to a Mask

One particularly helpful example of a tool you can use to place pixels onto an adjustment layer mask is the Gradient tool. This allows you to place a gradient on a layer mask, resulting in an adjustment that affects one side of the image completely but gradually tapers off in a given direction until it has no effect at the other side of the image. The most common example of using such a gradient is in a composition where you wish you had used a "graduated" neutral density filter over your lens while making the photo. A filter of this type consists of glass that is clear on one half and gray (neutral density) on the other half, with a feathered edge between the two areas. It's particularly useful in outdoor photography for darkening a bright sky without darkening the foreground of an image. You can re-create the effect that would have been provided by such a filter by creating an adjustment layer with a gradient mask in Elements (Figure 10.8).

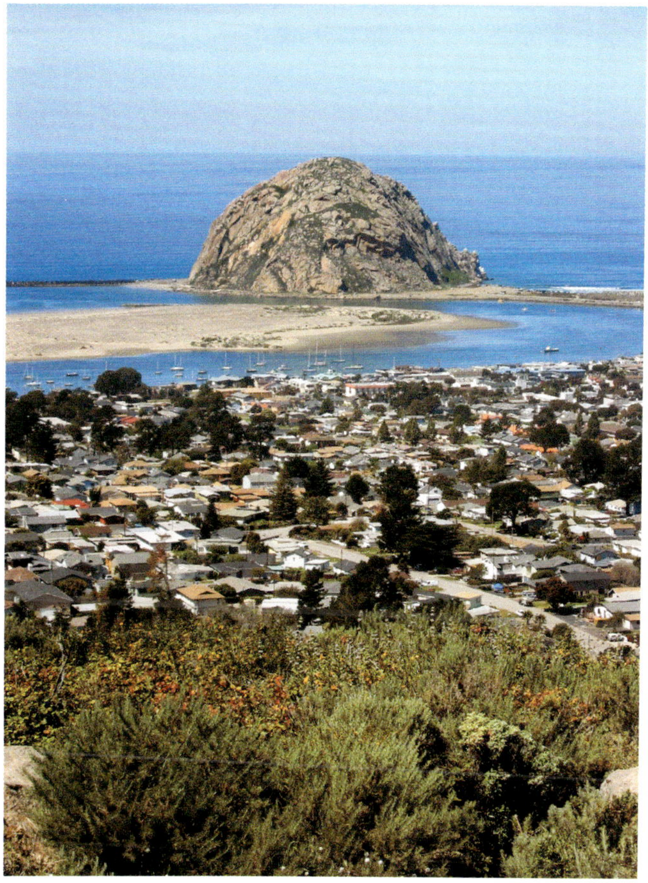

Figure 10.8 To darken this sky without darkening the foreground, a gradient on a mask for an adjustment layer will provide a perfect solution.

Start by creating a new adjustment layer that produces the desired effect in the area of the image that requires some modification. For example, you might create a Levels adjustment layer and use it to darken the sky in an image. After you've made the adjustment, select the Gradient tool from the Tools palette or press G on your keyboard.

On the Options bar near the top of the screen, click the drop-down list for the gradient editor; choose the first gradient thumbnail on the list, the Foreground To Background gradient. Next, select the Linear Gradient option from the set of five buttons that allow you to choose a style for your gradient (Figure 10.9). Finally, press D to set the colors to the defaults of black and white; set white to the foreground color (pressing X to switch foreground and background colors if necessary). You're now ready to create a gradient that will transition from white to black.

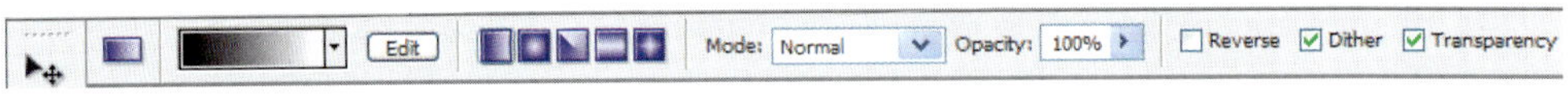

Figure 10.9 The Options bar for the Gradient tool provides the controls needed to produce the desired effect when masking an adjustment layer with a gradation.

Because you intend to create the gradient on the layer mask for the adjustment layer you just created, make sure that the adjustment layer is the active layer on the Layers palette. Then click and drag on the image to create a gradient. The foreground color will start at the point where you first click, with a smooth gradation to the background color at the point where you release the mouse. The length of the line you drag determines the distance over which the gradient will transition, and the direction determines the angle of that gradient. To lock the gradient to 45-degree increments, simply hold the Shift key as you drag.

If you're working with an image that calls for darkening the sky, click in the area of sky that represents the lowest area that requires complete adjustment—full darkening in this case. Then drag downward to the point where you do not want any darkening effect at all. If you're not happy with the initial gradient you created, simply press Ctrl/⌘+Z to undo, and then click and drag again to replace the gradient with a new one. After you're finished, the result will be an adjustment that blends smoothly (Figure 10.10). You will not see a harsh edge between the affected area (darkened sky) and the unaffected area.

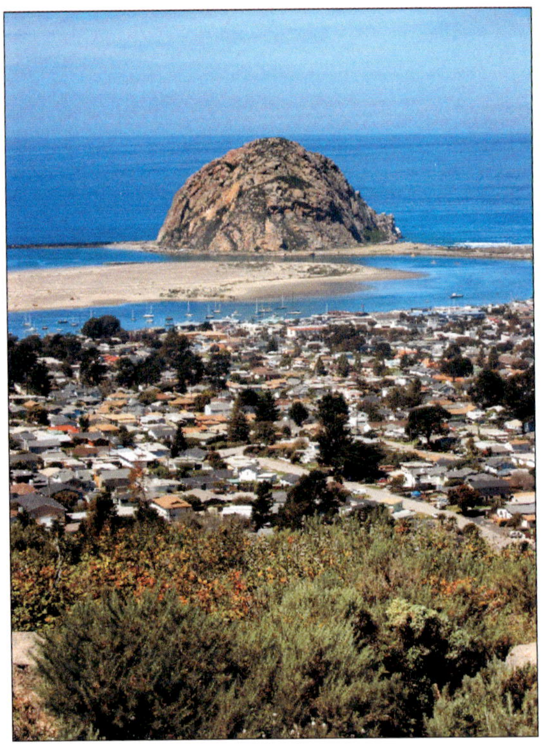

Figure 10.10 Applying a gradient to the layer mask for an adjustment layer produces an effect similar to using a graduated split neutral density filter when capturing an image.

Hitting Your Target

The topics in this chapter may seem relatively simple, and in a general sense they are. However, the opportunities they open up for your images are limitless. By enabling you to produce targeted adjustments for any area of your image, these techniques provide powerful capabilities. Practice making selections and targeting adjustments to specific areas of your images, and you'll be the master of your digital workflow.

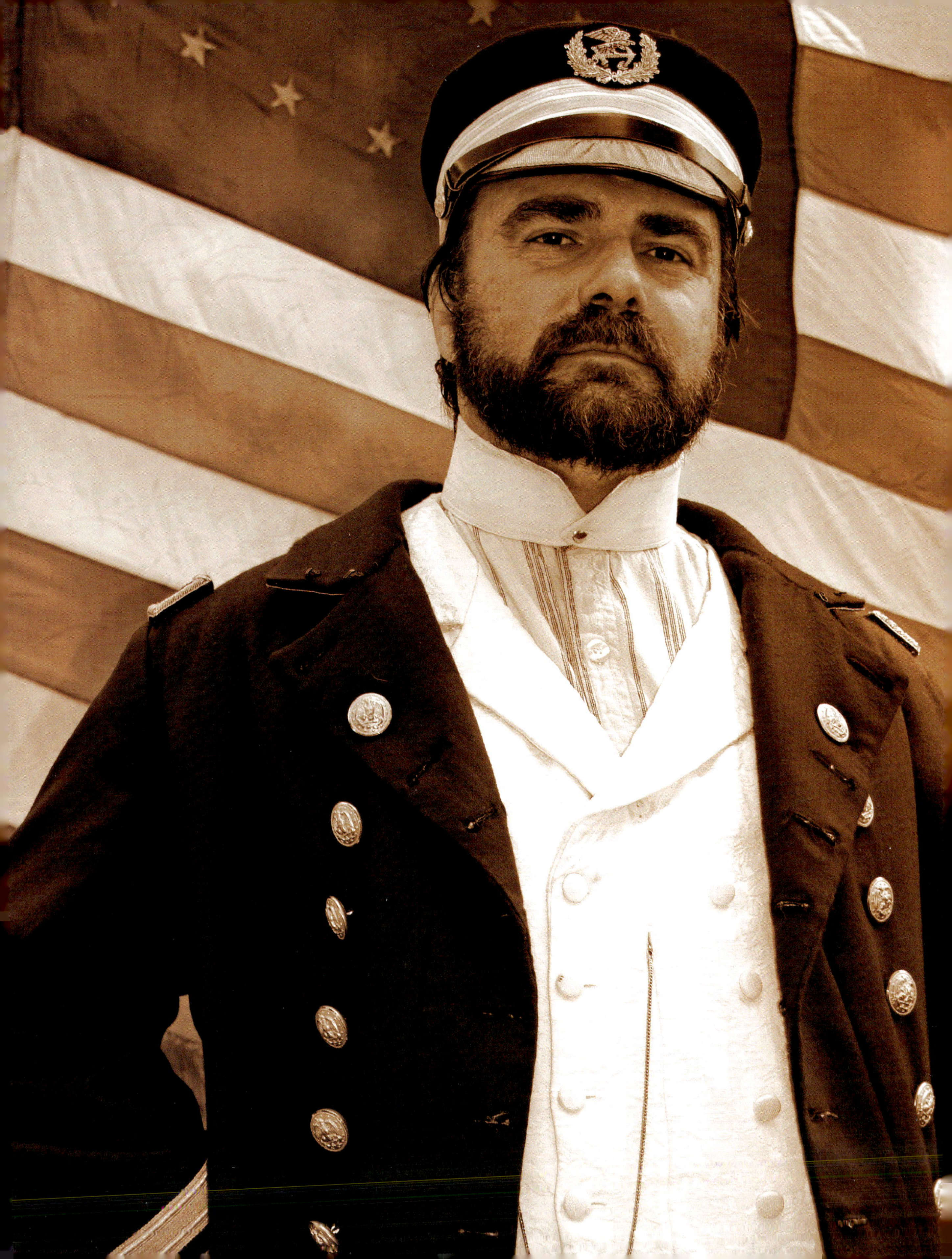

11 Creative Adjustments

Up to this point, we have presented components of an overall digital workflow that allow you to optimize images to achieve the best results that match your vision. However, all the methods presented have been aimed at producing a "normal" photographic image. Although this is the goal of most photographers with most images, at times you'll want to take some creative license and present a unique interpretation of an image.

Chapter Contents

Getting Creative
Colorize
Grayscale Conversion
High Pass Sharpening
Filters

Getting Creative

After completing the full workflow for optimizing your images, you're ready to think about any creative adjustments you'd like to make. We recommend waiting until this stage of the workflow before considering a more creative approach because that ensures you have focused on getting the best quality possible from your master image before considering entirely new interpretations of those photos. Even if you think you'll be presenting a black-and-white version of the image exclusively, we still recommend starting with an optimization of the color image. This will help ensure that the original master is of the best quality and will provide a better frame of reference as you apply creative adjustments.

In this chapter, we'll discuss only a handful of creative adjustments you may want to consider for certain images. As you reach the end of your workflow, you'll likely find yourself wanting to explore additional interpretations of your images more and more. Think of this chapter as an introduction to creative adjustments, providing some insight into what is possible with Photoshop Elements 5. Then, each time you reach the end of your optimization workflow, you'll be better prepared to think of new ways you could present some of your favorite images.

Colorize

In Chapter 5, "Tone and Color," and Chapter 8, "Advanced Color Adjustments," we discussed many aspects of the Hue/Saturation adjustment but didn't mention one of the available creative options. The Colorize checkbox provides a way to apply a color in such a way as to produce a monochromatic image, in which a single color is used at various tonal values. You can think of this as a monochromatic image that uses a colored ink instead of black (Figure 11.1).

Although it is possible to include both a basic saturation adjustment and the Colorize feature in a single Hue/Saturation adjustment layer, we recommend creating a new adjustment layer for the Colorize adjustment. This also makes it easier to switch between different versions of your image, choosing between the full-color and Colorize options by toggling the visibility of a single Hue/Saturation adjustment layer. Therefore, the first step is to create a new Hue/Saturation adjustment layer for your image.

In the Hue/Saturation dialog box, select the Colorize checkbox, which will cause some aspects of the controls to change (Figure 11.2). The Hue slider changes to a representation that includes zero at the far left rather than center and has a scale from 0 to 360 rather than from –180 to +180 (these numbers represent position on the color wheel as an indicator of actual color value). The Saturation slider's original range of–100 to +100 changes to a range of 0 to 100. Adjusting these sliders will change the color (Hue) of the image as well as the intensity (Saturation) of that color.

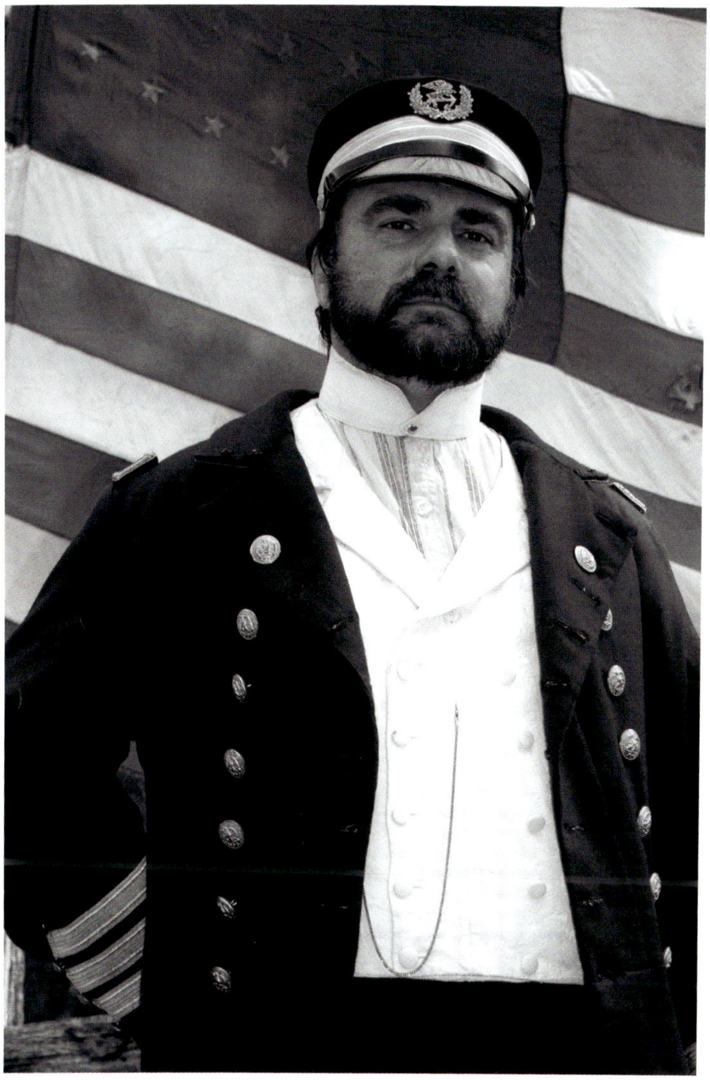

Figure 11.1 The Colorize option in the Hue/Saturation dialog box allows you to produce monochromatic images from a full-color original.

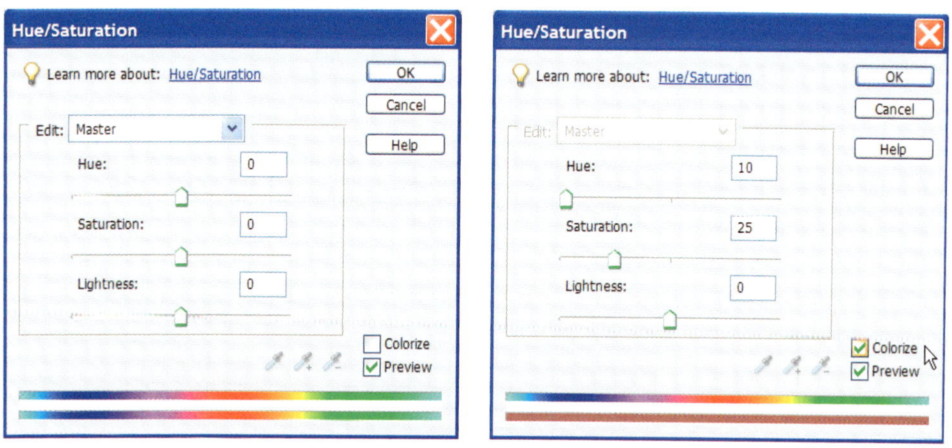

Figure 11.2 When you select the Colorize checkbox in the Hue/Saturation dialog box, the controls change.

You'll also notice that at the bottom of the Hue/Saturation dialog box, the color bar representing the "after" value for colors changes to reflect only the single color that will now exist within the image. The Edit drop-down list becomes disabled because you aren't able to adjust individual color channels when working with Colorize.

Experiment with the Hue slider, and you'll notice that it changes colors. Select the particular color you'd like to use for the Colorize effect. Think about the psychology of the colors you're considering and the context of the image. For example, scenes with snow and water tend to look good with cooler colors such as cyan or blue, and images with metal or "rugged" subjects tend to look better with warmer tones such as red or magenta. You have tremendous flexibility and can choose any color of the rainbow (Figure 11.3), but it is generally best to find a color that suits the subject of the photo.

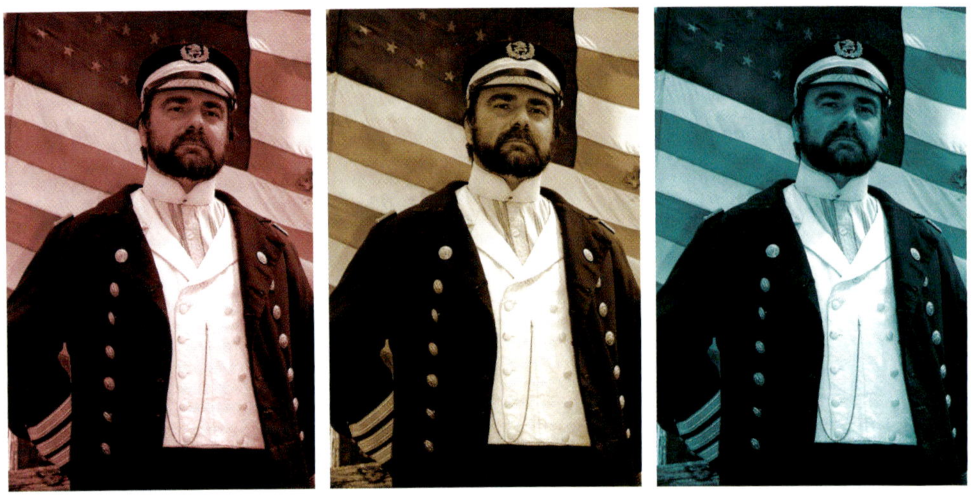

Figure 11.3 You can use any combination of settings for Hue and Saturation for the desired effect with the Colorize option. These images show Hue/Saturation settings of 0/20 (left), 50/25 (center), and 195/27 (right).

After you have selected the basic color for the image, use the Saturation slider to adjust the intensity of the color. Start by experimenting with relatively low Saturation levels, in the range of about 15 to 25. Sometimes you might want an image that looks like a black-and-white at first glance but elicits an emotional response because of the perception of a color element that the viewer doesn't immediately recognize. Other times you may decide to make a more dramatic statement with an image by using a higher Saturation level, perhaps as high as 35 or 40; beyond that, the image will seem to have excessive color. The key is to find settings that you like for the image (Figure 11.4).

Note: Many photographers like to add a "sepia tone" effect so their image will resemble an old photo from the 18th century. That is also a popular effect possible when processing black-and-white images in a traditional photography darkroom. To achieve a sepia tone, use the Colorize option with a Hue setting of about 50 and a Saturation setting of about 20, and do some fine-tuning of these values until the image matches your preferences.

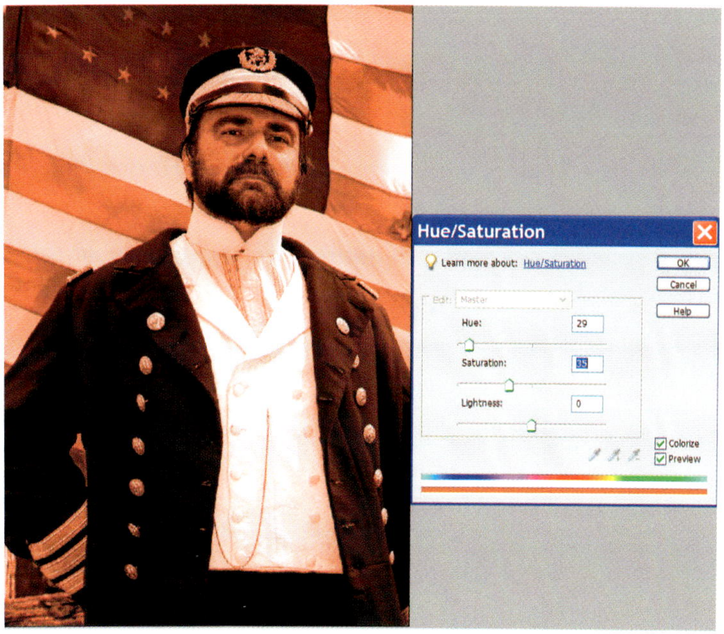

Figure 11.4 Use the Hue and Saturation sliders with the Colorize checkbox selected to find the values that work best for the image based on your preferences.

Because you're using this Hue/Saturation adjustment layer for the sole purpose of adding an artistic effect to your image, it is a good idea to rename the adjustment layer so you'll know in the future why it is there. To do so, double-click the name of the new Hue/Saturation adjustment layer you created, type a new name (such as *Colorize*), and press Enter/Return (Figure 11.5).

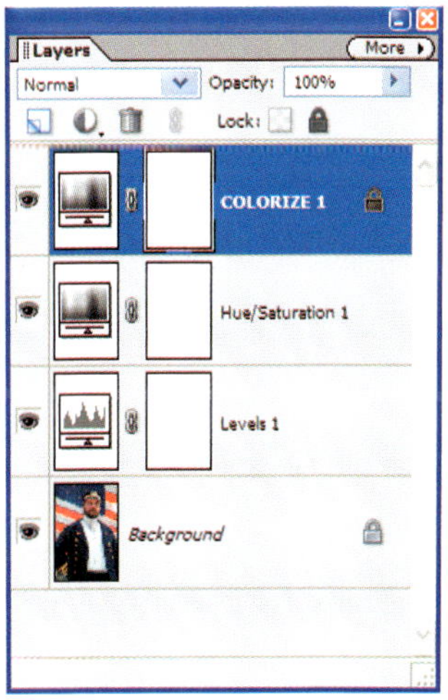

Figure 11.5 Renaming the Hue/Saturation adjustment layer you created to apply the Colorize effect will help you stay organized when reviewing or revising your images later.

Grayscale Conversion

Although digital cameras default to capturing images in full color and most photography is captured in color, many photographers still enjoy producing black-and-white versions of their images. You can convert a color image to black-and-white in a variety of ways. We recommend using only methods that preserve the original color data in the image, because that will retain maximum detail in the final result while providing greater flexibility. Primarily we use two methods for producing these conversions.

Using Convert To Black And White

Adobe has provided a simple yet very versatile and intuitive tool for converting images to black-and-white. Before experimenting with the many available options, be sure to create a copy of your Background image layer by dragging the thumbnail for that layer to the Create A New Layer button on the Layers palette. You can accomplish the conversion by choosing Enhance > Convert To Black And White from the menu. Elements converts the image to monochrome, and a large dialog box opens (Figure 11.6) showing Before and After versions of the photo. You can then select a style, such as Portraits, Scenic Landscape, or Urban/Snapshots, and your displayed image, as well as the After version in the box, will change. The change is primarily in overall contrast from high to low and in tonal values; certain tones are lighter or darker, depending on the style selected.

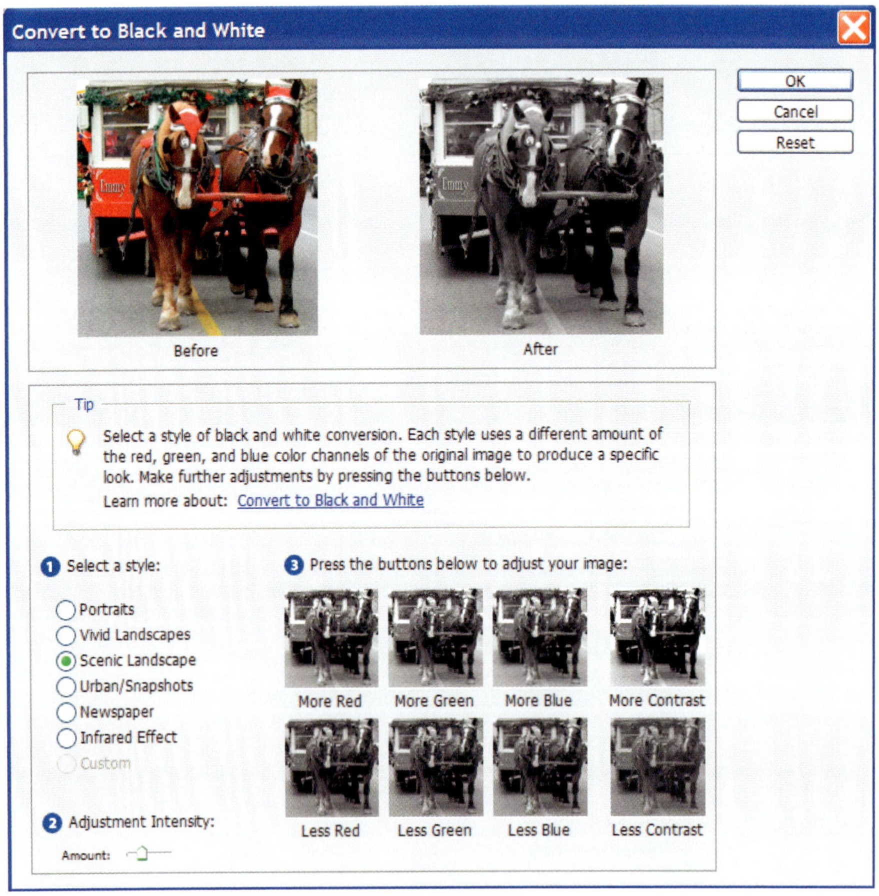

Figure 11.6 The Convert To Black And White dialog box offers a simple method for converting images to monochrome but also provides a wealth of options for modifying the appearance of the image.

Instead of trying to explain the exact change that occurs with each style (Figure 11.7), we recommend spending a couple of minutes trying each of these options. In our experience, the most pleasing effect for most types of images is the Portraits or Scenic Landscape style. You must select one of the options before moving on to adjusting your image. Other options consist of thumbnail images that allow you to increase or decrease the amount of red, green, and blue, as well as overall contrast. It may sound odd to mix amounts of red, green, and blue in an image that should be perfectly neutral. If you recall that every pixel in a color image has individual values for red, green, and blue, this makes a bit more sense. You can think of an RGB image as the combination of three monochrome channels that get represented as red, green, and blue. By blending those monochrome channels at varying percentages but not applying color information, you can achieve a wide range of options for your final monochrome image.

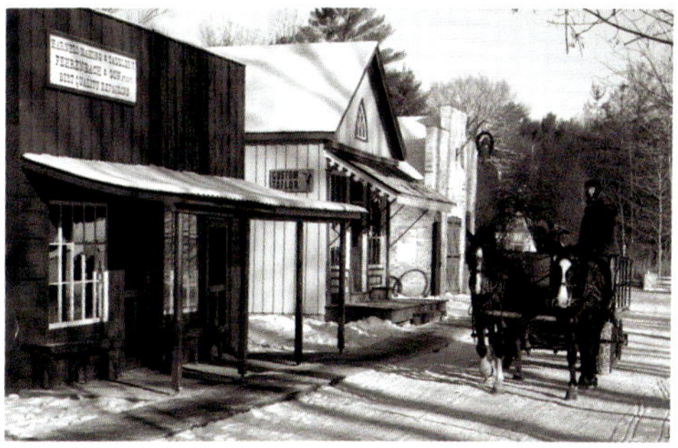

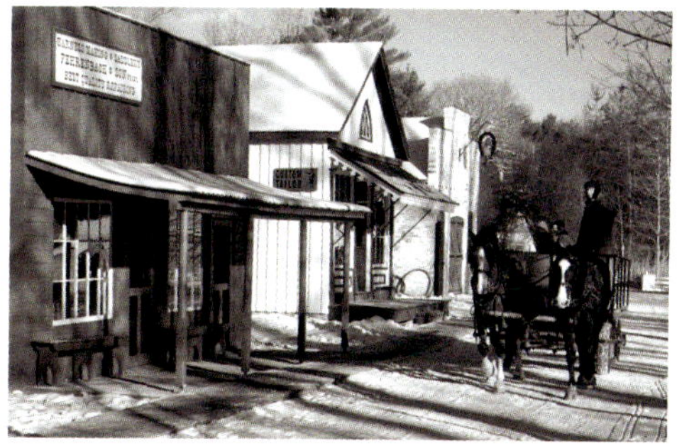

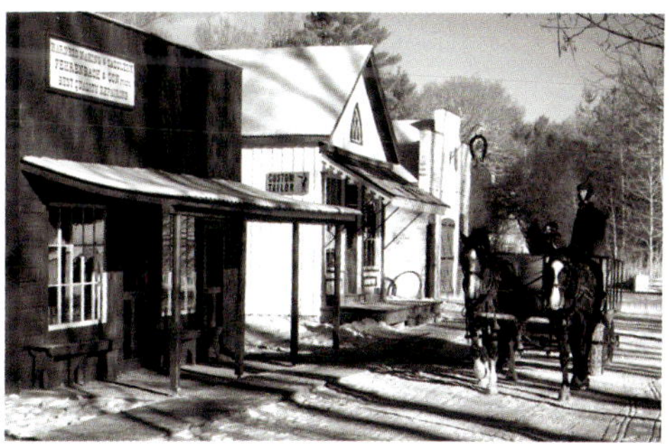

Figure 11.7 We made these three images by using the Portraits, Vivid Landscapes, and Infrared Effect styles, respectively, but you can also select Scenic Landscape, Urban/Snapshots, or Newspaper.

Photographers who have enjoyed using black-and-white film are familiar with the concepts of using "contrast" filters of different colors over their lenses for modifying the relative darkness and lightness of certain tones. Convert To Black And White does not provide filters, but it does offer Red, Green, and Blue controls that produce a change in tonal values, and to some extent, in contrast.

Note: Although we mentioned using colored filters in black-and-white film photography, the Red, Green, and Blue color controls in Convert To Black And White do not produce comparable effects. For example, More Red does not darken blues or lighten reds as a red filter would if you were using Tri-X film, for example, in a 35mm SLR camera. And yet, the Red, Green, and Blue options in this utility do alter the overall look of the image in terms of tonal values—the relative lightness and darkness of various tones in the image that has been converted to monochrome. The change, however, is not the same as you would expect if using colored filters in black-and-white film photography.

We recommend experimenting, especially with the More Red, Green, and Blue controls (Figure 11.8). Set the highest level available with the Adjustment Intensity slider and practice with More Red, clicking several times for even greater intensity until the image no longer looks natural. This exaggerated approach provides a quick learning experience as to how more or less of a color will affect your images. Afterwards, click the Reset button to return to the original (pre-adjustment) image and begin experimenting with the Green control, and later with the Blue control option.

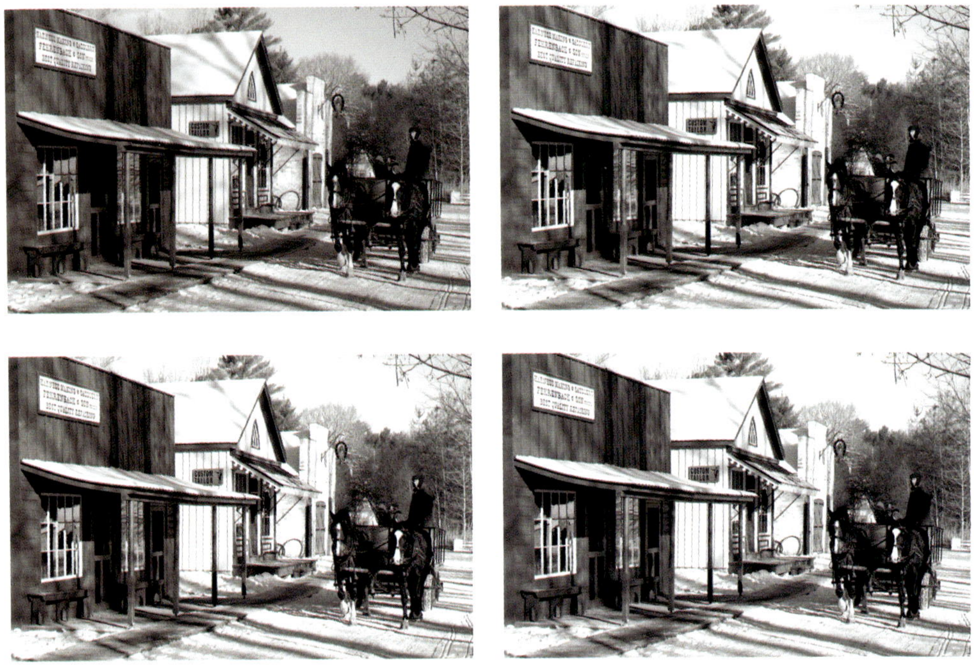

Figure 11.8 When experimenting with the three color controls in the Convert To Black And White utility, you'll notice a substantial difference in the effect that each produces even with a single click when using the high-intensity level. For these illustrations, we used the Scenic Landscape style and the following settings: no adjustment (top left), More Red (top right), More Green (bottom left), and More Blue (bottom right). Additional clicks provide even more dramatic results but frankly, a more subtle effect is usually preferable.

Later, when you're ready to start optimizing your best photos, we suggest taking a conservative approach, using the *lowest* Adjustment Intensity level. For example, if a slight bit of More Green provides a pleasing but not adequately striking effect, click More Green again. When working at the lowest intensity level, each click will produce a moderate though visible change. If you decide that you've gone too far by clicking More Green too often, click Less Green as often as necessary until your image exhibits the desired effect.

The Less controls provide the only way to moderate the change in tonal values because Adobe does not provide any Step Backward option to cancel a single adjustment step when Convert To Black And White is used, although you can click the "opposite" thumbnail button to get the same effect. For example, if you click More Blue and don't like the effect, you can click Less Blue to effectively reverse the adjustment. A Reset button is available in the dialog box but that simply reverts the image to its pre-adjustment state. Note too that Reset also reduces the Intensity level control to the default, the midpoint, so you may need to adjust that slider (usually, to the lowest level) before starting again.

Immediately after converting an image, you should also experiment with the Less options for each color, although we predict that you will rarely use those except for moderating an effect after applying one of the More options. When used as the primary tool, Less simply produces a flat, dull effect without the rich dark tones and bright whites that you will probably want for black-and-white photos. Of course, you could try various combinations of More and Less: More Green at medium intensity and then Less Red at low intensity, for example. Contrast control is also available, with More and Less thumbnail buttons, but we recommend ignoring those controls. Other Elements tools, particularly Levels but even Brightness/Contrast, offer much greater and more precise contrast control because you can adjust the black and white points individually with Levels while Brightness/Contrast causes both to always be adjusted to the same effect.

Grayscale Hue Shift

You can use another method for converting images from color to monochrome, but it's not nearly as simple and intuitive as using the Convert To Black And White dialog box. Still, this special technique—involving a Hue/Saturation adjustment layer—is worth trying because it provides greater user control. And this solution is not really complicated; it provides the simplicity of adjusting a single slider to produce variations in the grayscale interpretation of the image.

To use this method, start by creating an empty image layer at the top of your stack of layers on the Layers palette. You can do this by first clicking the topmost layer on the palette and then clicking the Create A New Layer button. Fill this layer with black (or any neutral value) either by choosing Edit > Fill Layer or by pressing D to set the colors to their default values, holding Alt/Option, and then pressing Delete. Change the blending mode for this image layer to Color by using the drop-down menu directly below the Layers tab. Doing so ensures that only the color of the underlying image will be affected. The result will be a black-and-white image, but you still need to apply an adjustment to change the result based on your preferences (Figure 11.9).

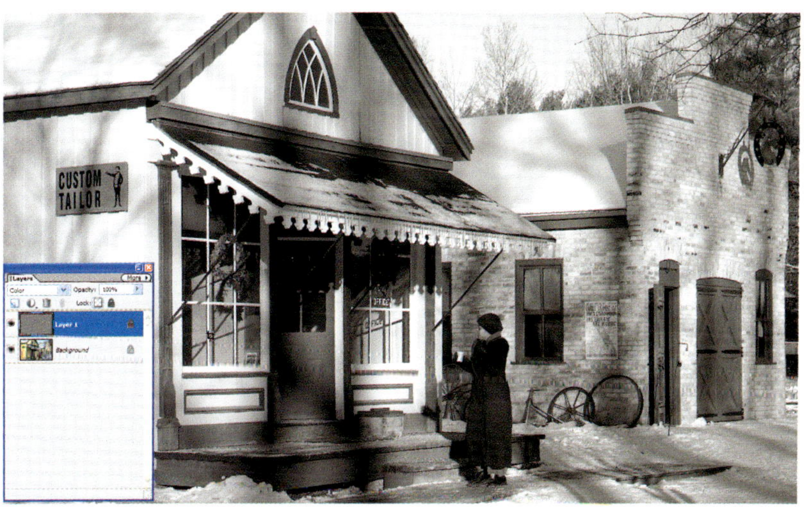

Figure 11.9 To produce a black-and-white image that you will alter with controls provided by a Hue/Saturation adjustment, create a new empty layer, fill it with black (or another neutral value), and change the blending mode to Color.

Now you're ready to fine-tune the appearance of your monochrome image. Create a Hue/Saturation adjustment layer. This one should be placed directly below the new layer you just added, so first click the layer below the new layer and then create a new Hue/Saturation adjustment layer.

In the Hue/Saturation dialog box, slide the Hue slider to various positions to create a range of different interpretations for the image (Figure 11.10). What's happening is that you're changing the color values in the underlying image, which in turn changes the tonality of those colors. However, you're not seeing the underlying color shift because the topmost new layer you created allows you to view the image only in a black-and-white form. You can also use the Saturation slider as a rudimentary brightness/contrast adjustment. However, it doesn't offer much control, so we recommend adding a Levels Adjust Color Curves adjustment to the top of the Layers palette and using that utility to further fine-tune the tonality of your black-and-white interpretation of the image.

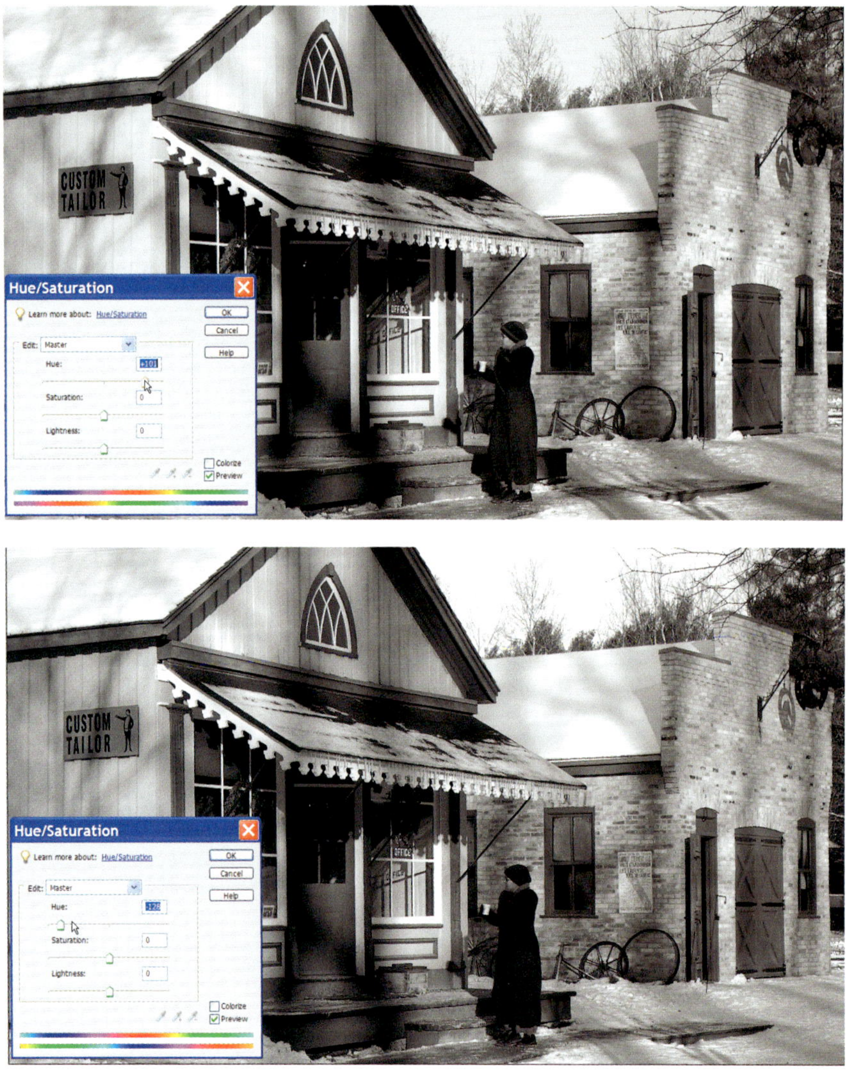

Figure 11.10 Adjusting the Hue slider in the Hue/Saturation dialog box when using this method will allow you to produce various interpretations of the black-and-white image.

High Pass Sharpening

In addition to conventional methods for sharpening discussed in Chapter 13 , you can use another technique when using the High Pass filter. In our experience, this is most useful for images containing smooth textures that need sharpening (Figure 11.11). That may sound a bit odd, but when you try the technique, you'll agree that it makes sense. The method enhances edge contrast, making it similar to sharpening with Unsharp Mask, for example. However, it doesn't enhance noise, grain, or small artifacts, and it works great as a creative application of a sharpening effect.

Figure 11.11 An image such as this one, which includes smooth textures, is an ideal candidate for the High Pass sharpening technique.

The first step is to create a copy of your background image layer (for example, by choosing Duplicate Layer from the Layers palette menu). Then change the blending mode for this new layer to Overlay (Figure 11.12). Initially, the effect will be stronger contrast and color saturation within the image, but you'll change the effect by applying a filter.

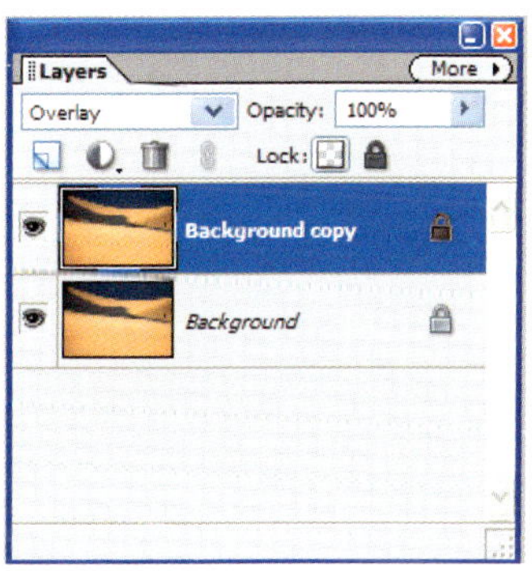

Figure 11.12 To use the High Pass sharpening technique, first create a copy of the background image layer and change the blending mode for this copy to Overlay.

Choose Filter > Other > High Pass from the menu, which opens the High Pass filter dialog box (Figure 11.13). This filter produces something of an embossing effect within the image, producing many middle gray pixels, and brighter and darker values along contrast edges within the image. Because you're using the Overlay blending mode, this is similar to dodging and burning along contrast edges within the image. Adjust the Radius setting to achieve the desired effect, and click OK (Figure 11.14).

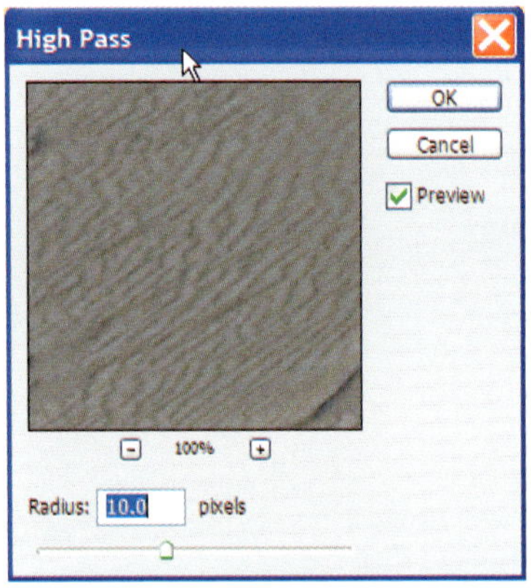

Figure 11.13 The High Pass filter applies an embossing effect to the image, and you can control the strength of the effect by adjusting the Radius slider.

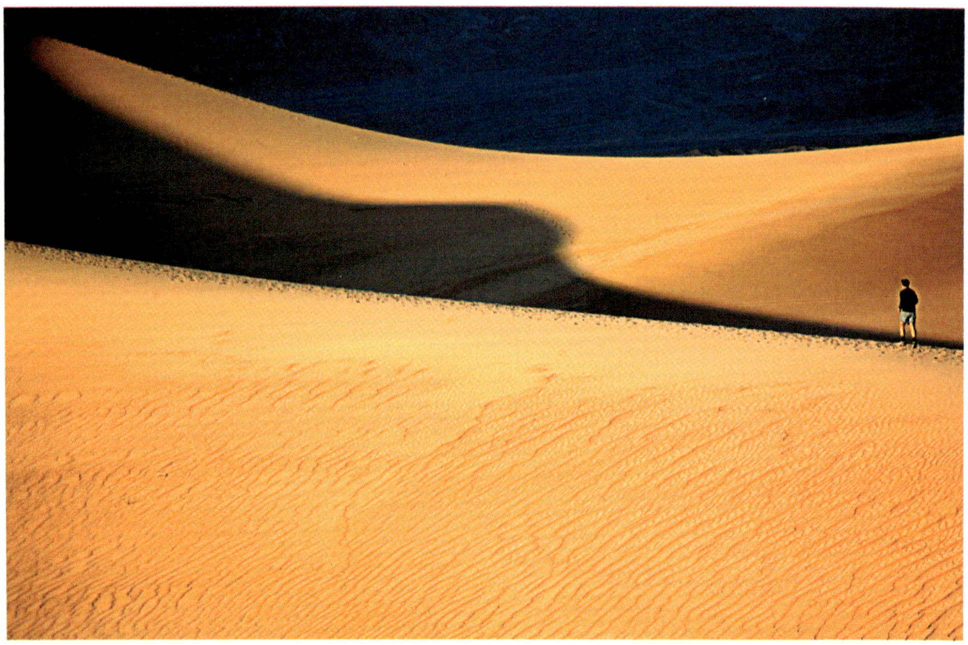

Figure 11.14 When you've found the desired Radius setting for High Pass, click OK to apply the final result.

Note: In most cases a Radius value of 10 pixels in the High Pass filter produces the best effect with this technique, but you should experiment to find the value that produces the results you find to be most suitable with various types of images. And keep in mind that because this effect is on a separate layer, you can always adjust the Opacity slider on the Layers palette to help control the strength of the effect.

Filters

When you really want to produce creative interpretations of your images, some of the many filters available within Photoshop (or third-party plug-ins) can be great for extending the possibilities. A wide variety of filters exist, all of which produce some distortion in the image. In some cases you may want an effect that's minor, whereas in others you may want a more dramatic effect. Even better, you can mix various filters to produce a completely new interpretation of an image.

Because filters directly adjust pixels within the image, it is important to start by creating a copy of your background image layer (for instance, by dragging it to the Create A New Layer button on the Layers palette). That way you can apply artistic filters without directly affecting the pixels in your original image.

Filter Gallery

The best way to apply filters with maximum flexibility is to use the Filter Gallery. It is certainly possible to apply individual filters one at a time by selecting them by name from the Filter menu. However, the Filter Gallery allows you to select from a broad variety of filters, and to apply multiple filters at one time to an image, similar to the use of adjustment layers on the Layers palette. You can then mix and match various filters, adjusting the settings for each as desired (Figure 11.15). You can launch the Filter Gallery by choosing Filter > Filter Gallery from the menu.

Note: Not all filters found under the Filter menu are available in the Filter Gallery, but most of the "artistic" ones are included.

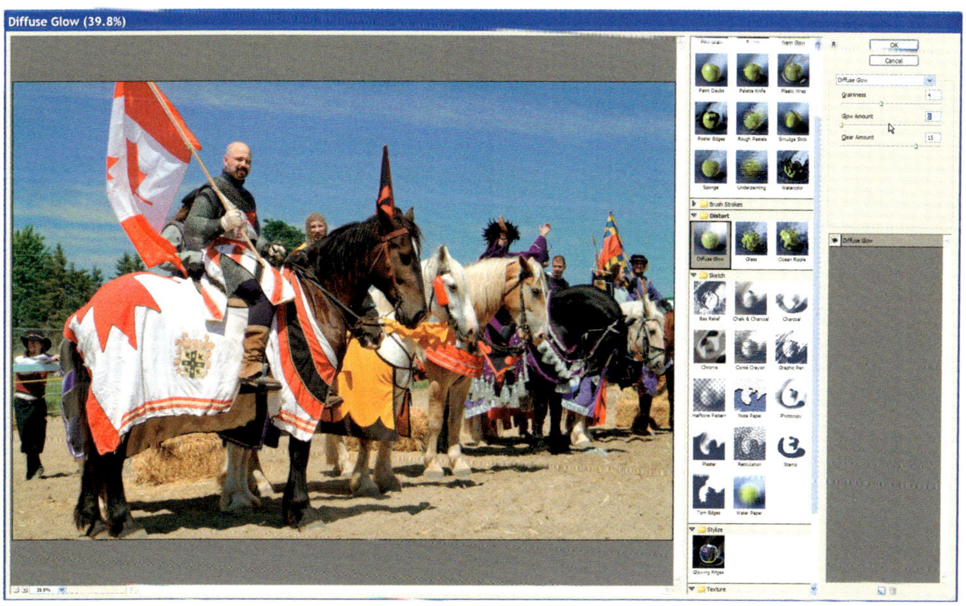

Figure 11.15 The Filter Gallery allows you to apply multiple filters at once to an image, adjusting the settings for each filter until you achieve the desired result.

When you first launch the Filter Gallery, a single filter will be listed in the bottom-right of the dialog box (Diffuse Glow, in this example). You can then expand the various categories of filters to the left—for example, Distort, Stylize, or Texture—by clicking the right-pointing arrow to the left of each category name. Thumbnail previews of the filters will appear, and you can click any thumbnail to apply that filter to the current filter layer within the Filter Gallery.

After you've selected a particular filter, the settings that are pertinent to that type of filter will be displayed on the right side of the dialog box. Adjust each of the controls as desired, using the preview image on the left to evaluate the effect at each level of intensity. If you'd like to apply multiple filters, simply click the New Effect Layer button at the bottom of the Filter Gallery. This will initially create a duplicate of the same filter you're using, but you can then click a new filter from the thumbnails to change that filter layer and then change the settings for the filter being applied.

You can also change the order of filters, which can change the appearance of the final result, by dragging them on the list. As you're working, you can also toggle the visibility of individual filter layers by clicking the eye icon to the left of the layer.

After you've found the combination of filters and settings that produces the effect you like, click OK to apply the filters all at once to your image (Figure 11.16).

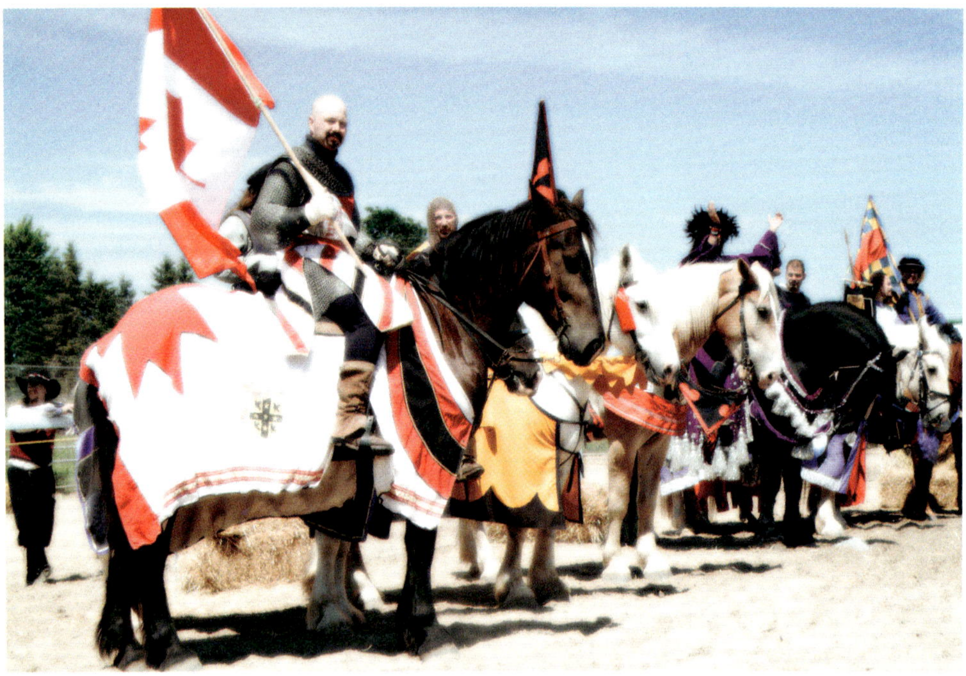

Figure 11.16 After you've established the desired filter settings, you can click OK in the Filter Gallery to produce the final result in your image.

Just the Beginning

The techniques in this chapter are not presented with the intent of making you a creative genius but rather to show you some of the ways you can apply (and extend) the techniques covered in earlier chapters to produce creative interpretations of your images. Think of the techniques presented in this chapter as a sampling of a few of the many possibilities. By gaining a better understanding of the topics covered in previous chapters and by thinking more creatively about your images, you'll be able to create your own techniques (or modify those learned elsewhere) to enhance your skills and creativity. You'll quickly discover that Elements provides a tremendous amount of power when it comes to adjusting your images, and you are limited only by your own imagination. If you can imagine a final result, there's almost surely a way to achieve that in Elements.

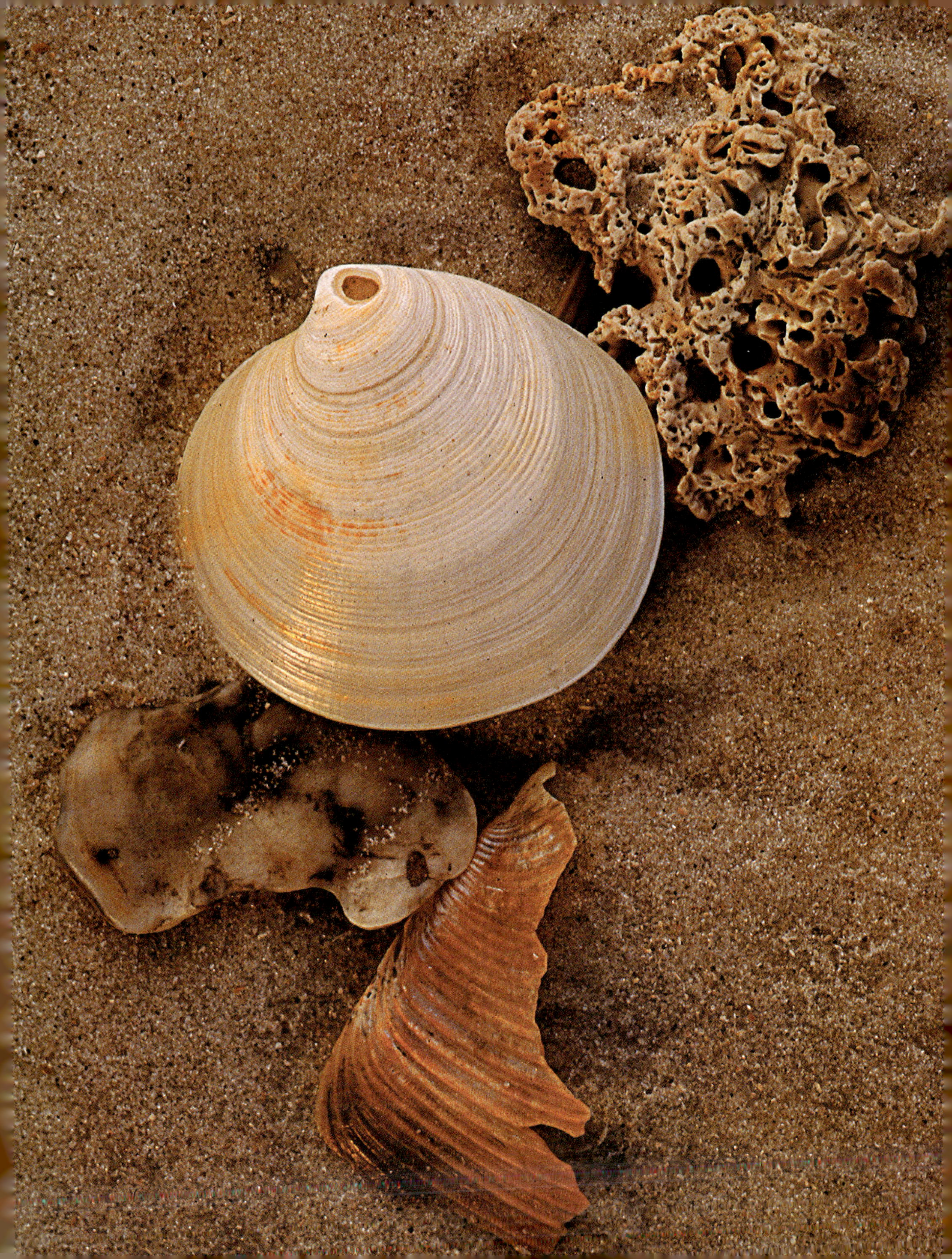

IV

Finishing the Workflow

Many photographers might assume that the workflow ends after the image has been optimized to perfection by using layers in various ways as outlined in previous chapters. However, a key part of the workflow is "closing out" the process and achieving your ultimate goal. That includes saving the image files after you've optimized them, as well as preparing them for the final output, which is most often a print. Part IV will focus on these topics, as well as providing some tools for automating portions of your workflow.

Chapter 12 **Saving Files**
Chapter 13 **Output Processing**

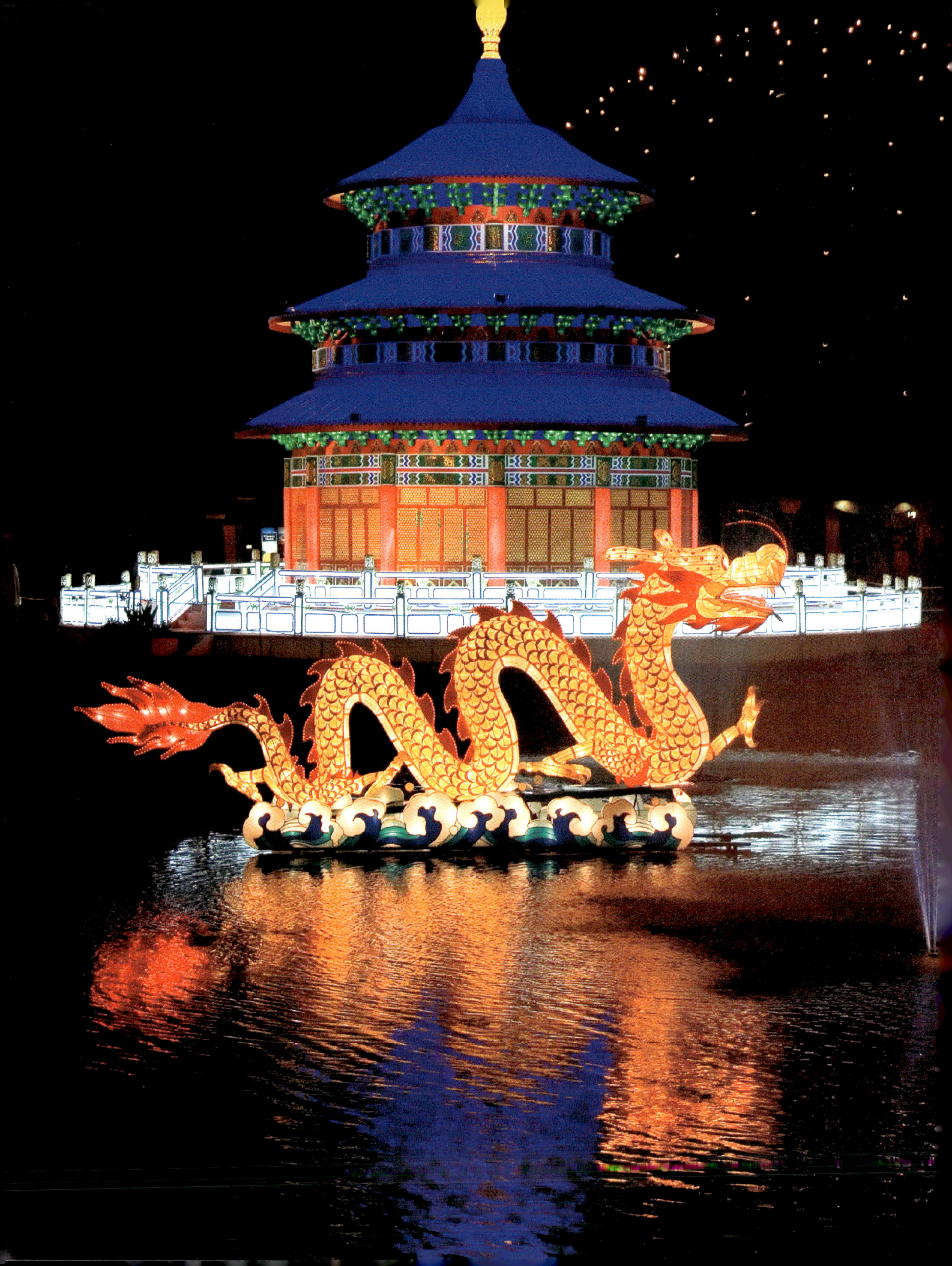

Saving Files

The most efficient workflow and all the optimization tips in the world aren't going to do you much good—at least not for long—if the efforts you've made are lost as soon as you close the image. Saving your image file is a critical conclusion to your image-optimization workflow, and this chapter will help you understand the issues involved with saving your files properly.

12

Chapter Contents

Master Image Concept
Filenames, Locations, and Formats

Master Image Concept

Throughout this book we've focused on techniques for adjusting your images within a workflow process that preserves your original pixel values, utilizing layers to change the appearance of the image without altering the original data. This approach provides maximum flexibility, enabling you to return later to modify the adjustments you've made, as long as you have saved images with the layers open. At the same time, it provides maximum protection of your image by ensuring that you aren't permanently discarding image detail you might want to recover later.

After you've optimized the image, investing time and effort in the process, the result is a master image that contains your complete interpretation of the image (Figure 12.1). In fact, you might even include multiple interpretations of the image within a single image file by using different adjustment layers for each interpretation.

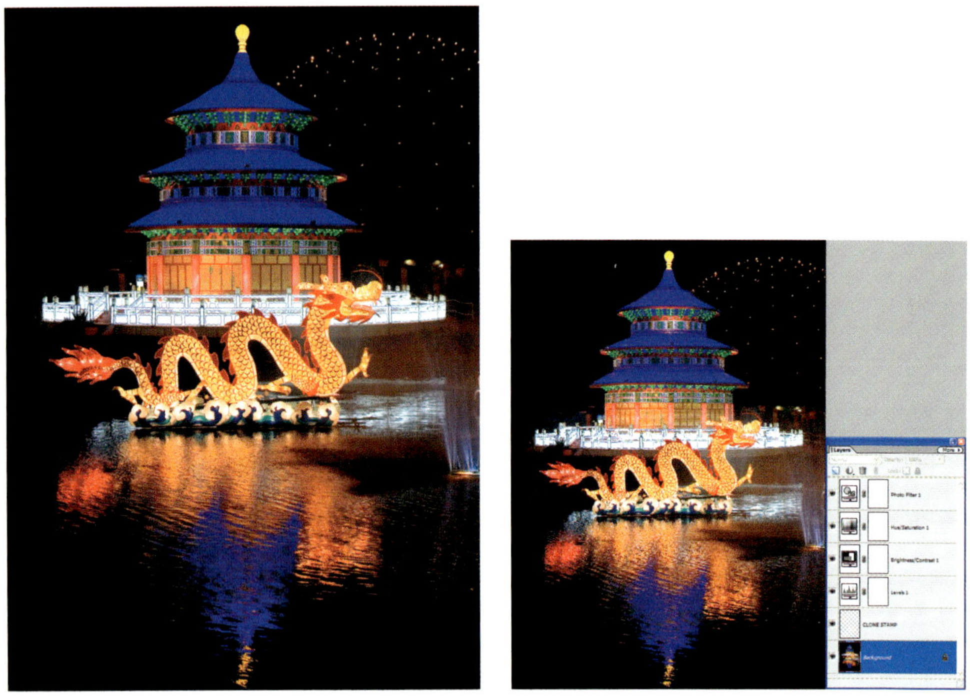

Figure 12.1 After you've perfected your image by using the steps outlined in previous chapters, the result is a master image that should be saved for all future output.

Note: Although we're discussing saving the image now, it is important to remember that you should save the image early in the workflow and save it often throughout the process of optimizing the image.

It is important to save the final image containing all layers as the master image, which will serve as the starting point for all future output from that image. This master image file should contain the original, unaltered pixel data from the digital capture or film scan, with no resizing and with no changes applied directly to the background image layer. Of course, in the case of a RAW capture, what you're storing is the image file that was processed during RAW conversion, which is why we also recommend archiving the original RAW capture. Furthermore, you should save all adjustment layers and image layers used in addition to the background image layer to produce the final result.

To be sure, saving a master image file in this way can result in very large files. However, this is a worthwhile investment in the quality and flexibility of the image. You may be tempted to flatten the image to reduce the file size after you feel confident you've achieved exactly the results you were hoping for, but we believe it is important to preserve the original image data along with your modifications. For one, your tastes may change with time. By maintaining the original image data as well as all adjustments within the same file, you can comfortably change your mind later and revise the image as desired. Also, you may learn new techniques at a later date that will allow you to produce even better results. Saving a master file with layers intact (as well as any RAW file) enables you to take full advantage of any future preferences or opportunities.

The bottom line is that you've invested considerable time perfecting your image (Figure 12.2). That effort deserves to be preserved in such a way that if you change your mind about the best interpretation of the image, or you learn new techniques that allow you to improve your results, you don't have to start over.

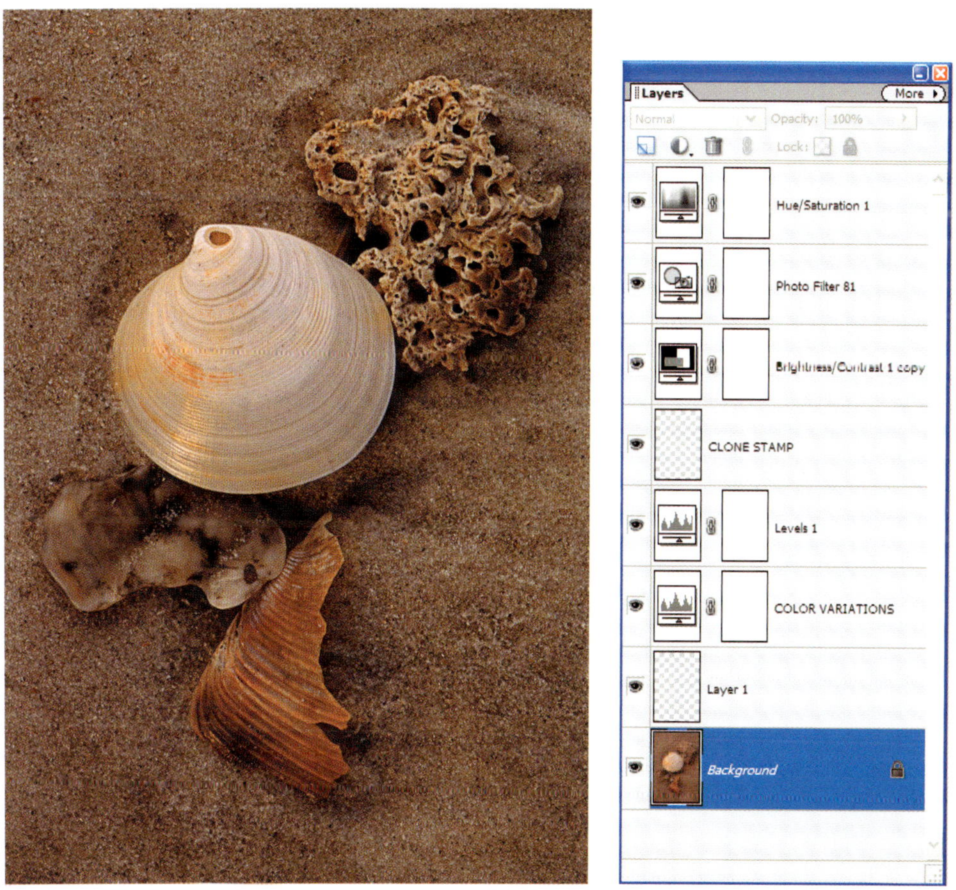

Figure 12.2 After spending considerable time achieving exactly the results you desire, including the creation of many layers to optimize your image, you should save the master image file with maximum information to maintain quality and flexibility. (Photo by Gabby Salazar)

When to Sharpen

There tends to be a lot of discussion about the proper time and method for applying sharpening to digital images. The simple fact is that just about all digital photos need to be sharpened to some degree, whether they are digital captures or film scans. The question is when that sharpening should be applied.

We recommend against applying any sharpening to your master image. Sharpening by its nature is a destructive process, in that it changes pixel values. Furthermore, resizing an image after sharpening can mitigate sharpening or exaggerate artifacts that were caused by sharpening. Also, you should tailor your sharpening settings to the specific output size of the image—the size of the print you intend to make, for example. In addition, resizing will probably be required. Because the master image contains the original pixel dimensions of the digital capture or film scan, it won't likely match the exact image dimensions—or aspect ratio—of the final output, such as an 8″×10″ or 13″×19″ print. For all these reasons and more, we prefer not to apply sharpening to the master image. Instead, we apply sharpening when preparing the image for the final output, after it has been resized for that purpose.

We'll cover sharpening in the output workflow in Chapter 13, "Output Processing."

Filenames, Locations, and Formats

Saving your master image file means you need to decide on the file format you'll use. You really need to consider only two file formats for the master file: the native Photoshop Document (PSD) and Tagged Image File Format (TIFF, or TIF) formats. Both will allow you to save all your layers and saved selections as part of that file.

What about JPEG?

Although the JPEG file format is perfectly acceptable for use in digital capture, it isn't an ideal format for saving images as a master file after you've worked on them. For starters, JPEG does not support layers, so you cannot save an image with layers preserved. In addition, further JPEG compression can degrade image quality. You don't need to convert your JPEG captures to another format if you haven't adjusted the images, so by all means keep those original JPEG files as they are until you decide to work on each file. After you have worked on the file, you'll want to preserve the master image in another format: TIFF or PSD.

In addition to being viable for capture, JPEG is an excellent format for saving images for digital slideshows, websites, email, and other purposes for which a small file size is at least as important as image quality.

The first time you save the image file, you'll need to choose File > Save As from the menu (Figure 12.3). In fact, if you choose File > Save from the menu without having previously saved the image (or after adding adjustment layers to an image that was already saved in a file format that doesn't support layers), the Save As dialog box will automatically be invoked. In the Save As dialog box, you'll first need to select the location where you'd like to save the image file. You can make this selection from the Save In drop-down list. If necessary, you can use the Save In drop-down list to navigate to a specific drive, and then double-click the desired folder (or multiple folders in turn) to navigate to the folder to be used for storing the image file. You can also create new folders at any time by clicking the Create New Folder button in the Save As dialog box and then typing a name for the new folder.

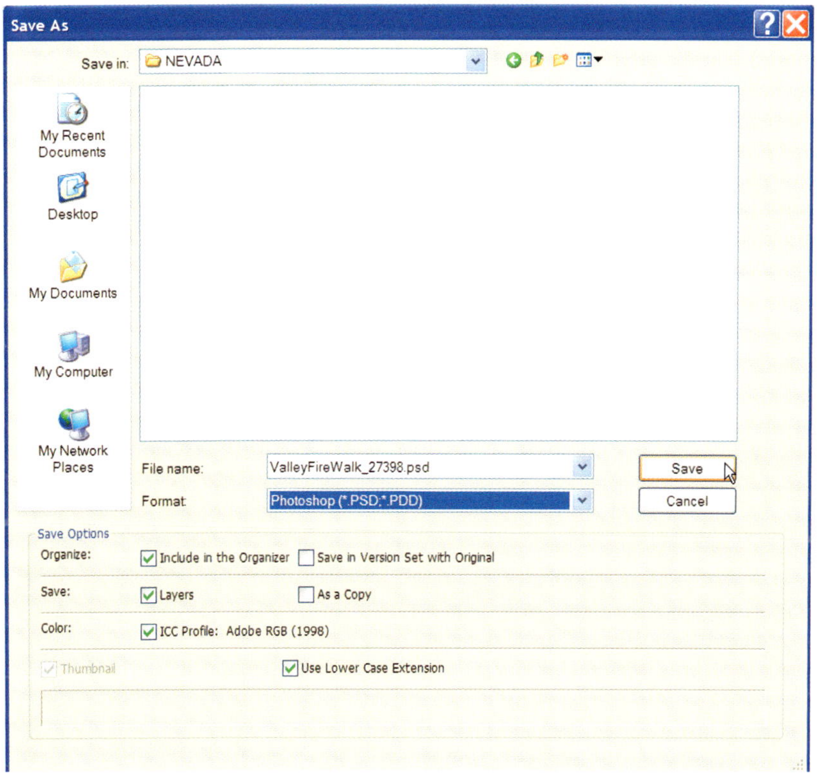

Figure 12.3 The Save As dialog box allows you to select the location, filename, and file format to use when saving your master image file.

Note: Your first step in keeping images organized will be deciding where the file will be saved. We recommend saving all image files in a single primary folder, using subfolders within that main folder to organize images into categories that are appropriate for your type of photography and suit your method for staying organized.

The next step is to provide a name for the image file. It is important to select a useful name so you'll be able to easily identify the image later. In fact, we recommend utilizing the filename as another method for staying organized. By naming your image files with useful names, you can search for filenames or otherwise keep them organized.

You can even use names that allow you—within reason—to know what the contents of the image are without even opening the file.

It is important to get organized early with your filenames. Develop a system that works for you to organize and categorize your images, and that enables you to search for filenames by doing a rudimentary keyword search. However, it's also wise to incorporate serial numbers as part of your file-naming system so you can have a collection of images saved with the same basic name but a unique number to identify each.

With the location and filename established, the only other major option you need to select is the file format you'd like to save the image file in, which can be selected from the Format drop-down list (Figure 12.4). Although many options are available on this list, you really need to choose between only the Photoshop PSD and TIFF file formats.

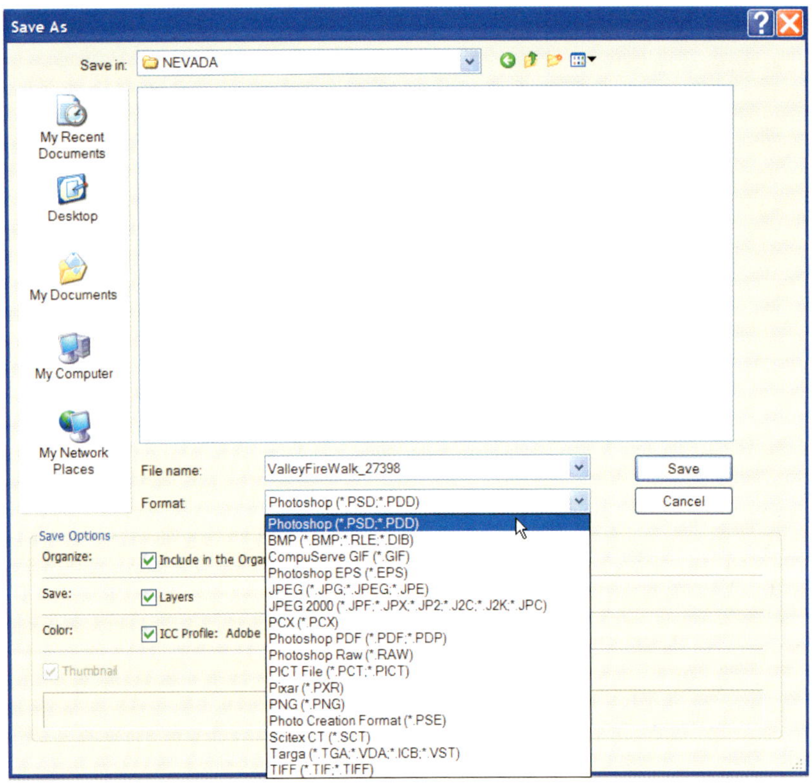

Figure 12.4 Although many options are available when saving your image files, the only two you really need to consider are Photoshop PSD and TIFF.

Photoshop PSD Format

The Photoshop PSD file format is well suited to saving your master image files. Because it is the native file format in Photoshop, you can trust that it will preserve all of the adjustment layers, image layers, and saved selections. All of these features are supported, so you can be confident that everything you've done to your image can be preserved in the master image file you save.

The Photoshop PSD format utilizes lossless compression, which means the file data is stored efficiently without changing any pixel values. The compression reduces the overall file size without any risk of image degradation.

To save the master image file in the Photoshop PSD file format, select Photoshop PSD from the Format drop-down list and click Save. The image will be saved in the location and with the filename that you specify.

Note: After you've saved the image once (which should really be done early in the workflow process), you should update the saved file on a regular basis. Every time you make a significant adjustment, choose File > Save or press Ctrl/⌘+S to save the file with updates. This ensures that the most recent version of the image is always the one saved; that can be useful in case of a power failure or other event that shuts down your computer.

TIFF Format

The Tagged Image File Format (TIFF) has gone through various iterations over the years, and the latest version of TIFF, when used in Adobe Photoshop and many other programs, supports the saving of multiple image and adjustment layers. That was not the case at one time, making PSD the most suitable format for archiving images. Today, we consider TIFF to be equal to PSD in terms of the features supported. In other words, anything you do to your image, including all of the techniques covered in this book, are equally supported by PSD and TIFF.

To save an image in the TIFF format, simply select TIFF from the Format drop-down list in the Save As dialog box and click Save. When you do so, an additional TIFF Options dialog box will be presented, providing special options unique to the TIFF format (Figure 12.5).

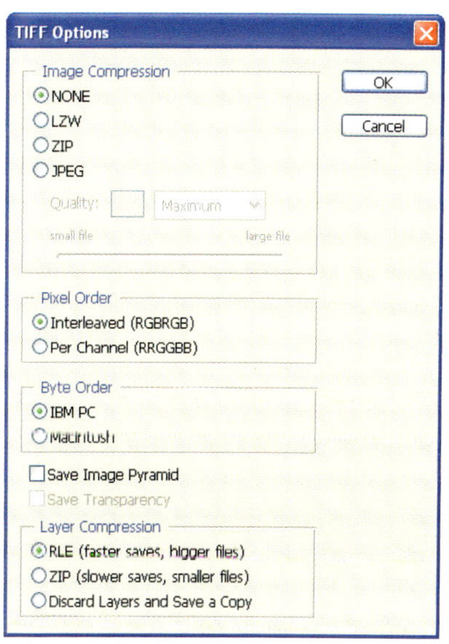

Figure 12.5 As you are saving an image in the TIFF file format, a TIFF Options dialog box will allow you to set compression and byte order options before the image is actually saved.

The first section of the TIFF Options dialog box allows you to select the Image Compression type to be used. The None option will not apply any compression to the image, resulting in a relatively large file size. The LZW option applies the Lempel-Ziv-Welch compression algorithm (named after the three people who developed it) to the file but doesn't compress image data, only the file itself. In other words, this provides lossless compression that will reduce the file size without any effect on image quality. The ZIP option also provides lossless compression and often results in file sizes that are slightly smaller than when LZW is used, but ZIP takes much longer in the save and in the subsequent reopening process.

Both LZW and ZIP will reduce the file size, but there is a compatibility concern with both of them. Not all software that can read TIFF files can support LZW or ZIP compression. (By the same token, not all imaging software can read layered TIFF files.) LZW has broader support than ZIP compression, but both have limited support. However, because you aren't likely to send your master image files to others, you could certainly take advantage of either of these options for your own purposes. (If you do need to send files to others, ask them if they use Adobe or other software that supports LZW or ZIP compression.) We prefer LZW compression because the process is quick and has broader support among image-editing software.

The Pixel Order options allow you to determine in which order the pixel values will be recorded in the image file. The options are Interleaved or Per Channel. In some prior versions of Elements and in Photoshop, only the interleaved option was available. The Per Channel option offers the potential to improve the read and write speed of the file, as well as to provide better compression, so it's the best choice.

Note: Although Per Channel pixel order is available with both LZW and ZIP compression, this pixel order is not supported by Elements Organizer. So if you intend to use Organizer, you will want to use the Interleaved pixel order option to save TIFF files. Note too that Per Channel is not supported by many other imaging software applications that can read TIFF files.

The next section in the TIFF Options dialog box allows you to determine whether the IBM PC or Macintosh byte order should be used. In theory this allows you to choose between compatibility on a Windows or a Macintosh PC. However, the term *IBM PC* is a dated definition based on a generic description of the Windows platform. Both Mac- and Windows-based computers are perfectly capable of reading files with either byte order set, so the choice you make is not important. You may decide to choose the byte order option appropriate to your platform, but there's no need to be concerned about additional byte order compatibility issues.

Finally, the Layer Compression options allow you to determine how layers should be saved. The RLE option applies run-length encoding as a compression algorithm to the layers in the file. This reduces the overall file size somewhat and processes quickly, making it useful because of speed. The ZIP option applies different compression methods, yielding smaller file sizes, but the processing time is longer. Although the differences aren't generally significant, we prefer to stick with RLE. The Discard option will cause the image to be saved as a flattened version without any layers. This is helpful if you're saving a second copy of your image file to send to someone else, but is obviously detrimental to the master image concept and shouldn't be used for your main image file.

After you've established the appropriate settings in the TIFF Options dialog box, simply click OK, and the image will be saved.

Choosing between PSD and TIFF

As you've probably gathered, there are only minor differences between the PSD and TIFF file formats, which often leads to confusion when trying to decide which format to use. Quite honestly, you could use either format without any problems; both support all the features that are important to you in saving a master image file.

The primary difference between the two comes down to compression. Although the Photoshop PSD file format does utilize some lossless compression, it isn't as powerful as the LZW or ZIP compression available with TIFF files. Therefore, in most cases the TIFF file with LZW or ZIP compression is preferable, because it's considerably smaller than the same layered file saved as a PSD.

So, if file size is an important consideration, select the TIFF file format with LZW compression. However, you may still decide to utilize the PSD format for master image files as Tim does. Although the PSD files are slightly larger than they would be if saved as TIFF with LZW compression, saving as PSD can provide a slight organizational benefit by saving all master image files in PSD.

That's because this approach—if used consistently—provides some differentiation between file types. It allows you to think of a TIFF file as one without any preserved layers while PSD files can be considered as images with layers intact. Tim uses this approach, saving master image files as PSD files and saving any copies made for other purposes (such as for publication in a book or magazine) as TIFF files without layers. By using this system, he can look at a list of files in a hard drive folder and instantly recognize master image files vs. the copies without layers that are intended for another purpose.

This is a minor consideration, but it may be of value after you accumulate thousands of image files. You'll have your own priorities and can make your own decision now that you have a better understanding of the issues involved with each file format.

Safely Saved

After you've safely saved your master images, you've completed the full workflow. Of course, it is also critical that you back up those important master image files so a hardware or media failure won't cause you to lose your images. Ideally, the backup copies should be stored in a different physical location than your primary storage. We recommend using CD-Rs or DVD-Rs, and not the RWs, because studies have shown that RW discs deteriorate more quickly. Try to find "archival" CD or DVD products, with a high permanence rating, such as the Mitsui Gold or Delkin Archival Gold series. If your budget is tight, do some research on the Verbatim DataLife series. Afterward, you can pat yourself on the back for processing images through a workflow that has helped you optimize them to produce exactly the results you envisioned at each click of the shutter.

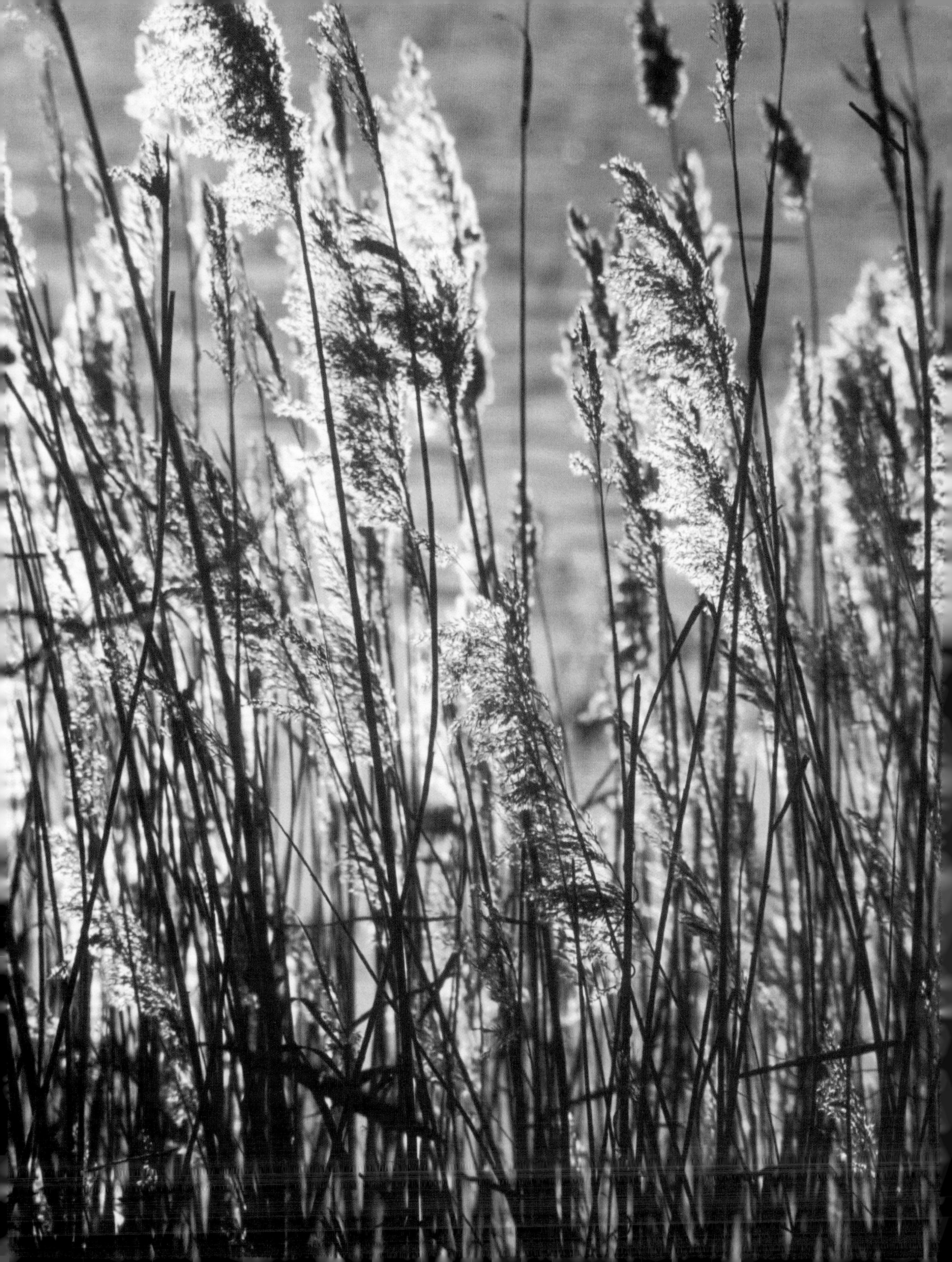

Output Processing

The ultimate goal for most photographers putting an image through the paces of an optimization workflow, as has been presented through the chapters of this book, is to prepare an image to share with others. This generally means producing output in some form, most commonly as a print. To preserve the work you've put into the original image and to ensure the best output quality possible, it is important to follow an output processing workflow.

13

Chapter Contents

Following an Output Workflow
Preserving the Master Image
Processing a Working Copy
Sharpening Your Images
Saving a Copy

Following an Output Workflow

The output workflow we recommend is a process that helps ensure you don't lose any information in your master image file (Figure 13.1). Throughout this book we have demonstrated methods of working with your images in Elements that will preserve the original information contained in your image in the form of the Background image layer and will also preserve in discrete packets all of the adjustments you've made in the form of adjustment layers and additional image layers (Figure 13.2).

When producing output from your images, you will need to perform tasks that will destroy some of the information in your image. Therefore, a workflow that insulates you from the risk of permanently losing that information is important.

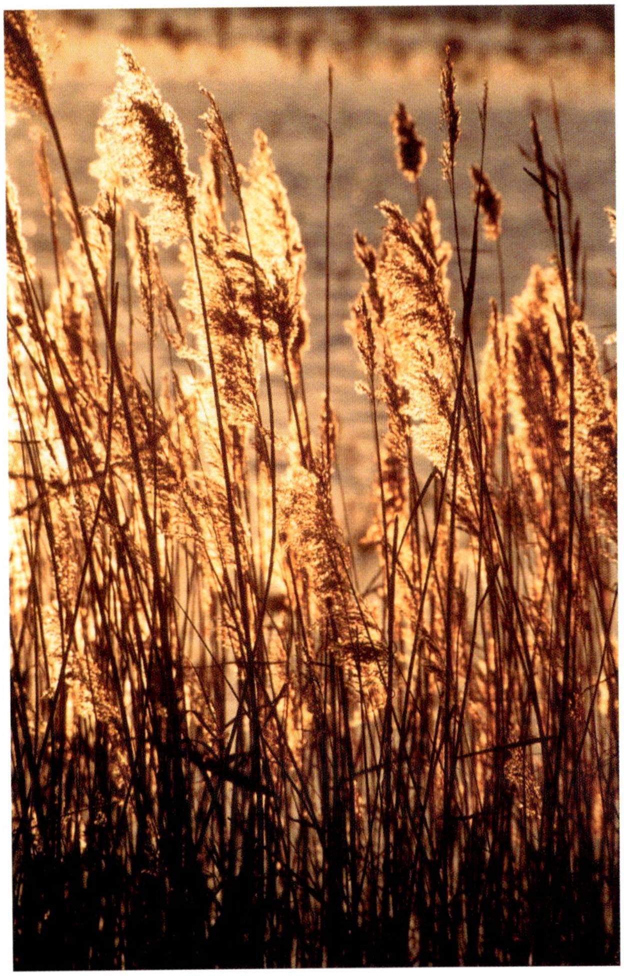

Figure 13.1 When you've put the effort into optimizing your image to produce exactly the result you intended, preserving that information in a master image file is important. (Photo by Gabby Salazar)

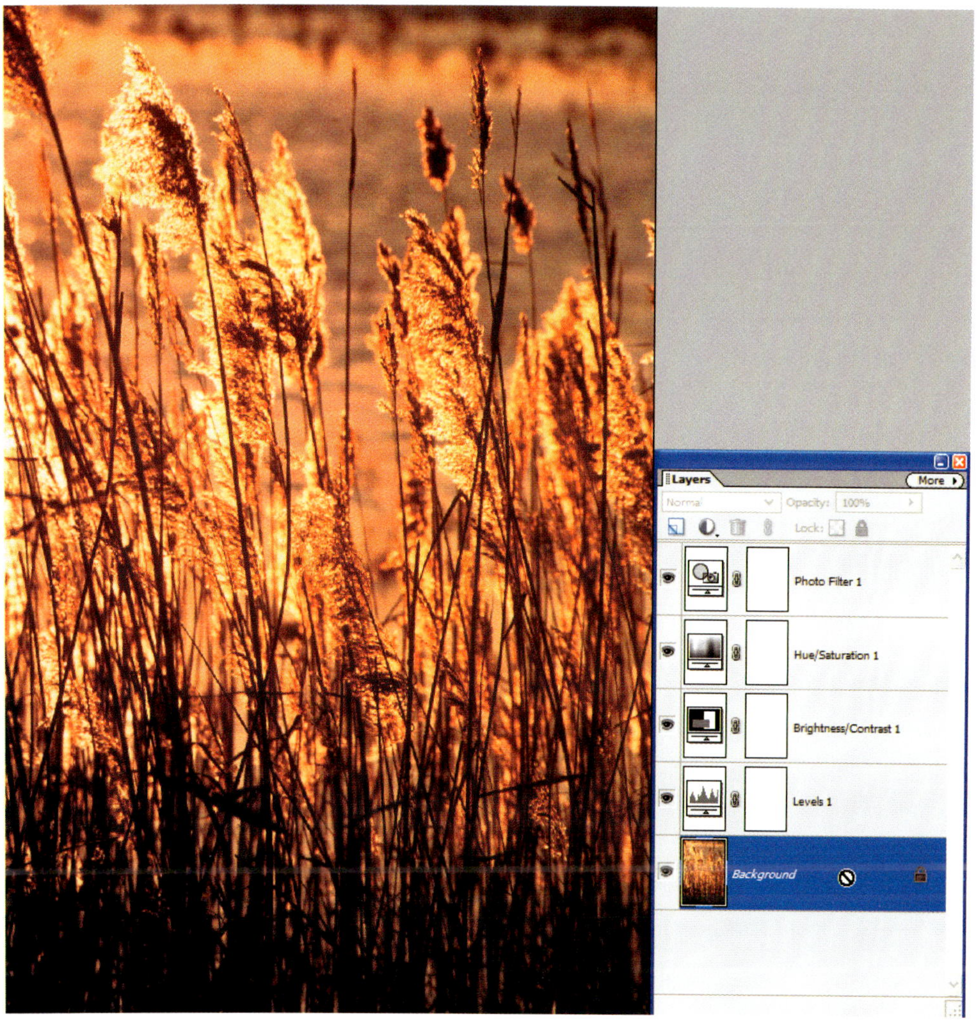

Figure 13.2 The master image file preserves the original image by maintaining a Background image layer that isn't modified and other layers that perform the actual adjustments.

Preserving the Master Image

The first step in preparing your image for output is making sure you've preserved the information contained in that image file. As discussed in Chapter 12, "Saving Files," when you have completed the process of optimizing your image by using the workflow techniques discussed in this book, it is important to save the file with all layers included in that file. This file, typically saved as either a Photoshop PSD or TIFF file, becomes your master image file (Figure 13.3). It contains both your original capture information and all information about the adjustments you've made to improve the image. It is critical that this information be preserved to provide you with maximum quality and flexibility later should you choose to revise your adjustments.

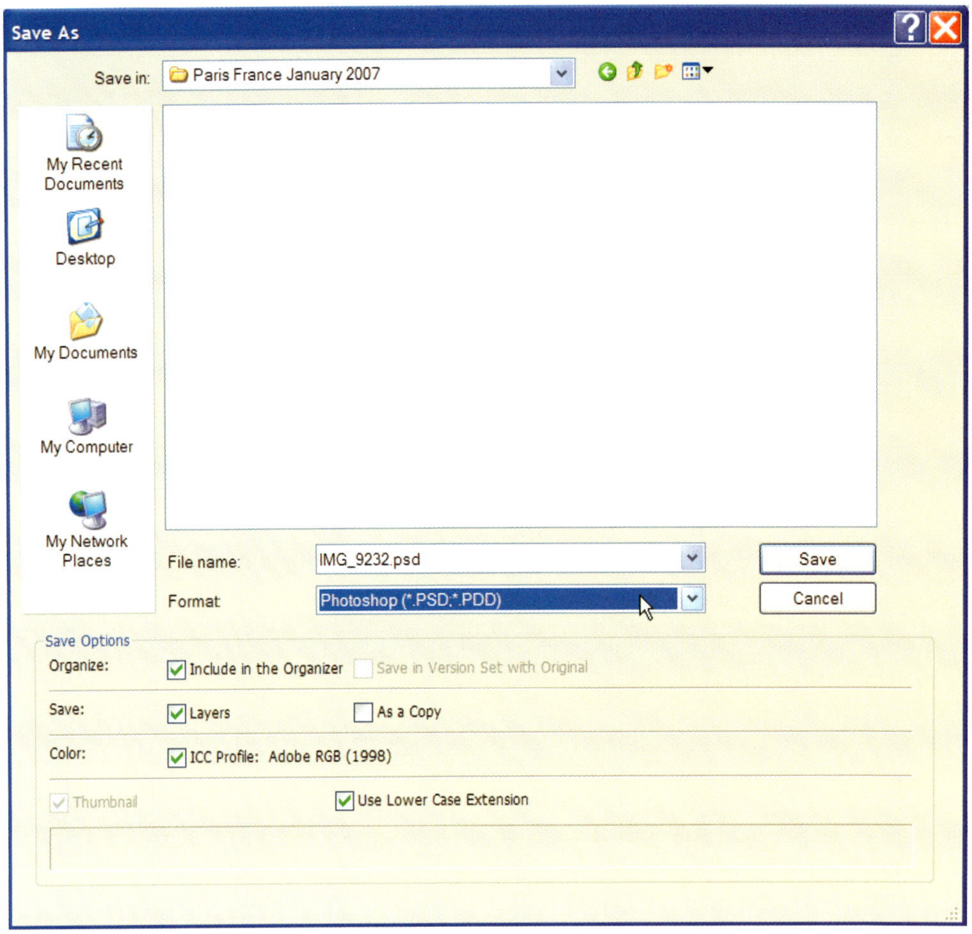

Figure 13.3 Saving your master image file as either a Photoshop PSD or TIFF image ensures that you'll maintain all layers used to optimize the image.

Before you move on to preparing an image for output, be sure you have indeed saved the master image file. If you make any changes to this master image file, be sure to save it again so you don't lose those changes.

Note: Saving your master image file—with layers intact—is important for obvious reasons, but it is also important that you back up your essential files. We recommend using external hard drives for this purpose, because they provide a fast, convenient, and scalable backup solution. But any system that works for you is good, as long as you're safely backing up your images.

Processing a Working Copy

With the peace of mind that comes from knowing your master image has been saved, you're ready to start processing your image to produce the intended output. This involves a series of steps that will prepare the image to be printed or displayed in the final form you have planned. By processing a working copy of the image, you'll be able to work without any concern that you'll harm your master image file.

Open the master image file for the photo you want to prepare for output, and you're ready to get started with the output preparation workflow.

Duplicate Image

The first step in assuring the long-term safety of an image is to create a working copy before you start planning to make a print, for example. To do so, choose File > Duplicate. The Duplicate Image dialog box will appear, allowing you to enter a name for the new image document (Figure 13.4). The name in the text box will simply be the name of the document you are duplicating with the word *copy* appended to it. You can enter a different name if you like, perhaps appending *duplicate* instead of the word *copy*, when setting a filename. Using the word *duplicate* can be helpful if you plan to save a copy of the processed image as well (to be discussed later in this chapter), but otherwise you can just accept the default name.

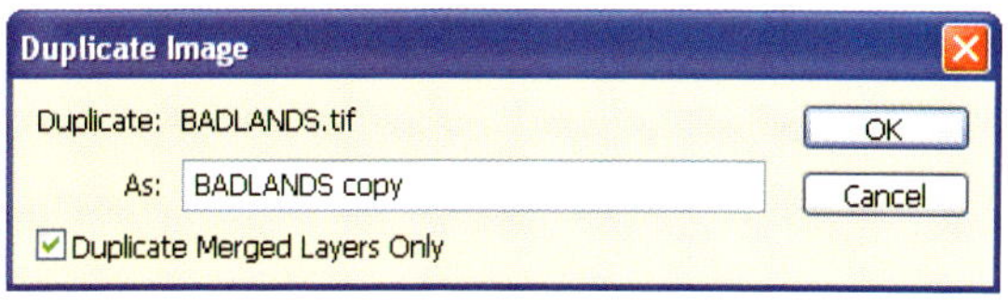

Figure 13.4 Using the Duplicate command allows you to create a working copy of your image so you can work without worrying about accidentally replacing your master image file with a degraded version.

The Duplicate Image dialog box also contains a checkbox labeled Duplicate Merged Layers Only. This checkbox will be enabled only if the image you're duplicating contains multiple layers. If you select this checkbox, the duplicate image will be a flattened version of the original image; that is convenient and useful, because at this time, you are ready to flatten the image, merging all layers into a single layer. After you click OK to create the working copy of your image file, you can close the original master image.

> **Note:** You can bypass the Duplicate Image dialog box by holding the Alt/Option key as you choose Image > Duplicate from the menu. The image will be duplicated with the default name but without flattening the layers.

Flatten Image

If you didn't flatten the working copy of your image in the process of creating the duplicate copy, we recommend flattening at this point by choosing Layer > Flatten Image.

Generally speaking, it isn't necessary to flatten the image before printing it or saving it for other output. For example, you can most certainly send an image with many layers to your printer, because Elements will send the data based on the final appearance, so no problems are created for the printer. However, we still recommend flattening the image at this point. You can feel perfectly comfortable doing so because you've already saved your master image file and are now processing a working copy.

There are also some benefits to flattening the file now. For starters, flattening the file reduces the memory footprint. In other words, there is less data, so the file will not consume as much memory and the processing time will be shorter. This is generally a small benefit, but it can be significant for large images. Another benefit has to do with sharpening. For most output methods you'll want to sharpen the image. Sharpening, as with any filter, can be applied to only one image layer at a time. If you have additional layers for cloning, compositing, or other purposes, you'd need to sharpen each of those layers individually. By flattening the image, you need to sharpen only once.

If you didn't already flatten the image during the Duplicate Image step, you can do so now. All layers will be merged into a single layer, preserving the appearance of your image (Figure 13.5).

Note: In Photoshop Elements the side menu for the Layers palette is labeled More and offers easier access to many of the same options you'll find on the Layers menu at the top of the Elements interface—including the option Flatten Image.

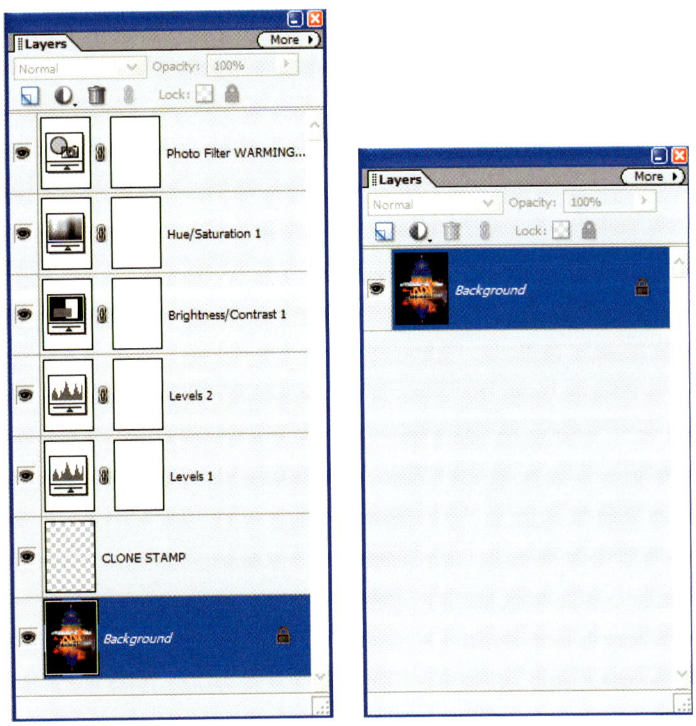

Figure 13.5 When you flatten an image, all layers from the original are merged into a single layer while maintaining the appearance of the image.

Image Size

Chances are the native size of your image doesn't match the final output size you're targeting, so you'll need to resize it. This requires setting the resolution for both the final output and the actual output size. To change the size of the image, choose Image > Resize > Image Size, which opens the Image Size dialog box (Figure 13.6).

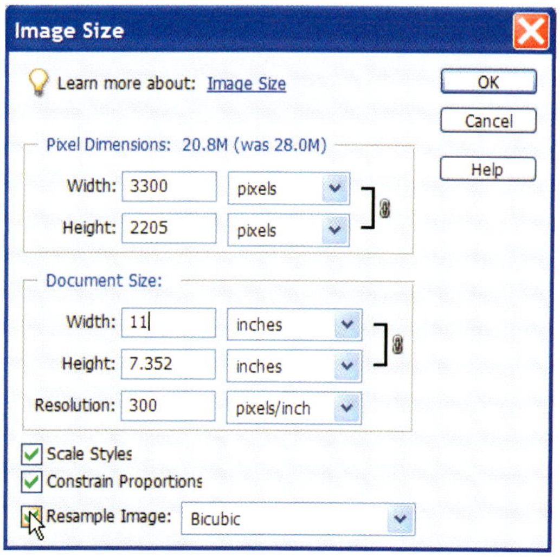

Figure 13.6 The Image Size dialog box allows you to resize the image to exactly the output size you need.

Although you would typically start at the top of a dialog box and work your way down, it makes more sense to start at the bottom and work your way up the list of options in Image Size. At the bottom, be sure the Resample Image checkbox is selected to ensure that the file size will be changed.

The drop-down list to the right of this checkbox provides options for the algorithm that Elements will use for interpolating the data in your image. Bicubic is the sort of "all-purpose" best option and the one we generally recommend. If you're creating a particularly large enlargement from your original, the Bicubic Smoother option is a good choice because it retains image quality without introducing artifacts. We cannot recommend the use of Bicubic Sharper, which is designed to maintain sharpness when reducing the size of an image. That option does apply sharpening so it can save time, but you may not be satisfied with the amount of sharpening used by the automated system. It's better to use Bicubic and apply exactly the right amount and type of sharpening algorithm yourself. The other two options, Nearest Neighbor and Bilinear, are not appropriate for producing high-quality photographic output and should not be selected.

The Constrain Proportions checkbox should always be selected. Doing so ensures that the aspect ratio of the image is maintained. If you clear this checkbox, the image may be stretched horizontally or vertically when it is resized. Although this isn't a problem when done to a very small degree, it can produce a distorted result if taken too far. Eliminate that possibility altogether by keeping the checkbox selected.

The Scale Styles checkbox determines whether layer styles will be scaled. In other words, the effects you have applied will maintain the same relative size relationship to the image, so as the image gets larger, the styles (such as a drop shadow) get larger as well. This isn't an issue at this point because you have already flattened the image. However, if you were resizing an unflattened image, it would be wise to keep this checkbox selected because you generally want to scale any layer styles along with the image.

In the Document Size section of the dialog box, the Resolution box determines how the pixels will be distributed when the image is output. The amount entered here plays a role in determining the number of pixels required in the final image. For printing it will depend on the output method being used. Ink-jet printers generally provide excellent results with 240 ppi to 360 ppi (pixels per inch) resolution. For this application, 300 ppi is a suitable standard value. For images to be viewed on a monitor or for digital projection, 96 ppi is adequate.

Note: Typical computer monitor resolution is 72 ppi or 96 ppi; that's why images designed for websites are typically set for only 72 ppi. When you send an image to a printer, however, it's a different story. A printer needs to squeeze more pixels per inch in order to reveal more detail in the image. Therefore, images that will be output using an ink-jet printer should have a target resolution of at least 240 ppi for a finely detailed print. Have you ever printed a 72 ppi graphic from a website and thought, "This image looks terrible?" That's understandable. An image that looks fine in an electronic display may not translate well to the printer because it does not contain enough pixels per inch to fully define the details.

Although Adobe uses the correct term for resolution—*ppi* for *pixels per inch*—the term *dpi* (dots per inch) is more frequently used conversationally; in truth, dpi is also used in some published documents. The term dpi is not correct for defining resolution for anything other than printed output but it is very commonly used. Although dpi and ppi tend to be used interchangeably, dpi is technically used for print, and ppi for digital displays.

Note: If you're working with film scans, it's particularly important to keep an eye on the resolution setting. If you've scanned a slide or negative at 4,000 ppi, you don't want to resize to a 20″×30″ print without changing the resolution to a more appropriate value. If you fail to make the change, to 300 ppi for example, the resulting file size will be immense. This makes sense if you do the math, and multiply 4,000 by 20 inches, and then multiply 4,000 by 30 inches to obtain the total pixel size. The resulting 2.5-gigabyte file would call for an absolutely huge increase that would take forever to complete and would likely crash your computer.

The next step is to set the actual output size. For printed images this should be done in the Document Size section, setting either the Width or the Height. You can change the unit of measure with the drop-downs to the right. If you have the Constrain Proportions checkbox selected (as recommended), then you can set one dimension and the other will be set automatically. Often you will want to size the image to fit the paper size that you will print to, although obviously in some situations you'll need to set a more specific output size.

If you leave the Resample Image option unchecked, changing the Width or Height of the image will automatically cause the Resolution number to increase or decrease, as necessary to maintain the same number of pixels in the image file. Selecting the Resample Image checkbox—and setting the desired ppi, such as 240 ppi or 300 ppi—will cause Elements to change the file size as required for the intended output at the desired resolution.

Note: When you make adjustments in the Image Size dialog box that affect the pixel dimensions of the image, the current size is displayed after the Pixel Dimensions label, and the starting size is shown in parentheses.

For images that will be displayed on a monitor or digital projector, the size should be adjusted by using the Width or Height text boxes in the Pixel Dimensions section. The Resample Image checkbox (at the bottom of the dialog box) will be selected in this situation. This allows you to set the specific pixel sizing for your intended purpose. For a digital slideshow, for example, you might set these dimensions to fit within the resolution of your digital projector. For a website, you might set them to a standard output size that you deem appropriate for your specific site design.

When you change your image size by adjusting the pixel Width or Height, Elements performs a calculation to discard pixels or generate additional pixels; the strategy depends on whether you want to decrease or increase file size. Keep in mind that the image quality can be affected. If the number of pixels is *decreased*, detail will be lost; of course, that would be relevant and noticeable only if you subsequently decided to make a large print from the smaller file. And if the number of pixels is increased, Elements must guess at what pixels need to be copied in order to add pixels; this process will also produce some image softness because some loss of detail will occur. The next section will cover some sharpening techniques that can help to correct this problem, providing the increase in the number of pixels was not extreme.

Note: For more discussion of preparing your images for all types of output, see the book *Photo Finish* by Tim Grey and Jon Canfield (Sybex, 2004).

After you've established the sizing parameters in the Image Size dialog box, click OK and the image will be resized accordingly.

Sharpening Your Images

Virtually all images that are being prepared for output in any form need to be sharpened to some degree in order to optimize their appearance and compensate for the loss of sharpness that occurs at the time of output. The only exceptions are images that don't contain any real detail you want to enhance. However, this is generally a rare exception, so you can assume that all images need to be sharpened. Also, remember that sharpening should be the final step, after your image has been resized for a specific output, such as an 8.5″×11″ or 13″×19″ print.

Two distinct sharpening utilities are available in Elements 5, including Unsharp Mask and Adjust Sharpness. Each employs a different technology and algorithms to achieve its effect.

Unsharp Mask

To apply this sharpening method, choose Enhance > Unsharp Mask from the menu. This brings up the Unsharp Mask dialog box, which allows you to adjust three values for modifying the sharpening effect: Amount, Radius, and Threshold (Figure 13.7).

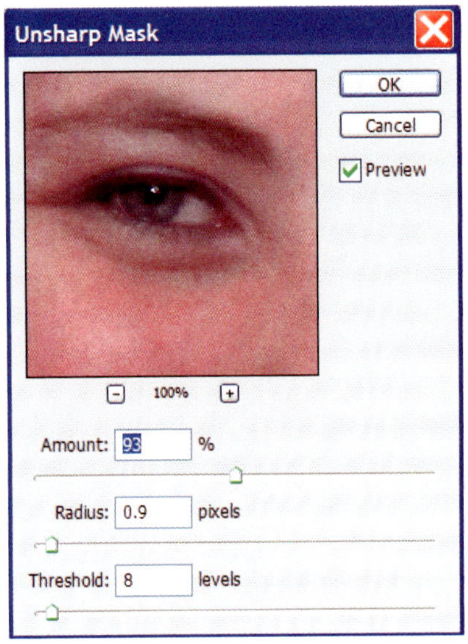

Figure 13.7 The Unsharp Mask dialog box allows you to adjust the sharpening effect by specifying values for Amount, Radius, and Threshold.

Unsharp Mask (USM) operates by enhancing contrast along the edges of objects within your image. In other words, it enhances contrast where contrast already exists. Adjusting the controls in the Unsharp Mask dialog box allows you to change how this contrast enhancement is applied.

The Amount setting determines the extent to which contrast is enhanced along edges. You can think of this as an intensity control. The higher the setting, the more intense the edge contrast will be in your image. As a general rule you will probably work in a range from about 100% to 300% for Amount.

The Radius setting allows you to determine the size of the area to be affected by the boost in contrast along edges. For images with a great deal of intricate detail, you'll generally want to have the impact affect only a small area for each edge, so work in a range of around 0.4 to 1.0 pixels. For images without much intricate detail, a Radius setting of between 2.0 and 3.0 is probably best. When in doubt, work in a range from about 1.0 to 1.5.

The Threshold setting provides something of a "damage control" function. It determines how much contrast must exist between two pixels for them to be considered as defining an edge. With a minimum Threshold setting of 0, virtually all pixels will be affected by sharpening. As you increase the value, fewer areas will be sharpened because they must exhibit a certain amount of contrast before sharpening will be applied. This enables you to maintain smooth textures in areas of the image where that is important.

For high-detail images, you'll generally want to use a very low Threshold setting, between 0 and 4. For images with areas of smooth texture that you want to preserve, such as skin in a portrait, a setting of between 8 and 12 is probably appropriate.

It is important to evaluate the effect of USM on a 100% preview of an image. However, you don't need to zoom in to a 100% scale on the image itself when using USM. It's actually much more convenient to start by resizing the image to fit the screen (by pressing Ctrl/⌘+0) so you can see all of it at once. Then use the full image to decide where you want to focus your view when evaluating the amount of sharpening that you might want to add.

The preview within the Unsharp Mask dialog box defaults to a 100% scale, so you can use that to evaluate the effect of various amounts on small sections of the image. In addition, you can click and hold your mouse on the preview image in the Unsharp Mask dialog box to see the "before" version, releasing the mouse button to see the "after" version again. By using this method, you can quickly click on various parts of the image to preview the sharpening effect in key areas (Figure 13.8).

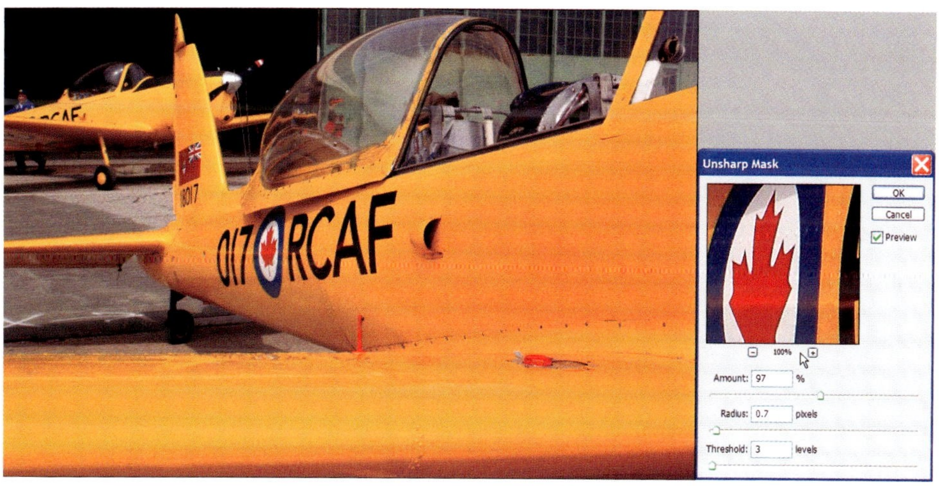

Figure 13.8 By keeping the image sized to fit your display, but the preview in Unsharp Mask set to 100%, you can easily navigate around your image and check the effect of your sharpening settings on various areas.

After you've established your settings for Unsharp Mask, click OK and the effect will be applied.

Note: If you are interested in a more detailed review of the aspects of sharpening, check out the e-book *Photoshop Sharpening* by Tim Grey. It is available for purchase and download as a PDF from www.wiley.com.

Adjust Sharpness

Unlike earlier versions, Elements 5 omits simplistic sharpening tools: Sharpen, Sharpen Edges, and Sharpen More. That's just as well because none of those three were recommended for serious image enhancing. Instead, Adobe provides an entirely new tool, simply called Adjust Sharpness (Figure 13.9). Available by choosing Enhance > Adjust Sharpness, this one is based on algorithms that were developed for the Photoshop CS2 utility which is called Smart Sharpen. Adjust Sharpen allows you to select from three distinct options and offers Amount and Radius controls for controlling the effect of sharpening.

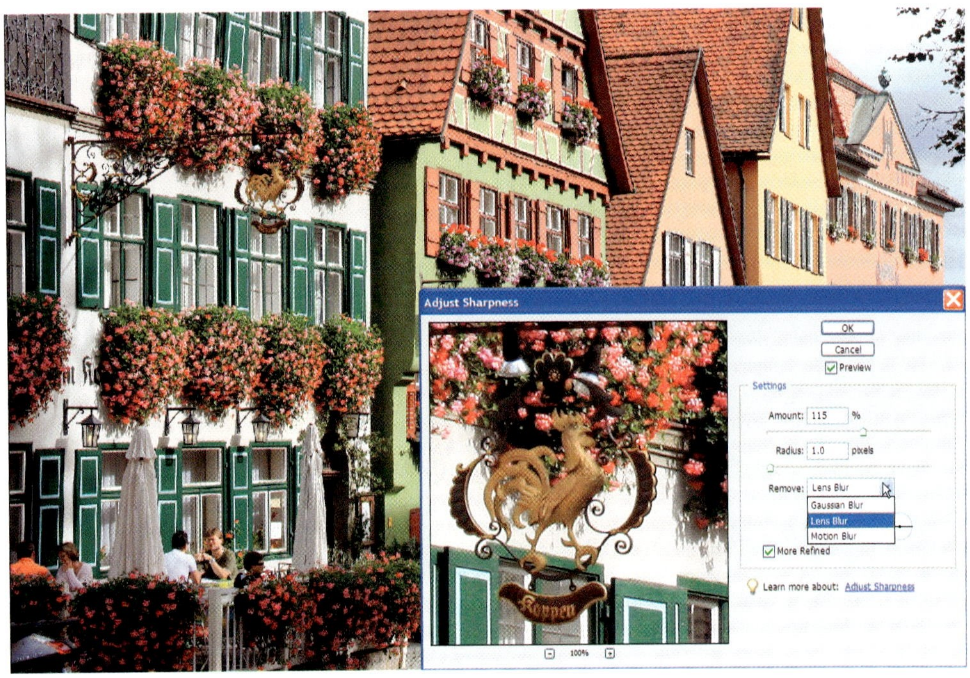

Figure 13.9 Not available in previous versions of Elements, Adjust Sharpness is a versatile utility that employs more-sophisticated algorithms than Unsharp Mask.

As with USM, Amount determines the intensity, or the extent to which contrast is enhanced along edges. Radius allows you to determine the size of the area to be affected. Again, when working with images with a great deal of intricate detail, you'll generally want to have the impact affect only a small area for each edge, so use a low Radius amount, under 1. For other types of images you may want to use a Radius of up to 3.

Beyond those general suggestions, there is no rule of thumb as to the settings that are suitable for any image. When setting the Remove drop-down list to Lens Blur, experiment with Amount settings from about 100% to 200% and Radius settings from 0.8 to 3 (Figure 13.10). Avoid oversharpening. Watch for halos appearing around sharp edges within the image; when those become visible, reduce the sharpening Amount.

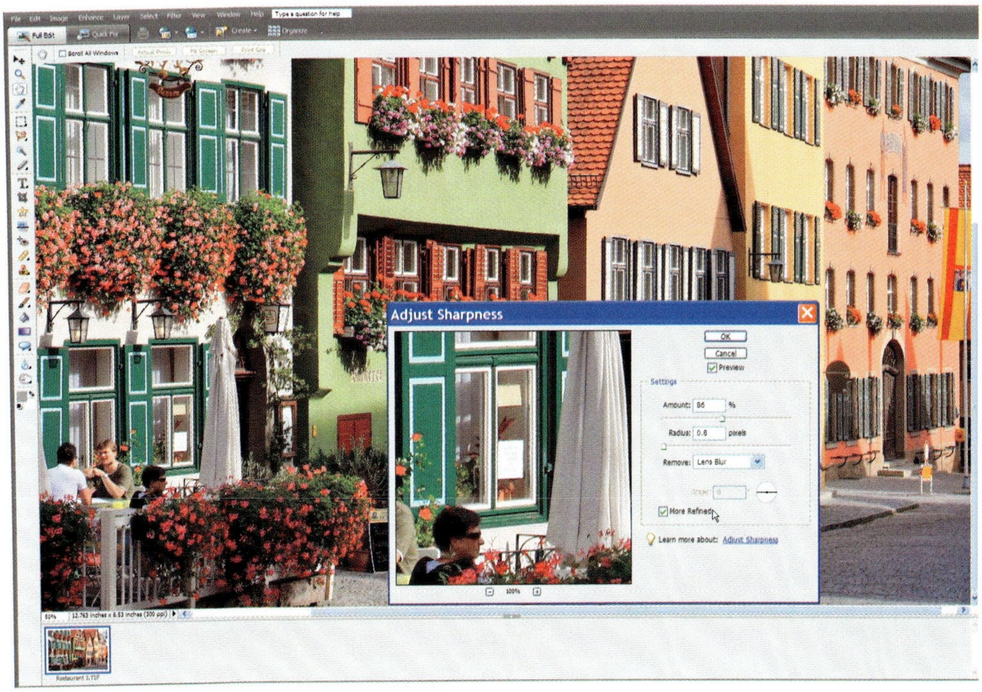

Figure 13.10 In our experience, Lens Blur is the most valuable option within Adjust Sharpness, particularly when used with the More Refined checkbox selected.

The second option in the Remove drop-down list, Gaussian Blur is designed to remove the blurring effect caused by the micro lenses or low-pass filters used in most digital cameras' sensors. According to Adobe, Gaussian Blur provides an effect that's similar to Unsharp Mask; frankly, USM provides greater user control with a Threshold tool that can be useful. However, Lens Blur can be a valuable alternative to USM. This option employs more-sophisticated or "intelligent" edge-detection algorithms. For the best results, make sure that the More Refined checkbox is selected. That does increase the time required to complete sharpening because the system runs two passes on the image, but it is more effective, particularly on images with a great deal of intricate detail.

Note: When the More Refined checkbox is selected while you are using any of the three Remove options, Adjust Sharpness provides more-sophisticated sharpening. However, this can also sharpen grain in a film scan or a digital noise pattern. When that is obvious in the preview, experiment by clearing the More Refined checkbox. Frankly, Unsharp Mask is a more suitable sharpening tool than Adjust Sharpness for images with a prominent grain or digital noise pattern because it provides a Threshold control. For very grainy or noisy images, set the Threshold to a high level, as high as 30 or 40, and increase the Amount as necessary to achieve a sharper subject without accentuating the grain or noise pattern.

The third option in the Remove drop-down list is Motion Blur, designed to correct for blurring caused by the movement of a subject or the camera while the image was being made (Figure 13.11). Frankly, this does not really correct blurring caused by a sloppy photographic technique, such as camera shake, but it can minimize the blurring effect. In our view, it's primarily intended for correcting motion blur, as in action photos.

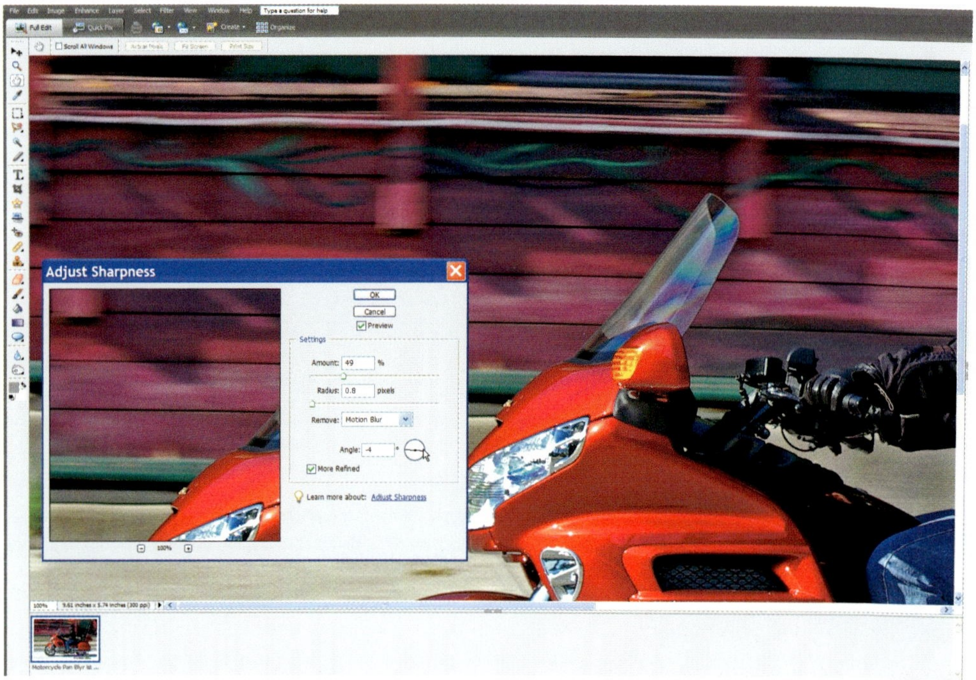

Figure 13.11 The key to success with the Motion Blur option is to identify the angle of the blur with some accuracy. That's easiest to do by viewing various areas of the image at high magnification.

When you select Motion Blur, you can also enter the angle of blur found in the image. That may be vertical (as in an image of a high jumper, for example) or horizontal (as in an image of a racing car). View the image at 100% or 200% magnification to determine the exact direction of camera shake or motion. Then click and drag on the circular control to set the indicator to the same angle as the motion in the image.

Image Output

The image is now prepared for final output. If you are preparing the image for a digital slideshow or Web display, you can simply save the file. If, however, you are going to print the image, this is the time to do so, making sure to use the appropriate settings for your printer. By using the workflow presented in this chapter to prepare your image, you can rest assured that the master image file is safely protected and that the quality of the final print will be the best possible.

Note: For more details on sending your prepared image to the printer with all appropriate settings to ensure accurate results, see Tim's book *Color Confidence, Second Edition* (Sybex, 2006).

Saving a Copy

Naturally, if you're preparing an image for use in another software application, such as when you're building a web page or producing a digital slideshow, you'll need to save a copy of the file. To do so, simply choose File > Save As from the menu, specify a location, filename, and file format, and click Save. For these types of usages, it is generally most appropriate to save the file in a JPEG format, with the Quality setting based on the priority between quality and file size (for example, on the Web, file size is more important, whereas for digital slideshows the quality is a higher priority).

Note: If you are preparing your image for digital display, such as on a monitor or digital projector, and the application used to present that image doesn't support color management, it is a good idea to convert the image to the sRGB color space before saving a copy of the image. To do so, choose Image > Convert Color Profile > Apply sRGB Profile (if this field is disabled, the image is already in sRGB).

If you've prepared the image for printed output, saving a copy of the result is optional because you already have the master image file saved. That master image file should be the starting point for any future output, so the only real reason to save a copy of the final file is for convenience if you plan to make prints of the same size often from that image. Then you can simply open the finalized version and print it; that eliminates the need to go through the full output processing workflow each time you want to make a print at that size. After your printing is finished, you'll need to decide whether to retain the finalized file. That depends on whether you think you might want to make prints again in the future and whether that's likely enough to warrant consuming additional hard-disk space with this extra file.

If you do choose to save a copy of the finalized file for print purposes, we recommend saving the file in either the TIFF or Photoshop PSD format. As mentioned in Chapter 12, you might want to save finalized files in the TIFF format, if you saved master image files (with layers intact) in the PSD format. That distinction can be useful when scanning a list of files because you'll know at a glance which are the finalized copies for printing (TIFF) and which are master image files (PSD). Otherwise, there is no advantage to either TIFF or PSD; either format is fine, although TIFF files are smaller if you used compression such as LZW.

Workflow Complete!

As you conclude this book, you've made it through the complete workflow from capture to print, with an emphasis on the process of optimizing your images in Elements 5. We hope that you feel a sense of accomplishment in having learned to make the most of your images in an efficient manner, with a focus on preserving the information in the original image. Using the techniques presented in this book, perhaps with a bit of review from time to time, you'll be able to take full control over your photographic images, producing exactly the result you envisioned when you clicked the shutter (Figure 13.12). Have fun putting your workflow to work for you!

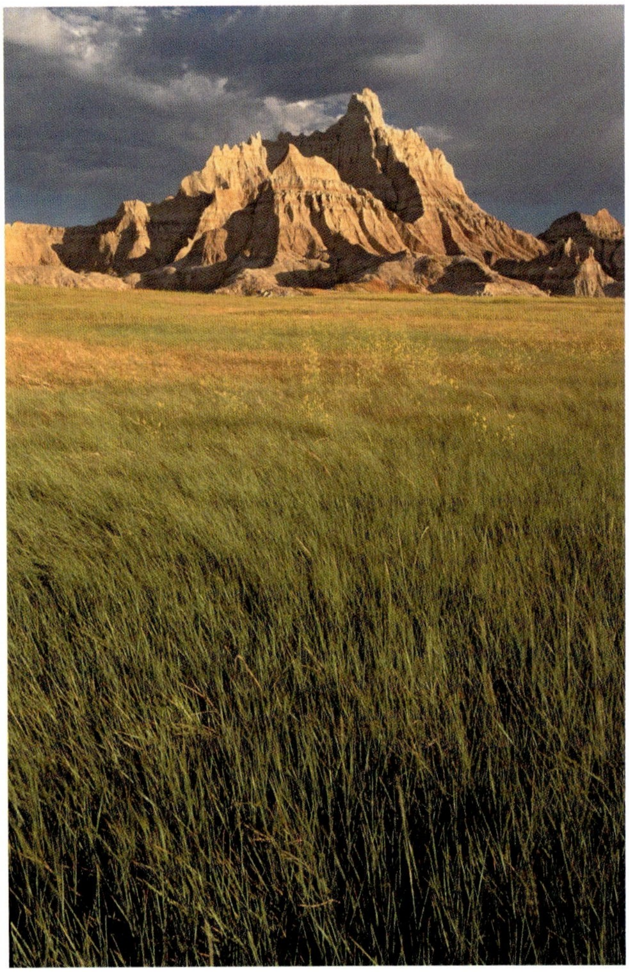

Figure 13.12 The workflow process presented in this book will help you achieve exactly the results you intend for your images. (Photo by Alice Cahill, www.alicecahill.com)

Appendix: Sample Workflow Checklist

This book has presented a logical workflow for optimizing your images. However, because the chapters offer considerable detail about how to perform each step, in this appendix we have provided a basic checklist to use as you developyour own workflow. Think of this as a way to remind yourself of the order in which we have recommended performing the steps of an image-optimization workflow; also use it as a guide for developing a workflow that works best for you. We have included a reference to the chapter that contains details on performing each step.

Sorting

- Download your images from your digital camera or memory card (Chapter 2).
- Use the Organizer (Organize button at the top of Full Edit or Quick Fix mode) in Elements to quickly review thumbnails and discard the obviously unacceptable images (Chapter 2).
- Use a preview view in Organizer, or an aftermarket program, to review your images more closely, discarding those that do not seem to be worth keeping; also identify images that are your favorites (Chapter 2).
- Evaluate your favorite images with great scrutiny to make sure they are worth the effort of a complete image-optimization workflow (Chapter 2).

Initial Image Preparation

- Convert RAW captures into image files with Adobe Camera Raw after making the basic adjustments to the raw data file; that will allow you to later optimize them in Elements (Chapter 3).
- Perform basic rotation to place the image in the proper orientation (Chapter 4).
- Perform basic cropping and rotation to eliminate unwanted pixels around the periphery of the image and to fix the horizon if crooked, respectively (Chapter 4).

Basic Optimization

- Perform a basic tonal adjustment by using Levels to set the black point, white point, and middle-tone values (Chapter 5).
- Perform a basic adjustment to deal with any color cast in the image (Chapter 5).
- Perform a saturation adjustment with Hue/Saturation (Chapter 5).
- Clean up dust, scratches, and other blemishes by using the Clone Stamp and Healing Brush tools (Chapter 6).

Advanced Adjustments

- Perform advanced tonal adjustments with utilities such as Adjust Color Curves. Then take advantage of painting with light or the Dodge & Burn tools using a duplicate layer technique (Chapter 7).
- Perform color adjustments targeted to specific color values by using Hue/Saturation, Solid Color, and Average Color Removal (Chapter 8).
- Perform targeted color fixes and saturation painting (Chapter 8).
- Create and save selections that isolate areas requiring targeted adjustments (Chapter 9).
- Make targeted adjustments to specific areas of your images by both creating selections and painting on masks (Chapter 10).
- Perform any creative adjustments such as Colorize, Convert To Black And White, or applying Filters (Chapter 11).

Workflow Wrap-Up

- Decide on a file-naming and organization plan determining the best locations for storing files (Chapter 12).
- Save your master image file, preferably in the PSD file format (Chapter 12).
- Prepare your master image files for output so they can be shared with others (Chapter 13).

Index

Note to the Reader: Throughout this index **boldfaced** page numbers indicate primary discussions of a topic. *Italicized* page numbers indicate illustrations.

A

ACDSee Photo Manager, 23
ACR. *See* Adobe Camera Raw (ACR)
active area in selections, 193, *194*
Actual Pixels (100% view) option, 38
Add To Sample eyedropper, 172
Add To Selection option
  Lasso, 199
  Magic Wand, 209–211, *210*
  Marquee tools, 197
  Polygonal Lasso, 201
  saved selections, 217
Adjust Color Curves feature, **153–155**, *154*, *156*
Adjust Color For Skin Tone utility, 117, *117*
Adjust Color Intensity scale, 113
Adjust Highlights slider, 154
Adjust Hue/Saturation command, 93
Adjust Shadows slider, 154
Adjust Sharpness tool, **270–272**, *270–272*
Adjust Size Of Thumbnail slider, 32
Adjustment Intensity slider, 238
adjustment layers
  benefits, **102**
  brightness/contrast, 96, 99
  visibility of, 100, 127
Adobe Camera Raw (ACR), **51–53**, *52*
  alternatives, 64
  batch processing, 62
  bit depth, 63
  conversion, 63
  navigation tools, **53**, *53*
  noise reduction, 61
  saturation, 61
  settings, **53**
  shadows, 59
  white balance, **54–58**, *54*, *57*
Adobe Photo Downloader, **19–22**, *20–22*
Adobe RGB color space option, 45
Advanced Options
  Adjust Color Curves feature, 154–155, *154*
  Photo Downloader, 22
After Copying, Do Not Delete Originals option, 22
After version for grayscale conversion, 236
Aligned option
  Clone Stamp, 130
  Healing Brush, 137
Alt/Option key
  clipping preview, 109–110, *109–110*
  Clone Stamp selection, 132
  Eyedropper, 185–186
  Magnetic Lasso, 205
  Marquee tools, 194
  masking, 225–226
  Polygonal Lasso, 202
  Selection Brush, 207
Ambient Light Temperature slider, 118
Amount setting
  Adjust Sharpness, 270
  Unsharp Mask, 268, *268*
analog-to-digital conversion, 51
anchor points
  Magnetic Lasso, 203–205, *204*
  Polygonal Lasso, 201–203, *201*
angle of blur, 272
Anti-alias option
  Elliptical Marquee, 197
  Lasso, 199
  Magic Wand, 211
  Magnetic Lasso, 203
Apply sRGB Profile command, 273
archiving
  images, **28–29**
  RAW captures, **64–65**
artistic cropping, 72
As Shot setting, 55
aspect ratio
  cropping, 72, 76, 78–79
  image size, 265
  selections, 195
Auto Color Correction tool, 116, *117*
Auto Color option, 119
Auto Launch Adobe Photo Downloader On Device Connect option, 21
Auto Levels option, 119
Auto Sharpen option, 119
Auto Smart Fix tool, 116
Auto White Balance (AWB) feature, 48–49, 55
Automatically Fix Red Eyes option, 21
Automatically Suggest Photo Stacks option, 21
average color removal, **180–182**
AWB (Auto White Balance) feature, 48–49, 55

B

Back To All Photos option, 35
background and background color
  for average color removal, 181, *182*
  with cropping, 77
  with masking, 228
backup systems, **28**
balance
  color, **112–118**, *113–118*
  white. *See* white balance
batch processing Camera raw images, **62**
Before version for grayscale conversion, 236
Bicubic option, 265
Bicubic Sharper option, 265
Bicubic Smoother option, 265
Bilinear option, 265
bit depth, 51, **63**
black point setting, **106–111**, *107–111*
blending and blending modes
  average color removal, 181
  Clone Stamp, 129
  color range, 171
  Healing Brush, 139
  sharpening, 241–242
  solid color, 178
  targeted color painting, 184
  targeted saturation painting, 187–188, *188*
  tonal adjustments, 157
blocking with masking, 221
Blue option, 237–239
blur
  Adjust Sharpness, **270–272**, *271–272*
  with masking, 223–224, *223*
Blush slider, 118
Border option for selections, 215, *215*
Borderless option for contact sheets, 44
Brightness/Contrast adjustment
  levels, 106
  tonal adjustments, **95–102**, *95*, *97–101*
brightness in RAW conversion, **60**
Browse For Folder dialog box, 24
Brush tool
  with masking, 224
  painting with light, **160–162**
  targeted color painting, 184–185
  targeted saturation painting, 187–188
  tonal adjustments, 158
brushes
  Clone Stamp, 128–129, *128*, 132–133, *132–133*
  Dodge, 162
  Healing Brush, **136–139**, *137–139*
  Selection Brush, **205–207**, *206*
  Spot Healing Brush, 136, **140–141**, *140*
  tonal adjustments, 158–159, *160*
Burn tool and burning, 157, **161–163**, *162–163*

C

Caps Lock key, 185
Caption option, 36
Capture One PRO software, 64
capturing high-bit data, **51**, *51*
cards
  reformatting, 25, **28–29**
  transferring images from, **25–27**
cast, color, **176**, *177*
  average color removal, **180–182**
  solid color, **178–180**, *178–180*
categories for tags, 34
checklist, workflow, **275–277**
cleanup, **123**
  Clone Stamp. *See* Clone Stamp tool
  Healing Brush, **136–139**, *137–139*
  Spot Healing Brush, **140–141**, *140*
  workflow, **124–125**, *124*
clipping
  overview, **103–105**, *105*
  preview, **108–111**, *108–111*
Clone Stamp tool, **125**
  configuring, **125–130**, *126–129*
  fixing cloning mistakes, **134–135**, *135*
  painting with, **132–134**, *132–134*
  source selection for, **130–132**, *131*
cm metric selection measurements, 196
Collections feature, 37
color, **91**, **112**
  Adjust Color Curves feature, **153–155**, *154*, *156*
  balance, **112–118**, *113–118*
  clipping preview, 110
  Hue/Saturation. *See* Hue/Saturation utility
  with masking, 228
  prioritizing adjustments, **93–95**, *94*
  Quick Fix, **119–120**, *120*
  ranges
    customizing, **169–173**, *170–172*
    eyedroppers for, **172–173**
    inverse, **173–176**, *174–176*
    preset, **168–169**, *169*
  saturation, 61, **92–93**, *92–93*, **118–119**, *118–119*
  targeted color painting, **183–186**, *184–186*
  targeted saturation painting, **187–188**, *187–188*
color casts, **176**, *177*
  average color removal, **180–182**
  solid color, **178–180**, *178–180*
Color Noise Reduction slider, 62, *62*
Color Picker dialog box
  solid color, 178–180, *179*
  targeted saturation painting, 187–188
Color Saturation level setting, 61
color temperature, 48
Color Variations feature, 112–115, *113*, *115*

Colorize adjustment, **232–235**, *233–235*
Columns option for contact sheets, 44
compensation, exposure, 58
compression, 256–257
consistency, workflow for, **7**
Constrain Proportions option, 265–266
contact sheet printing, **44–45**, *44–45*
Contiguous option, 211, *212*
Contract selection option, 216
contrast
  grayscale conversion, 237
  RAW conversion, **60**
  tonal adjustments, 95–96, 99
conversion
  16-bit files, **101**
  analog-to-digital, 51
  grayscale, **235–236**
    Convert To Black And White command, **236–239**, *236–238*
    hue shift in, **239–240**, *239–240*
  RAW. *See* RAW images
Convert depth option, 101
Convert To Black And White command, **236–239**, *236–238*
Copy pictures to a folder on my computer using Scanner And Camera Wizard option, 23
copying. *See* Clone Stamp tool
Correct Camera Distortion utility, 80–82, *81–82*
corrective cropping, 72
Create Adjustment Layer button, 96, 98
creative adjustments, **231–232**
  Colorize, **232–235**, *233–235*
  filters, **243–244**, *243–244*
  grayscale conversion, **235–240**, *236–240*
  sharpening, **241–242**, *241–242*
Crop To Original Size option, 88
Crop To Remove Background option, 88, *89*
cropping and Crop tool, **69**, **76–78**, *76–77*
  basic, **72–73**, *73*
  perspective with, **80–82**, *80–82*
  rotating with, **83–85**, *84–86*
  from selections, **73–76**, *74–75*
  sizing with, 76, **78–79**, *79*
Custom Rotate tool, **86–88**, *87–88*

D

Darken Highlights slider, 147, *147*, 150, *150–151*, 153
Date View, 35
DCIM folder, 26
Delete From Catalog option, 32
Diffuse Glow filter, 244
Digital Negative (DNG) format, 63
Discard option, 256
Display & Cursors dialog box, 76–77, *77*
Distort filter, 244
DNG (Digital Negative) format, 63
dodging and Dodge tool, 157, **161–163**, *162–163*
dots per inch (dpi) resolution, 266
Downloader Pro, 23
downloading images, **17–18**, *18*
  Adobe Photo Downloader for, **19–22**, *20–22*
  confirming, **26–27**, *27*
  manual copying, **25–27**
  master folder for, **18–19**, *19*
  Scanner And Camera Wizard for, **23–25**, *24–25*
  third-party software for, **23**
dpi (dots per inch) resolution, 266
Duplicate Image dialog box, 263, *263*
Duplicate Layer option, 112
Duplicate Merged Layers Only option, 263

E

Edge Contrast setting, 203–204
Effect mode, 129
efficiency, workflow for, **5–6**
Elliptical Marquee tool, 193, 195, 197–198
Eraser tool
  cloning errors, 135, *135*
  tonal adjustments, 164, *164*
evaluating
  images, **37–40**, *39*
  sharpness, **40**
Events category, 34
evolving requirements, **13–15**, *14*
EXIF data, 36
Expand selection option, 216
exposure
  with Dodge, 162
  with RAW images, **50–51**, *50*, **58–59**
eyedroppers and Eyedropper tool
  color range, **172–173**
  with Magic Wand, 208
  settings, **185–186**
  targeted color painting, 184–185

F

Face Tagging option, 35
Favorites category, 34
Feather option
  Lasso, 199
  Magnetic Lasso, 203
  for selections, 195, 197, 216, 222
filenames
  renaming, 21
  in saving files, **252–254**, *253–254*
fills
  in grayscale conversion, 239
  with masking, 226

filters and Filter Gallery
applying, **243–244**, *243–244*
density, 227–228
High Pass, **241–242**, *241–242*
Find By Visual Similarity option, 35
Find command, 36, *36*
Fit On Screen option, 38, 40
5 By 5 Average option
Eyedropper, 185
with Magic Wand, 208
Fixed Aspect Ratio option, 195
Fixed Size mode, 195–196, *196*
flattening images, **263–264**, *264*
flexibility in workflow, **10–11**
flipping vs. rotating, 71
focus on results, **9–10**, *10*
folders
for downloading images, **18–19**, *19*
names for, 253
foreground color with masking, 228
Foreground To Background option, 227
formats, file, 252, **254–257**, *255*, 273
formatting, memory cards, 25, **28–29**
Frequency setting with Magnetic Lasso, 204
Full Edit section, 153
Full Screen View, 33

G

gapping, 103, 105–106
Gaussian Blur
Adjust Sharpness, 271
with masking, 223–224, *223*
General Fixes, 119–120, 153, *153*
gradients for masks, 226–228, *227–228*
grayscale conversion, **235–236**
Convert To Black And White command, **236–239**, *236–238*
hue shift in, **239–240**, *239–240*
Green option, 237–239
groups, names, 24
Grow option, 216
Grow Or Shrink Canvas To Fit option, 88

H

halos in sharpening, 53, 270
Hand tool
for Camera raw, 53, *53*
with Lasso, 200
with selections, 194
working with, **38–40**
Hard brush, 129
hardness of brush
Clone Stamp, 128–129, *128*
Healing Brush, 136–137, *137*
Selection Brush, 206
Healing Brush, **136**, *137–139*
configuring, **136–137**, *137*
healing with, **137–138**, *138*
minimizing healing, **138–139**, *139*
Height setting
cropping, 78–79, 81
image resizing, 266–267
selections, 195–196
high-bit data captures, **51**, *51*
High Pass filters, **241–242**, *241–242*
Highlights option
Burn, 163
for exposure, *59*
Shadows/Highlights, **146–153**, *146–153*
histogram display
for exposure, *58*
for levels, 103–106, *103–105*
Hue/Saturation utility, **168**, *168*
color ranges
customizing, **169–173**, *170–172*
eyedroppers for, **172–173**
inverse, **173–176**, *174–176*
preset, **168–169**, *169*
Colorize, 232–235, *233*
grayscale conversion, 240, *240*
Quick Fix, 118–120
saturation, 93, *93*, **118–119**, *118*
hue shift in grayscale conversion, **239–240**, *239–240*
Hue slider
color ranges, 168, 173
Colorize, 232–234, *234*
grayscale conversion, 240, *240*

I

Image Compression setting, 256
Image Size dialog box, **265–267**, *265*
in-camera overrides, 4
in (inches) selection measurements, 196
Increase Midtones option, 153
Infrared Effect style, 237, *237*
Interleaved option, 256
interpolation in image resizing, 265
Intersect With Selection option
Lasso, 199
Polygonal Lasso, 201
for saved selections, 217
inverse color ranges, **173–176**, *174–176*

J

jagged lines in selections, 215, *216*
JPEG file format, 4, **252**

K

keyboard shortcuts, **42–43**

L

Landscape orientation option, 44
Lasso tool
  Magnetic Lasso, **203–205**, *204*
  Polygonal Lasso, **200–203**, *201–202*
  working with, **198–200**, *199–200*
Layer Compression options, 256
layer masks, 220
layers
  benefits, **11–12**, *12–13*, **102**
  brightness/contrast, 96, 99
  with Clone Stamp, **126–127**, *126–127*
  for masking. *See* masking
  renaming, 126
  for tonal adjustments, 157–158, *158*
  visibility of, 100, 127
Lempel-Ziv-Welch compression algorithm, 256–257
Lens Blur setting, 270–271, *271*
Less Red option, 239
levels, **102–103**, *103*
  basic adjustments, **106–107**, *107*
  grayscale conversion, 240
  problem signs, **103–106**, *104–105*
Levels Adjust Color Curves adjustment, 240
light, painting with, **160–162**, *161*
light table analogy, **29–30**, *30*
lightbox view, **31–33**, *31–32*
Lighten Shadows slider, 147, *147*, 150, *151*, 153
Lightness slider, 168, 173
Linear Gradient option, 227
Load Selection dialog box, 217, *217*
loading selections, **216–217**, *217*
locations in saving files, **252–254**, *253–254*
lossless compression, 257
loupes, 29
Luminance Smoothing slider, 61
LZW option, 256–257

M

Magic Selection Brush tool, 207
Magic Wand tool, **207–213**, *209–210*, *212*
Magnetic Lasso tool, **203–205**, *204*
Make Group Custom Name A Tag option, 21–22
marching ants, 221
Marquee tools, **193–198**, *193–198*
marquees
  with Crop, 76
  with Zoom, 38, 42
masking, **219–221**, *220–221*
  gradients for, **226–228**, *227–228*
  by painting, **224–228**, *225*, *227–228*
  Selection Brush, 206–207
  from selections, **221–224**, *222–223*
Master color range option, 168
master folders, **18–19**, *19*
master images
  preserving, **261–262**, *262*
  working with, **250–251**, *250–251*
media for saving files, **257**
memory cards
  reformatting, 25, **28–29**
  transferring images from, **25–27**
metadata, 22, 36
metric selection measurements, 196
middle-tone setting, 106, 111, *111*
Midtone Brightness slider, 154–155, *156*
Midtone Contrast slider, 147, *147*, 151–154, *152–153*
Midtones option
  Burn, 163
  Dodge, 162
mini-lab adjustments, 94
mm metric selection measurements, 196
modes, selection, **197–198**, *197–198*
More Blue option, 238–239, *238*
More Green option, 238–239, *238*
More Red option, 238–239, *238*
More Refined option, 271
Motion Blur setting, 271–272, *272*

N

names
  folders, 253
  groups, 24
  layers, 126
  in saving files, **252–254**, *253–254*
  selections, 217
navigation tools for RAW conversion, **53**, *53*
Navigator palette, **41–43**, *41–42*
Nearest Neighbor option, 265
New Layer dialog box, 157–158, *158*
New Selection option
  Lasso, 199
  Marquee, 197
  Polygonal Lasso, 201
No Restriction cropping option, 76
noise reduction, **61–63**, *62*
noncontiguous selections, 212

O

off-kilter images, 85
opacity
  average color removal, 181, *182*

Clone Stamp, 130
color, 116
cropping, 76–77
Healing Brush, 139, *139*
solid color, 179–180, *180*
targeted color painting, 184
targeted saturation painting, 188
threshold selection technique, 213–214, *213*
tonal adjustments, 159–160
Open Organizer When Finished option, 22
optimization checklist, 276
Options bar
Clone Stamp, 128–129, *128*
Dodge, 162
Lasso, 199
Magic Wand, 207–208, 212
Magnetic Lasso, 203
Marquee, 195
Polygonal Lasso, 201
Selection Brush, 206
Spot Healing Brush, 141
tonal adjustments, 159, *160*
Organizer, 21–22, *22*
for RAW captures, 27
sorting images in. *See* sorting images
support for, 256
output processing, **259**
duplicating images, **263**, *263*
flattening images, **263–264**, *264*
image size, **265–267**, *265*
master images, **261–262**, *262*
saving images, **273**
sharpening, **267–272**
workflow, **260**, *261*
working copies, **262–263**
Overlay mode
sharpening, 241–242
tonal adjustments, 157
Overlay Color mode, 206

P

painting
with Clone Stamp, **132–134**, *132–134*
with light, **160–162**, *161*
masking by, **224–228**, *225*, *227–228*
targeted color, **183–186**, *184–186*
targeted saturation, **187–188**, *187–188*
Paper Size option, 44
Pen Pressure option, 204
People category, 34
Per Channel option, 256
perspective with cropping, **80–82**, *80–82*
Photo Downloader, **19–22**, *20–22*
Photo Stacks option, 21
Photoshop Document (PSD) format, 252, **254–255**, **257**
Picture Name And Destination page, 25, *25*
Pixel Dimensions settings, 267
Pixel Order settings, 256
pixels per inch (ppi) resolution, 266
Places category, 34
Point Sample option
Eyedropper, 185
with Magic Wand tool, 208
Polygonal Lasso tool, **200–203**, *201–202*
Portrait orientation option, 44
Portraits style, 237, *237*
position of selections, 194
posterization, 106
ppi (pixels per inch) resolution, 266
Preference dialog box, 21
presets
color ranges, **168–169**, *169*
white balance, **55**
preview
ACR files, 53
clipping, **108–111**, *108–111*
preview view, **33–34**, *33*
Previous Conversion option, 62–63
Print Photos dialog box, 44–45, *44–45*
Print Size option, 38
printing contact sheets, **44–45**, *44–45*
priorities
tone and color adjustments, **93–95**, *94*
workflow, **7–8**, *8*
PSD (Photoshop Document) format, 252, **254–255**, **257**
px (pixels) selection measurements, 196

Q

quality
output settings, 273
workflow for, **4–5**, *6*
Quick Fix tools, **119–120**, *120*

R

Radius setting
Adjust Sharpness, 270
sharpening, 242, *242*
Unsharp Mask, 268, *268*
Range option
Burn, 163
Dodge, 162
ranges, color
customizing, **169–173**, *170–172*
eyedroppers for, **172–173**
inverse, **173–176**, *174–176*
preset, **168–169**, *169*

RAW images
  captures
    archiving, **64–65**
    Organizer for, 27
    quality, **4–5**
    saving, 250–251
  conversions, **47**
    Adobe Camera Raw, **51–53**, *52*
    alternatives, **64**
    approach to, **63–64**
    benefits, **48**
    for exposure errors, **50–51**, *50*
    for high-bit data capture, **51**, *51*
    navigation tools, **53**, *53*
    noise reduction, **61–63**, *62*
    tonal adjustments, **58–61**, *60*
    for white balance, **48–49**, *49*, **54–58**, *54*, *57*
Rectangular Marquee tool, 74, *74*, 193–195, *194*
red-eye correction, 21
Red option, 237–239
Red Eye Fix option, 119
reformatting memory cards, 25, **28–29**
Remove Color Cast tool, 114–115, *114*, *116*
Remove From Category option, 35
renaming
  files, 21
  layers, 126
requirements, evolving, **13–15**, *14*
Resample Image option, 265, 267
resizing images, **265–267**, *265*
resolution
  cropping, 78–79
  image resizing, 266–267
results, focus on, **9–10**, *10*
revealing with masking, 221
reviewing images, **37–40**, *39*
revising workflow, **13–15**, *14*
RLE option, 256
Rotate Left tool, 30
Rotate Right tool, 30
rotation, **69**
  basic, **70–71**, *70–71*
  with Crop, **83–85**, *84–86*
  custom, **82**, *83*
  with Custom Rotate, **86–88**, *87–88*
  in sorting, 30
  with Straighten, **88–89**, *89*

S

Sample All Layers option
  Clone Stamp, 130
  Healing Brush, 137
  Magic Wand, 212
Sample Size setting, 208
sample workflow checklist, **275–277**
sampling Eyedropper tool, 185
saturation and Saturation slider
  color, **118–119**, *118–119*
  color ranges, 168, 173
  Colorize, 232–234, *234*
  increasing, **92–93**, *92–93*
  RAW conversion, **61**
  targeted saturation painting, 187–188, *188*
Save As dialog box, 253, *253*, 261–262, *262*
Save New Camera Raw Defaults option, 53
Save Selection dialog box, 216–217, *217*
saving, **249**
  filenames and locations in, **252–254**, *253–254*
  formats in, **254–257**, *255*
  master images, **250–251**, *250–251*, **261–262**, *262*
  media for, **257**
  output, **273**
  selections, **216–217**, *217*
Scale Styles option, 265
Scanner And Camera Wizard, **23–25**, *24–25*
Scenic Landscape style, 237
Selection Brush tool, **205–207**, *206*
Selection mode, 207
selections, **191**, *192*
  cropping from, **73–76**, *74–75*
  Lasso tools
    Magnetic Lasso, **203–205**, *204*
    Polygonal Lasso, **200–203**, *201–202*
    working with, **198–200**, *199–200*
  Magic Wand, **207–213**, *209–210*, *212*
  Marquee tools, **193–198**, *193–198*
  masking from, **221–224**, *222–223*
  modifying, **215–216**, *215–216*
  saving and loading, **216–217**, *217*
  Selection Brush, **205–207**, *206*
  threshold technique, **213–214**, *213–214*
  Tools palette, **192**
  working with, **217**
sepia tone, 234
Set Background Color tool, 175
Set The Background Color option, 187
Set The Foreground Color option, 187
shadows
  Dodge, 162
  RAW conversion, **59**, *60*
  Shadows/Highlights, **146–153**, *146–153*
shape of Clone Stamp brush, 128, *128*
Sharpen tool, 270
Sharpen Edges tool, 270
Sharpen More tool, 270
sharpening, **267–268**
  Adjust Sharpness, **270–272**, *270–272*
  high pass, **241–242**, *241–242*
  master images, **252**
  in RAW conversion, 53
  Unsharp Mask, **268–269**, *268–269*

sharpness, evaluating, **40**
shield for cropping, 76–77, *77*
Shift key
  for brush hardness, 129, 136
  with cropping, 76
  with gradients, 228
  with masking, 222, *223*
  for selections, 193, 197–198, 202, 211, 213
shortcuts, keyboard, **42–43**
Similar option, 216
Single Photo View mode, 32, *32*, 36
16-bit file conversions, **101**
size
  Clone Stamp brush, 128, *128*, 132–133, *132–133*
  with cropping, 76, **78–79**, *79*
  Dodge area, 162
  Healing Brush, 136
  images, **265–267**, *265*
  paper, 44
  selections, 195–196
skin tones, 117, *117*
Smart Fix option, 119
Smooth selection option, 215, *216*
Soft Light option, 157
Soft Round brush
  Clone Stamp, 129
  tonal adjustments, 159
Solid Color adjustment layer, **178–180**, *178–180*
sorting images, **29**
  features for, **35–37**, *36–37*
  light table analogy, **29–30**, *30*
  lightbox view, **31–33**, *31–32*
  preview view, **33–34**, *33*
  strategies, **30–31**
  tags for, **34–35**, *35*
  workflow checklist, **276**
source selection for cloning, **130–132**, *131*
Sponge tool
  for Dodge and Burn, 162
  for targeted saturation painting, 187
Spot Healing Brush, 136, **140–141**, *140*
standards, changing, 14
straight lines and edges with selections, 201–202
Straighten And Crop Image command, 85
Straighten Image command, 85
Straighten tool, **88–89**, *89*
straightening off-kilter images, 85
strategies in workflow, 8
Stylize filter, 244
Subtract From Sample eyedropper, 173
Subtract From Selection option
  Lasso, 199
  Magic Wand, 209, 211
  Marquee tools, 198
  Polygonal Lasso, 201
  for saved selections, 217

T

Tag palette, 22
Tagged Image File Format (TIFF), 252, **255–257**, *255*
tags, **34–35**, *35*
Tan slider, 118
targeted adjustments. *See* masking
targeted color painting, **183–186**, *184–186*
targeted saturation painting, **187–188**, *187–188*
temperature in white balance, **56–58**, *57*
Texture filter, 244
third-party software
  for downloading images, **23**
  filters, 243
3 By 3 Average option
  Eyedropper, 185
  with Magic Wand, 208
Threshold selection technique, **213–214**, *213–214*
Threshold setting, Unsharp Mask, 268–269, *268*
thumbnails
  brush stroke previews, 129
  Navigator palette for, 41
  Organizer, 21
  for sorting images. *See* sorting images
TIFF (Tagged Image File Format), 252, **255–257**, *255*
tint in white balance, **56–58**, *57*
Tolerance setting for Magic Wand, 208–211, *209–210*
tonal adjustments, **58**, **91**, **95**, **145**, *161*
  Adjust Color Curves, **153–155**, *154*, *156*
  brightness, **60**
  Brightness/Contrast, **95–102**, *95*, *97–101*
  contrast, **60**
  Dodge and Burn for, **162–163**, *162–163*
  exposure, **58–59**
  levels, **102–103**, *103*
    basic, **106–107**, *107*
    grayscale conversion, 240
    problem signs, **103–106**, *104–105*
  mistake correction, **164–165**, *164*
  painting with light, **160–162**
  prioritizing, **93–95**, *94*
  saturation, **61**, **92–93**, *92–93*
  selective, **155–157**
  setup, **157–159**, *158–160*
  shadows, **59**, *60*
  Shadows/Highlights, **146–153**, *146–153*
Tools palette, **192**
trapezoid sliders, 171

U

Undo Rotate command, 87
Unsharp Mask (USM), 241, **268–269**, *268–269*
Use Photo Ratio option, 78

V

vertical bars for color range, 171
visibility of adjustment layers, 100, 127
Vivid Landscape style, 237, *237*

W

white balance, **54**
  adjusting, **55–56**
  presets, **55**
  RAW for, **48–49**, *49*
  temperature and tint, **56–58**, *57*
white point setting, **106–111**, *107–111*
Width setting
  cropping, 78–79, 81
  image resizing, 266–267
  Magnetic Lasso, 203
  selections, 195–196
workflow, **3**
  benefits, **15**
  cleanup, **124–125**, *124*
  for consistency, **7**
  for efficiency, **5–6**
  establishing, **7**
  for flexibility, **10–11**
  focus on results, **9–10**, *10*
  layer-based, **11–12**, *12–13*
  output, **260**, *261*
  priorities, **7–8**, *8*
  for quality, **4–5**, *6*
  revising, **13–15**, *14*
  sample checklist, **275–277**
working copies, processing, **262–263**

Z

zero sharpening in RAW conversion, 53
ZIP option, 256–257
Zoom tool
  for Camera raw, 53, *53*
  overview, **38**, *39*
  shortcuts, 43